GLORIOUS, ACCURSED EUROPE

THE TAUBER INSTITUTE SERIES
FOR THE STUDY OF EUROPEAN JEWRY

Jehuda Reinharz, *General Editor*
Sylvia Fuks Fried, *Associate Editor*

The Tauber Institute Series is dedicated to publishing compelling and innovative approaches to the study of modern European Jewish history, thought, culture, and society. The series features scholarly works related to the Enlightenment, modern Judaism and the struggle for emancipation, the rise of nationalism and the spread of antisemitism, the Holocaust and its aftermath, as well as the contemporary Jewish experience. The series is published under the auspices of the Tauber Institute for the Study of European Jewry—established by a gift to Brandeis University from Dr. Laszlo N. Tauber—and is supported, in part, by the Tauber Foundation and the Valya and Robert Shapiro Endowment.

For the complete list of books that are available in this series,
please see www.upne.com

Jehuda Reinharz and Yaacov Shavit
  Glorious, Accursed Europe: An Essay on Jewish Ambivalence
Eugene M. Avrutin, Valerii Dymshits, Alexander Ivanov, Alexander Lvov,
  Harriet Murav, and Alla Sokolova, editors
  Photographing the Jewish Nation: Pictures from S. An-sky's Ethnographic Expeditions
Michael Dorland
  Cadaverland: Inventing a Pathology of Catastrophe for Holocaust Survival
Walter Laqueur
  Best of Times, Worst of Times: Memoirs of a Political Education
Rose-Carol Washton Long, Matthew Baigell, and Milly Heyd, editors
  Jewish Dimensions in Modern Visual Culture: Antisemitism, Assimilation, Affirmation
Berel Lang
  Philosophical Witnessing: The Holocaust as Presence
David N. Myers
  Between Jew and Arab: The Lost Voice of Simon Rawidowicz
Sara Bender
  The Jews of Białystok during World War II and the Holocaust
Nili Scharf Gold
  Yehuda Amichai: The Making of Israel's National Poet
Hans Jonas
  Memoirs

GLORIOUS, ACCURSED EUROPE

AN ESSAY ON JEWISH AMBIVALENCE

JEHUDA REINHARZ
YAACOV SHAVIT

Translated by M. Engel

BRANDEIS UNIVERSITY PRESS
Waltham, Massachusetts
Published by
University Press of New England
Hanover and London

BRANDEIS UNIVERSITY PRESS
Published by University Press of New England,
One Court Street, Lebanon NH 03766
www.upne.com
© 2010 by Brandeis University
All rights reserved

This book is a revised version of the Hebrew edition,
which originally appeared as *Eropah hamehulelet vehamekulelet*
(Tel Aviv: Am Oved Publishers), 2006.

Manufactured in the United States of America
Designed by Eric M. Brooks
Typeset in Chaparral Pro and Goshen by Passumpsic Publishing

University Press of New England is a member of the
Green Press Initiative. The paper used in this book meets
their minimum requirement for recycled paper.

For permission to reproduce any of the material in
this book, contact Permissions, University Press of New England,
One Court Street, Lebanon NH 03766; or visit www.upne.com

Library of Congress Cataloging-in-Publication Data
Shavit, Jacob.
[Eropah ha-mehulelet veha-mekulelet. English]
Glorious, accursed Europe: an essay on Jewish ambivalence /
Jehuda Reinharz, Yaacov Shavit; Michelle Engel, translator.
    p. cm. — (The Tauber institute for the study
of European Jewry series)
"This book is a revised version of the Hebrew edition,
which originally appeared as Eropah hamehulelet vehamekulelet
(Tel Aviv: Am Oved Publishers), 2006."
Includes bibliographical references and index.
ISBN 978-1-58465-843-6 (cloth: alk. paper)
1. Jews—Europe—History—19th century. 2. Jews—Europe—
History—20th century. 3. Jews—Europe—Identity. 4. Europe—
Civilization—19th century. 5. Europe—Civilization—
20th century. 6. Israelis. I. Reinharz, Jehuda. II. Title.
DS135.E83S5413   2010
305.892'404—dc22   2009052107

5 4 3 2 1

*We are thoroughly European
in all our thoughts and sentiments.*
MORDECHAI EHRENPREIS,
"Whither?" *Hashiloach*, 1897

———

*I longed to dwell in Europe,
where I was born—but in vain.*
URI ZVI GREENBERG,
"In the Land of the Slavs,"
Albatross, 1923

———

*Israel passes over Europe like the sun;
at its coming new life bursts forth;
at its going all falls into decay.*
WERNER SOMBART,
*The Jews and Modern
Capitalism*, 1911

CONTENTS

INTRODUCTION 1

1
Europe Discovers Itself, Jews Discover Europe 11

2
The Glorious Nineteenth Century—Europe as Promised Land 23

3
The Accursed Century—Europe as an Ailing Culture 42

4
The Emergence of the Modern European Jew 54

5
Antisemitism as an Incurable European Disease 86

6
Old Europe or New Europe? 100

7
Manifold Europes 121

8
I Am in the East, and My Heart Is in the West 134

9
Europeanness and Anti-Europeanness in Palestine 154

10
Europe, Old or New? 179

CONCLUSION
Between "Real Europe" and the "European Spirit" 192

Notes 197
Bibliography 253
Index 291

GLORIOUS, ACCURSED EUROPE

INTRODUCTION

This is not a book about Europe, nor is it about the history of the Jews in Europe.[1] Instead, its aim is to describe some aspects of the complex relationship between Jews and Europe during the past two hundred years.[2] Several chapters deal with Jews' attempts to understand the essence of Europe, with their perceptions of Europe, and with the various images and topoi of Europe within their worldview; we are concerned with how Jews imagined and invented the idea of Europe and how it existed in the collective memory of an elite group of Jewish thinkers and writers, the ways in which these thinkers interpreted the experience of living in Europe as Jews, and the influence and impact of European heritage on Jewish culture. A discussion of this sort, in our opinion, will not only shed light on how Jewish thinkers and literati understood and interpreted key issues in both modern European and modern Jewish history, but will also —we hope—contribute to an understanding of those very same issues. In other words, the book also deals with the reality that existed beyond images and perceptions, and we argue that modern Jews are European Jews in the sense that a large and central part of their values, culture, and behavior is European.

In the historian Heinrich (Zvi) Graetz's "The Correspondence of an English Lady on Judaism and Semitism," Edith (the lady) posed a rhetorical question: "can you de-Europeanize us?" Could the educated classes of Jewish society, she asked, be saved from the "Europeanness [that] fills the entire field of vision?"[3] This question had occupied Jews since the beginning of the nineteenth century in various, and rapidly evolving, environments, and it continued to occupy them after Europe rose against them and attempted to destroy them. The variety of answers to the question about Europeanness notwithstanding, it is abundantly clear that Jews were neither able nor willing to erase the European heritage from the Jewish experience.

This book examines several different subjects: interpretations, images, perceptions, and even prophecies on the one hand; and beliefs, values, and cultural practices on the other hand. With respect to the latter, it deals with the influence of Europe and Western culture on Jewish society and culture, particularly in Germany, Eastern Europe, and Jewish Palestine, and the relationships among perceptions and images, and cultural reality. By "cultural reality" we refer, in the European context, to processes of acculturation and, in the context of Palestine, to the influence of the European heritage and its cultural assets on the construction of the new Jewish society and culture there—as well as the role that the antinomy between West and East played in that construction. As we will discover, the terms "Europe" and "Europeanness" became rallying cries, labels, and standards for judgment and evaluation in Israeli society, and they now form part of the struggle over the character of Israeli culture and the *Kulturkampf* taking place within it.

Our book deals with Jews rather than with *the* Jews: in other words, it examines a varied group of thinkers, literati, and political figures who operated in different environments—primarily in Eastern and Central Europe (including Germany). These thinkers do not represent all of the camps and streams of thought that have been part of the modern Jewish world—a world that, during the nineteenth century, became more pluralistic than ever and that was divided by profound internal disagreements over, among other things, how Europe should be approached. The figures whose work we will cite here represent several aspects of the climate of the time, and they demonstrate Jews' polar and complex attitudes toward Europe as it was and as they imagined it to be, beginning at the start of the nineteenth century. The texts we cite, primarily in the second and third chapters, reflect the general moods of optimism and pessimism during the period, expressing European superiority on the one hand, and a consciousness of crisis and decline on the other hand. However, Jews had their own reasons to believe that Europe represented the pinnacle of human achievement, and simultaneously other good reasons to keep an anxious eye on expressions of "degeneration" and "decline." They had many good reasons to follow what was unfolding in Europe—expectantly, hopefully, but also with concern—to try to understand Europe, and to prophesy its fate.

WHY EUROPE?

We begin with three quotes, which emphasize three different points of view about Jews' relationship with Europe, and Europe's relationship with Jews.

> Europe is ours; we are among those most responsible for its creation. Over the course of eighteen hundred years, we have, relatively

speaking, contributed no less to it than any of the great "Western" nations. However, beyond that, we began creating Europe long before its common beginning—long before even the Athenians began to create it. For the chief characteristics of European civilization—discontent, the "struggle with God," the concept of progress; that very gulf between the two conceptions of the world manifested in the antithesis of two beliefs—in the "Golden Age" and in the "Messiah," an ideal of the past and an ideal of the future—these characteristics are ones that we bestowed upon Europe long before our forefathers arrived there. As for the Bible, we brought it with us fully formed.

Perhaps more than any other nation, we have the right to say that "Western" culture is bone of our bones, flesh of our flesh, spirit of our spirit. To renounce "Westernness," to adhere to what is typical of the "Orient," signifies denial of our selves. I refer, of course, to moral "Europe."[4]

These words belong to Zeev Jabotinsky, a Zionist leader who was without a doubt one of the more enthusiastic Europhiles among the Zionist leadership,[5] and they reflect an image of Europe that was part of the worldview of several Jewish circles during the nineteenth and twentieth centuries. In truth this was far more than an image: it was, rather, a far-reaching claim that Jews had actually invented Europe. Europe was not only a continent, which in 1925 had a population of 9.2 million Jews (about 63 percent of the world's Jewish population, which also included 4.8 million American Jews, nearly all of whom had emigrated from Europe); nor was it merely a place of which Jews formed an inseparable part. Far more than this, Europe was a culture and civilization whose character had been created and shaped by Jews under the defining influence of the Jewish heritage, first and foremost the Hebrew Bible. In this view, Jews were clearly *Homo europaeus*; it was they who had created Europe and determined its worldview and fundamental values. Jewishness (*Judensein*) and Europeanness were consequently one and the same. Without Jews there could be no Europe; every positive aspect of Europe had a Jewish source, while every negative aspect originated elsewhere.

More than forty years earlier, in 1882, Moshe Leib Lilienblum, who was a leading figure in the Jewish national movement in the last quarter of the nineteenth century, experienced a revelation. One night—"as I lay in bed"—he discovered the painful truth: "We are strangers . . . we are strangers not only here [in Russia] but in the whole of Europe, for it is not the homeland of our people . . . Yes, we are Semites . . . among Aryans; the children of Shem among the children of Japheth . . . foundlings, uninvited guests."[6] Jews were uninvited guests, and the gaping chasm between them and non-Jews—Lilienblum used the terms "Semite" and "Aryan," which were part of the lexicon of the nineteenth century—could never be bridged. The consequence was that incurable malady: Judeophobia and modern antisemitism.

The writer and thinker Michah Yosef Berdichevsky, a native of Podolia who had emigrated west (to Germany) in 1890, wrote in 1899:

> My heart emptied of ancient history and filled instead with new ideas and emotions which brought me to a state of intoxication, to a state of ardor. My being, my existence, my belonging, and my desires shrank down into a single point, and from this point I beheld and examined the entire world. This point was Western culture. To the West! I knelt and bowed before the name. My most heartfelt wish was that God might spread the spirit of Western culture over all life, that the land might be filled with its knowledge and thought.[7]

In Berdichevsky's opinion, Europe had not become Jewish; instead, the Jews must become Europeans—or, more precisely, Western Europeans.

Jabotinsky's rather pretentious argument, as we will see in chapter 4, was an expression of the desire to declare that modern Jews had a place in Europe, and of a sense of belonging, identity, and partnership with Europe and especially with its values. This claim emerged in the nineteenth century in order to serve as Jews' admission ticket to the modern era, and it expanded over the course of the century into a claim that the Jews had made a decisive contribution to the creation of modernity, in all its aspects and manifestations, and were in fact its primary creators and progenitors. Here was an unequivocal response to the description of Jews as uninvited and unwanted guests in Europe, alien to it and its spirit not only in their religion, but also with respect to character and race, to use the vocabulary of the time. This declaration of belonging to Europe—even of being responsible for it—acquired an entirely different meaning in the anti-Jewish literature, which not only described the Jews as an alien minority within Europe but also encouraged and disseminated the false claim that, rather than a feeble minority, the Jews were a terrifying force that had managed to dominate Europe and even Judaize it.[8] The conclusion was that in order to rescue the authentic Europe and extract it from the Jewish domination over its body and soul—a domination that was the very source of and reason for the profound crisis in which Europe found itself—the Jews must either leave Europe of their own will or be uprooted from it.

Despite deeply different attitudes to Europe and to the role Jews played in its history (and to the future they might expect there), Jabotinsky, Lilienblum, and Berdichevsky shared a great admiration for Europe: not necessarily for the concrete historical European reality, but rather for its basic values—that is, for Western culture. And all three feared that both antisemitism and Jews' disappointment in Europe, which had not fulfilled their expectations, would lead to a Jewish rejection of every European cultural asset. The three referred in their work not to any particular part of Europe, but rather to Europe as a single historical and cultural entity.

Yet Europe and Europeanness were not invented by Jews, nor were they the product of Jews' presence or influence. It is true that during the modern era, Jews were part of Europe and contributed significantly to the creation of its various national cultures, as well as to modern European culture in general. Many among them took pride in this contribution and publicized it. However, to speak of Jews in general, or to attribute specific attributes or abilities to them collectively, amounts in our opinion to constructing a mythical Jew and is both mistaken and misleading. The unavoidable result of such generalizations was to attribute to Jews the responsibility or blame for the emergence of capitalism and socialism, nationalism and cosmopolitanism—in other words, to see traces of Jewish influence in every development and every event.

Before Jews could claim to belong to it and identify with it, Europe had to develop flesh and form and become at once a historical entity and a utopian concept (see chapter 1). And before Jews could claim full partnership in and identify with any particular national culture, nationalism itself had to emerge, take shape, and become a dominant phenomenon. Only then, beginning at the start of the nineteenth century, did Jews need to take a position in regard to the European entity—to define their approach to it and to the ideals of Europe and Europeanness. And only since the beginning of the nineteenth century were they required to define their ties to the various nation-states and national cultures that took shape during this time. These attitudes and positions were expressed in their lifestyles, in a repertoire of perceptions and images, and in attempts to understand and interpret the meaning of "Europe" and "Europeanness" and the distinctions among Europe's national cultures. They had to define their expectations of Europe and to determine which European values were worthy of adoption. In other words, from the start of the nineteenth century, the attempt to understand Europe became a central part of Jews' worldview.

It is highly tempting to describe Jews' attitude toward Europe as dichotomous—as a bipolar attitude of adoration and disgust, hatred and love, rejection and influence. Europe was beloved and admired, its culture perceived as the acme of human progress and a treasury of spiritual and cultural assets that must not be forsaken; but at the same time, it was also perceived as a decadent, corrupt world—a place where Jewish people were persecuted and murdered. Europe was at once both glorious and accursed.

Yet a dichotomous description of Jews' approach to and perceptions of Europe would be ahistorical. As captivating as such a description might be, it does not offer a full picture of Jews' encounters with Europe—a picture that must be dynamic, layered, and complex. There was more than one Europe.

EUROCENTRISM AND JUDEOCENTRISM

Given the discussion above, our point of view may be considered both Eurocentric and Judeocentric.

It is Eurocentric because until World War II, Europe was in many ways the center of the world—and not only for Jews, who were not the only group to encounter Europe.[9] During the nineteenth and twentieth centuries—and, indeed, well before then—Europe saw itself as the apotheosis of human development and a torchbearer of enlightenment and progress. It was Europe that named those parts of the world that lay beyond its borders and, from its perspective, discovered them. Europe was the model to which the others who lived outside of it compared themselves and were in turn compared, the ideal to which they aspired and whose challenges they strove to meet, and the standard by which they were judged and judged themselves.[10] At the same time, Europe's conception of itself was perceived as a clear declaration of superiority that permitted the oppression of the others and imposed upon them a worldview and values extrinsic to their own. As a result, it became a mirror through which they examined themselves, a challenge to which they responded, and an enemy that they had to confront.

After World War I, there arose in Europe voices of lamentation and tidings of Europe's decline. Other voices began to express doubts regarding its centrality and especially the universality of its values. Despite this, it cannot be said that Europe's influence on other nations declined.[11] In contrast, after World War II—during the postcolonial era—these doubts increased, and Europe's influence did weaken. Once again Europe was confronted with the questions of what its values were and where its borders lay—of the meaning of Europe and Europeanness. Once more it was devoured by doubts, despair, and self-criticism, filled with the foreboding that *finis Europae*—the end of Europe—was in sight. Yet while the Eurocentric worldview has declined considerably, Europe today remains a model to others, a subject of admiration and aspiration.

Ours is also a Judeocentric point of view—not only because of the importance we attribute to the history of Europe's Jews, and not only because the so-called Jewish Question was the central issue that occupied Europe in the modern age, but because, in our opinion, an analysis of how Jews understood Europe offers a unique perspective on the history of Europe and Western culture over the past two hundred years. The Jewish encounter with Europe, or the Jewish experience in Europe, is more than a central part of Jewish history, more even than a source of explanations for the tragic conclusion of that experience. In our opinion, it also offers a unique vantage point from which we may try to understand the history of Europe itself. This is because in contrast to other peoples outside of Europe, Jews were not part of the world of which European colonialism and imperialism took control, and upon which they imposed the processes of westernization. They were an integral part of the history of Europe, and as a result they observed it both up close, from within, and at a distance, as strangers.[12]

Jews thus had a dual perspective regarding Europe: they were insiders, who saw themselves as flesh of Europe's flesh and were involved in European life and the European experience; and they were outsiders, who approached Europe from the position of a minority or other group caught between two worlds. Jews created their topoi of Europe through a combination of knowledge, preconceptions, and stereotypes. Some Jews even compared themselves to the scientific instruments that detect earthquakes. An example of such claims appears in the anthology *Kehiliateinu* (Our community), which reflects the worldview of a small group of radical Zionist pioneers in Palestine during the early 1920s: "We—the youth of Israel—have experienced the life of Europe, its tremors, and its anxieties with all the fervor of our youth. We were like a seismograph that recorded every slight tremor."[13] According to this assertion, the Jews' dual status within European society and their great sensitivity to developments there were what made them able to sense omens before others. The poet Uri Zvi Greenberg, for example, declared in 1926 that Europe in the twentieth century had been "robbed of heaven" and that only Jews walked in her midst as astrologers (*etztagnin*); according to him, they alone could understand the depth of European reality and foretell Europe's future and destiny.[14]

WHICH EUROPE?

With which Europe are we concerned here? With Europe as a unified cultural entity, or as a combination of multiple identities and multiple cultures and values? In fact, with both. Jews were well aware of the profound differences among the various European cultures. They even emphasized these differences and demonstrated (as we shall see in chapter 7) entirely different attitudes toward individual national cultures. As a result, there were differences in their expectations of the processes of civil and cultural integration in various countries. Moreover, during the nineteenth century, Jews began to believe—some hopefully, some fearfully—that the unity of the Jewish people belonged to the past, and that this was a new age of Jewish Germans, Jewish Frenchmen, Jewish Russians, and so forth. Yet at the same time, some Jews believed that in many respects national borders were meaningless, and that cultural assets and values extended beyond borders to create a single Europe, and consequently a single European Jewish people as well.

The attempt to understand Europe and Europeanness, and on the strength of this understanding to forecast the future that awaited it and the Jews, occupied Europe's Jewish elite since the French Revolution, the Enlightenment, and emancipation. The questions asked and the answers given have undergone countless changes and evolutions over the course of the past two hundred years. Various historical contexts raised new questions, which led to different answers. The desire on the part of Israeli Jews to understand all matters relating to Europe and Western culture[15] stemmed—and still stems—from three necessities:

1. To determine the borders and domain of European culture's actual and desired influence on society and culture in Israel (in fact, in Jewish Pal-

estine since the 1880s). This is related to the struggle being waged over the cultural composition of Israeli society, the definition of its identity, its cultural affinity, and its geographical and political belonging.

2. To take a position on the political events that have taken place in Europe since the 1990s, as well as to select one of the following options: to remain a backwater of this unified civilization from an economic and political point of view;[16] to become an inseparable part of it; to bind Israel's fate to the American empire; or to be part of the Arab-Muslim Middle East.

3. To take a position on the issue of the antisemitism, both open and concealed, which has once again emerged in Europe.[17] In this context, a question arises: which is the real Europe—the irrational, fanatical, imperialistic, antisemitic, and racist Europe, or the rational, tolerant Europe, which exhibits openness, curiosity, and impatience, and strives for wholeness?

Two answers to this question have appeared in Israeli discourse. According to the first, Europe at the close of the twentieth century and the birth of the twenty-first is realizing the ancient ideal of a federative continent—a continent that has shed nationalism and put an end to international wars and imperial arrogance. But according to the second, materialism, technological advancement, comfort, self-satisfaction, and serenity at the end of the twentieth century will not be able to prevent the rebirth of the forces of darkness of the not-so-distant past, with antisemitism at the forefront. The second answer raises additional questions: Is this simply a case of mistaking shadows for mountains, and does the criticism of Europe stem not from existential fear but from Jewish or Israeli paranoia, a hatred of Europe, and an inability to understand that Europe in the second half of the twentieth century is not Europe in the first half, but an entirely new entity? Or are Jews indeed the sensitive seismograph picking up signals from the depths, able to discern that the fault lines of calamity still lie within the magic mountain (*Zauberberg*) of Europe?[18]

The reality of the dichotomous Jewish opinion of Europe—and of what Europe symbolizes and represents—was born and formulated during the nineteenth century and persisted throughout the twentieth. Despite the Holocaust, Jews' basic views regarding Europe changed little even at the start of the twenty-first century. Is it desirable or possible to remove Europeanness from modern Jewish culture, or should it be cultivated?

Should the State of Israel be part of Europe, or should it turn its back on Europe—and Western culture? These questions continue to be asked with great intensity by a Jewish society that exists outside of Europe. This fact reveals, among other things, that Europe and Europeanness hold a central place not only in the Jewish memory, but in Israel's present and its future as well.

EUROPE DISCOVERS ITSELF, JEWS DISCOVER EUROPE

Ah, Europe, Europe!
FRIEDRICH NIETZSCHE,
Beyond Good and Evil[1]

There will be a time when no one in Europe will ask any longer, who is a Jew and who is a Christian.
JOHANN GOTTFRIED HERDER,
Reflections on the Philosophy of the History of Mankind[2]

For hundreds of years, the word "Europe" denoted a geographical location whose borders were not precisely defined; it did not appear to describe a specific, well-defined human or social entity. Jews who read Greek encountered the word "Europe" as a geographical reference in Jewish literature from the Hellenic period—for instance, in Flavius Josephus's *Jewish Antiquities*,[3] in *The Book of Jubilees*, and in *The Sibylline Oracles*. Jewish literature borrowed the word and the geographical area it denoted from contemporary Greek geographical and ethnographical literature, which devoted special treatises to descriptions of Europe and defined it in opposition to the external world.[4] Furthermore, it borrowed the Greek division of the world into three continents. Within Jewish Hellenic literature, there was an effort to apply the three-continent model to the description of the world in Genesis 5.[5]

The Jews who lived in Europe during the Middle Ages were not aware that they lived in the part of the world labeled Europe. The tenth-century *Book of Josippon* does not mention Europe in its geographic descriptions; as far as we know, the name does not appear in any Jewish text from that period. This is not a consequence of limited geographical knowledge on the part of the Jews; Europe's Christians were also unaware that they resided in Europe, and they defined themselves in terms of provinces and countries that were part of the Christian world. To be sure, Europe as a geographical concept did not, over the course of generations, disappear from descriptions of the world in literature and cartography, and at times it was also used for rhetorical purposes. However, it was known primarily to the intellectual elite. Scribes in Charlemagne's court thus used the terms "European" and "Europeanness" as synonyms for "Christian" and "Christianity," and in the poem "Karlus Magnus et Leo Papa" (Charlemagne and Pope Leo), an anonymous court poet described Charlemagne as *"rex, pater Europae"* (king, father of Europe) and *"regnum Europae"* (king of Europe—that is, from the Pyrenees to the Elbe River).[6]

THE BIRTH OF EUROPE AS REALITY AND CONCEPT

In reality the correspondence between Europe as a geographical region and the region controlled by Western Christianity was not precise, and local geographical consciousness was far stronger than any regional consciousness. Until the seventeenth century, it was primarily the Muslim enemy at the gate that inspired a pan-European rhetoric: the battle of Poitiers was portrayed as a critical confrontation between the inhabitants of Europe and the Arabs (then called Saracens). The Ottoman Empire was described as a foreign, threatening force encroaching on Europe, and hence it was necessary—as Pope Pius II declared in 1464—"to drive the Turks from Europe." Not only did the humanist pope (né Aeneas Silvius Piccolomini) use the word "Europe," but he also coined the adjective "European" to widen the gulf between the inhabitants of the West and the "Asiatic," "barbaric" Turks, and in order to present Europe as "coherent" and "collective."[7] However, this was not merely rhetoric for the purpose of uniting the Christian world against the enemy. The Roman Catholic Church created Europe as a region composed of a many-branched family tree of nations,[8] and the classic Christian heritage endowed it with a common background and with characteristics of a shared identity, both spiritual and physical. Both during and after the Renaissance, writers, thinkers, and scholars preferred the term "Europe" to *"Christanitas,"* cultivated a cross-European consciousness (*nostre Europe*), and searched for kernels of a culture and consciousness common to all the continent's nations, past and present. Humanists—part of the *Gelehrtenrepublik* (republic of scholars) who, like the scholars and students of the Middle Ages, traveled without difficulty from country to country—spoke a common language (French, rather than the Latin of medieval times), and exchanged ideas;

they transformed the word "Europe" from a geographical concept and lexicographical entry into an idea and a vision.[9] They were the first to speak of Europeanness and "the European," emphasize cross-European identity, and highlight the affinity among Europe's various regions. They considered Europe the center and crowning jewel of the known world.

Voltaire expressed the consciousness of this new identity thus: "Today there are no more French, Germans, Spanish, or even English. There are only Europeans." Europeans, wrote Voltaire, did fight among themselves, just as the Greeks had fought each other; but individual Europeans from different countries behaved so politely when they met, that an observer would think they were compatriots. Jean-Jacques Rousseau asserted that individual cultures no longer existed; there were only Europeans, "all [with] the same tastes, the same passions, the same manners."[10] The conservative British historian Edmund Burke wrote in 1796 that "no European can be a complete exile in any part of Europe."[11] Voltaire, Burke, and others saw Europe—at least, Western Europe—as a blessed region and the cradle of intellectual development, enlightenment, science, and art, which made it the most developed and enlightened civilization of all: *ex Europae lux* (the light comes from Europe).[12] The conservative idealist writer Novalis (Friedrich von Hardenberg), in contrast, looked forward in his 1799 essay "Europe or Christianity" to a reunification of Western Christianity accomplished through the merger of the Catholic and Protestant churches.[13] Others, like Heinrich Heine, looked forward to the harmonious melding of biblical Judaism and Hellenism—that is, of the traditional spiritual and aesthetic foundations of European civilization. Such a merger would bring Europe to a full realization of its calling. The Europeans, in this idealistic worldview, were of the same utopian cut as the Greeks—though, according to the classification laid out in the *Panegyricus* by the Athenian rhetorician Isocrates, their name attested not to a common origin (genus) but to a shared mentality (*dianoia*) and similar culture and education (*paideia*).[14]

Recognition of Europe's unity, not only in theory but in practice, increased after the Napoleonic wars. The French historian and statesman François Guizot was the first to write about the history of Europe, in his 1828 *Histoire générale de la civilization en Europe*,[15] which Heine later described as a cultural Tower of Babel, with many nations having taken part in its construction over the course of hundreds of years. Nietzsche wrote that "morality in Europe today is herd animal morality,"[16] but elsewhere he prophesied that trade and industry, postal communication, the distribution of books, and increased mobility would necessarily blur the divisions between nations and finally obliterate those divisions to give birth to a new, mixed race—a strong race "of European man."[17] In truth, Nietzsche maintained, a common European background had existed for a long time, since in every aspect of morality, Europe spoke a single language, which was expanding outside of Europe as well. In any case, the accepted view was that Europe possessed a common set of basic principles and a unique understanding of the world—a Western worldview. In the mid-nineteenth century, another shared factor appeared. The Industrial Revolution created a cross-European working class whose universal interests were expressed in the opening declaration of *The Communist Manifesto* in 1848 that a specter—that of Communism—was haunting Europe. In contrast to the opinion of Otto Bismarck, the German chancellor, Europe was far more than a geographical term. During the calm between the two world wars, José Ortega y Gasset described "the common property of Europe" as deeper and more rooted than any of these differences of opinion.[18]

Many of these images of Europe were the fruits of imagination, utopia, and delusion, and were the province of a small community of intellectuals.[19] In reality, Europe's inhabitants did share a common religious background, philosophical framework, and cultural heritage. But the idea of a universal Europe, which arose as an attempt to obscure differences and disputes, was not fully realized. Reading even a fraction of European travel literature shows that a Frenchman did not need to stray as far as the Balkans, Poland, or Russia to comprehend the cultural differences between himself and the inhabitants of other nations. Madame de Staël, one of the originators of the concept of Europe, asserted that "in these modern times, one must be European," but in her *Littérature du Nord et littérature du Midi* (Literature of the north and literature of the south, 1800), she followed in Montesquieu's footsteps[20] and divided Western Europe into north and south—two regions with profound differences in cultural mentality, each embodying a separate side of Europe's character.[21] Germans or Englishmen who traveled south in order to discover classical Italy or Greece imagined meeting people with character traits different from theirs and did not always grant them a flattering characterization.[22] Climatic theories differentiated not only between the character traits of Europe's inhabitants and those of other continents, but also among the character traits of inhabitants of different parts of Europe characterized by different climates.

Needless to say, the eastern part of Europe—part of the Hapsburg Empire and all of the Russian Empire—was perceived by the West as a part of the world characterized by barbarism, fanaticism, and ignorance, light years away from cultured Europe. This image emerged during the Enlightenment, which "invented Western Europe and Eastern Europe together, as complementing concepts, defining each other by opposition and adjacency."[23]

At the same time, an opposite process was taking place. In parallel with their growing particularistic consciousness, the broadening of Europeans' geographic horizons in the wake of geographic discoveries exposed them to new worlds and new cultures.[24] This development prompted Europe's desire to define the cultural borders that separated it from the pagan civilizations—several of which, such as India and China, could claim numerous impressive achievements in various cultural and scientific fields, as Europe discovered to its surprise. Thus in parallel to the appearance, in the late eighteenth century, of an outlook in which nations and people (*Volk*) were considered organic entities—and in which Europe itself was composed of such separate entities—there also appeared a perspective in which Europe was a single civilization that had developed and crystallized according to its own rules and principles. Up until the nineteenth century, the European sense of superiority was based not on racial advantages but on the achievements of the Renaissance, the scientific revolution, the Industrial Revolution, and the Enlightenment.[25] In Samuel Johnson's *Rasselas* (1759), the prince's companion Imlac, who has seen the world, explains that the peoples of Northern and Western Europe are "almost another order of beings" who are "in possession of all power and all knowledge." They are more intelligent and stronger; "in their countries . . . a thousand arts, of which we never heard, are continually labouring for their convenience and pleasure; and whatever their own climate has denied them is supplied by their commerce." These traits were God-given gifts.[26] Similar but more authentic words came from the East. Mustafa Sami, a former chief secretary of the Ottoman embassy in Paris, wrote in 1840: "thanks to their science, Europeans have found ways to overcome plague and other illnesses, and have invented many mechanical devices to mass-produce various items." His and other Turks' expressions of wonder were accompanied by astonishment about how "the smallest of the continents" had attained such power and influence.[27] The collective European genius—its vibrant creative spirit—was later explained in other ways. Some theories claimed it originated in the nature of the relationship between human society and the natural properties (that is, environmental conditions) that were unique to Europe. Montesquieu, for example, believed that the origin of the European spirit of liberty lay in the continent's topographical structure, which did not lend itself to the creation of (necessarily despotic) large empires. Anthropological theories maintained that the source of Europe's unique nature and of its superiority over all other peoples was its population's racial heritage, Caucasian or Indo-European. The result of all these explanations was that predictions regarding the future also dealt with the destiny of Europe—both in its own right and in relation to other civilizations—not as a collection of empires and states, but as a single entity with a common past and for which a common future was expected.

Thus two opposing views appeared and matured during the nineteenth century. According to the first, the concept of a unified Europe was a cloak obscuring the reality of a Europe whose individual nations and peoples each cultivated and broadened their own sense of self and uniqueness, among other means by emphasizing their differences and contrasts with all the others. According to the second view, cross-European cooperation was the reality, and the nations' emphasis on their differences and their attempts at individuation were a result of the fact that they were but newly born and were thus obliged to invent a distinct identity for themselves. Nietzsche wrote that in Europe a "nation" was more a *res facta* (product) than a *res nata* (natural phenomenon); in fact, the European nations were almost a *res ficta et picta*—an imaginary and thoroughly new entity. In contrast, he wrote, the Jews were an ancient and everlasting people.[28] José Ortega y Gasset wrote in a similar spirit that France and Spain did not exist "as unities in the depths of the French and Spanish soul . . . before France and Spain came into being"; Frenchmen and Spaniards were "things that had to be hammered out in two thousand years of toil." Nationality was a product, not a cause. As a result, Ortega y Gasset believed that an annulment of particularistic nationality would not be a change of earth-shaking proportions, and that the creation of a Europe without nationalities was entirely possible;[29] it was not a matter of establishing an artificial structure, but one of returning to the reality that existed before the nineteenth century:

> The souls of the French and English and Spanish are, and will be, as different as you like, but they possess the same psychological architecture; and, above all, they are gradually becoming similar in

content. Religion, science, law, art, social and sentimental values are being shared alike. Now these are the spiritual things by which man lives. The homogeneity, then, becomes greater than if the souls themselves were all cast in identical mould . . . To-day, in fact, we are more influenced by what is European in us than by what is special to us as Frenchmen, Spaniards, and so on.[30]

In any case, even before the age of nationalism, Europe was factious, split, and dissentious; it possessed no consciousness of any sort of unity that was not based on religion.[31] The deciding role in the creation of modern Europe was played by the French Revolution and Napoleon's campaigns.[32] These were the driving force of nationalistic awakening and of the myth of nation and homeland, but at the same time they turned Europe into a stage for events that would create a profound impulse toward reciprocity between the nations. From this point on, the discussion of Europe, its common future, and European civilization became a matter of course.

This development was not lost on Jewish *maskilim* (proponents of the Enlightenment). Even from their provincial vantage point, the great changes taking place in Europe were very clear.[33] The *maskil*, historian, and popularizer Kalman Shulman of Vilna inaugurated the description of the new era in his *Sefer Divrei Yemei Olam*, which was the first universal history (*Weltgeschichte*) written in Hebrew. He cited two events that, according to him, shook "the foundations of the world": the French Revolution and the Napoleonic wars. Both of them, wrote Shulman, "flew as a spark" from "one end of Europe to the other." The result of these earth-shaking events in France would be that "the rest of Europe too would stir and take up arms." The widespread assumption was that the French Revolution and Napoleonic wars had begun a process that would weaken Europe's religious background and, as a result, would lead to the crystallization of the concept of a universal European identity based not on religion but, as we have stated, on values, tastes, lifestyle, shared historical consciousness, and common cultural background. From the Jewish perspective, it seemed that "the universe, with all its old laws, had turned upside down, and a new land [Europe] and new order were created under Heaven," and that the "iron wall" of religious hatred had collapsed.[34] It was in this spirit that the Russian Jewish *maskil* Isaac Baer Levinsohn (known by the acronym "Rival") wrote in 1834: "But like the passing of night and its heavy clouds, so will the thickness and foolishness which have obscured Europe until now disappear, and the sun of wisdom and enlightenment will rise from the East . . . until even the nations' throngs who walked blindly in the dark will see a great light . . . and all nations of Europe, large and small, will strive to correct their manners and desire the love of Mankind."[35]

JEWS DISCOVER EUROPE AND THEIR OWN EUROPEAN IDENTITY

Beginning in the latter part of the eighteenth century, and especially after the Napoleonic wars,[36] the modern Jewish intellectual elite began to realize that events taking place in one part of Europe had an effect on developments in every other part, as well as on the situation of the Jews who lived there. The elite insisted that cross-European phenomena consisted not only of policies and wars, but of developments in economics, society, culture, and technology as well. The elite realized in addition that modern Europe had a cultural identity as well as a religious one, and that as a result it was important to examine Europe's nature carefully. In other words, Europe was transformed in the eyes of this elite from a geographic concept and a political reality into a cultural entity, and therefore a subject for discussion and consideration in that light.

In his January 1770 response "An einen Mann von Stande" (To a man of high rank), Moses Mendelssohn wrote about "the great kingdoms of Europe" that might, Heaven forbid, become involved in a general war.[37] The Sanhedrin, which gathered in Paris in 1806 on Napoleon's orders, discussed "European policy" and referred to the Jews as "Children of Israel and residents of Europe," who were promised a better future and a more secure existence under Napoleon's regime than they had had in the past.[38] There is no hint in either of these two texts of a perception of Europe as a single cultural entity. But that perception was expressed in a speech made by Josef Mendelssohn (1770–1848), Moses Mendelssohn's son and a wealthy banker, at the 1792 meeting that established the Society of Friends (Gesellschaft der Freunde), a society of educated Jewish bourgeois. The younger Mendelssohn spoke—in the spirit of optimistic rhetoric that characterized the *Haskalah*, or Jewish Enlightenment—about the "light of enlightenment that has shone on all of Europe in our century [and] has also cast its blessed influence on our nation for the last thirty years." In his opinion, this universal European "light of enlightenment" was expressed in a desire for religious reform, in whose wake the Jews would be able to separate "the kernel from the husk in the religion of our forefathers."[39] The intellectual members of the Society for Culture and Science of the

Jews (Verein für Kultur und Wissenschaft der Juden), which was founded in 1819, also believed that Europe was not merely a political concept, but an embodiment of the universal spirit (within European borders, naturally) and of "universal reason." Eduard Gans, one of the founders of the society, declared in October 1822 that Europe was not born by chance, "but is the necessary result of thousands of years of effort by the rational spirit, which can be observed throughout world history." According to this view, European life and the universal Europe were not identical to German national and *Volk* culture, to the idea of the *Deutschtum* (Germanness), or to the seemingly authentic and autochthonic attachment to the German *Vaterland* (fatherland).[40] The idea that Germany's unification was inseparable from the cosmopolitan nature of German culture was widespread among various circles at the start of the nineteenth century. August Wilhelm Schlegel, for example, a historian of literature who translated Shakespeare's works into German, saw the German nationalistic patriotism that sprang up after the Napoleonic wars as no more than passing childishness and provincialism, and opined that Germany's destiny was to become the *Mutterland* (motherland) of Europe.

In 1864, in Eastern Europe, the radical *maskil* and poet Y. L. Gordon described Jews' integration into European society and culture as follows: "How many of Israel's nobility and of its wealthy, who are Jewish in their hearts and faces and appearance and clothing and manners, will you find respectable in the eyes of the government as children of Europe? Now let us be calm and trust in our God, because there is hope for the last of us, and we have a future."[41]

Jewish intellectuals' allegiance to the universal European idea at the start of the nineteenth century was in part the result of a desire to consolidate a supernational framework for Jewish belonging—a theoretically universal framework similar to European civic society, which would be superior to any national culture. If Jews could not be natural Germans because they were born without any feeling of German nationalism (*volkstümlich*), there was nothing to prevent them from being European bourgeois or intellectuals, because they were citizens of the new European civilization. In this way, the philosopher Johann Gottfried Herder's dream might be fulfilled—that "there will be a time when no one in Europe will ask any longer, who is a Jew and who is a Christian; because the Jew will also live by Europe's laws and contribute to the good of the nation." In other words, Jews would become part of European humanity (*Humanität*).[42]

Gans wrote: "the good fortune and significance of the European lie in the fact that he may freely choose his own status for himself from the multiplicity of positions available in bourgeois liberal society, and in the fact that he will sense every other social status in the status that he chose."[43] The Jews would not disappear, but they would be absorbed into the European world. Despite this, Jewish values would not die out and would continue to contribute to Europe: "only the bothersome independence" would be destroyed, not the independence necessary for wholeness. Judaism could integrate with the European unity, wrote Leopold Zunz, because it was a culture that originated from an ancient common spirit.[44] When a Jewish writer wrote about his feeling of belonging to humanity, or to the general culture, he meant the culture of Western Europe. It is no wonder that from the conservative Orthodox perspective, "enlightened Europe" seemed like a "desert wasteland"—a world of atheistic heresy, in which Voltaire played the part of the seducing serpent and which opened its gates to the Jews in order to bring about the end of Judaism.[45]

These semantic and ideological shifts reflected changes in worldview and historical recognition. The intellectuals and men of letters of the late eighteenth and early nineteenth centuries generally spoke of the kingdoms of Europe because the model on which their thinking was based was that of the state—that is, enlightened absolutism. They also spoke occasionally of the peoples of Europe, because they were aware that the French Revolution and Romanticism had raised the people to the historical center stage as an active historical subject, and also moved the homeland to center stage as the object of belonging and attachment. The Jewish elite of the following generations, by contrast, also began to speak of European culture, or the culture of Europe.[46] Thus at the start of the nineteenth century, the word "Europe" primarily symbolized institutions of power and sociopolitical ideas, while later Europe would signify culture (*Kultur*)—that is, language, literature, free inquiry, music, art, theater, and the values and customs of urban bourgeois society.[47]

Jewish awareness of identification with Europe, or at least declarations of that identification, increased at the end of the nineteenth century, and the trend continued with vigor during the twentieth century. Jews described Judaism as a central partner in the historic creation of Europe and, moreover, described themselves as bearing a responsibility for Europe's destiny and future—and as holding the keys to its salvation in their hands. Thus, for example, the Jewish German journalist and author Moritz Goldstein wrote in a 1912 article titled, very typically, "Wir und Europa" (We and Europe), that ever since Moses Mendelssohn's generation, European Jews had seen themselves as "possess[ing] European culture in all respects" and "instinctively [had felt] entirely at home in Europe." This was a spiritual belonging (*geistige Zugehörigkeit*). Not only that, but it was they who endowed Europe with its moral pathos—its spiritual dimension. At the same time, the Jews had learned from Europe to develop their own nationalism and understood that they would be able to realize their individualism only outside of Europe.[48] The final conclusion of the European doctrines was that the Jews must become hyper-Europeans (*hypereuropäisch*) so that world redemption (*Heil*) would once again come to the world from Judah. Rabbi Dr. Mordechai Ehrenpreis, who traveled frequently throughout Europe between the two world wars, wrote that his understanding of "the innermost core of the essence of Western life" and his "very great [affinity] to the European spirit," was a result of his visits to Europe's small nations and their capitals. That was where he discovered "the average European man, with all his nationalistic limitations, virtues, and shortcomings," and where his "comprehensive view of today's European citizen" matured. In a trip to Prague, Lisbon, Czernowitz, and Geneva he found a looking glass to the European world and discovered "the inner soul of our [European] generation."[49] In discussions of Palestinian Jews' attachment to Europe, emphasis was also placed on their direct spiritual attachment to Europe's natural (local) landscape, because their distance from it prompted a yearning for it and a search for a worthy replacement. Meir Yaari, the spiritual leader of the Hashomer Hazair group, wrote the following in the same spirit in 1920 from Galilee: "While we dug holes to plant trees, we never heard the sounds of the forest around us. There are those who sometimes discourage yearnings for the faraway specter of the forest, to its mists and nectar, to the satyrs of the forest. But we planted young olive and nut trees, and are already dreaming of forests and moss, of mushrooms and bubbling swamps."[50]

Moreover, identification with Europe led to identification with the idea that Europe had a civilizationist mission. In December 1858, the maskilic newspaper *Hamagid* published a series of articles called "The Spirit of the Time," glorifying and praising Europe, which had disseminated its culture throughout the world: "Europe's actions are not miserly ones; it does not hide the seeds of knowledge in its own deep soil alone, but by the fruit of its actions it may be said to feed the whole world; it sends the springs of knowledge to water even strange lands at the edges of the world and corners of the earth. In the spirit of wisdom they destroyed the borders of India, China, and Japan, in order to serve as dew to those lands as well, and revive even faraway fields."[51]

By the end of the nineteenth century, there were Jews who identified with the West's universalist mission and saw themselves as representatives of European civilization and as taking part in its design, just as they considered themselves full partners in Europe's consciousness of its superiority. The bitter irony was that not only did Jews identify themselves as Europeans; so did those who were not overly sympathetic toward the Jews. In 1793 the German nationalist philosopher Johann Gottlieb Fichte had described the Jews as forming a "nation within a nation" throughout Europe: "in almost every country in Europe there sprawls a giant nation with hostile intentions which is engaged in an eternal war against all the rest . . . that nation is Judaism."[52] Almost eighty years later, in September 1870, Bismarck described the Jews as having "no real home, they are generally Europeans, cosmopolitan, nomad." (But he noted in 1892 that "the Jews bring to the mixture of the different German tribes a certain *mousseux* [sparkle], which should not be underestimated.")[53] Statements of this sort taught Moshe Leib Lilienblum the fact that—as he wrote in his article "The Revival of Israel in the Land of our Fathers" in 1882—"we were regarded as strangers in Europe . . . against our will we were exiled from our land to Western Europe and from there to Poland."[54] Europe was merely the place where Jews resided. It was not a permanent home for them, but a place through which they wandered—sometimes of their own free will, sometimes not—without belonging to any place at all.

THE GLORIOUS NINETEENTH CENTURY— EUROPE AS PROMISED LAND

The living, enlightened, edificial time,
The nineteenth century, praised and sublime.
YEHUDA LEIB LEVIN,
"Sheelot Hazman" (Questions of our time)[1]

And yet throughout Europe the Jews see the light of
liberty and live a vibrant, multifaceted life.
MORITZ LAZARUS,
Was heisst national? (What is a nation?)[2]

Jews were not alone, of course, in appraising the nineteenth century and placing it on the scales for judgment. Once the century had ended, it was possible to reflect and draw conclusions. Some Jews extolled the century, while others regarded it with disappointment; everyone was concerned with the question of what form Europe might take in the new century—would the twentieth century continue along the path of positive and far-reaching changes seen during the nineteenth century, or was the nineteenth century a time of distortions that would only grow more acute and more powerful in the next century? Opinions were divided between optimism and pessimism: where some saw decline, others found reasons for reassurance.[3] "Our nineteenth century," Karl Marx declared in 1856, was characterized by forces of industry and science that "no epoch of the former human history had ever suspected." At the same time, however, it revealed signs of far greater decline than those seen in the twilight of the Roman Empire: "in our days everything seems pregnant with its contrary."[4] In 1849, in contrast, in his opening address to the International Peace Congress held in Paris, Victor Hugo described a vision of a Europe united in peace that would be the acme of the nineteenth century: "the nineteenth century will be—let us say it openly—the greatest page in history."

During this century the various European nations would, without losing their distinctive qualities and glorious individuality, become "blended into a superior unity and constitute a European fraternity." According to Hugo, the railroad and steamship contributed greatly to European unification, and through its colonies, Europe would bring not barbarism but civilization to other continents: "civilization will replace barbarism."[5]

In the following two chapters, we will describe the evaluation of the nineteenth century by Jewish thinkers and journalists at the end of that century. By "nineteenth century," we mean, of course, the European century; this is the century that was placed on the scales. We will examine Europe's achievements first, and its failings afterward.[6]

THE TWO FACES OF THE NINETEENTH CENTURY

The intellectual Jewish elite assessed the nineteenth century from both a Jewish and a European point of view—that is, Europe's fate concerned the elite because it considered itself an inseparable part of Europe. As a Jewish elite, it asked which of the expectations, hopes, and wishes that had occupied it during most of the period in question had been fulfilled, and which had met with disappointment; similarly, it dealt with the question of what might be expected from Europe during the next century. In this context, the Jewish elite evaluated itself as well: where had it been correct, and where mistaken; had it successfully understood the essence of Europe; and might that understanding deepen at the start of the twentieth century?

The portrait drawn of the nineteenth century by the Jewish elite—and by non-Jewish elites in Europe's various countries—had, as we have mentioned, two sides. One side depicted Europe as the pinnacle of mankind's achievements, a perfect mix of civilization and culture, of material comfort and moral refinement. "We live in a time that recalls the glory days of the Renaissance and the Reformation," declares a character in Theodor Herzl's 1898 *Die Güter des Lebens* (The assets of life).[7] On the other side, the Jewish elite described the century as an age of myriad afflictions and illusions—a world of moral decline, loneliness, and emptiness. From the Jews' perspective, the nineteenth century was a time in which they were granted citizenship and equal opportunity, but it was also a period that saw the appearance of the incurable plague of modern antisemitism, and one in which profound schisms were revealed that created unprecedented divergence in the Jewish world.

Let us begin with the positive side of the century.

EMBRACING EUROPE

From the modern Jewish perspective, the nineteenth century opened with soaring hopes and expectations. David Frankel, one of the founding editors of the first Jewish periodical in German, *Shulamit* (founded in 1806), expressed those hopes as follows: the "people of Abraham" were attempting, despite all the difficulties placed in their path, to attain recognition as equals in humanity, and *Kultur* (culture) would enable them to "embrace Europe."[8] According to this optimistic view of the future, it was not Europe that would embrace the Jews who lived within its borders, but the Jews who would embrace Europe. In other words, it was the Jews who needed to change and improve in order to become worthy of Europe's loving, accepting embrace.

The longing for Europe's firm embrace originated in the perception that the European spirit (often represented, as we have seen, by the German spirit) was the pinnacle of humanity: a blessed and welcome combination of reason, intellectual achievement, education (*Bildung*), and aesthetic sensitivity. Earlier we quoted Eduard Gans, who described Europe in Hegelian terms: "Europe is not the work or the outcome of chance which would have been different, better or worse, but the inevitable result of the effort made, through many millennia, by the Spirit of Reason which manifests itself in world history." Gans expressed his vision as follows: "This, then, is the demand of present-day Europe: the Jews must completely incorporate themselves into Europe's social and cultural fabric. This demand, the logical consequence of the European principle, must be put to the Jews. Europe would be untrue to itself and to its essential nature if it did not put forth this demand. Now the time for this demand, and its fulfillment, has come." If so, the Jews must be an inseparable part of European culture; but, he added, Europe was "a plurality whose unity can only be found in the whole," while the Jews were a "unity which has not yet become a plurality."[9]

Leopold (Yom-Tov) Lipmann Zunz, one of the foremost Jewish scholars of his time and a distinguished member of the Wissenschaft des Judentums (Science of Judaism movement), concluded an 1832 book with a highly optimistic picture: "From now on, the light must shine not from Babylon, but from Germany, our homeland." "Religious persecutions, spiritual oppression and social disintegration," he continued, "can no longer withstand the forces of the new era." According to Zunz, Europe—in particular Germany, rather than France, as Germany was the pinnacle of culture and civilization, its inhabitants noted for a wondrous blend of patience and energy, wisdom and innocence—had shaken off the last remnants of barbarity and demonstrated a steadfast spirit and sense of compassion. Nothing could successfully oppose "enlightened Europe's mighty strides" and prevent the triumph of liberty and civilization. The heritage of medieval times had been erased as though it had never existed, and little time would elapse before this European civilization, its conflicts ended, would shed its light on czarist Russia as well.[10] "The injustices of the Middle Ages," promised Moshe Leib Lilienblum in May 1881, "will never be renewed."[11] At the same time, Nathan Birnbaum, a Zionist who later moved to the Haredi (ultra-Orthodox) camp, declared at the start of the twentieth century that "the Jewish people will belong to European civilization, or it will not exist at all"; this was because the Jewish nation (*Volkstum*) belonged to the great partnership of European civilization.[12] However, as we shall see, his opinion on this subject was not consistent.

The question arises: what inspired this optimistic, even messianic, picture of the future regarding the Jews' full integration in Europe, and Europe's readiness to embrace them?

BETWEEN REVOLUTIONARY EUROPE AND THE EUROPE OF ENLIGHTENED ABSOLUTISM

The late eighteenth-century Enlightenment in Europe impressed the perception upon the Jewish *Haskalah* that a new era was dawning in Europe, one entirely different from its predecessors. This view was expressed to some extent by modern Jews' orientation toward and rhetoric regarding the future.[13] Historical time was now seen as moving forward, along a path of both material and spiritual innovation that would lead to an age of light. In the few surviving written reactions about the Jewish response to the French Revolution and the Napoleonic wars as they were taking place, there is a noticeable belief that these were a victory for reason and a joining of hearts that would bring about a profound change in the nature of political rule in Europe. *Hameassef* (The gatherer), the newspaper of the *Haskalah*, published an ode in 1790 to France's great committee, describing the national assembly as a body laboring to enforce the principle of universal justice, and expressing the author's hope that the situation of the Jewish people would improve:

> O House of Jacob! Fed on sorrow,
> Thou hast fallen terribly, through no sin of your own;
> Be of good courage, for there is yet hope,
> A year of salvation draws nigh
> Your righteousness shall shine forth . . .
>
> Blessed are you who sow justice,
> The generation of your fathers rejoices in you;
> You have constructed a memorial,
> On which the world may perch like the moon . . .[14]

In its early years, the French Revolution was seen as an event that "removed the yoke [of injustice] from Europe's nations." The revolution was perceived as disseminating religious tolerance and civil liberty, and therefore as bringing an end to religious fanaticism and the medieval "clouds of darkness."[15] After Napoleon, "the world and all its ancient laws were overturned and a new land and new order were created under the sun."[16]

Naturally, there were also doubters. First and foremost was Moses Mendelssohn, who believed that the course of human history was one of peaks and valleys, and that Jews would therefore do well to be wary and not pin their hopes on what only seemed to be invincible progress. Indeed, during the 1820s, the French Revolution, the Reign of Terror, and the Napoleonic wars were already portrayed as a period of chaos—a regime of violent terror and boastful tyranny. The blame was attributed to, among others, the aesthetic philosophers, headed by Voltaire and Rousseau, under whose influence France had become a "dangerous, rabid man" and brought about the deaths of "thousands and tens of thousands in Europe."[17] From the perspective of the 1860s, Kalman Shulman wrote that the French Revolution had brought "tens of millions of ignorant men, the rabble and dregs of society, who fear neither God nor King" to the historical forefront.[18] In 1869, Lilienblum wrote that after the revolution, European history "overflowed with rivers of blood, and Europe's nations have become as savage as the beasts of the field."[19]

Despite this ominous view of European civilization as overflowing with abominations, it is difficult to find evidence of nostalgia for previous generations. The new generation, even with its flaws and maladies, was perceived as the end of Old Europe—in Shulman's words, that home of "all criminal evil, all murderous killing . . . and all the abominations of Man and God." Since France was not considered a fitting representative for the new century, that torch should be passed to another country; Shulman elected Prussia. He described it—despite its wars against France, Denmark, and Austria—as the nation of education and culture: "On the basis of the knowledge that it produces, [Prussia] was praised in all corners of Europe; the Prussians all bent their ears to learning as well, until almost no man could be found in Prussia who did not possess rudimentary education."[20] He regarded the Prussian victory over France—"this great and wonderful thing"[21]—as a victory over a savage people who were prisoners of fantasy. If formerly Shulman had believed that Prussia was plotting "to extinguish the flame of enlightenment and the brightness of civilization and culture, whose origin is France and its inspiration all the rest of Europe," he now believed that France was actually the threat to culture.[22] Czar Alexander II was also lauded and described as a *"hasid"* (a righteous man) who had liberated Russia's serfs, enacted regulatory reforms "based on the foundations of justice and honesty," and "sounded the horn of enlightenment in such an exalted way that within not many days Russia had ascended a hundred rungs on the ladder of learning and science." The czar had opened "the gates of all the schools and institutions of knowledge and science" to the Jews, and ushered the whole of Russia through the gates of civilization: "Commerce increased during the days of the exalted Emperor, and agriculture and all forms of labor and industry flourished like a vine. The railroad and telegraph were built and installed across his domain by his word."[23] In this way, Jewish *maskilim* from Eastern Europe adopted the opinion, born in the seventeenth century, that Russia had ceased to be an Asiatic country and had become part of Europe.[24]

In the eyes of the *maskilim*, enlightened absolutism was perceived as a regime that implemented the Enlightenment's values of tolerance, suppressed religious fundamentalism, instilled stability and order, and reined in the masses' radical outbreaks and passions, which were apt to lead to new tyranny. Enlightened absolutism was depicted as an ideal regime, which could effect gradual changes without upheavals or turbulence. Shulman was not the only one who believed in the optimistic picture of the future put forth by Levinsohn during the first half of the nineteenth century. In 1851—after the failure of the Revolutions of 1848 (called the Spring of Nations)—Shmuel Joseph Fuenn, another Jewish Russian moderate *maskil*, described the achievements of enlightened absolutism: "Suddenly a gleaming light appeared in Europe's skies and with the glory of the gentile nations it illuminated the entire land; wisdom and intellect were brought together; justice and peace embraced."[25] Enlightened absolutism was therefore seen as having brought Europe out of the "darkness of barbarity" and the anarchy of revolutionary mass rule, and into an age of refined, tolerant, and humanistic culture. The absolute ruler was sometimes described in the contemporary literature as the "Cyrus of our times" and as a messiah: "the duty of the Israelite to the King" was, according to the Bible, to "heed him and obey his commands to us with love and faith; to fear him, to love him, and to pray to the Lord God for his health and for peace in his domain."[26]

From the Jewish perspective, there was no doubt that Europe during the second half of the nineteenth century was a world of stability and progress. Despite all uncertainties and differences of opinion, Jews regarded the period after the Revolution of 1848 as a far better age than any of its predecessors. Everything then considered worthy of emulation by Jews was European. In spite of the cultural differences among its various nations, Europe was perceived as a single world with a common background of values, whose history was a universal history following the course of progress and modernity. The prevailing opinion was that the spirit of Enlightenment had spread throughout Europe and would eventually arrive in other countries, even if it tarried in doing so. In his 1864 programmatic poem *Hakitza Ami* (Awake, my people), Y. L. Gordon wrote that czarist Russia had become an inseparable part of Europe:

> Awake, my people! How long will you sleep?
> The night has passed, the sun shines through.
> Awake, cast your eyes hither and yon
> Recognize your time and your place . . .
>
> The land where we live and are born
> Is it not thought to be part of Europe?
> Europe—the smallest of continents
> But the mightiest of all in wisdom and knowledge.
>
> This land of Eden [Russia] is now open to you,
> Its sons now call you "brothers."
> How long will you dwell among them as a guest,
> Why do you reject their hand?[27]

According to this vision, the concepts of equality that had been born in France would slowly and gradually arrive in Russia as well, and that country was destined soon to become a paradise, integrated with the new European world. The Jews' woes and travails throughout Europe had not yet come to an end, but all doors were now open to them, and they could begin to contribute their talents to various cultural fields as in "the best of the European nations." The day was not far off, Shulman added, when the Jews of czarist Russia would experience emancipation and "become the equals of all the citizens of the land, in all civil laws and in all governmental positions of seniority and authority."[28] The fulfillment of these tidings of salvation for Russia's Jews was tied to the westernization of Asiatic Russia.

As we will see in chapter 3, this was not the only forecast. The disillusionment felt by Leopold Lipmann Zunz over the failure of the Revolution of 1848 stirred him to issue doomsday prophecies about the dark, impending barbarism that would oppress or enslave enlightened Europe. Another medieval night threatened to darken Europe's skies; the days of culture would vanish. The disappointment and disillusionment evident at the close of the century were even greater. After the so-called Southern Storms (a series of pogroms in southern Russia), Gordon amended his optimistic worldview and wrote: "who was wise enough to have foretold that such an outrage would take place in our time?"[29] And the writer and thinker Michah Yosef Berdichevsky, living in Berlin, threw cold water over optimistic predictions when he wrote, following the first international conference on antisemitism in Dresden on August 14, 1891:

> Our Russian brothers are building castles in Spain . . . little do they know that in the West, too, life is corrupt and mercenary. Little do they know that here, too, the foundations of society are corrupt, and that the groundwork of morality and decency have been totally eroded! Social justice has been crushed. Instead, the wealthy devour the labor of the poor, who toil away, destitute. Little do they know of the desolation, loneliness, and isolation that prevail here! Little do they know that here, too, people have no qualms about devouring each other alive! That here too everyone is out for himself. Whoever says that the sun shines in the West is mistaken.[30]

During the nineteenth century, there were many events and developments that brought about disappointment and disillusionment: pogroms; the Damascus Affair and other blood libels against Jews; and a new type of antisemitism.[31] Yet despite their disappointments and concerns, it appears that Jews remained optimistic. Europe's negative aspect was seen as shadows that only occasionally took center stage, or as delusional visions that arose from Europe's past and invaded its present—not as characteristic of modern Europe. Most Jews believed that Europe would not return to a medieval darkness, and that progress was inevitable. In his speech at the Third Zionist Congress in Basel in 1899, Max Nordau said: "I openly declare that I do not believe that the catastrophes of our past will be reenacted in the future . . . Today there is a European conscience, a conscience of humanity, limited indeed, but requiring at least the appearance of a degree of honesty and it could hardly tolerate preposterous mob crimes."[32]

As the nineteenth century gave way to the twentieth, the historian Simon Dubnow expressed his confidence that the rule of religion, which had flooded the rivers of Europe with blood during the Middle Ages, would not return, and he added that "the time is near when the theory of oppressing minorities will be totally repudiated, since it endangers the existence and integrity of the state."[33] In its December 28, 1899, issue, *Der Israelit*, the weekly newspaper of German Jewish Orthodoxy, summarized the improvements in the Jews' situation that had taken place during the nineteenth century as follows: "Since exiting the Ghetto, Jews [had become] partners in creativity in all areas of life" in Europe. Although blood libels and the Dreyfus Affair had placed the stamp of barbarism on the nineteenth century, the Jews' situation in Europe was tolerable. In Germany, they had been granted full equality under the law, and public antisemitism had disappeared, though it continued to exist covertly among the upper classes. The situation in the Austro-Hungarian Empire was not good, because of internal unrest for which Jews were paying the price. In Russia, some discriminatory laws had been repealed, and these developments raised hopes; in France, the Dreyfus Affair had hurt the Jews' self-confidence; in England and the United States, the situation was excellent, and the Jews had been granted equal rights and had integrated seamlessly into society. The shadows were therefore numerous, but it could be hoped that they would disperse during the following century and that a new age would dawn.[34] The liberal *Allgemeine Zeitung des Judentums* also wrote that the Jews had every reason to look back with satisfaction: the national liberation of Germany meant equality for the Jews, as embodied in political and civil freedom, interpersonal relations, personal treatment, and material situation. The Jews were full of appreciation for these achievements, as well as for the unification of Germany—an achievement for the sake of which they, as well as others, had shed their blood. However, there still existed a great distance between the ideals that had been declared at the start of the century and the de facto situation: equality of rights was brutally trampled, and in its place rose the accursed antisemitism. This was the curse of the magnificent century, and as it erupted primarily at its close, the newspaper noted: "we therefore expect that during the new century things will change."[35] According to this analysis, the Jews' situation depended on the internal political situation of each European country and would be influenced by processes that would take place between those countries and Europe as a whole. In 1899, Emil Lehmann, one of the founders of the German-Jewish Community Alliance, wrote: "The Middle Ages, in which the Jews were persecuted, have passed . . . , and so has the time of all the despicable elements that characterized the age of religious Romanticism . . . The cultured nations of Europe and America have already solved the problem, if religious faith is independent and is not tied to civil or political rights."[36] In these assertions, the authors echo the optimistic words of the prominent German-Jewish scholar Moritz Lazarus, who noted in a lecture in December 1879 at the Hochschule für die Wissenschaft des Judentums in Berlin: "throughout Europe the Jews see the light of liberty and live a vibrant, multifaceted life."[37]

The mood at the end of the nineteenth century was full of hope and confidence that developments would follow a positive trend.

EUROPE BETWEEN SCIENCE AND TRADITION

With admiration and excitement, as well as trepidation and concern, the Jewish intelligentsia observed the factor that most influenced Europe's transformation into a single entity: the enormous achievements of science and technology. The intelligentsia tracked them, reported them to other Jews, and discussed their relationship to ethics and international politics. Technological and scientific achievements and resulting improvements in living conditions were seen as a clear sign of progress[38] and modernity. The telegraph, electricity, steamships, railroads, and many other inventions during the latter half of the nineteenth century were described as the work of man, completing and improving upon God's creation.[39] So, for example, the moderate *Haskalah* weekly *Hamagid* summarized the first half of the century in a series of articles titled "The Spirit of the Times," published in December 1858, with the author's unambiguous conclusion that progress was increasingly taking place throughout the world thanks to Western achievements in science and technology.[40] These provided mankind with the tools to overcome and control nature, and to alter not only values and patterns of government, but the entire human experience of life.

Several other summaries were compiled in this spirit at the end of the nineteenth century. One was written in 1893 by Zvi Hermann Shapira, a rabbi and professor of mathematics at the University of Heidelberg. He noted:

> Ours is a generation of industry, a generation of railroads and steamships. Telegraph poles are planted from one end of the world to the other. We capture sunlight and electrical energy, gathering and storing them in vessels like a man drawing water from a cistern. We speak and our voices resound from one end of the world to the other . . . People are amazed by the wonders they see and hear . . . Entire fields of knowledge have sprung up before our eyes and will develop in our hands and spread new light on many subjects that had lain beyond our reach until only yesterday.[41]

The newspaper *Hatzfira*, which was published in Warsaw and sought—according to its motto—to disseminate "knowledge, science, and news about the world and nature," declared in a December 31, 1889, article titled "The First Good Days":

> How fortunate the future generations! Even a thick and hefty volume will not suffice to contain a fraction of all the advancements in science and industry that have been made in the nineteenth century; and indeed we will be able to take pride in the idea, for even an old man living today has seen more inventions born before his eyes than all the generations of the past two thousand years.

Another article in *Hatzfira*, titled "From the Four Corners of the Earth" and published on December 24, 1889, stated:

> If you are traveling in a steam or electrical carriage—if you traverse great waters in a steamship, and gaze at the lights, great and small, at electrical lights that illuminate the night in the big city squares . . . and sit in your bedroom at the telephone and converse with your friend who is seated in another city—when you peer with the aid of rays of hidden light [x-rays] and behold your own skeleton without flesh or tendons, and when you hear your own voice addressing you from the phonograph—you think to yourself and know that merely a century ago all these were but vague ideas and impossible dreams.

Nahum Sokolow, the editor of *Hatzfira*, waved the banner of technological and scientific achievements that would lead humanity toward a new era.⁴² Nachman Syrkin, a Socialist-Zionist thinker, wrote in the same spirit that technology had changed life entirely, and as a result the eyes of all the world were focused on the coming century "with hope and confidence, because it will fortify the human race and imbue it with lofty ambitions."⁴³

These and other articles did not address the question of what factors were responsible for the fact that the industrial, scientific, and technological revolutions had all occurred in Europe. However, it is clear that in the eyes of the authors, the affinity between this revolution and the European spirit was self-evident, just as the profound difference between advanced Europe and the backward world beyond its borders was self-evident. This was also why nearly everyone debated the connections between a civilization's technological progress and the state of its culture in the context of Europe.

Machines, electricity, trains, and other technological and scientific innovations, which were foundations of the modern world, were not generally perceived as leading to disintegration or decay. "This century," Herzl wrote in 1895 in his introduction to *Der Judenstaat* (The Jewish state), "has given the world a wonderful renaissance by means of its technical achievements." During the century, new assets were endlessly created, and it "brought us a valuable revival through technological achievements," which could be utilized in solving humanity's problems. "At the same time," he added, "its miraculous progress has not yet been employed in the service of humanity."⁴⁴ Despite Herzl's criticism of the situation in Europe, his Zionist utopia was based on nineteenth-century "scientific Messianism"—that is, on confidence in the power of science and technology to settle the contradictions inherent in this social reality—and, of course, in their ability to take the Zionist idea from potential to implementation and to shape a new Jewish society in Palestine.

Prior to formulating his plan of action for the creation of a new Jewish society, Herzl revealed an ambivalent attitude regarding the influence of science and technology on society. In several stories and *feuilletons*, he hesitantly described the effect that various inventions would have on the life of the common man. The most famous of these tales is "Solon in Lydia": in the story, there is free bread for everyone, which emancipates humanity from the need to work. In other stories, Herzl displayed a more positive attitude toward technology and science. In the story "Das Automobil" (1899), he described the effect of automobiles as follows: "Every owner of an automobile has, in the distance, his own small house surrounded by a garden. Life on the main roads is more pleasant . . . The modern lifestyle cultivates a new type of people, in whom the farmers' culture and the urbanites' power are combined." Herzl's optimism came with qualifications. According to him, technological sophistication did not guarantee human sophistication: "How rapid our journey . . . how sluggish our wisdom."[45] Still, after visiting an automobile exhibition in Paris, where he admired "the new American Cleveland automobile," which was powered by electricity, he wrote in his diary on June 21, 1899: "The automobile was created for us. We will have cement roads, fewer rails, and from the start we will install our new forms of transportation."[46] In the 1896 story *Das lenkbare Luftschiff* (The dirigible airship) Herzl again expressed his doubts when he wrote about the new "toys" that were bringing about unexpected changes:

> Now the horseless carriages begin to go forth into the world. What changes will they wreak? Every innovation in transportation is likely to bring about enormous and unforeseen changes. Soon enough, and strangely enough, the effects begin to emerge in the lives of the masses, in their successes and in their morals. New diseases are born, though the human race is becoming healthier. Living conditions change rapidly these days that had never before changed at all.

The airship in the story is developed by Joseph Müller, a genius whose inventions also include an automatic brake for trains and a puncture-proof bicycle tire. Müller decides to destroy the airship, claiming that humans were fit for inventions such as corkscrews and gaslights, but not for the ability to fly. The Doctor, one of the characters in this story, approves Müller's decision. If the airship remained in human hands, he says, it would be used as a weapon and bring about great bloodshed; furthermore, it would increase the wealth and pleasure of those who possess wealth and power on the one hand, while spreading new forms of poverty and misery on the other hand. Some of the characters wonder if it should therefore be considered a destructive invention. "The Parisian" supplies an optimistic summary of the discussion: Müller "should not have concerned himself with those living in our times and certainly not with the poor folks around him. Anyone who shapes the future must look forward from the present. Eventually, humanity will become good."[47] Herzl's 1896 pamphlet, *The Jewish State*, is uniformly optimistic; during the 1830s, he wrote, many conservatives had not believed in the railroad, yet now it was established fact.[48]

The relationship between progress and morality thus concerned Herzl, as it did many members of his generation; he saw both sides of the coin. In an article in August 1893, he compared the suffering of machinists in factories to the suffering of the Jews, and wrote that it was not revolutionary socialism's misleading eschatological rhetoric that would bring the workers salvation, but rather the scientific revolution. However, it was also possible that their creations would create new troubles.[49] Yet on June 8, 1895, Herzl wrote in his diary: "My view is that socialism is a purely technological problem. The distribution of nature's forces through electricity will eliminate it. Meanwhile our model state will have come into being."[50]

On March 21, 1897, Herzl sent a copy of *The Jewish State* to the aging British philosopher Herbert Spencer (1820–1903) and requested his opinion. In a letter he included with the book, Herzl wrote that once a Jewish state was created, it would be possible to see "how the beginning of this undertaking was reflected in the great mind of Herbert Spencer."[51] Here Herzl was referring not to social Darwinism, with which Spencer was associated, but to Spencer's belief in progress arising from the power of scientific thought and achievement—a belief that made Spencer very popular in Central and Eastern Europe, where his views became important weapons in the struggle against autocracy. Spencer's influence on Herzl is evident in statements such as: "We know, after all, what phases the human race has passed through from its primitive to its civilized state. Its progression tends ever upwards."[52] Herzl was one of the great believers in social progress and innovation through all the modern methods. Like Spencer and other liberal thinkers, he believed that a liberal industrial society was a prerequisite for peace, love for mankind, and happiness. In order to convince others that his plan of a Jewish state was realistic, Herzl repeatedly emphasized that by means of science and technology—in particular, trains and electricity—Palestine could be transformed into a modern country. The modern technology of the present and the future would provide the tools necessary for realizing the Zionist enterprise. On June 17, 1895, Herzl wrote in his diary that the difference between him and Shabtai Zvi was that "in the last century it was impossible. Now it is possible—because we have machines."[53] *The Jewish State* begins with the declaration: "The world now possesses slaves of extraordinary capacity for work, whose appearance has been fatal to the production of handmade goods. These slaves are the machines." The steam engine, he added, had crowded workers into factories, while electric power would liberate them and create better working conditions. In a lecture he gave in London's East End in July 1896, he enumerated the advantages of modern society:

> And there is another advantage in modern civilization that will make the terms of our new migration unique and without any model in history. The results of geographical surveys, of sea travel, of research, of engineering and steam-locomotion, will serve our new migration . . . Our people, an intelligent people, will adopt the most modern methods.[54]

In his 1902 utopian novel *Altneuland* (Old-new land), Herzl described the fulfillment of this idea: modern Palestine was well stocked with all the accoutrements of comfort and all the technological innovations needed both to develop and modernize the land—thanks to electricity, the "old new land" was transformed into a flowering garden—and to create a model society. "The nineteenth century," claims the novel's protagonist, David Litwak, "was an oddly lame age—one foot far forward, the other dragging behind . . . At the beginning of that curious era, the most muddle-headed visionaries were taken seriously while the most practical inventors were regarded as mad." Nonetheless industrialization, which led to the creation of the exploited industrial proletariat, also led to the creation of a futuristic nation. According to Litwak, social planners had never before had access to such technical powers: "Even at the end of the nineteenth century technical methods were already advanced. We only had to take the inventions of the Western world and use them."[55] The assets of technology and science that the Jews brought from Europe to Palestine and the knowledge amassed in all of the cultured nations—including turbines, generators, electric power, steam engines, and railways—enabled them to exert control over nature, develop the land, and fulfill the "springtime of humanity"; the power that science provided did not trample the Jews, but launched them forward. "In short, we needed the entire yield of the year 1900"—the yield of modern civilization's accomplishments. These achievements, Herzl wrote, created a unified world: "With regards to science and art, all the borders have already vanished."[56]

Thus there is no doubt that Herzl's outlook on the subject was shaped by belief in human willpower, supported by science and technology. Humans could raise cities from scratch: "Will is what raises a city. I might point anywhere and say 'Let there be a city here!' and a city will rise," he wrote aboard ship in his diary on September 30, 1898, as the Dutch capital, The Hague, came into view.[57] In contrast to the chilling picture painted

The Glorious Nineteenth Century   37

by H. G. Wells in his 1899 novel *When the Sleeper Wakes*, which describes the world in the twenty-second century as a cruel and awful megalopolis, albeit brimming with technological inventions—a world which made the nineteenth century seem like the Stone Age—Herzl described the city of the future in *Altneuland* as a modern and humane place.

In his Zionist writings, Herzl was therefore distant from the depressed mood of the *Kulturpessimismus* (the culture of pessimism) and from the consciousness of decadence and the "craving for gloominess" which it created, in Max Nordau's words. Herzl did not regard the processes of urbanization and industrialization with terror, nor did he describe them as creating a hell on earth.[58] Despite profound and copious criticism, he did not accept the "impassioned image of little old Europe."[59] On the contrary, he believed it was possible to create a modern, sophisticated, and just society of the future. In this, his vision of the new era resembled that of the positivists and utopianists of his time (some sixty utopian works were published between 1850 and 1900):[60] this was an age of material comfort, freedom, and moral conduct, and the growth of knowledge and the advancement of technology would make the twentieth century even better. Herzl agreed with the naturalist Alfred Russel Wallace, a contemporary of Darwin who had also developed a theory of evolution based on the principle of natural selection. In his 1898 *The Wonderful Century: Its Successes and Its Failures*,[61] Wallace summarized the achievements and inventions of the nineteenth century and their positive effects on people's lives, though he did not ignore the gap between technological progress and the state of morality.[62] Herzl's almost childlike amazement at the abundance of new inventions was expressed in passages like the one he wrote in his diary on June 8, 1895: "A department of innovations, with correspondents in Paris, London, Berlin, etc., immediately reports on all novelties, which are then tested for their usability"; and he stated elsewhere, "what one man discovers belongs to the whole world an hour later."[63]

More than a decade earlier, on June 19, 1882, the Istanbul office of Bilu—the elite group active in the First Aliyah (immigration to Israel)—composed a circular to European and American students that was never sent out. Its substance was that Bilu intended to create a model settlement in Palestine that would inject "the neglected Jewish economic reality with new foundations according to the latest conclusions drawn from the science of our times and according to the latest word of European culture in our generation"[64]—that is, of the culture of Western Europe. Bilu's members therefore shared Herzl's belief in the importance of industry and of scientific messianism. A worldview that stressed the role of science and technology in the formation of the future was also held by other members of the Jewish elite at the end of the nineteenth century, bourgeois and revolutionaries alike. However, there is no doubt that of all the Zionist leaders and businessmen, it was Herzl—a journalist and author—who devoted the most profound attention and accorded the most central position to science and technology, and he extended his enthusiasm for the achievements of science in general to the Zionist context.

The philosopher Martin Buber was profoundly critical of Herzl's "scientific messianism": Herzl "loved to think in technological terms. When he began to explain his plan [regarding] the time of technological conquests, which brought us those 'mighty slaves,' the machines, he said it had thus brought us 'a wonderful renaissance.' He, who always knew how to choose his words appropriately, did not even sense how mistaken he was in seeing technological progress, even great amounts of it, as a renaissance, a cultural revival."[65] Buber, an idealist, considered Herzl's enthusiasm for science and technology an obsession, but he was mistaken in describing him as a materialist, aloof to the spiritual and cultural contents of a society. Herzl was deeply interested in the spiritual and cultural content of modern Jewish society.

Max Nordau, who shared Herzl's vision, was also deeply critical both of such pessimists and of the phenomenon of deterioration in Europe and its literary culture. In his books *Entartung* (Degeneration, 1883), *Die Conventionellen Lügen der Kulturmenschheit* (The conventional lies of our civilization, 1883), *Paradoxe* (Paradoxes, 1885), and *Die Krankheit des Jahrhunderts* (The malady of the century, 1887), he described them as the symptoms of a pathological culture. Nordau was a great admirer of European bourgeois culture, in which he saw the embodiment of normal European values.[66] He believed that the decadent and naturalistic literature and art produced by European modernism dealt with sick and abnormal phenomena, and that they steered European society away from rational, universal values and toward nihilism and political demagoguery, from which he, like Herzl, recoiled; this led to antirationalism and anti-intellectualism, and from there to nationalism and antisemitism, until Europe would resemble a large mental institution. At the same time, Nordau, again like Herzl, saw science—the clear product of rational thought—as the antithesis of and cure for theology and metaphysics. He too raised the key question: how would mankind utilize science? His response was that the common man was a creature of deep-rooted and sturdy optimism, who knew how to use the achievements of science and technology in order to cure Europe of the "malady of the century"—a term coined by the French poet Alfred de Musset in the 1830s. Nordau distinguished between scientific pessimism and practical pessimism, and he believed that optimism was man's basic outlook that expressed the human life force: *dum spiro, spero* (while I breathe, I hope). Only such belief could form the basis for Nordau's view that the Jews were an inseparable part of the positive layers of European culture, and that to drive a wedge between them and Europe would be impossible.

However, as we will see in chapter 3, Nordau too was not exempt from the apocalyptic inclination:

> Europe will not be able [for] very much longer to escape a great and violent rending asunder of its nationalities . . . The twentieth century can hardly come to an end without seeing the conclusion of this drama in the world's history. Before then a considerable portion of Europe will see much distress and bloodshed, many acts of violence and crimes . . . People[s] will be raged against and races pitilessly crushed; side by side with tragedies of human baseness will be played tragedies of lofty heroism; hordes of cowards will allow themselves to be emasculated without resistance; and brave armies will perish gloriously in fight. The survivors, however, will then enjoy the full possession of their national rights, and in word and action will always and everywhere be able to be themselves.[67]

In the same chapter, he prophesies a European struggle for existence, over the course of which Europe's population would spread to other continents until "the entire earth will be subject to the plough and the locomotive of the sons of Europe." However, the tables would eventually be turned. He concludes: "And then? Yes, what will be then I do not know. Here a black future will become still blacker; I am utterly unable to distinguish anything more, and therefore am compelled to bring this tale to an end."[68]

The late-nineteenth-century doomsday prophecies and visions of an approaching battle between good and evil,[69] which we will examine in chapter 3, arose from a feeling of discomfort with the condition of society and culture in Western Europe and from lack of faith in science and technology. In the pessimistic climate at the turn of the century, many prophecies emerged of cultural decline (*Untergang*), and of decadence that would commit crimes against the entire fabric of life and transform Europe into a diseased entity and eventually an invalid whose death would quickly approach. In spite of this mood, the intellectual Jewish elite considered the Europe of the "long nineteenth century" (which extended to 1914) a world of material and cultural progress. Urbanization, industrialization, global trade, and the like did not inspire the same fears of modernity among most Jews that they did among the European petite bourgeoisie and rural population.[70] From their perspective, nineteenth-century Europe was a reality that should be embraced warmly, and they hoped that it would continue to embrace the Jews.

It is thus no wonder that from the perspective of the gloomy 1930s, the none-too-distant past of the previous century was seen through rose-colored glasses. The shadows of the nineteenth century were forgotten. It was depicted as an enchanted century—as "the good century," *la belle epoque*, a shining period, and a lost paradise,[71] and as the century in which the flag of political and creative freedom was raised and a recognizable improvement in the quality of life began. However, even during the 1930s, when Europe approached the most profound schism in its history and revealed its monstrous side, it was impossible to ignore the fact that the previous century had been one of cruel imperialism, exploitative and oppressive capitalism, and national militarism. It was indeed a century of dishonor, but—as Jabotinsky wrote in 1937—despite all of its flaws, the twentieth century was in comparison a "swindling century," a century that betrayed all the values and ideals of its predecessor. The twentieth century was one in which "all the forces of unenlightened reactionism form a powerful and giant army."[72] Still, despite their great disappointment and fear of what was to come, Jabotinsky and many other Jews still believed at the end of the 1930s that the moral and aesthetic nineteenth century could be revived, and that the dark, opposing trends they faced did not represent the true nature of Europe and Western culture.

THE ACCURSED CENTURY—
EUROPE AS AN AILING CULTURE

Our unfortunate nineteenth century.
FYODOR DOSTOEVSKY[1]

In *Notes from the Underground*, Dostoevsky's protagonist discovers that civilization neither tames mankind nor makes men less violent or thirsty for war. In "our unhappy nineteenth century," he declares, "blood is being spilt in streams . . . as though it were champagne."[2] In contrast, in Chekhov's novella *The Duel*, the zoologist von Koren mocks the lamentations of the clerk Ivan Andreitch Laevsky—"how we have been crippled by civilisation!"—noting that while Laevsky "has scarcely sniffed at civilisation," it had already brought him disillusionment and disappointment; he sought to undermine it "only to justify and conceal [his] own rottenness and moral poverty."[3]

These two opposing opinions reflect the debate that unfolded within the Russian intelligentsia. Pro-Westerners saw Russia as a pauper pounding on the gates of civilization, with the West its yearned-for ideal. Slavophiles believed that Russia superficially imitated values foreign to the authentic Russian spirit. The West was the looking glass into which the Russian intelligentsia had been peering since the eighteenth century, in an attempt to examine both the good and the bad in Russia and to find a path to the nation's rejuvenation.[4] In the self-confident West, pessimistic historical consciousness and fear of what was to come had an entirely different character. So, for example, in 1897, as Britain began its lavish celebration of Queen Victoria's diamond jubilee, Rudyard Kipling wrote in his poem "Recessional" that he sensed a troubling optimism in the air, and wondered whether beyond Britain's might and global power lay the same bitter fate that had overtaken the great powers of the past, such as Nineveh and Tyre.[5] H. G. Wells evoked this cosmic pessimism in his novels *The Time Machine* (1895) and *When the Sleeper Wakes* (1899). In

Germany,[6] Austria, France, Poland, and Russia, new literary works and philosophical and historical treatises disseminated this mood of cultural pessimism and criticism and conjured a nightmarish vision of a rapidly approaching apocalypse.[7] Beneath Western civilization's facade of bountiful, world-changing scientific and technological achievement, and behind the scenes of Europe's rule over a great portion of the world, fears and concerns set in, some real and some imaginary. Once again, it seemed that barbarians were closing in and that, as in the ancient past, Europe's self-confident culture would collapse. These fears crossed the Atlantic and made their way to the New World. Brooks Adams, in *The Law of Civilization and Decay* (1895), and his brother, Henry Adams, in *The Education of Henry Adams* (1907), both described a West mired in the process of decay and descent into a cesspit of vulgarity.[8] This abundance of prophecies and predictions reflected an orientation toward the future, its integral role in the nineteenth-century worldview, and attempts to envision the world to come.

THE CLIMATE AT THE END OF AN ERA

Fear, pessimism, and the Europhobia that was an inseparable part of them also appeared in Jewish literature and journalism at the end of the nineteenth century. There, too, writers looked backward on the closing century with disappointment and disillusionment, and looked forward to the coming century with deep anxiety and even terror. Disappointment and fear were not only a reaction to the emergence of modern antisemitism, but also the result of intense identification with and admiration for Europe—hence, the concern that it might be drawn into an inescapable crisis.

A twilight atmosphere of looming demise had also emerged at the end of the fifteenth century—the "autumn of the Middle Ages," as the Dutch historian Johan Huizinga called it. A sense of approaching doom prevailed then, rising from the decay that seemed to spread throughout European society.[9] The great difference between these two periods lies in the fact that the nineteenth-century awareness of decline and destruction came at the end of an age seen as an incubator for a new European world—one that would be "the best of all possible worlds," to use Voltaire's well-known phrase without his irony. It was for this reason that the fear of decline was so severe. Born in the middle of the century, the fear grew stronger during the *fin de siècle*, as the 1880s and 1890s came to be known. That term became widely used to refer to various phenomena; as a French rhyme put it in 1891, "*Fin-de-siècle* . . . stands for everything."[10] Max Nordau, meanwhile, wrote in his introduction to *Degeneration* that the "mental state" known as *fin de siècle* was ubiquitous.[11]

The name given to this historical period chiefly connoted a feeling of malaise and a sense of profound, irreparable cultural and social decadence.[12] According to the mood then in vogue, humanity (that is, the West) was heading irrevocably toward disintegration and loss. Not only had technology failed to heal the ills of Western society, it had also spawned destructive forces: ethical bankruptcy, alienation, emptiness, exploitation, horrific poverty, and even biological degeneration.[13] Those who predicted decline had a ready audience, but they were also portrayed as false prophets who projected their own spiritual condition onto reality. According to von Koren, Chekhov's protagonist, pessimism seemed an expression of egotistical wretchedness. The German Jewish writer Berthold Auerbach described the literature infused with *Weltschmerz* (the sorrows of the world) as *Ichpoesie* (self-centered writing) that projected the private, subjective world—that is, the authors' private predicaments—onto reality, and thus distorted it.[14] Nordau had a similarly decided opinion: *Weltgefühl* (one's sense of the world) and objective reality were separated by a broad chasm. The mania for distress, as he put it, that was evident in fashionable pessimism testified to the triumph of the power of imagination over reality. In *Degeneration*, Nordau proposed a clinical diagnosis according to which the authors of pessimistic and nihilistic literature were possessed of a decadent personality and were, in fact, mentally unwell. The pessimism and egotistical individualism they created were the malady of the century. The radical *maskil* Yehuda Leib Levin, who would later spare few harsh words in his criticism of the nineteenth century, wrote in 1899 that the Eastern European Jewish intelligentsia's "consciousness of decadence" was a fashionable illness, contracted from the Russian and German intelligentsia. This was a regrettable consequence of confused ideas, romantic decisions, and the tendency to follow intellectual and literary vogues.[15]

We might claim, from the perspective of the twenty-first century, that the pessimism expressed by Jewish writers and thinkers was not *Ichpoesie* but rather a product of sensitivity, intuition, and foresight. These writers and thinkers sensitively plumbed the depths of the crisis of modernity and thus were best able to foresee the calamity it heralded. Their pessimistic and even apocalyptic mood was not simply an imitation of intellectual and literary fashions, but also a result of their alertness to existing undercurrents and the dangers these posed to Europe's future. It was because of this that they adopted the consciousness of decline and the mood of cultural pessimism, became filled with the sorrows of the world, and thought of Europe as sick—even moribund. This was all done without regard to the deep affinity between German prophets of decline such as Paul de Lagarde and Julius Langbehn—as well as the nostalgia they cultivated for the medieval German world, the sanctuary to which they wished to flee in the face of alienation and the false idols of capitalism, materialism, individualism, and liberalism, all destroyers of authenticity—on the one hand, and the antisemitic and racist *völkische* ideology, on the other hand.[16]

A CRITICALLY ILL EUROPE

The *maskilim*'s faith in progress and in the myth of enlightenment was already a target of criticism in the first half of the nineteenth century, but few critics focused on modern Europe and its fundamental values. One who did was the learned Paduan rabbi Shmuel David Luzzatto (known by the acronym Shadal). In 1841 he published a poem in the Frankfurt journal *Tzion* (Zion) titled "Derech Eretz or Atheism: A Poem by Shadal to His Generation" (*derech eretz* here signifies a combination of traditional and religious morality). This poem expresses his bitter disappointment in the fruits of emancipation and sketches a bleak portrait of European culture. Luzzatto conceded that religious zealotry and political despotism had been reined in, and that Europe had made remarkable technological and scientific achievements; nonetheless, civilization (that is, European culture) was built upon a flawed and corrupt foundation. "Our generation's civilization is half good and half bad," he wrote elsewhere, claiming that the good half was derived from Jewish roots, and the bad half from Greek.[17]

This gloomy portrait also found its way to Jewish *maskilim* in the remotest places in Europe during the latter half of the century. As early as 1878, Yehuda Leib Levin—whom we have cited as believing that Europe was a homeland to the Jews in every respect—described the European nineteenth century—that "enlightened, intellectual, and glorious" century—through the eyes of a bitterly disappointed optimist. In his poem "Sheelot Hazman" (Questions of our time), he wrote:

> This time, this century, perfection unblemished!
> Alive! Nineteenth! Perfection in beauty!

> What new power has this century, I ask myself,
> That it bears such great praise without stumbling?
> Can it really be? It soars so far up the scale,
> And the brilliance of its intellect penetrates all;
> Its leaders and thinkers—are they all superhuman,
> Enlightened in thought and action—victorious?
> Or is this perhaps a vain dream, a delusion,
> Its gleam pale and putrid, mere spray upon the shore?[18]

Europe's glorious nineteenth century was a century not of enlightenment and progress, but of evil, cruelty, and the triumph of force. Jews could expect nothing good from such a century, and Levin prophesied: "The days march on, the Jews' plight deteriorates. How will you act on the day when calamity strikes like lightning and destruction rains down like a storm, and the pleasures in which you delight wither all of a sudden while you gape open-mouthed, your faces distorted, fit for contempt! Perhaps then you will repent within your souls for the blood of your brothers, which was spilled due to your pride."[19]

The best-known expression of the idea that Europe at the end of the nineteenth century was in a grave and deteriorating physical and spiritual condition was supplied by the young author Mordechai Zeev Feierberg, in his short novel *Le'an?* (translated as *Whither?*), published in the periodical *Hashiloach* in 1899.[20] Feierberg maintained that those who predicted a pleasant future for Europe were "small prophets" (false prophets), while the true prophets were those who forecast decline. He described decadent Europe as follows:

> Europe is sick. Everyone can sense that society is crumbling; its foundations have long been rotten. Humankind is weary, thirsty for the word of God, for a prophet and a seer. Little prophets arise and strengthen it from time to time; Kant kept society alive for a century. Perhaps Darwin will be vital for another. But a great prophet and seer who would pronounce the word of God to the weary and the stumbling, who would inspire society—we have none. Society is now groping aimlessly; until the time when God's spirit will be poured out upon us in a mighty draught, and Civilization will be satiate for thousands of years.[21]

The historian Heinrich Graetz also painted a gloomy portrait of Europe in "The Correspondence of an English Lady on Judaism and Semitism" (1883): "You, culture enthusiast, do you have any idea how sick our highly civilized Europe really is?" According to him, the disease was evident not only in the signs that a new, full-scale European war was about to break out over control of the Ottoman Empire, but also in Europe's social and moral condition. Europe's social organism was ill, and the continent appeared to be on its deathbed; a clear symptom of its licentiousness and moral corruption was the extensive spread of syphilis and prostitution. In this case, it was impossible to believe that *putrescat ut resurgat* (decay begets revival). Edith, the "English lady," countered this depressing description with omnipresent examples of progress: railways, steamships, urban planning, parks and gardens, science institutes, and museums. Could it be that among all these wonders, which had improved the quality of life beyond recognition, hidden ailments lurked and were devouring Europe from within? "You have robbed me," she scolded Graetz, "of my gilded illusion."[22]

Two years later, in 1885, Edmund Menachem Eisler published his utopian novel *Ein Zukunftsbild* (An image of the future) in Vienna. In it, he painted a portrait of the Jewish kingdom destined to rise in Palestine and described the laws by which it would be governed. With honed sarcasm, Eisler addressed Europe: "How pleased you must be, oh Europe, that your Jews have all departed."[23] Prophets predicted that after the Jews' removal, Europe would be rid of the root of its troubles and enjoy happy, thriving days. But instead, Eisler wrote, Europe's troubles only multiplied. Europe fell ill; its exploits frothed and seethed like a witch's stew. Not only did its indecent, corrupting vices wreak havoc, but they were accompanied by further evils that, artificially cultivated during the last wave of violence, now flourished, sprouted, and spread abominably.

Eisler then described how militarism was gaining strength and political dominance in Germany; how Russia hovered on the horizon of Western Europe like an ominous cloud threatening to destroy every achievement of civilization; and how Great Britain was declining abruptly:

> This is the vision of Europe, that imagines that by driving out her Jews she will find the key to her happiness. The Jews were therefore not the cause of her illness . . . Europe's power weakens from old age, and a malignant contagion has spread throughout her flesh; but Europe's first wound, which spread its foul pus over her entire face, was the rancid, putrid bog of antisemitism.[24]

Articles in this spirit proliferated as the end of the century approached. In an article titled "Toward the End of the Nineteenth Century," Rabbi

Dr. Shimon Bernfeld wrote that the nineteenth century had brought forth only perversions and disappointment; it had "fallen miserably short regarding capital and man's advancement in morality and thought." Despite scientific progress, morality and culture had failed to overcome the animalistic urges of the masses. It was true that progress had improved the quality of life, but at the same time, the "culture of the masses" that arose during the French Revolution had eroded human culture: "the spirit of the masses now lies over the entire culture; it is a coarse spirit and lacks the noble quality it had possessed in generations past."[25]

Surprisingly enough, the century was defended against its detractors by Yehuda Leib Levin, who had become a radical *maskil* over the two decades since the publication of his pessimistic poem. In a series of articles titled "The End of the Century," published in *Hamelitz* during April and May of 1899, Levin wrote that Bernfeld was expressing a conservative attitude and engaging in nostalgia for the days when "refined" nobility ruled with an iron hand, before Europe was "infected by the plague" of mass culture. Levin believed that "the reckoning of Ages" was an artificial concern, and that the year 1900 was neither the beginning nor the end of an age, as far as the unfolding of historical processes was concerned. However, he too assessed the nineteenth century, and proposed an explanation for the internal contradiction it contained. He also pointed out the century's deficiencies. According to him, what caused the "evils of the nineteenth century" was not the flaws of mass democracy, but the gaping chasm between "impassioned minds and ossified hearts." In other words, material civilization and morality were not equivalent; technology and science had no "feeling or compassion" and were simply instruments to be used. It was morality ("the heart") that must determine how civilization's advancements should be utilized. In contrast to the English historian H. T. Buckle, whose book had much influence over the European intelligentsia,[26] Levin believed that material progress had weakened rather than strengthened social morality, because it gave "the immoral" new and powerful means to carry out evil. Social Darwinism had become a political doctrine extolling power and militarism on the one hand, and exploitative and violent capitalism on the other: "mammon [capital] belonged to Almighty God, and the men of culture all prostrated themselves to it." If so, "civilization marches forth in sound and fury and storm, and the human spirit sinks downward," and "Europe's intellect has become a fatal drug." According to Levin, this chilling awareness of impending destruction was not a projection of *Ichpoesie* on reality, but the result of a social, radical, and realistic understanding of reality. Another article, by an unknown author, described Bernfeld as denouncing modern culture, even though the only flaw he could identify in it was the democratic system and "the broadening of the sciences in the sense of superficial and fragmented knowledge"—and there he contradicted his own role as a popularizer of science.[27]

But Bernfeld was not alone on the pessimistic front. Moshe Leib Lilienblum, for example, depicted Europe as a degenerate monster, awash in blood and evil urges, and he noted: "both in the Middle Ages and today, the nations of Europe have been entirely licentious." After being surprised by the anti-Jewish riots that took place in czarist Russia in 1881, Lilienblum wrote that it was clear that the naive utopianists who believed that humanity's great achievements in the realm of science would draw humans ever closer to moral perfection were mistaken. On the contrary, it turned out that science had provided mankind with more sophisticated weapons, and "humanity's evil impulses have not abated, and there is no hope that they will do so in the future."[28] In an article titled "The End of the Century," which marked the birth of the phrase as cliché and was published in *Hamagid* on January 12, 1899, the writer Reuven Brainin wrote that progress had increased neither happiness nor morality. Enslavement to machines, to the flood of new knowledge, and to pleasure had brought only embarrassment and confusion:

> Is there not a great measure of truth in the criticism that technological modernity has diminished the humanity of Man? The shape of our generation is that of a coin, and our breath is that of a steam engine. Our wildflowers have wilted from the chimney soot and smoke, our poetic genius is dulled, and the coin on the one hand and the steam engine on the other have bewitched the moral and virtuous . . . for our generation is made entirely of vanity and vice.

In Elchanan Leib Levinsky's utopian work "Masa Leeretz Israel Bishnat 2040" (A voyage to the land of Israel in the year 2040), which was written in 1892, Europe was empty of wars; yet "despite that, all of Europe is like a battlefield, like a giant camp armed not against an external enemy but against an internal one. This is the more terrible war: the war over property and labor."[29] Similarly, in a 1901 *feuilleton* titled "Thoughts and Deeds," Levinsky wrote: "I was born during the golden age of the previous century . . . But it is true that I grew up and saw her far from the desired ideal: . . . old and weak, about to die, dragging her feet . . . I saw her in disgrace."[30]

In December 1901, the historian Simon Dubnow summarized the nineteenth century as follows: "The nineteenth century, which began with a wave of glowing youthful hopes, came to a close worn out and enfeebled and in an esthetic and ethical condition described by the term *fin-de-siècle*."[31]

HAD EUROPE GONE MAD?

If this was the face of the nineteenth century, what could be expected from the twentieth? In 1901, Levinsky prophesied: "Considering its beginning, it is difficult to hope that the end of the new century [the twentieth century] will be peaceful. Man seems to have been condemned since the time of Creation to be born and die, century by century, in times of war. Each and every age, each and every century has a war of its own."[32]

Nordau, who believed in the power of science and technology to refine moral behavior and to contribute to the creation of a society grounded in a morality of solidarity (*Solidaritätsmoral*), offered "a glance into the future." This glance revealed a horrifying, rather than utopian, vision. In one part, as we have seen, Nordau predicted that vicious wars would break out among Europe's nations. In another section, his crystal ball revealed the solution to the problem of nationalism: the smaller nations of Europe would disappear and be absorbed into the "four or five great nations." However, he wrote, this process of assimilation would be the result of Darwinian selection rather than choice. A unified Europe would thus reach a state of internal equilibrium, and its entire population would become a single family sharing a common culture. In this European paradise, moreover, modern technology would eliminate the need for manual labor. This vision might seem to predict the "end of history"; in effect, in Nordau's vision of the future, a population surplus would prompt white Europeans to conquer other continents and "the inferior races" who lived there, until "the entire earth will be subject to the plow and locomotive of the sons of Europe." The Europeans would treat the "black" and "yellow" races as they treated wild animals: the white race "will extirpate them root and branch." Still, even Europe's global domination would not bring history to an end; the aggressiveness of the Europeans who had emigrated to other continents would increase, and the surplus population would set out to roam like "a pack of wolves on the borders of the magic circle" of European civilization, but "they will be driven back into their icy deserts by the energetic lords of these lands of bliss." Nordau's racist, Darwinian apocalypse about the "clash of civilizations" ended thus: "And then? Yes, what happens next I cannot tell; here the shadowy future darkens sevenfold, until I can discern nothing more and our tale comes to a close."[33]

This vision of horrors was not concrete. No Jews had predicted before 1914 that a full-scale European war was just around the corner, despite their seemingly seismographical sensitivity. Only after World War I broke out did there seem to be any evidence that Europe was indeed ill, even mad. About two years before the war, in October 1912, Ahad Haam wrote from his residence in London:

> Behold: Sennacherib has come and wreaked havoc on the world . . . You, who live across the sea, are fortunate you need not witness "Europe" in its disgrace, or feel so strongly the emptiness and void that now govern our world . . . The Germans speak ad nauseam of *Kultur*, the English and their allies (including the Russians) of justice and honesty. How odious to hear words that only yesterday were sacred emanating from the mouths of wild beasts roaring over their prey.[34]

A month later, Ahad Haam predicted that the Balkan wars would drive the Ottoman Empire out of its holdings in Europe and perhaps even in Asia, and these would then be divided among other countries. However, he added: "as to how this will affect our venture, no prophet can foretell."[35] In any case, he did not expect that the Balkan wars would develop into a general European war. He was astonished to find at the end of 1914 that "the world has lost its mind" and devolved into chaos, and that Europe had descended to "the depths of depravity" and to wholesale slaughter—"the handiwork of that contemptible animal known as 'Man.'" In this somber mood, he wrote of his yearning to escape far from "civilization" to a place where "the stench of humanity" would not penetrate.

Ahad Haam was not the only one caught unaware by the war. In Istanbul in November 1912, David Ben Gurion wrote to his father in Pinsk about the Balkan war, describing the Russians as "the enemy some three hours distant from Istanbul." He predicted that the war would end quickly and that, "in any case, it is clear that we are facing rare historical developments that will determine an entirely new course for politics in Europe."[36] Ben Gurion predicted neither World War I nor the collapse of the Ottoman Empire. Even after the Young Turk Revolution, moreover, he believed that the empire had a long future ahead of it. He believed that the victory of the capitalist powers, Britain and France, would spur the rise of despotic regimes in the Middle East, and there would be no one left to halt "victorious Slavic imperialism." Consequently a strong Turkey was necessary for Zionism.[37]

On June 28, 1914, Chaim Weizmann expressed his despair at the possibility that "the world is fully prepared to slaughter itself using all the innovations of the twentieth century," and his belief that "a peaceful settlement will still be reached."[38] In October 1914, Dov Ber Borochov wrote from his residence in Italy that "it is not possible or even imaginable that the German spirit will penetrate everywhere and drive out Europe's variety, that Deutschland will extend *über alles in der Welt*." He believed that "Germany has lost its mind and is infecting Austro-Hungary with its rising madness. Austria will reap all the consequences. It will pay more than any other actor. That is clear to everyone."[39] In an article called "Horoscope," published in *Odesskiya Novosti* on January 1, 1912, Zeev Jabotinsky wrote, with foresight: "The first item on the list of events in Europe is a great war . . . between two (or more) first-class powers, with all the grandiose madness of modern technology . . . [and] with an incredible number of human casualties."[40] On May 18, 1915, he predicted that a victory by Britain and France would strengthen the czarist regime for years to come,[41] and he was certain that Germany would remain a great power even after its defeat: "In terms of wealth, culture, and military power, [Germany] will remain, first of all, a great center of energy. Energy demands expansion; if it is prevented from expanding in the logical directions, it will necessarily explode. The policy of preventing Germany from every natural expansion is, in our opinion, suicidal."[42]

It is not our intention, in citing these extracts, to judge the authors' prophetic ability regarding the nature of the postwar world. What is important to note here is the fact that their representation of Europe as a decaying continent hurtling toward self-destruction did not translate into a prediction of an impending all-European war that would destroy the old political order. On the contrary, most of the authors believed that the multinational empires of the day would continue to exist indefinitely, albeit becoming more liberal and democratic. As a result, the outbreak of the war, its duration, its events, and its results were deeply surprising. It was hard to understand how Europe, that realm of culture, had allowed itself to be swept up in a war so harrowing and destructive. Had the prophets of doom been correct while all the others, full of hope and optimism, had been blind to fathom Europe's true character? Was this world war simply a unique spasm, the result of Europe's growing pains in a modern world? Or did an even more dire future await Europe, like the "rough beast" destined to spring again that William Butler Yeats foretold in his 1919 poem, "The Second Coming"? In *Lapis Lazuli*, Yeats described a hysterical woman who sees airplanes and zeppelins burst from the sky, scattering bombs and reducing cities to rubble. Planes were also the instruments of destruction that devastated France and Italy by means of poison gas, in Hans Gobsch's prophetic novel *Wahn-Europa 1934, Eine Vision* (Madness in Europe 1934, a vision), which was published in 1931 and translated into Hebrew in 1932. The novel describes the beginning of a European war, ignited by a quarrel between Albania and Yugoslavia, that put an end to the ideas of pan-Europeanism and the creation of a unified European nation.

Was this, then, a war that aimed to destroy European culture in the name of the rebellion declared against it by the prophets of decline? Was it a war that would tear down the old world and create a new and better world in its place? Or would the true Europe have the strength to overcome the forces of destruction and rise again? After the collapse of the old European world order, the nineteenth century was often tinted with a soft, nostalgic cast, its many ailments apparently forgotten. The Europe of those days now seemed an orderly place where life proceeded at a moderate pace, with no dark passions or extremism—"an ordered world with definite classes and calm transitions, a world without haste." Shocked by the war, the Jewish Austrian writer Stefan Zweig described it as an atrocious betrayal that destroyed the secure, tranquil life that had existed in nineteenth-century Europe. So secure and tranquil had that existence been that the impending darkness had not been presaged in even the worst nightmares. Zweig's conclusion was that he had failed to foresee the coming war because "it is an indisputable law of history that one does not notice the great movements that determine the course of one's own time, and which are already underway." His senses honed by this lesson, he strove to decipher the voices that rose from the depths of postwar Europe. Others also whetted their senses after the war, in order never again to be caught unawares. The lesson they learned was, as Zweig put it, that in one's own time one must be more alert to the "great movements" that determine the course of history and "are already underway."[43]

What lesson, then, did Jews learn from World War I with respect to their European heritage and the future they could expect in twentieth-century Europe?

THE EMERGENCE OF THE MODERN EUROPEAN JEW

Why does Europe create such a powerful, magical, alluring impression on us, no matter who we might be?

FYODOR DOSTOEVSKY,
Winter Notes on Summer Impressions[1]

What Europe owes to the Jews? Many things, good and bad.

FRIEDRICH NIETZSCHE,
Beyond Good and Evil[2]

The Jews of France and Germany, England and Italy strive with all their might to be French and German, English and Italian, and to be Jewish no more. Their country's tongue and ways are now their own . . . They have forgotten their roots, and the bonds between them and their brothers in other lands have been broken.

Y. L. GORDON,
"A Vial of Perfume"[3]

We are part of the household of Europe, and we consider ourselves children of the land in which we were born and raised, whose language we speak and of whose knowledge the foundations of our spirit are built. We are Germans, Frenchmen, Englishmen, Magyars, Italians, and more.

ADOLF JELLINEK,
"A Conversation with Pinsker"[4]

The nineteenth century in Europe was called, among other things, the *Judenjahrhundert*—the Jewish century. Nietzsche offered one explanation for this label in *The Dawn of Day*, describing Jews' prominence in all dimensions of the European experience as nothing less than a "Jewish conquest," which he considered both desirable and necessary for Europe's future. In his opinion, European Jews—by which he meant the Jewish German bourgeoisie and intelligentsia—were a people of great vitality; they were becoming increasingly European both physically and spiritually, and they "distinguish[ed] themselves in all departments of European distinction." He predicted that the turning point in Jewish history was rapidly approaching, and that the question of the day would be whether Jews would "become masters of Europe or . . . lose Europe, as they once, centuries ago, lost Egypt." Jewish control over Europe, he added, would not be a result of conquest or violence; rather, "some day or other Europe may, like a ripe fruit, fall into their hands" and they would become "the pioneers and guides of the Europeans." In this way, "Israel shall have changed its eternal vengeance into an eternal benediction for Europe."[5]

A similar vision was cultivated and disseminated by antisemitic literature, which depicted Jews as striving, both in broad daylight and under cover of night, to achieve control over Europe, or effectively controlling it already. The Jews were Europe's masters; they were the agents of modernity, who propagated values in Europe that undermined the foundations of its society; it was they who had brought the world all the ailments of modern society: alienation, cosmopolitanism, and capitalism[6]—or, antithetically, revolutionary radicalism.[7] In 1879, Wilhelm Marr's *Der Sieg des Judenthums über das Germanenthum* (The victory of Judaism over Germandom) presented a vision of Jewish control over society, politics, and religious thought, in which 1,800 years of attempts to conquer and enslave the Germans had resulted in victory for the Semite Jews. In another infamous book, Eduard Drumont described how Jews had usurped control of France.[8] Other antisemites wrote that Jews had taught the rich how to exploit the poor through modern methods such as usury and capitalism—or, conversely, that the Jews had taught the poor to despise the rich, just as the nineteenth-century proletariat did. In his 1874 novel *Metamorphosis*, the Polish writer Józef Ignacy Kraszewski declared that Jews had imposed their values on European culture: the prophecies had come to pass, the Kingdom of Israel had arrived, and Jewish bankers were now the masters of the world.[9] This cross-European antisemitic literature warned of the negative consequences of Judaizing Europe. Such warning cries against increasing Jewish control were perceived as a crucial and effective method of self-defense against Jewish influence—whether real or imaginary—in order to save Europe's soul.[10]

THE "JEWISH CENTURY" AND
THE JEWISH REVOLUTION

These two opposite, fabricated depictions—one of complete, harmonious Jewish integration in European society, and the other of Jews as conspicuous and controlling Europe—as well as Jews' conceit that they had a moral mission to fulfill in Europe, developed in part because of the emergence of a new Jewish archetype: the modern European Jew. The nineteenth century was not really the Jewish century, but it was the century in which the modern Jewish revolution took place, during which the so-called Jewish Question came into being,[11] and which determined the fate of Jews throughout the next century. This was a revolution because processes of change, change—and awareness of change—in multiple spheres, and agendas for change and initiatives to realize them were all involved.

Jews in nineteenth-century Europe did not become European because they were ensnared by the charms and temptations of Western culture, fell victim to its allure, and thus abandoned their identity—in fact, they were eventually betrayed by Europe, which declared a crusade of destruction against them. They became European because it was not possible for them to become modern Jews—that is, to adapt to the modern world and adjust Jewish life to it—without actually becoming, in one sense or another, European. The main reason for this was that, in contrast to inhabitants of lands under Western colonial rule, the Jews encountered the full spectrum of Western culture (or cultures)—and not through the intermediary of literature or through representatives of colonial rule, but in a direct and intensive way. Because of this, the process of their Europeanization was general and comprehensive.[12]

The Jews of medieval Europe were also European. This is not only due to the fact that they lived in Europe, but also because they were never, in any part of it, a closed society, disconnected and isolated from their environment; their culture was influenced by and reflected many dimensions of Christian culture. Nonetheless, the Europeanism of nineteenth-century Jews was an entirely new development. It was created by the influence of the range of processes and phenomena that gave rise to the modern European world: demographic growth; industrialization and urbanization;[13] the strengthening of nationalistic movements and the emergence of nationalist states; political and social radicalism; and civil wars and revolutions. All these destabilized and reconstructed every layer of the Jewish experience—in different ways, of course, depending on the circumstances of time and place. It might be said that to a great extent the outside penetrated the Jewish world, while the inside (the Jews) penetrated the outside (non-Jewish) world to a great extent as well. The magnitude of this process is also evident in its influence beyond Europe, in every region touched by European influence. The desire for "European forms of culture," Graetz wrote, spread even to the Middle East and North Africa.[14] In other words, Jews in Europe were European because they underwent similar processes of change, transformation, adaptation, and adjustment wherever they lived in Europe.

Jews in Europe were sometimes described as Europhiles in the days before any inhabitant of Europe was called European, and during the period when other nations searched for a more general framework for themselves in ideas like pan-Slavism and pan-Germanism.[15] However, to call Jews the only Europeans would be a pretension that conflicted with reality. There were Europeans with a sense of European identity far before that perception existed among Jews, and many Jews made an effort to emphasize their attachment to the particular state and culture in which they lived—a phenomenon that Stefan Zweig described correctly in his *The World of Yesterday* as "a longing for homeland, for rest, for security," which "urge[d] them to attach themselves passionately to the culture of the world around them."[16]

However, a distinction should be drawn between declarations of beliefs and self-image on the one hand, and cultural reality on the other hand. The Jewish elite not only adopted cultural values that were identified with particular European cultures, but it also adopted values and ways of life that were widespread in European culture as a whole. Naturally in the age of nationalism, much weight was placed on the differences between various national cultures. Even so, ideas, values, and the cultural repertoire were not bound by strict national or political boundaries, instead crossing these boundaries by means of cultural agents, being adopted into new cultural environments, and becoming an inseparable part of them. This process of Europeanization influenced not only the elite but also—in various ways and to varying extents—other groups within the Jewish population.

In the research literature, examples are frequently cited of the processes of adaptation and integration of central figures in the Jewish world, tracing their awareness of these processes and their misgivings toward all that related to defining their identity. In many cases, the literature highlights the great tension between declarations on the subject of full integration and disappointment and despair. However, concepts such as personal identity, collective identity, and true nature are hazy and difficult to define,[17] nor are groups like German Jews, Russian Jews, or Polish Jews monolithic. The result is that the use of generalizing terms paints a one-dimensional and integrative picture, while the reality consisted of a hybrid situation in which new and traditional norms existed side by side, their relationship evolving over time. The variety and dynamism of that relationship is a clear testament to the profound transformations that took place in Jewish life during the nineteenth century. Thus instead of discussing essence and identity, we find it preferable to examine the Jews' real culture, values, and "habitus"—in other words, the pre-arranged models that shaped Jews' lives and informed their conduct in specific situations according to their social standing.[18] These models reflect the social and cultural norms that different groups follow in their everyday lives, rather than vague and general declarations.

This is a matter not only of behavioral patterns in society and culture, as we see, for example, in the 1833 description by Michael Benedict Lessing of the extensive transformations that had taken place in Jews' language, lifestyle, pastimes, attributes, and customs, which he illustrated by comparing the East European Jewish world to its urban German counterpart: "In the last half of the eighteenth century—in contrast to the first half of the nineteenth—it was impossible for one to encounter Jews at concerts, parties, balls, festivals, cafés, or trading floors, taking interest in the daily newspapers, participating in musical, artistic, or scientific circles, or in any intellectual or other circles, to find Jews who were not inferior to the rest of society in manners or knowledge."[19] This description is exaggerated with regard to the start of the nineteenth century, but accurate with respect to its latter half.

The nineteenth-century Jewish revolution brought about the most radical transformations in Jews' circumstances since the destruction of the Second Temple. Its revolutionary nature—as Benjamin Harshav correctly described it—was expressed not only in transformations that took place in various aspects of the Jewish experience, but also in the fact that "it was the framework that reconstructed the various details that characterized the whole as an inclusive, entirely new phenomenon."[20] In other words, this was a matter of reconstructing the entire scope of Jewish life, and in doing so, forging a new tradition.[21] The fundamental questions regarding identity, belonging, and the desirable boundaries of Jewish culture and the surrounding European culture appeared on the Jews' agenda because at the start of the nineteenth century, Jews were required to work out for themselves—and to explain to others—how Judaism could exist in its new environment. The success of their integration and acculturation was measured not only by how Jews evaluated the outcome of these processes, but also—perhaps primarily—according to the reaction of the non-Jewish environment. In order to answer this pressing question for themselves, Jews formulated various strategies to deal with everything related to the construction of their new identity and its desired character. The strategies that were proposed created different camps in European Jewish society and brought about a war of ideas and perspectives that continues to this day. Indeed, one of the central expressions of the Jewish revolution in the nineteenth century was that new ways of life and new self-definitions became available to European Jews as a whole—as well as, for the first time, as individuals; these were determined by the broad freedom of choice and action that was granted to them by various European societies. One could now choose not only whether to be Jewish, but what sort of Jew to be.

The nineteenth-century revolution also created entirely new criteria concerning everything related to the boundaries between Jews and their environment.[22] These criteria may be grouped as follows:

1. The extent of Jews' presence in all fields of general cultural activity, whether as creators or as consumers. This presence was described as participation in or contribution to Western culture.[23]
2. The extent to which Jews identified with a specific nation or the national culture in which they lived—that is, the manner in which Jews expressed an awareness of their belonging to the nation in which they lived, and the ways in which they identified with it.
3. The nature and content of the Western cultural models and repertoire of cultural values that Jews adopted and internalized—that is, the nature of the processes of Jewish integration and acculturation into their environments.[24] The desired results, or those actually achieved, were a broad range of transformations that were described in many ways—as identity, growing proximity, integration, acclimatization, absorption, and assimilation—and were evaluated as positive or negative.
4. A comparison between nineteenth-century Jewish norms and values and those of Jews in equivalent social groups during previous generations. What, for example, was the difference between what was seen as normative in traditional society, and what was considered normative in Jewish society in the modern era?

5. The reactions of the non-Jewish environment to the processes of adaptation, acclimatization, and integration, and the boundaries it set for these processes.

EUROPEAN JEWS—BETWEEN NATIONALISM AND EUROPEANISM

Which Europe is at issue here?

During the first half of the nineteenth century, the cultural characteristics of East European Christian society were described in Jewish literature as a product of social standing rather than as ethnic or national differences.[25] Thus this period had not yet experienced the creation of a repertoire of stereotypes for the characteristic aspects attributed to various peoples. This repertoire began to appear toward the latter half of the century as a result of the discovery of peoples, and of folk identity, in the various European societies according to typical group traits.[26] The *maskil* Baruch Lindau, for example, proposed the following observations in his 1788 book *Reshit Limudim*: the Portuguese were indolent, miserly seamen, wholly unskilled for labor; Spaniards were lazy and coarse; the French were "intelligent and crafty," skilled in every science and discipline; Germans were industrious in science and lovers of knowledge; Italians were easygoing and particularly talented in painting and music; the British loved art, knowledge, and science; and the Swedes were "hard of heart and weak of mind."[27] Another example of the use of this repertoire of national characteristics is Herzl's opening speech at the Second Zionist Congress, in which he noted "the Germans' industry, the Romanians' nimbleness, the Slavs' endless patience," and so forth.[28]

The national characteristics that were attributed to Europe's various nations and perceived as expressing their deeply rooted collective essence were eventually depicted as qualities that also cast their mark on, and shaped the identity of, the Jews who lived in these nations. Differences among the various types of Jews, or between different Jewish populations in Europe, were delineated according to these typical characteristics.[29] As Richard Cohen has noted, "the construction of German, Italian, English, Dutch, or Austro-Hungarian identity was an inseparable part of the modern Jew's historical experience."[30] Thus European Jews were classified as German Jews, Russian Jews, and so forth, and one could speak of their Britishness, Germanness, or Russianness. Over the course of the nineteenth century, Jewish society in Europe became more divided and heterogeneous than ever. The great Jewish center in Germany dissolved, and the differences between German Jews and the Jews of Eastern Europe became increasingly stark throughout the nineteenth century.[31]

East European Jews were depicted in the West as old-fashioned and frozen in time, mired in ignorance and characterized by religious zealotry; in other words, they were not considered a cultured group. The rift was especially profound in all that concerned the East European Jewish Orthodoxy's relationship to German Jews, but modern non-Orthodox Jews in Eastern Europe also had an ambivalent attitude toward German Jews. Even a radical *maskil* such as Y. L. Gordon, for example, disliked what he saw in Berlin in both the Reform and neo-Orthodox movements: "None of what I have seen thus far in Berlin has brought me pleasure or peace of mind."[32] Nonetheless, the fissure between German and East European Jews was even deeper than another fissure, that between East European and West European Jews generally.

During the 1880s, following the emergence of national revival movements in Eastern Europe, Gordon maintained that Jews' integration into various national cultures had divided European Jews according to their affiliation with one national type or another. In 1882, the Viennese scholar and preacher Dr. Adolf Jellinek wrote to Leon Pinsker, whose pamphlet *Autoemancipation* had just been published, that Jews were at once both Europeans and members of the nations in which they lived. Jews were "children of Europe, and [we] see ourselves as part of the lands in which we were born and raised, whose tongues we speak and whose cultures shape our intellectual being. We are German, English, Hungarian, Italian, etc., in every fiber of our being. We have long since ceased being true racial Semites, and a long time has passed since we lost the sense of Hebrew nationalism."[33] Simon Dubnow claimed that Jews did adhere to an overall Western culture—but that because there was no single culture truly shared by all of Europe, and instead there existed a "culture of nationalist form ... built on the language, education, and literature of a nation's people," it became inevitable that "each branch of the Jewish Diaspora would have acquired the national culture of the land in "which it settled." According to him, Jews' education in school and at home "made [them] German, Russian, French—not Jewish."[34] Nathan Birnbaum wrote that life among the *Gattungskulturen*—the various types of European culture—created tribal divisions among Europe's Jews:

> Take heed! Cultural contrast! The issue is not that Jews in Poland exist on a lower cultural level but that they possess a different culture than that of the German Jews. They [Polish Jews] have acquired not the European culture but rather the medieval culture of the Ghetto Jew, which is, in the eyes of one who has been educated in Europe, un-aesthetic and not superior.[35]

The response Birnbaum desired was not assimilation into the dominant culture, but rather *Nationalisierung* (nationalization) and *Liebe zum Eigentümlichen* (love of one's unique identity), because taking pride in belonging to another people would never result in inner satisfaction.[36]

These stereotypes of Jewish traits according to Jews' provenance were destined for a long existence. They were used, for example, to describe the differences between *Ostjuden* (Eastern Jews) newly immigrated to Germany and longtime German Jews:

> It cannot be denied that there are differences between the "Yekkes" and the "Ostjuden." Some are really cultural differences, some are differences of habit, some are very profound differences in ways of thought . . . German Jews grew up at the knees of German idealism and the logical, Kantian, German way of thinking. Our brothers to the East have a more moderate way of thinking that has been defined to a greater extent by another form of logic . . . There are also differences in other areas . . . German Jews have been educated in a very formal manner. Etiquette carries great weight with them.[37]

Ahad Haam summarized the situation in a sad letter to Dubnow: "we can speak no longer of a single Jewish people, but rather of Jewish peoples."[38]

There is no doubt that the particular cultural experience of the European nations—language, literature, education, construction of sentiment, and collective historical memory—made a deep mark on the Jewish culture of each country. However, as we have seen, particularity need not obscure the existence of a shared, universal European background, which also informed daily life and conduct. Consequently, we should distinguish between, on the one hand, the results of Jews' integration and assimilation in various, particular European societies, and on the other hand, the manner in which they accepted and internalized universal European values.

HOMELAND, NATIONALITY, AND DIVIDED IDENTITY

Jews' adaptation to the reality of nineteenth-century Europe was expressed in their attempts to become an integrated part of the national society and culture of the countries in which they lived. These attempts took different forms and had different results in multinational, multiethnic countries than in more culturally homogeneous countries. Zeev Jabotinsky, who wrote a great deal on the subject, was not alone in pointing out the profound difference between life in unilingual and life in multilingual states. In a 1911 article titled "Letters on Nationalities and Oblasts: Jewry and its Attitudes," for example, he wrote:

> In Russia . . . the Jews live en masse among the Little Russians, Belorussians, Poles, Lithuanians, and Moldavians; they have the least contact with the Great Russians. Thus, even if they accepted Russification, the Jews would be assimilated not by the majority population around them but by a people that constitutes a weaker, scattered minority within the Pale of Settlement and dominates today only thanks to state coercion. In the event of the elimination of that coercion, the local national cultures would develop and thrive, forcing Jewry also to separate finally into a distinct cultural group. It would be impelled not only by the attraction of example . . . but also by necessity, born of a sense of political self-preservation.[39]

During the age of nationalism, it was possible to think of acculturation as an admission ticket to the universal European culture, but even more than that, it was a ticket to individual, nationalistic cultures. Entry into one of those cultures meant not only treating it as more than a temporary refuge, but also belonging to and identifying with it. Nation and location became homeland and home. One's homeland consisted of both the autochthonic human landscape and the natural surroundings. For example, Mendele Mokher Seforim described Jewish integration into these surroundings in his 1887 novel *Beseter Raam* (A secret thunder):

> And they lived together in friendship for many days, visiting each other and consulting each other when they had need. Many of them [the gentiles] visit the homes of their Jewish friends, know their children by name, are fond of them and play with them . . . and speak with them in Yiddish. When a Jew sees his sons wed and the *klezmer* [wedding band] plays, these "uncles" often come to the banquet, and when the jester plays they join the crowd in laughter.[40]

The Modern European Jew

From the middle of the nineteenth century onward, not only did Jews have neighborly relations with Christians in their immediate area, but they also were aware of belonging to a homeland and its national culture. The concept of homeland had appeared at the end of the eighteenth century; during the following century, it became, together with the concept of a nation, a fundamental idea that shaped the era. German Jews' patriotic awakening and the emergence of their feeling of belonging to a homeland, which began during the time of the Napoleonic wars, was clearly expressed in a proclamation titled *Zuruf an die Jünglinge* by Eduard Kley, a reform preacher from Berlin, and Karl Siegfried Günsburg: "O what a heavenly feeling to possess a fatherland! O what a rapturous idea to be able to call a spot, a place, a nook one's own upon this lovely earth."[41] National identity was applied to Jews both by themselves and by others.[42] From this point on, the extent to which one belonged to one's homeland and identified with it was measured by one's affinity for its national culture and the depths of one's patriotic sentiment.[43] Such a formulation of the consciousness of affinity and belonging appears in 1862, in Mendele Mokher Seforim's novel *Fathers and Sons*. Ben David, the protagonist, lives abroad but yearns for Russia, which is not only a place but a homeland:

> On beholding another man from my homeland, whether Jewish or not, I rejoiced at the sight of him as one would at the sight of God; I touched his clothes and their smell was the scent of those God-blessed fields . . . And I, as though arriving at the outskirts of my blessed homeland, knelt and kissed the ground and rejoiced in its soil and told myself with an overflowing heart: "I am a Russian man!"[44]

In February 1882, in response to pogroms and widespread persecutions, Haim Hissin—a member of the Bilu movement, a group committed to settling in Israel, founded in Russia in 1882; a physician; and one of the founders of Tel Aviv—wrote that he considered himself Russian and loved the Russian people, and therefore "absolutely could never leave Russia forever." He also wrote that he felt a spiritual connection with Russian folk song and the Russian peasant. However, the pogroms had brought him to the conclusion that "the Jews have no place in Russia," and that they must pick up "the age-old walking staff" and search for "a new home." On July 19, sailing from Odessa to Jaffa aboard the *Russia*, he wrote that in Russia "my dreams and heart's desire lie buried." He had grown up there, and it was there that his sentiments had taken form, but "you pushed me away, my beloved homeland."⁴⁵ It is hard to tell to what extent this attitude toward Russia as a homeland was shared by the young generation of the Jewish Russian intelligentsia and semi-intelligentsia, not to mention by broader groups.

In 1931, a seventeen-year-old student from Tarnow in Galicia, Salo Wittmayer Baron, who became a distinguished historian, responded to the assertion that Jews neither were nor desired to be Polish with a long essay in the weekly *Haivri*, which was published in Krakow. Not satisfied with describing the Jews' extensive involvement in Polish culture, Baron also declared that the unbroken Jewish presence in Poland over the course of six centuries granted them "a historical right" to define themselves as natives of the land, no less than the Poles.⁴⁶ In general, a positive and affectionate image of the Poles, and a sense of Polish patriotism, existed among Polish Jews until the end of 1942.⁴⁷

However, modern Jews did not wish to assimilate into the autochthonic human landscape, and certainly not into rural peasant society, which was considered an environment of dark ignorance. Their model was not the East European peasant, who was generally described in Jewish literature as "simple folk, by nature ignorant, unenlightened, coarse, and crude, tending to drunkenness and other 'bestial' passions."⁴⁸

Modern Jews wished to integrate into the nationalist society represented, in their opinion, by the urban, bourgeois, and intellectual classes, depicted as rational and "aesthetically refined." They wished to integrate into the Europe that was a product of "science and reason" and thus enlightened and tolerant. Such an environment already existed in their opinion in Western Europe, where "Jews live without fear and are not subject to persecution . . . Little by little they become closer to the native folk, will become loyal citizens to the nation of their birth, will stride with a mighty step on the path of knowledge . . . [and] will purify their customs"—so wrote Nahum Sokolow in "A General Outlook on the Year 1879 and Its Significance for Our Jewish Brothers," an 1880 article in *Hamagid* in which he predicted that in the future, such an environment would also arise in Eastern Europe.

Dubnow wished to distinguish between two foundations of patriotism, the first based on "civic consciousness of the common needs of all members of the state," and the second on the "natural feeling of love for one's homeland." Since "Europe has become a second fatherland for the majority of the Jewish people, they have developed a natural feeling of love of fatherland wherever they settled." Because the Jewish people formed their own culture, they could be a patriotic "nationality among nationalities" in any country they inhabited.[49]

Patriotism, civic awareness, and the awareness of a nationalistic belonging to a specific homeland and culture characterized sizable groups of Jews in both Western and Eastern Europe. The dilemma was, of course, whether it was possible to differentiate between patriotism, citizenship, and national bonds.

EUROPEAN CULTURE AND THE LIMITS OF ACCULTURATION

When the Orthodox weekly *Der Israelit* summarized the nineteenth century, it wrote, as we have seen, that "since exiting the Ghetto, Jews have been partners in creativity in all areas of life," and this partnership reached its peak during that century.[50] The extent to which Jews' integration was successful was measured according to the extent of their participation in all aspects of life, as well as the contributions they made over time to various fields of endeavor, and the degree to which they excelled or were prominent in those fields. The ability to integrate was considered a calling card that Jews must present when they knocked at the gates of European culture and society—a calling card on which they marked their successes in the present, their contribution to world culture in the past, and their qualifications to contribute in the future. In effect, this calling card represented a demand for the Jews to absorb the environment around them, which included "regeneration," "correction," and even fundamental change in, or a conversion of, their codes of behavior and values.[51] It was not enough to present accomplishments; it was necessary to point to their significance to the particular national culture.[52] Because the nations' cultural level and the quality of their cultural achievements were a primary measure of their merit and their status among other nations,[53] the Jews' active participation in this creation and their contributions to it—not to mention their qualifications to participate and contribute—became a new way to evaluate them. Jews seemingly wished to prove that they were able to fulfill—indeed, that they had already fulfilled—the expectations of the philosopher J. G. von Herder, who had looked forward to the day when Jews would "live by European laws and contribute to the good of the State's interests."[54]

At the end of the 1860s, when the *maskil* and popularizer Kalman Schulman, from Vilna, presented an impressive picture of Jewish integration in European culture and society, he took pride in the speed with which Jews had entered all the branches of European culture—an achievement unrealized by other groups "for many hundreds of years." The modern era granted Jews the opportunity to express "the precious merits and high talents which had slumbered within their souls during the dark years of oppression," and had allowed them to cultivate "great poets, wondrous rhetoricians, lauded authors in all realms, renowned mathematicians and engineers, astronomers, historians, men well versed in religion and law, and knowledgeable in all branches of the natural sciences, famous physicians, psalmists, musicians, diplomats, sculptors, visionaries. And there is no wisdom, art or craftsmanship in which the Jews did not engage, and they became famous in the land for their prowess."[55] In 1864, in the same spirit of spiritual uplift, Y. L. Gordon wrote:

> Now there is no city or state in which young Jewish men do not draw the clear waters of alien springs . . . You can count the specialist physicians employed by the state . . . how many young Jews you will find today who engage in writing and speak the language of their country fluently, or German and French, and all of them born in the last generation, products of the last decade.[56]

In 1839, the Russian Jewish *maskil* Isaac Baer Levinsohn described with admiration a similar calling card of the Jews: "There is hardly any field of science, art and the crafts, even among the most prestigious and honoured, in which there are no Jews today." In other words, Jews did not need to remain outside, or knocking at, the door of European culture because they had all the gifts needed for equal and active participation in it; the evidence was their ability to integrate into the modern European world.[57]

In 1858 Abraham Geiger, who was one of the leaders of the *Wissenschaft des Judentums* and of the Reform movement in Germany, responded to a Jew who wrote that he intended to leave the religion:

> Let me tell you—and do not accuse me of arrogance—that the Jews are proving an ability to develop that is likely to earn them much favor . . . Less than a century has passed since their situation became considerably more comfortable, and today an entirely different generation has quickly sprung up! Improving in every sense, enormously energetic in all their aspirations, spiritually alert and making great achievements in all spheres despite the fact that quite

a few professions are closed to them. This is not a decadent population; on the contrary, it is brimming with lofty talents . . .⁵⁸

A more impressive calling card presented the Jews as the begetters and instigators of modernism. Heine wrote that the Jews were the fathers of the *moderne Prinzip* (the modern principle) that was taking form in Europe.⁵⁹ Europe, wrote Graetz, had in the past been saved from the "Pagan filth" thanks to "our exalted prophets and poets, who injected a fresh spiritual wind into European history." During the Renaissance, Europe was rescued from the influence of the paganism of the classical world thanks to the revival of the *Hebraica veritas* (Hebrew truth) which was brought about by the Reformation.⁶⁰ According to Graetz, modern Europe could be saved from the ills of modernism only through the influence and inspiration of Jewish values. Only these could "prevent the chaos threatening the nations of Europe . . . If Judaism disappeared, then with it would disappear the moral demands it comprehends, upon which depend the continued existence of society and civilization." Graetz wished Edith, the "English Lady," to take cheer in what "the Jews have achieved in less than one century. They perform well in all branches of science and literature and in some they are the leaders." The "marvelous Jewish existence" which Graetz so admired included, among others, "the Rothschilds, who decide matters of war and peace"; the "sons of Jacob who dominate the European money market"; and the Jews who participated actively "in all branches of science and literature" and shaped public opinion as writers of front-page articles, political reports, and *feuilletons*.⁶¹

In a June 1895 letter to Baron Hirsch, Herzl too described the talents of the Jews who would join the Zionist movement, noting that these included "all the engineers, architects, chemists, physicians, technicians and lawyers who have emerged from the ghetto during the last thirty years."⁶² Dubnow, the ideologue of national cultural autonomy in Eastern Europe, wrote that Jews were not strangers in Europe: "History proves that the Jews are old inhabitants of Europe, that they established themselves in Europe even before the growth of European civilization and the spread of Christianity . . . The Jews are inhabitants of Europe since ancient times and their territorial rights are based not on property titles but on colonization and cultural influence."⁶³ By "cultural influence," Dubnow referred not only to past contributions—that is, to the fact that Jews brought the Old Testament to Western culture, and through it monotheism and the moral teachings of the prophets—but also to their contemporary contributions. In the nineteenth century, Jews contributed to Europe in all fields of excellence: economics, art, and science. Jews' entry into the modern world, wrote Arthur Ruppin, as well as their integration in and contributions to it, stemmed from modern man's characteristic traits: "sharpness, diligence, ease of movement and ease of understanding, the rule of mind over desire, and constant vigilance of thought."[64]

In other words, according to this perception, modern Jews were European because their creative activity was an inseparable part of the whole of European cultural creation, and because this activity was part of the forces sculpting the spirit of Europe. Probably by the end of the twentieth century, a unified Europe would be described as an embodiment of the Jewish essence, and some have already claimed that everything in Europe—both good and bad—stems from a Jewish source.[65] In reality, this was not a matter of a collective, organized effort on the part of the Jews; however, the fact that even the research literature that avoids the concept of contribution devotes chapters to the detailed description of the Jews' part in German and other European cultures demonstrates the wish to consider these achievements as belonging to a distinct group, as well as to emphasize its relatively large role in various realms of activity and creativity.

Alongside the declarations that the Jewish spirit had given birth to modernism, leading humanity to the pinnacle of achievement—and that the Jewish spirit alone could rescue Western culture from moral corruption and degeneration—warning cries were heard, and not only from the Orthodox camp. Germany's Jews were urged to abstain from the evils of modernism, which were apt to corrupt them as well. Modern European culture, which exerted a magical, exuberant, and sometimes irresistible pull on Jews— they were enchanted by what they saw, or imagined they saw—was nothing but the "temptation of sirens of the formal beauty of Hellenism, which many choose in these times." European education in the spirit of classical Greece and Hellenism brought about "the spirit of detached individualism, love for artificial pleasures, meaningless minutiae, luxuries, subservience to women, a tendency toward various frivolous pastimes, and all that we generally associate with gentile behavior. All of these traits, which are the substance of European civilization, corrupt body and soul."[66] A solution to the tension between the desire to adopt certain European cultural values and the desire to reject others was sometimes found in the claim that the cultural values which could and should be adopted were those perceived as universally relevant and valuable—part of European culture. These values, which personified the universal spirit, knew no national, ethnic, or religious boundaries; as a result, the distinction that modern Jews should make was between "positive acculturation" and "negative acculturation"—or, in other words, between "positive knowledge" and "counterfeit knowledge."[67] According to this view, a sort of controlled or selective acculturation could be possible, its boundaries determined by Jews.

In an 1886 *feuilleton* titled "A Vial of Perfume," Y. L. Gordon described a young Jew torn between the "wise and tasteful halls" of European culture and Judaism, which he saw as "the fields of Israel, mired in mud!" The wavering youth wrote to Gordon: "I am young and have been a supporter of the *Haskalah*. The source of my education has been European literature and culture . . . In short, I am a slave to the jewels of Japheth, and he has struck me with fever." However, he added, the riots against Russia's Jews brought him to a crossroads, and he knew not which path to choose: "whether the path called European culture or the path called nationalism!" This was Gordon's response:

> Our ancient fathers too carried Japheth's jewels into Shem's tent and drank their fill of the wisdom of their time, each man in his own way. And even if they are correct who say that the learning of the sons of Japheth is "flowers without fruit," they forget that while there are flowers without fruit there are no fruit without flowers; therefore, what will prevent us from constructing this wreath from the grapevines of Israel so that we may have both fruit and flowers and so that our tree of life may be both good to eat and pleasing to the eye? The *Haskalah* is not a concept that stands alone; it is not wisdom or learning which is already known. Enlightenment is treading the paths of reason and knowing to think things through, and this is necessary and a requisite for every man, whoever he may be, wherever he may be, whatever station he may possess. Enlightenment is fresh air to the soul . . . And who tells you that the fields of Israel must be mired in mud? If you are one of those who truly possesses culture, and if the light of Enlightenment shines upon you, then by that light you will walk, and when you return to narrow lodgings you will know to keep them clean of mire and refuse . . . Culture, which is Enlightenment, is useful and necessary for every Jew, including the most nationalist of nationalists.[68]

According to Gordon, therefore, only one culture existed—that of Europe—and he distinguished between true and counterfeit European culture. Viewpoints that were considered alien to the spirit of Judaism were described as counterfeit culture, as were phenomena that were perceived as negative and leading to heresy and licentiousness. In his 1899 short story "In Exchange for Shoes," Gordon painted a portrait of the heresy that resulted when the negative values of European culture dominated Jewish society:

> It is true that lately the generations have degenerated . . . now the crowd will jostle like bulls at the feeding trough of the supposed Enlightenment and will learn the ways of the gentiles around them and take after the most corrupt of them. Now the sons of Abraham, Isaac, and Jacob infest the theaters and circuses,[69] they are teeming like locusts . . . Group by group they will stroll in the gardens and orchards to see the gentile girls who dance in the vineyards, look in a pitcher and in what lies inside it, and listen to the voices of the singing women and court the daughters of gentiles; group by group, they will gather at dances in clubhouses full of the frolics of men and women, in which men and women are all intermingled, and play at cards and dice, and hurry from there to the dance halls where men wear women's clothing and women wear the clothes of men and disguise themselves with powders and masks until they can no longer tell the accursed Haman from the accursed Zeresh [tell the difference between men and women]. Alas for the generation whom this befell! Because from that day honor was exiled from the synagogues and *batei-midrash* [halls of study]. In the synagogue courtyards weeds will grow from the lack of traffic, and between the walls of the *batei-midrash* echoes will sound and coo like doves: alas for the sons exiled from their fathers' tables.[70]

Mendele Mokher Seforim also believed that "low culture" would lead to evil—yeshiva students would abandon their faith and play at dice and cards[71]—while Moshe Leib Lilienblum distinguished between *Haskalah*—"reason, questing for truth, pure virtue, and love for the natural sciences"—and culture—"Greco-Roman civilization, its taste and beauty and external delicacy." But he also found many positive ideas in European civilization whose adoption would bring about desired change in Jewish society: "All Jews [should] know how to recognize the value of life in this world, citizenship and civilization, and they should strive to end the chain that binds us to the days of darkness, with the Talmudic spirit and all the Asiatic wildness."[72] At the same time, Lilienblum maintained that "our faith will not be repaired in Europe, nor have we any life there";[73] the return to a full and authentic life could be achieved only in Palestine. Leaving Europe would allow Jews to distinguish between the good and bad foundations of Western culture and hold on only to what was necessary, good, and of the highest quality.

HOMELAND AND NATIONAL CULTURE

German Jews, perhaps more than any other Jewish group in Europe, made intellectual and emotional efforts to define their relationship to their country, homeland, and national culture; they also reformulated their Jewish consciousness (*jüdisches Selbstverständnis*). Even Heine—whose warning about what Jews could expect from "the scent of Germany of the future" (i.e., from German nationalism) we will discuss later—wrote in 1838 that Jews and Germans had been natural allies since the beginning of their histories, and that the ancient land of Israel had been a sort of "oriental Germany," just as nineteenth-century Germany was the fertile ground of prophecy and "the stronghold of pure spirituality" deriving from the Bible. Thus, Heine maintained, there was a profound kinship between the two peoples: both were moral people.[74] In Thomas Mann's *Doctor Faustus*, on the other hand, Saul Fitelberg, a Jewish music impresario born in Lublin—"provincial Poland"—who achieves greatness in Germany, says:

> To be German, that means above all to be national—and who expects a Jew to be nationalistic? Not only would nobody believe him, but everybody would bash his head in for having the impudence to try it on. We Jews have everything to fear from the German character, *qui est essentiellement antisémitique* [which is essentially antisemitic]; and that is reason enough, of course, for us to strive for the worldly side and arrange sensational entertainments.[75]

Gabriel Riesser, a resolute fighter for Jewish rights and the editor of *Der Jude* from 1832 to 1835, denounced those who proposed to deny Jews rights because of their different nationality: "The thunderous sounds of the German language, the works of the German poets, are what sparked and fed the sacred flames of liberty . . . We want to belong to the German fatherland; we *will* belong to it wherever we may be; it is possible and even likely to demand of us whatever one is entitled to demand of its citizens."[76] Germany's Jews hoped not only for a harmonious coexistence of the fraternal nations—the Jewish minority and the German majority—in which both peoples would live at peace with each other, but they also expected full entry as German Jews into German-educated, bourgeois society. Liberal Jews even found some similarity between Judaism and liberal Germany: both were imbued with patriotism, moderated by cosmopolitan humanism. In 1879, Moritz Lazarus issued an enthusiastic declaration of total belonging to Germany: "The Germans: these—we are—they are what we wish to be—we cannot be otherwise. The language itself makes us German. The land in which we live; the state which we serve; the law to which we are loyal; the science scholarship from which we learn; the education which lights our way; the art which uplifts us—all of these are German. Our mother tongue and fatherland, both German, together form our inner core."[77] In his 1915 essay *Deutschtum und Judentum*, the philosopher Hermann Cohen described Germany as the soul's homeland, not only with respect to German Jews but for all Jews everywhere.[78] Cohen, in fact, believed that modern Judaism was similar to Protestantism, and he faced severe criticism as a result. Jakob Klatzkin claimed that there was no common background between Germanness and Jewishness, because Germanness had never escaped its pagan, Teutonic background; this was a matter of "two expressions of two rich cultures opposed to each other from beginning to end."[79] Franz Rosenzweig's response, which he wrote as a young soldier in the German army, was entirely different:

> To be German means to feel responsibility for the German people as a whole; harmonize not only with Goethe and Schiller and Kant but also with the others, and especially with the inferior and average, with the assessor, the little public servant, the fat-headed peasant, the stiff *Oberlehrer* [senior teacher] . . . Cohen confused what he finds as a European in *Deutschtum* with what the German finds in it . . . In Cohen there is only *Europäertum*; he lacks genuine *Deutschtum*.[80]

According to Rosenzweig, then, true Germanness was not necessarily the Germanness of liberal thinkers and humanists (whose primary model was Friedrich Schiller), but the "deep-seated," "empirical" Germanness that Buber described as "a true, natural bond with the earth and culture of the nation."[81] From this perspective, the German language was seen not only as useful and necessary for civilian integration, but also—in the spirit of the times—as a clear expression of the inner soul of the German Jew. Thus Abraham Geiger wrote that the very fact that Germany's Jews had become entirely German in sentiment and being found its true expression in the German language, through which these Jews plumbed the depths of their souls and rose to the greatest heights; language was a matter not of appearance but of essence.[82] German Jews were described as "rooted in [their] old homeland even in difficult times."[83] The identification with Germany and its perception as the refuge of European humanism was expressed in Rabbi Leo Baeck's declaration in August 1914 that the war would determine Europe's morality and culture, and that Europe's fate rested in Germany's hands.[84]

Liberal Jews were not alone in this sentiment; it was also the position of neo-Orthodoxy. The neo-Orthodox German Jews did not lag behind in declarations of loyalty to the homeland. *Der Israelit* declared in 1870 that "we are the German Jews; we are Germans, and nothing more," and in 1881 that "we are Germans, both by birth and in mentality" and that the German *Bund* (the German union), was the new homeland, replacing the old. In effect, the neo-Orthodox Jews in Germany who followed the teachings of S. R. Hirsch were consumers of German (and European) culture, but their integration into German society and their involvement in German culture were very limited.[85]

The yearning for the complete removal of obstacles to this *Zweiheit* (double identity) and for complete integration from a position of equality—for the creation of an internally consistent integration, which became known as *Deutschjudentum* (German Jewishness)—led to a rift among German Jews and many personal crises. Those who accepted the perception that personality, whether individual or collective, was an organic and authentic entity could not fail to be aware of this rift and, as a result, to search for ways to blend in with the new authentic entity. The question at hand was thus whether that entity would be found outside of Judaism, within Judaism, or in the integration of the two worlds. Could Jews manage to free themselves from their essence and become integrated into a different, opposing essence? In 1862, Moses Hess wrote: "even in the West, a place to which Jews are bound by a thousand cultural threads and with which they are in direct contact, the *Haskalah* was unable to diminish the existence of Judaism and its traditions."[86]

Most of the members of the Jewish elite were conscious of this tragic trap of split identity. Modern Jews wished with all their might to belong to their environment, but they were rejected by it. This awareness created a crisis of identity and belonging and forced them to search for new ways to escape from the trap, to rehabilitate their identity, and to belong to a separate, unique framework of their own.

Many modern Jews' private crises stemmed not from the realization of how strong their ties were to the old Jewish world, but from the revelation that the path to true Germanness was blocked. It was obstructed not only by Jews' inability to shed their Jewish organic essence, but because non-Jewish society did not permit them to shed it. This was the sharp and painful conclusion reached, for example, by Leo Wolf, a student of philosophy and the protagonist of the 1892 novel *Werther, der Jude* (Werther, the Jew) by the forgotten German Jewish author Ludwig Jacobowski (1868–1900).[87] Wolf wishes to erase all traces of his Jewish identity, "to think and feel in a German way." However, this proves impossible—not because of the thousand threads that bind him to tradition, but because the German environment constantly reminds him that he is "an offshoot of an alien branch" and therefore not able to be "a native-born German" in the Germany he loved so well. As a result of this revelation, he takes his own life. In his poem "Dank" (Thanks), Jakobowski, who committed suicide in December 1900 at the age of thirty-two, wrote:

> O Germany, what will you grant me,
> in return for my generous gifts?
> Ah, bestow upon me love—
> love alone have I desired.
>
> Three thousand days have I toiled,
> twenty long hours each day;
> If my pay has been in searing wounds—
> these were the wounds of victory!
>
> O Germany, O terrible land,
> what will you grant your servants?
>
> Only a handful of sand for the living
> and sand for the grave as well![88]

In the same spirit, but in an entirely different historical context, the poet Karl Wolfskehl, who had escaped from Nazi Germany, wrote in 1933:

> A German province gave me life,
> It was German bread that nurtured me,
> Grapes plucked from the German Rhine
> A thousand years fermented in my blood.[89]

Jacobowski was one of the many German-Jewish intellectuals and literary figures who earned the title "Germany's stepchildren."[90] Not only

The Modern European Jew   75

were some of them able to continue to believe in the possibility of Jewish-German duality, but they even wished to be rid of the burden of the Jewish part of this dual identity, maintaining that it was impossible to create compatibility between Judaism (Semitism) and Germanness (Aryanness). Other Jews professed an unrestricted spiritual attachment to Germany, both the nation and its culture, and cultivated a hatred of their Jewish identity.[91] "My ancestors and I," the politician Walter Rathenau proudly declared, "were raised on German soil and in the German spirit and we have given the German people all that was in our power to give." Consequently, from his perspective, Jews were as much a Germanic tribe as the Saxons and Bavarians were.[92] Franz Oppenheimer classified the Jews of Western Europe as a tribe (*Stamm*) and the Jews of Eastern Europe as a people (*Volk*). In his opinion, the German Jews were not a part of Jewish culture but rather belonged to German culture. If he were to examine his own sensibilities, he wrote, he would find "ninety-nine percent Kant and Goethe and only one percent Old Testament."[93] The Jews of Russia and Poland belonged to the Jewish culture, which was a lesser culture—that of the ghetto and the Middle Ages—while Germany's Jews were "patriots of our landscapes, our homeland, our people, and our culture. We are not [in Germany] as 'guests.'"[94] Oppenheimer's article sparked profound controversy. Among other responses was the claim that, contrary to the views of the *Völkerpsychologie* school, that culture was not an acquired quality but rather an inherited identity, and as a result, German Jews belonged to the Jewish culture and were more closely related to East European Jews than to Germans. National identity was an organic trait, not a form of association. Other Jews claimed that Jews were an inseparable part of German civilization, but this was a way of life and not a quality; therefore, Jews could be partners and part of the family in the various civilizations among which they lived.[95] The debate also included the opinion that German Jews were able to distinguish between civilian duty, patriotism, and national sentiment, and nations demanded only the first form of attachment; furthermore, the German Jews may have drunk from the fount of German culture, but they were still part of the overall culture of humanity.[96]

However, during a period of nationalistic awakening and rising patriotism, it was sometimes difficult to distinguish between the German tradition of humanism and the awareness of belonging to Germany's national culture and national destiny—in other words, to distinguish between *Kultur* and *Volkskultur*. Such a distinction was also difficult because of the new separation between religious and national cultural identity. This gave rise to an entirely novel dilemma: religious conversion was effected by a symbolic act and was received not only as betrayal, but also as a pathological manifestation of a futile attempt to deny one's self[97] because it was a conversion to a different human essence—an exchange of one soul for another that was entirely different. In contrast, cultural integration and assimilation were multidimensional processes and were thus considered less binding than religious conversion. In theory, therefore, integration into the culture of *Bildungsbürgertum* (educated bourgeoisie) as it was manifested in thought, literature, music, arts, and education did not present an insurmountable obstacle.[98] However, if national culture was a unified and all-encompassing system of perceptions, concepts, values, and lifestyles—in effect, a system more demanding than religion because it was manifested not in supernational values but rather in values stemming from the unique spirit of the nation (or, as Hegel called it, "ein besonderer Volksgeist"[99])—the question arose as to whether Jews could integrate into that system, live in it, and build on its foundations. If culture, rather than religion, formed the foundation and focus of identity and uniqueness—the creation of the specific spirit (*Geist*) of a people (*Volk*) or even of a race—then surely foreigners, such as Semitic Jews, would never be able to change and become part of this different culture. And if modern European culture was indeed permeated by the Christian and the pagan Greco-Roman heritages, then it was clear that the boundaries between Judaism and secular European culture were insurmountable. Jewishness was an unalterable fact, not because Jews could not become Christians or because their Christianity would always be counterfeit, but because no Oriental could become a German.

German Jewish literature abounded with biographies, both real and invented, which involved this dilemma and recounted tales of self-denial and uprooting on the one hand, and of tragic awakening from the delusion of complete integration and assimilation on the other hand.[100] It is important to note that patriotic sentiment and identity with German culture were shared not only by assimilated, or liberal, Jews, but also by Orthodox Jews and Zionists. Most Jews in Germany saw themselves as German citizens and patriots and believed that they were an inseparable part of German culture. At least part of the quest to integrate and merge with a vague concept like "the German spirit," with the goal of erasing their duality, arose from Jews' desire to find an alternative to the limited social integration that Nathan Birnbaum hyperbolically described:

"First and foremost, the mutual distance between the Jews and others is reflected in the paucity of reciprocal connections. The full separation between Jews and non-Jews stands out in social clubs, public houses, and cafés... Even more significant is the rarity with which social relationships between Jews and non-Jews develop from their business relationships."[101] Birnbaum painted an extreme picture, and it is necessary to distinguish between personal ties in the private sphere (such as a gentile's visit to a Jewish home) and professional and social ties in the public sphere (schools, workplaces, etc.) on the other. German society was not closed off to Jews; it was, in fact, very open to them.[102] In any case, acculturation is not necessarily linked to social integration, and a minority may adopt values from its immediate environment without becoming assimilated to or integrated into it.

Six years after the illusion of Jewish-German symbiosis was shattered in 1933, Martin Buber wrote that there was indeed an organic bond between Jews and Germany. This was a true symbiosis that was expressed not only in Jews' participation in German culture, but also in "a special cooperation between the German spirit and the Jewish spirit." However, despite the tragic end to this symbiosis, Buber wrote that German Jews brought with them to Palestine, "in their Jewish bones[,] something of the noble spiritual foundation which their persecutors deny and strangle in their own people."[103] Though he saw the symbiosis as a "phantom in a void" and addiction to self-delusion, Gershom Scholem also refrained from criticizing the ensemble of values and cultural assets that Jews received from Germany.[104] Buber and Scholem evaluated the processes of assimilation and acculturation among German Jews on an idealistic scale, or according to the high bar of expectations set by some German Jews. However, it is impossible to evaluate the success of acculturation processes by such measures.

The reality in Eastern Europe was entirely different from the reality in Germany. Even ardent Jewish believers in Russification, for example, understood that they could not identify with organic Russian nationalism and that, from their perspective, being Russian in heart and soul merely meant using the Russian language as the language of culture. In effect, it was possible to integrate only into the middle class and liberal intelligentsia—or, in other words, into the Russian version of Western culture. A Jewish *maskil* in Odessa wrote in 1841 that "throughout Russia, Odessa is the only place where Jews try to be perfect Europeans."[105] Russification in the sense of social and cultural integration into the Russian middle class and intelligentsia was at first the concern of a small percentage of the Jews in czarist Russia and depended on place of residence—within the Pale of Settlement or in Russia proper.[106] The groups that underwent the process of Russification did so by entering defined social groups such as student organizations or, later, revolutionary movements. In January 1882, the writer Lev Levanda wrote in the journal *Russkii Evrei* that Russian antisemitism was propelling the Jewish intelligentsia "into the kingdom of darkness." However, if events changed, he would join the chorus that would be singing: "I am a Russian and love my land."[107] Osip Rabinowich, on the other hand, wrote in *Razvet* in 1861 that Jews in other European countries had learned the local tongue; only in Russia did they "persist in speaking our corrupted jargon [i.e., Yiddish]." Yet it was necessary for them to learn Russian as a gateway to the Enlightenment: "The Russian language must serve as the primary force animating the masses . . . Our homeland is Russia—just as its air is ours, so its language must become ours."[108] The weakness of Russian civil society made it difficult for the intelligentsia and the upper middle class to integrate into it, and in most cases, the integration was partial at best. Russification was expressed primarily in Russian language instruction, and afterward in active participation in various areas of secular Russian culture and the Western values that it absorbed and internalized.[109] In 1911, Alter Druyanov described Vilna as a "Yiddish-speaking" city—but only in streets where Jews lived. Outside those areas, one heard only "Russian, Russian, Russian." In the public library, he found that half of the books were in Russian, and that the Hebrew newspaper had at most 400 readers. His conclusion was that half of the Jewish intelligentsia in the city "do not know how to read a Hebrew book or paper, and there are quite a few sons in the homes of the intelligentsia who do not even know how to pray from a *sidur*." The Jewish intellectuals in Vilna, Druyanov wrote, made sure that lower-class children studied the Bible and Talmud, but sent their own sons to study medicine and law.[110]

In Russia, as in Germany, the extent and substance of Jews' participation in the national culture were topics for debate. Did a list of distinguished Jews who wrote in Russian suffice to demonstrate Jews' contribution to Russian culture—and, indeed, to the world and humanity? (It was on the basis of this contribution that the Russification of Russia's Jewish intelligentsia was derogatorily called "cosmopolitical.")[111] Zeev Jabotinsky proposed a criterion for evaluating the nature of this contribution: it was not the language in which literature was written that mattered, but the identity of the audience at which the writing was directed, and the issues that it raised.[112] The clear expression of the modernity of Jewish society in the czarist empire was its politicization, which was manifested in the political struggle for civic and national emancipation and the cooperation among many of the empire's internal constituents in the struggle to change the face of Russian society and the czarist regime.[113]

In Poland, the situation was different. Heine's image of the authentic Polish Jew, whose character was not heterogeneous, was no longer accurate after the middle of the nineteenth century. As the journalist Eliezer Eliyahu Friedman wrote in 1926:

> A notable phenomenon in the life of Polish Jews is the adaptation to Polish rule and culture . . . Were it not for the unconcealed antisemitism in Polish society, which does not permit Jews to approach it and thus relegates Jews to a separate existence, this process of "Polonization" would be very rapid . . . Even so the Jews are the Polonizers of the frontier, and not in Galicia alone. I'll give an example. The Third of May is a Polish national holiday. Radical Polish circles do not celebrate it, nevertheless one can find Jewish students in many villages participating in the parades, as well as the village firemen, who are mostly Jewish and participate in these parades and sing the national songs in a non-Polish environment.[114]

This description is quite exaggerated.[115] In Poland, the processes of modernization and westernization did not lead to assimilation outside of a narrow stratum, which displayed a deep attachment to the Polish homeland and the Polish state—that is, an identification with the land, its people, its culture, and its landscape—an identification that caused great distress among Jews when Poland, during the 1920s and 1930s, became a "step-motherland." In David Cohen's journal of his travels in mid-1930s Poland, he describes his renewed encounter with the "landscape of my homeland," which was accompanied by "the profound pain of a child who returns home only to be greeted by his step-mother." Cohen relates his visit to Wołyń, where a Jewish resident tells him:

> We were bound by birth to this land. What have the *goyim* [gentiles] not done to us? They have destroyed, robbed, massacred, and abused us. But we resembled a tree with many branches: they came with saws and axes and felled the trunk, but the roots remained, and we grew again, and bloomed again, and it was hard to uproot us. But now these Poles are uprooting the tree.[116]

Thus Poland was not just a place to do business, but also a place to live. It was a natural place for Jews to live as an inseparable part of the landscape, and a place where they became indispensable over the course of centuries, even if a great many of them were not partners in Polish culture and did not feel they belonged to it.

However, wrote Jabotinsky, assimilated Jews were the true outsiders in Poland; in contrast, traditional Jews, despite their demonstrated segregation from their environment, were an intimate part of "that intimate group called Poland," where "the tradition of neighborliness [lay] deep in the blood and bones" of its people.[117]

THE UNIVERSAL EUROPEAN BACKGROUND OF JEWISH MODERNITY

The emphasis on affinity and belonging to a particular European culture blurred the all-European nature of Jews' acculturation and modernization in Europe. These latter concepts became the subject of various analyses in the general academic literature, including, of course, in the context of Jewish studies.[118] By acculturation, we mean the adoption and absorption of cultural—and, in this case, modern—values and norms from the surrounding environment. Since Jews' acculturation was targeted at the modern strata of society and culture, there was a nearly complete identity between it and modernism. It is possible to distinguish between modernism—as a manifestation of the adoption of elements from the realm of the reality culture, which are neutral in a value-normative sense—and acculturation—as a manifestation of the adoption of elements from the realm of value culture. Indeed, modernism can in many cases be a neutral phenomenon that does not require changes in the normative system.[119]

Theoretically, European Jews could adopt various elements from the repertoire of modernism without influencing their own self-definition or the normative system according to which they lived. However, the process of acculturation for a subsociety or minority culture living within a modern majority society was also necessarily accompanied by the adoption of cultural values and the loss of some traditional values and norms.[120] Modern Jews could not avoid adopting at least a part of the majority's habitus—whether in order to better to resemble it and facilitate their integration and assimilation, or in order to rebuild the normative system of Jewish society itself.

There is not necessarily any essential antinomy between Jewish tradition and modernism. However, changes in patterns of social organization, the nature of occupations and livelihoods, dress, possibilities for social mobility, and the like are generally accompanied by changes in the system of values and norms. Fluency in a local language, for example, can simply serve utilitarian or pragmatic purposes, but it also grants access to the culture of the surrounding environment and throws open the doors to external influence. As a result, in many cases it is very difficult, at least in the context of European Jews, to distinguish between modernization and acculturation, and in effect these are two similar phenomena whose difference is solely a question of extent. Since modernism was a European creation and was identified with Europe, accepting and absorbing the values of modernism meant also accepting at least some of the values of European culture. Moreover, the fact that European society had undergone a process of secularization, which resulted in the conduct of life becoming less and less dependent on religious norms,[121] tightly bound the processes of acculturation and modernization among European Jews to the secularization of Jewish society. All the attempts to mark the desired boundaries of intercultural contact, and to define what was permitted and denied in all that related to the adoption of external values, could not absolutely and permanently determine the actual boundaries.

The way in which Jews dealt with this issue was to distinguish not only between the positive and negative aspects of European culture, and between culture and civilization, but also between *Kultur* in the nationalistic sense and *Kultur* in its overall European, humanistic, and even universal meaning—where these universal traits were manifested in the moral and humanistic understanding and in the values of *Bildung*, *Sittlichkeit* (morality), self-actualization, rationalism, freedom of thought, and humanism,[122] as well as rules of behavior and etiquette. These were all the values of liberal, bourgeois, civil society.[123] Rabbi Isaac Breuer, one of the leaders of German neo-Orthodoxy, insisted that this was a matter of new values that were not part of the old normative Jewish system. Breuer wrote that modern European culture had confronted traditional Judaism with a bitter foe: namely, individualism. Individuality in Jewish life—that is, individual self-awareness—was a European phenomenon that created a new Jewish prototype—the "solitary Jew," in the words of Eliezer Schweid,[124] who was not part of any organized community. Breuer wrote:

> We are accustomed to evaluate all the phenomena of life according to our traditional individualistic instinct. However, the moral in-

stinct of most German Jews is not at all different from the modern moral instinct of Western Europe in general. It will be no surprise, therefore, if the support of most German Jews will in fact be given to the German judge who overrules the Jewish Law, rather than to Jewish Law itself.[125]

Breuer pointed to the fact that acculturation did not mean only the adoption of external characteristics such as language, dress, or customs, but also the abandonment of traditional values in exchange for new ones. Modern Jews therefore transformed themselves into European Jews not only because they spoke European languages, appeared in European dress, and adopted the norms that delineated European private life (the age at marriage, family size and relationships, leisure pursuits, and the like). Nor were they European Jews simply because they read European newspapers or literature, were educated in kindergartens and modern schools[126] (both European institutions), studied at the university, or attended exhibitions and concerts. The reason they were European Jews was because they had undergone the process of acquiring a new culture. This was far more than simply a matter of etiquette and custom; it was a matter of various models of a broad habitus that encompassed all the domains of everyday life.[127] In Eastern Europe, the sizable Jewish population acted as a roadblock to processes of acculturation accompanied by absorption, but at the same time, it encouraged political involvement based on modern ideologies and modes of action. East European Jews' politicization from the latter half of the nineteenth century onward, and their involvement in local politics, were an integral part of the modernization of Jewish existence there.

Modern Jews, therefore, were European Jews because they thought about and interpreted the world, Judaism, and themselves in European terms, and imbued traditional values with European content.[128] In April 1915, Shmuel Hugo Bergman, who became a well-known philosopher, wrote his teacher Martin Buber from the front:

> Now that we have fought in the name of German culture, we sense more than ever how significant it is for us and how entirely it envelops us. I cannot imagine that our generation's ties to Biblical Judaism, Hasidic Judaism, etc., which were formed after all in an artificial manner, will ever be as natural as its ties to Fichte or to those European cultural figures who have shown us the way to the human experience. Only because we had Fichte and found ideas parallel to his in Jewish culture did we study our religion. There we were

educated; here we discovered revelations. But if so, only as Germans will we be able to enter Jewish cultural life.[129]

According to Bergman, the modern Jewish existence was Germanness in Jewish clothing, or Jewishness in German clothing; but it seems more accurate to call it Jewishness in European clothing, or Europeanness in Jewish clothing. This is also true with respect to Jews who adopted the views, concepts, and behavioral codes of the European counterculture—the revolutionary intelligentsia and the labor class's culture of sociopolitical radicalism. The Jews' involvement in the revolutionary movement clearly expressed the belief that Jews needed to take an active part in fundamentally changing the European world, and it expressed confidence that change for the good was possible. Not only the Enlightenment but European Romanticism and nationalism shaped the spiritual and intellectual world of the modern Jew.[130] Thus Europe was a store of values, ideas, and institutions from which one could borrow, among other things, Romantic nationalism and revolutionary radicalism; the model of a centralized state; and concepts of civil society, collectivism, individualism, and secularism.[131]

In recent years, there has been a trend in the research literature toward emphasizing the tension between maintaining Jewish uniqueness and integrating into the surrounding society, and emphasizing the impact of the Jews' confrontation with their environment. The emphasis is not solely on processes of adaptation, adjustment, integration, or even assimilation, but on the processes of reconstructing Jewish society and its identity in response to and as part of this encounter.[132]

The construction of a new ethnocultural identity is perceived as a way in which a group forms a new foundation for reciprocal relations between itself and other groups, rather than as a form of assimilation and loss of its unique identity.[133] A clear expression of this is the transformation of the concepts "tradition" and "culture" into the chief delineators of Jewish culture and its contents. The research on this subject has for the most part accepted Nietzsche's claim in *The Dawn of Day* that the Jews were characterized by values and a way of life that distinguished them from their surroundings: family values, flexibility, spiritual intelligence, and more.[134] This was the source of the observation that inherent Jewish traits and ingrained cultural traditions were what prevented a large number of Jews from integrating fully into European cultures, and that as a result, the main consequence of the acculturation process was the reconstruction of the unique Jewish identity, its contents, and its institutions. According to this view, the acculturation and modernization of a minority do not equate to its full integration into the host society. Nor is acculturation an act of imitation, but rather a process of selectively accepting and adopting borrowed cultural values; this process also involves internal changes in the acculturating society and its value system. If so, in the Jewish case—as in others—the processes of modernization did not lead to the loss of the Jews' unique identity; on the contrary, they forged new paths toward national and cultural renewal and revival.

However, the great emphasis placed on describing the preservation of traditional Jewish foundations in the modern Jewish culture, and on the vital necessity of these foundations, demonstrates the awareness of an essential difference between traditional and modern society. The correct means by which to evaluate the results of the acculturation, modernization, and cultural change that Jews underwent is to examine the scope of the new repertoire of insights, worldviews, and social and cultural norms that modern Jews accepted and internalized, which had not been part of their culture or way of life in previous generations. Such an examination cannot focus only on specific figures (generally intellectuals, writers, and the like[135]); it must include the entire Jewish population in all its layers. Such an examination would reveal that even when it was careful to preserve some of the components of the traditional Jewish identity, and even when it created new Jewish values, a large part of the modern Jewish world that was forged in the nineteenth century was in fact a European world in Jewish dress, or a Jewish world in European dress. While this world had a different character in the framework of Europe's various national cultures, an important part of it reflected a universal European background. Highlighting the contrasts created through the influence of national cultures and their presentation as oppositions blurs this shared European background. In one way or another, Jews in Europe were not only German Jews or Polish Jews, but European Jews as well. The system of values that they adopted was taken from the general store of European culture, and over time it became self-evident, to the extent that its particularistic origin became largely inconsequential.

ANTISEMITISM AS AN INCURABLE EUROPEAN DISEASE

> *Many have been asking with horror, "Have the Middle Ages returned?" In my opinion, yes!*
> MOSHE LEIB LILIENBLUM,
> "The General Jewish Question"[1]

Europe's fate and the swing of the pendulum between enlightenment, tolerance, and progress on the one hand, and decline, degeneration, and cruelty on the other hand, deeply preoccupied the Jewish intelligentsia. However, they were at least as preoccupied with the question of what the future held for Jews in Europe. This future would be shaped primarily by modern antisemitism; indeed, it became clear in the mid-nineteenth century that not only had enlightenment and progress not cured Europe of this affliction, but modern antisemitism was more dangerous than its previous incarnations, combining as it did Christian theological and popular hatred of Jews with neopagan and pseudoscientific hatred. From the Jews' vantage point, then, Europeanness represented not only the positive side of Western culture, but also—and sometimes primarily—anti-Jewishness and antisemitism. From such a vantage point, Europe and the Jews appeared as two distinct entities separated by an unbridgeable and eternal chasm.

It is not our intention to elaborate here on the rich and diverse research literature dealing with the origins of modern antisemitism. Instead, we wish to focus on two questions that have troubled Jews since at least the mid-nineteenth century and trouble them to this very day: Was antisemitism indeed a European illness, incurable and apt to erupt in waves, in various places and guises, but always with similar roots and substance?[2] And how was it possible to explain the fact that members of the enlightened European culture believed blood libel accusations, adhered to ancient prejudices, and were unable to escape them?

ANTISEMITISM: A MEDIEVAL FICTION?

Throughout 1840, as news of the Damascus Affair—a blood libel against the Jews of that city—spread around the world, many Jews believed it was now clear that those nations that stood at the forefront of enlightened civilization would not come out in defense of justice, morality, or even rationality. For example, Heine wrote on July 30, 1840: "We stand in wonder and ask ourselves: Is this France, the birthplace of enlightenment, the land in which Voltaire laughed and Rousseau wept? Are these Frenchmen, who had once bowed before the goddess of reason at Notre Dame?"[3] But the Damascus Affair involved the Orient—not Western Jews—and therefore, even if the arrival on the scene of the Jewish Question as an international problem inspired ideas which flourished only toward the end of the nineteenth century, Western Jews certainly could not forecast their future by its light.[4]

In response to the Damascus Affair, Moses Hess wrote:

> The way and manner in which the persecution of the Jews is looked upon in Europe, and even in enlightened Germany, must necessarily cause a new point of departure in Jewish life. This tendency demonstrates quite clearly that in spite of the degree of education to which the Occidental Jews have attained, there still exists a barrier between them and the surrounding nations, almost as formidable as in the days of religious fanaticism. Those of our brothers who, for purposes of obtaining emancipation, endeavor to persuade themselves, as well as others, that modern Jews possess no trace of a national feeling—have really lost their heads. These men do not understand how it is possible that such a stupid, medieval legend, which was only too well known to our forefathers under the name of *Mamserbilbul*, should be given credence, even for a moment, in nineteenth century Europe.[5]

Hess saw Germany as the source of modern antisemitism, since "the sympathetic Frenchman assimilates with irresistible attraction every foreign element . . . The German, on the other hand, is not at all anxious to assimilate any foreign element . . . He lacks the primary condition of every chemical assimilative process, namely, warmth." To the question of how it was possible that in nineteenth-century Germany people could be tempted to believe in "medieval legends," Hess responded that Germany was still Teutonic in spirit, reactionary and nationalistic, and that its liberalism was nothing more than a ripple on the water's surface.[6]

Antisemitism as a European Disease

The historian I. M. Jost wrote in July 1840:

> Where now is the demi-god needed to fight the Hydra of our times which shoots out its many-hundred heads each with its innumerable hissing tongues? The very spirit of Evil was required to create such a monster; and our century is fighting it . . . all in vain. A poison has entered the very organs of peace and love and who knows for how long it will continue to do its work. What good are the protestations of innocence, the reliance on justice and the confidence in prevailing morality, when innocence is held suspect, when justice is subject to error, and when the masses, so susceptible and barely weaned from prejudice, are deceived by these phantasmagoria which . . . restore the thorns of hatred?[7]

Indeed, it was primarily the antisemitism in nineteenth-century Germany—a nation viewed by many Jews as the pinnacle of European culture—that was received with shock. But Germany was not an isolated case. In the wake of a series of events—including the blood libel in Damascus in 1840; the pogroms during the Revolutions of 1848; the appearance of organized antisemitism in Germany during the 1870s; the pogroms of the 1870s and 1880s; and the Dreyfus Affair in France during the 1890s—doubts arose as to whether the age of rational enlightenment and tolerant liberalism would indeed bring an end to the hatred of Jews. Even those who predicted the explosion of antisemitism were astonished at its intensity. Thus, when Smolenskin was notified of the pogroms in Odessa in 1871, he wrote the following emotional words in the monthly *Hashachar* (The dawn):

> Do not believe those who say that this is an age of wisdom and an age of love for mankind; do not turn to the words of those who praise this time as a time for human justice and honesty; it is a lie! Just as murderers in the times of the Crusades and the reign of Isabel in blood-drenched Spain thirsted for innocent blood, so it is during this age.[8]

The Jewish writer Lev Levanda, an explicit supporter of Russification, predicted the pogroms that erupted in April 1882. They would happen, he wrote, because Russians saw the Jews as a power that must be taken into account and that therefore must be weakened.[9] On April 19, 1895, in the second article of his series about the French intellectual Ernest Renan in the St. Petersburg newspaper *Hamelitz*, the historian Josef Klausner wrote that he was deeply saddened by the fact that the *fin de siècle*—so proud of its intellectual progress, triumphs over nature, inventions, and lofty ideals—was still home to evil and sinful men. This was a cause for profound despair, because none of the inventions and improvements of the time had proved able to help humanity or overcome its impulse for evil. A day earlier, on April 18, the Paris correspondent for *Hamelitz* had reported on Eduard Drumont's great popularity and wrote that it was hardly surprising, as the Catholic hatred for Jews had existed since Europe's earliest days. More than a few essays toward the end of the nineteenth century cautioned against the threat of German antisemitism and maintained that its goal was to destroy the Jews. We will mention two of these essays here, both pamphlets: *Die Judenfrage und die Zukunft* (The Jewish question and the future), written in 1891 by Gustav Cohen, a Zionist merchant from Hamburg (who later moved to Manchester) and the father-in-law of Otto Warburg; and *Vor dem Sturm: Ernste Mahnworte an die deutschen Juden* (Before the storm: Grave warnings to German Jews), written in 1896 by Dr. Bernhard Cohen, a physician from Berlin. In 1891, the Reform rabbi Dr. Kaufmann Kohler, who had emigrated from Germany to the United States, decided to his despair that the growth of antisemitism in Europe and its appearance in the United States demonstrated that modern antisemitism must be a universal European phenomenon. Its new ideas and motifs flowed easily from country to country, and from culture to culture. The Jews' optimism in the New World was premature, Kohler felt:

> How rudely have we all been roused from our dream! How shocking were all the illusions of the beginning of the nineteenth century destroyed by the facts that developed at its close! What a mockery this so-called Christian civilization has turned out to be! What a shame and a fraud this era of tolerance and enlightenment has become![10]

From a historical perspective, these warnings obviously were correct. However, they were outnumbered by other voices that urged calm and depicted the demonstrations of modern antisemitism as a disturbing phenomenon, yet maintained that there was no need to exaggerate their power and influence or raise unnecessary fear. The Jews who downplayed the warnings believed that antisemitism could not delay the process of integration and acclimatization, or the development of new models of autonomous Jewish organization and activity. In this spirit, for example, Herzl wrote in June 1895 to Bismarck, the German chancellor, that the Jewish Question was merely a remnant of the Middle Ages. And to Hess's question about how it was possible that nineteenth-century Europeans could be tempted to believe medieval accusations of blood libel, Herzl replied that the antisemitism of modern cultures was their attempt to exorcise a "ghost from out of their own past."[11]

The belief that modern antisemitism in Europe was a regrettable but marginal phenomenon that would not delay the victory march of tolerance, integration, and acclimatization triumphed over the view that antisemitism was a permanent phenomenon and an inseparable part of Western culture. The question of whether the latter opinion arose from self-delusion or temporary blindness was much discussed in the years after the Holocaust, but by 1935, the Jewish German intellectual Ismar Elbogen had already proposed the following answer in his book *Geschichte der Juden in Deutschland* (The history of Jews in Germany): "The German Jews of the nineteenth century had done the best that they could to assimilate and therefore felt secure. What they failed to realize was that the liberal era had come to an end."[12] And in fact, the general impression is that the German Jews during the 1870s and 1880s exhibited a "slow response to the revival of antisemitism," partly because it raised the question of whether they "could . . . ever really become German"—a question to which few wished to respond in the negative.[13]

This spirit of optimism was not unique to Germany. Despite his disappointment with the nineteenth century, Simon Dubnow, for example, believed that political reactionism was not an inseparable part of nationalism,[14] and that the nations of Europe would understand that protecting the rights of national minorities—including, of course, the Jews—would only be to their advantage. Although the pogroms of 1905 shook his beliefs and roused in him "feelings of fear and apprehension for the future" that Russian Jews faced at the hands of "Amalek's government,"[15] causing him to support organized Jewish emigration to the United States, Dubnow did not lose hope that Jews in the Russian Empire would attain national autonomy.[16] Jabotinsky went so far as to believe that the Russian intelligentsia was not antisemitic.[17] The Jewish intelligentsia was therefore unable to agree on whether modern antisemitism was a remnant of Europe's dark past, or an inherent manifestation of Western culture.

The consequence of this second opinion was that any Jewish attempt to integrate and acclimatize was in vain. As noted, Herzl wrote to Bismarck that antisemitism was merely a ghost, but in fact he had concluded that it was a fatal and universal European illness: "The whole world [all of Europe] sips from the well of antisemitism and absorbs it slowly, almost imperceptibly. It penetrates every pore. It is accepted with the most passionate enthusiasm by those who deal more than most with books and speech: priests and teachers."[18] The results of this conclusion prompted Herzl to predict a horrible future, which was—in the words of *Altneuland*'s Friedrich—"a denunciation of Old Europe":[19]

> Finally we must end up at the bottom, rock bottom. What appearance this will have, what form this will take, I cannot surmise. Will it be a revolutionary expropriation from below or a reactionary confiscation from above? Will they chase us away? Will they kill us?
>
> I have a fair idea that it will take all these forms, and others. In one of the countries, probably France, there will come a social revolution whose first victims will needs be the big bankers and the Jews...
>
> Anyone who has, like myself, lived in this country [France] for a few years as a disinterested and detached observer can no longer have any doubts about this.
>
> In Russia there will simply be a confiscation from above. In Germany they will make emergency laws as soon as the Kaiser can no longer manage the Reichstag. In Austria people will let themselves be intimidated by the Viennese rabble and deliver up the Jews...
>
> So they will chase us out of these countries, and in the countries where we take refuge they will kill us.[20]

The socialist Zionist thinker Dov Ber Borochov reached a similar conclusion—namely, that "hatred toward Jews is not an economic phenomenon but a psychological and sociological one, born of emotions, and even a social revolution cannot change that."[21]

Nietzsche was therefore mistaken when he wrote in *Human, All Too Human* that the Jewish problem existed only in countries where the indecent custom of blaming the Jews for any trouble had taken root. In fact, the spirit of antisemitism existed everywhere; both Left and Right participated.[22] Nietzsche also wrote that "I have not met a German yet who was well disposed toward the Jews," and that anti-Jewish sentiment was a firmly implanted instinct among the Germans.[23] Chaim Weizmann expanded this claim, writing in October 1913: "[What European can] say that he is free of antisemitism? A man must be Jewish to be free of it!" The blood libels, Weizmann added, "are not a Russian monopoly; not many years ago we had blood libels in Germany and Austria, and who knows that they might not return?"[24] If all the modern phenomena—

nationalism and revolution, reactionism and progress, conservatism and modernity—indeed gave birth to antisemitism, this could not be a coincidental combination of circumstances and causes, but a phenomenon nourished at the very core of the European soul. Only this could explain the fact that although Europe had entered a new, enlightened age, hatred toward Jews still welled up in it, and not only in Eastern Europe, but in the West as well—the stronghold of progress. Only this could explain why antisemitism did not belong only to the lower classes or the reactionary circles, but to the liberal and enlightened circles as well. And only this could explain why antisemitism was targeted not only at traditional Jews but also, and perhaps primarily, at westernized Jews.

Thus the outbreak of popular and official antisemitism during the 1870s and 1880s in Western and Eastern Europe, along with the appearance of racial antisemitism, undermined the foundations of Jews' hope for the nineteenth century and shook the optimistic worldview held by most of the Jewish elite. These events led to the diagnosis of antisemitism as a collective, inherited, and contagious European spiritual illness: the Jews were Europe's nightmare, and antisemitism its antidote. Hatred of Jews took on different forms, but it was eternal; and the German people were the most affected by that illness. The modern hatred of Jews was born in Germany, renowned for its intellectual developments (and in particular for pan-Germanism); the Russians and Poles learned from Germany and imitated it.[25] The Orthodox rabbi and mystic Elchanan Hyle Wechsler was apparently the first to respond along these lines to the pamphlet published by Wilhelm Marr and to articles written by the historian Heinrich von Treitschke in 1879. In 1881, Wechsler published the pamphlet *Ein Wort der Mahnung an Israel* (A warning to the people of Israel) and asserted that here was a new type of hatred against Jews. Antisemitism was a "thousand-tongued Hydra," a cross-European phenomenon that first attached itself to Germany. The emergence of racial antisemitism— the "spirit of Amalek"—was, Wechsler wrote, "a phenomenon even more terrible and threatening" than the antisemitism of the past. Marr and Treitschke had described the Jews as a foreign, Semitic element, and in doing so had ridiculed the Jews' prediction of successful integration and decreed an end to all their foolish delusions.[26] A year later, on June 5, 1882, and in a different place and context, the staff of the central office of Bilu, in Odessa, wrote: "we are, as history shows, strangers everywhere."[27] This antisemitism was not simply the animalistic outburst of a dark, cruel rabble left behind by the march of progress—as the Southern Storms pogroms were depicted in 1881–82—but a collective pathology, an incurable Judeophobia that was an inseparable part of the collective European personality.

This was the prognosis proffered in 1882 by Dr. Leon Pinsker in his pamphlet *Autoemancipation: A Call to His Brethren from a Russian Jew*.[28] Europe's Jews, he declared, were in an unsalvageable situation: the utopia of a Europe without nations was as probable as the coming of the Messiah, but it was impossible for Jews to assimilate into Europe's various nations. Pinsker's radical prognosis was not widely accepted; the majority of the Jewish elite objected to it decisively. Objectors maintained that it gave Europe a bad name, encouraged antisemitism, and spread romantic delusions about a dubious new homeland waiting somewhere beyond the horizon:

> Free yourself then, my dear friend [Pinsker], of your harsh thoughts, and do not despair of our historic genius. In the great inventions of our time there lies promise not only for the military powers, but also for the enslaved and impoverished. The telegraph, the steamboat, and the railroad spread word of all the world's happenings at a wonderful speed . . . Get thee to Italy, your heart is ill; but your head, I hope, will become recharged and refreshed in Italy's fields. In Rome every ruin will speak of the might of the ancient world, but in spite of Vespasian and Titus, we are still alive to this day . . . The Roman she-wolf is dead and the Jewish lion-cub is alive and well. Go in peace, and on your return to Russia you will find that the wrath has passed, whether in large part or in small.[29]

The front-page article in the Russian Jewish weekly *Voskhod* on October 8, 1882, declared that Pinsker had ignored the great struggles in which Europe was embroiled. Despite the manifestations of reactionism that were once again evolving in the nineteenth century, progress would not retreat: antisemitism was not particularly successful, even in Germany. Russians, asserted the weekly, were by nature kindhearted.[30] Isaak Rülf, the rabbi of Memel, Lithuania, wrote to Pinsker reassuringly: "The Berliners are not so bad as you think. They merely want another good shock and upheaval to shake off the dust of assimilation and so forth that sticks to them. We will leave this task of purification to antisemitism. Believe me, the latter has an important role yet to play in the story of our national revival."[31]

This optimism sprang from the assumption that antisemitism was not a natural phenomenon but a historical one, which would disappear from the world along with the factors responsible for it. Thinkers and columnists from the socialist camp saw antisemitism not as an inherent and universal European disease—an explanation that would have put an end to their belief in the possibility of improving European society—but as a result of nationalism and the internal contradictions of bourgeois society. In this spirit, Nachman Syrkin, for example, claimed that the source of antisemitism was the middle class, and that it was a revolutionary movement encompassing every class of society.[32] Others proposed distinguishing between different types of antisemitism according to nationality. In 1923, Zeev Jabotinsky wrote that Europe's Jews were trapped between Scylla and Charybdis,[33] and that they were the first victims of every revolution—and, on the flip side, of every reaction;[34] but he added that even though the Poles hated the Jews, the tradition of good neighborliness would at length emerge victorious, because it lay deep in their blood and was stronger than hatred and madness, which resembled a layer of dirt obscuring the true nature of that nation. "Poland will yet be a nation of peace," he wrote,[35] and Polish antisemitism was nothing more than "rhetorical antisemitism"; that is, it was the objective result of demographic pressures and economic competition. It was true that in Poland there were hooligan elements, Jabotinsky wrote after harsh manifestations of public antisemitism,[36] but Polish society had almost no substantial hatred toward Jews. In contrast, German antisemitism was "a people's antisemitism"—that is, a psycho-cultural phenomenon "imbibed with the [German] mother's milk."[37]

Jabotinsky's words are a far cry from those of Uri Zvi Greenberg, who saw in Poland "the end of all exile"—the place in which Christian Europe was destined to settle its final bloody score with the Jewish people. A macabre irony of history, Greenberg wrote, was that the disaster would take place in wicked Poland, where Jews felt a deep-rooted sense of belonging: "We have been paying room and board to Europe until now. And now this Europe does not want to tolerate us in her lands and even rejects our Einsteins . . . Every nation is joining wicked Poland and raising its voice against its Jews: To Palestine!"[38]

The need to compare different types of antisemitism in Europe grew stronger after the start of the 1830s. Thus, for example, some claimed that the assimilation of German Jews was the main reason for Germany's antisemitic reaction, but then how could one explain the existence of antisemitism in Poland, where assimilation was a far less pervasive phenomenon? Nahum Sokolow, who had by then replaced Chaim Weizmann as president of the Zionist Organization, returned in 1934 from a journey to Poland (his homeland), and wrote that Poland was now headed by a "great European Pole"—Marshal Józef Piłsudski—whose government rejected *Volkist* nationalism based on racial principles. Poland's government, wrote Sokolow, lacked the foundation that supported German antisemitism; the latter form of antisemitism "expresses itself entirely in the cult of origin and race, in dreams and hallucinations of Polish national unification."[39] But Sokolow also warned that the growing power of the popular nationalist parties was apt to bring about the rise of an antisemitic government in Poland: "a Hitler regime is near,"[40] and "Polish Hitlerism" would draw after it "a tidal wave and volcanic flow of antisemitism." Sokolow believed, in other words, that while in Germany antisemitism grew "from top down"—from the government to the people—in Poland it rose "from the bottom up"—from people to government—because "the people are infected with the disease of antisemitism to a greater extent than the government."[41] Thus, in the absence of a government that might check this growth, Poland would follow in Germany's footsteps.

In the Yiddish poem "In Malchus fun Tzelm" (In the kingdom of the cross), Uri Zvi Greenberg asked: "How is it possible that those Europeans who worship Bethlehem [i.e., Christians] and sanctify the books of the Bible are also the same savages who dream of the destruction of the last Jew among them?"[42] Words of warning were sounded, sometimes in harsh language that presented disaster as inevitable and built into Europe's history, and that was intended to rouse public opinion. However, until the mid-1930s, the dangers of modern antisemitism in Europe were noticed primarily to the extent that they displaced Jews from their livelihoods and made it difficult for them to support themselves, or to the extent that it injured their pride. It was still unimaginable to think that Europe would plan and execute the physical destruction of the Jews.

THE ASHKENAZI APE

Toward the end of the nineteenth century, Jews began to protect the Jewish collective and to explain Jewish foreignness not in religious terms, but in racial and morphological terms—in terms of differences in "race."[43] Race was the source of the "collective essence," and racial differences were the reason for what Nahum Sokolow called, in 1882, "eternal hatred for an eternal people."[44] The new explanation proffered for antisemitism's vigor in the last quarter of the nineteenth century was that it was the unavoidable result of the eternal chasm separating Jews from Europeans, as a result of their racial disparity. In his 1890 novella "Shem and Japheth on the Train," Mendele Mokher Seforim ridiculed the Germans: they were reverting to the dawn of human history—that is, to the biblical conception of the world (Genesis 8)—and describing themselves as children of Japheth (Aryans), while calling the Jews children of Shem (Semites):

> The Germans, who perform miracles of science, have turned the clock back a thousand generations, so that all of us at this day are living in the time of the Flood. Nowadays they call the Jew "Shem," and the Gentile "Japheth." With the return of Shem and Japheth the customs of that far-off age have returned too, and the earth is filled with violence. The non-Semites are hostile towards the Semites.[45]

In Mendele's story, the train is where a Jew and his Polish friend meet and share the same fate. In the intellectual Vladimir Harcabi's story about his journey by rail from Vilna to Moscow in the summer of 1864—"From the Days of the Flood"—a train plays an entirely different role. There are no divisions between him and the Polish student seated opposite him; these are not Żyd and Pan (Jew and Gentile), but two students belonging to the same world—the student community. Harcabi quotes from Paul's Epistle to the Galatians (3:28): "there is neither Jew nor Greek."[46] The first story is a pessimistic one: not only did the dividers not fall, but modern antisemitism raised the barrier of race, a barrier that could not be overcome even through religious conversion. The second is an optimistic tale: the divisions between the Jewish and non-Jewish intelligentsias fall, and the two have common values.

Mendele Mokher Seforim was probably unable to imagine that Jewish writers would adopt the views in "From the Days of the Flood" and accept the opinion that antisemitism was an inevitable result of the fact that the Aryan nations of Europe possessed a fundamentally different national spirit and soul (*Gemüt*) from those of the Semitic Jews—in other words, that this was a question of different ontological entities, and that it was the profound difference between them that prevented the Jews from becoming part of European culture. Mendele discovered the boundless opposition between Aryan and Semite in a railway carriage, while Lilienblum—as noted earlier—discovered it in a revelation in 1882: "We are strangers not only here, but in the whole of Europe, for it is not the homeland of our people . . . Yes, we are Semites . . . among Aryans; the children of Shem among the children of Japheth, a Palestinian tribe from Asia in the countries of Europe."⁴⁷

Lilienblum wrote to the poet Y. L. Gordon that his investigation had "led me to a well-known path, of which I, so preoccupied by everyday matters, had till then taken little note. This is the natural difference between the children of Israel (and perhaps all the children of Shem) and the children of Japheth, at that time the Aryan family, the first of which were Greek, whose brethren later followed in their footsteps."⁴⁸ Earlier, however, Lilienblum had written an article in which he expressed his opinion that German antisemitism had been invented by Bismarck for political purposes, while the pogroms in Russia were the result of Russian Jews' lack of equal rights—and that after Bismarck's political goals were reached, and after Russian Jews were granted equal rights, "this entire disaster will go away."⁴⁹ At the same time, however, he believed that the source of European antisemitism lay in the character of its society, whether German or Russian. His views shifted radically after the Southern Storms.

In 1882, Lilienblum dubbed German antisemitism "the Ashkenazi Ape." This ape was admittedly created in Germany for the purposes of political manipulation, but its creation demonstrated that "the earth excels in raising up creatures like these." The fertile ground that nourished antisemitism was not religious hatred or the dark ignorance of the Middle Ages, but hatred of foreigners founded on the concepts of nationalism and race—the household gods that appeared in Europe as replacements for earlier religious ideals. Since the Jews were neither Slavic nor Teutonic but children of Shem, they were strangers in Europe whether they liked it or not—children of an alien race. Hatred of the Jewish stranger was therefore a natural and organic phenomenon. As a result, even modern European civilization was of no help to the Jews. It did not demand that Jews leave their faith or change their beliefs, but, as Lilienblum wrote, neither could it accept them as part of itself: "Can you demand that I take a stranger into my home and consider him a son?"⁵⁰ The German Orthodoxy also used the new concepts of race; in 1880, for example, Rabbi Shimshon Raphael Hirsch addressed assimilated Jews from the pages of *Der Israelit*: "As much as you may divest yourselves of every Jewish matter, the race will exist to eternity."⁵¹ The *Rassenjude* (racial Jew) thus replaced the *Religionsjude* (religious Jew) even in Jewish literature.

It is impossible not to notice the bitter irony hidden in these words, against the background of the widespread antisemitic claim that the threat Jews posed to Europe derived not from their Semitic racial characteristics, but from the idea that it was they who had created and disseminated the universal values of the West. Consequently, they were responsible for the disintegration (*Zersetzen*) of the organized European societies, and thus the way to save Europe was to destroy the Jews.[52] It is also impossible not to sense the bitter irony of Jews' invocation of terms from the field of collective psychology, and their diagnosis of antisemitism as a manifestation of a collective pathology. While antisemitic literature depicted Judaism as a hereditary illness, Jews diagnosed antisemitism as a hereditary illness in the Western, Christian world.[53]

WAS ONLY EUROPE GUILTY?

However, it was not only Europe that was responsible for antisemitism: some placed the blame on European Jews. The two rival movements—Orthodox Judaism and the Jewish nationalist movement (including both the Bund and the Zionist movement)—were thoroughly agreed on the subject of Jewish responsibility for the situation. Both felt that the reason for antisemitism was assimilation—that is, the attempt by Jews to resemble Europeans and to become integrated through self-deprecation and shedding signs of religious or national cultural singularity. It was assimilation that gave rise to the antisemitic reaction, whose goal was to drive the assimilated Jews out of Germanness, or out of Polishness. In the eyes of the Orthodox, the guilty parties were the liberal and Reform Jews, and their rejection of their religion. "Before, we were abused because we were too Jewish; today we are abused because we are not Jewish enough," wrote Rabbi Rülf in 1883.[54] Herzl and other Zionists placed the blame on the "financial Jews," and Herzl did not shy away from using the epithet *Mauschel*, commonly found in the antisemitic German press—meaning a degenerate Jew, of defective character, attempting to escape both his religion and his race, making peace with antisemitism and in fact provoking it.[55] Herzl wrote: "Antisemitism, too, probably contains the divine Will to Good, because it forces us to close ranks, unites us through pressure, and through our unity will make us free."[56]

This negative depiction of "exilic Jews" was adopted in Zionist literature. Herzl described European Jews as "the waste product of modern humanity [from which] we will create happy, confident people, just as the waste products of factories, which in the past were unutilized, are used today to produce beautiful aniline colors."[57] Others placed the blame on Jews' cursory acculturation, which adopted only superficial, trivial manners. In December 1914, Chaim Weizmann wrote to Ahad Haam about a conversation with Lord Balfour during which Weizmann maintained that German antisemitism stemmed from the fact that the formative element in Jewish society had been assimilated and absorbed by German society—to the detriment of the Jewish people—and society responded with antisemitism. Weizmann added: "We are in agreement with the cultural antisemites, in so far as we believe that Germans of the Mosaic faith are an undesirable demoralising phenomenon."[58] According to this outlook, antisemitism was a response to Jewish assimilation in German society. Jabotinsky also wrote, in a similar vein, that "the mad wave of assimilation in Germany has wreaked its revenge on us."[59]

No wonder that these and similar words, which adopted the negative stereotypes of Jews, were perceived as a clear manifestation of Jewish antisemitism. It is also no wonder that some saw, in this antisemitism or self-hatred, a foolish attempt by Jews to reinvent themselves in order to adapt to criteria dictated by European antisemitism.[60] Modern antisemitism, they claimed, would pass from the world only when Jews abandoned the attempt to become Europeans in Europe, or when they left Europe forever.

OLD EUROPE OR NEW EUROPE?

*One of the spectacles which the next century
will invite us to witness is the decision regarding
the fate of the European Jews.*

FRIEDRICH NIETZSCHE,
The Dawn of Day[1]

In his novel *Der Mann ohne Eigenschaften* (The man without attributes),[2] the Austrian writer Robert Musil wrote that at the beginning of the twentieth century—that magical date—some Jews clung to the old, while others pinned their hopes on the new. The internal crises that rocked European nations after World War I prompted fears not only that Europe would remain unstable, but that forces of destruction continued to lurk beneath the surface, increasing in power and momentum, and apt to explode in violence. Apprehension and misgivings about the future once again gave rise to a torrent of apocalyptic prophecies regarding the inevitable decline and fall of European civilization.[3] The most famous of these prophetic works was Oswald Spengler's monumental *Der Untergang des Abendlandes* (The decline of the West), which was published in installments beginning in late 1917 and ending in 1922.[4] It is important to note that in addition to the morphological, deterministic schema promoted by Spengler and others, a contrasting outlook developed that might be called relativistic. This outlook did not support the idea of redeeming the Occident through a return to the Orient, nor did it believe in European values such as Occidental rationalism—rather, it claimed the existence of multiple modernities. In other words, it was not a Eurocentric perception of universal history and did not observe the world outside of Europe as a projection of the European self-image.[5]

In any case, Spengler and his notion of decline created many responses and numerous imitators. One of the oddest, the bizarre Jewish American publisher and poet Samuel Roth, published a poem in 1919 titled "Europe: A Book for America," in which he attempted to bare Europe's "true face," hidden behind the facade of progress. Roth maintained that Europe was spiritual heir to the licentious and morally bankrupt classical world, and that there was no possibility that the 1919 Treaty of Versailles could establish stability on that quarrelsome continent. In his poem, an ailing Europe, having satisfied its brutish desires, calls for a doctor who might bring it relief:

> Europe,
> After you have made the rounds of your cruelest lusts,
>   and spat out a million devils
> You make a wry face
> And clamor for a doctor.
>
> Europe, let me be your doctor!
> With hammer let me break open those iron jaws and pour
>   a pail of your bitterest spleen down your throat.
> O, I know a way to make eunuchs of the most terrible men;
> For twelve months I would like to feed you on a diet of dung.
>
> You are a sick, sick Europe.
> You need medicine.
> Let me be your doctor![6]

BETWEEN THE WARS: THE PENDULUM OF EXPECTATIONS

In Europe itself, World War I was depicted as both a purifying and a refining experience—one of destruction and reconstruction—and as a testament to the irreversible decline of European culture.[7] In his poem *Mefisto*,[8] Uri Zvi Greenberg—influenced by Spengler or by *Upadek cywilizacji zachodniej* (The decline of the West, 1921), a book by the Polish sociologist Florian Znaniecki, and certainly by his own experiences in the Austro-Hungarian military as an army medic at the front—depicted Europe as a continent "given to evil."[9] A sick continent, it had sold its soul to the devil and unleashed all the forces of evil and destruction that had been buried within.

Still, this dismal picture did not dominate the mood of the day, just as images of destruction had not dominated the end of the previous century. At least during the 1920s, it was generally believed that the crises Europe endured after the war were simply the pangs of rebirth; Europe, still licking its wounds, had learned its lesson and would not permit a new general war to break out. This optimism translated into plans to establish a new Europe and to implement the idea of a federative Europe—an idea whose seeds first appeared, as we have seen, in the fourteenth century, and whose embers again began to glow in the seventeenth century.

The general consensus was that Europe, now mature and experienced, would become a continent free of national borders, armies, and wars. Before World War I, Sir Norman Angell—an author and member of Parliament, and the winner of the 1933 Nobel Peace Prize—published a book titled *The Great Illusion: A Study of the Relation of Military Power in Nations to their Economic and Social Advantage*, to great acclaim. After the war, the book's title took on an additional and unintended meaning, immortalized by Jean Renoir's 1937 film, *The Grand Illusion*.[10] Ivan Bloch's 1898 six-volume *The Future of War* was highly successful and was translated into twenty-five languages.[11] Bloch claimed that war was not an unavoidable phenomenon, and that economic and moral progress would bring about an end to war in Europe; because modern weapons were sufficiently powerful to turn wars into mass genocides, the nations of Europe would refrain from risking self-annihilation.

Optimistic—or perhaps naive—visionaries such as the Czech philosopher (and later politician) Tomáš Masaryk, the Austro-Hungarian count Richard Nikolaus von Coudenhove-Kalergi, and the French politicians Aristide Briand and Eduard Herriot called for the reorganization of East and Central European nations, and for the founding of a pan-European organization that might spare the continent from yet another vicious war. The Spanish thinker José Ortega y Gasset called for the establishment of a single great European nation that would inject new blood into the continent's veins; he believed this possible because nationalism was a relatively new historical movement without any deep roots.[12] He also rejected the assessment that Europe was increasingly in decline and losing its vitality, while the United States was poised to take its place—a prediction popularized in books such as Waldo Frank's 1929 *The Rediscovery of America*. Ortega y Gasset maintained that no other culture could inherit the culture of Europe (i.e., of France, England, and Germany). Nor was there the slightest indication of a civilization that might inherit it: America was incapable of ruling. Benedetto Croce rejected the "pessimism and voices of decadence, which were heard in pre-war literature" and "now heard once more." He also predicted in 1932 that although Europe was hovering on the brink of war, and despite the rise of communism and fascism, a unified Europe could still coalesce, and prewar Europe—that "orderly, rich Europe, overflowing with trade and movement, exuding comfort and convenience"—might be reborn. Europe, he wrote, was a vast world of common spirit, thought, art, and culture. Nationalism and communism had carved an immense chasm between liberal and fanatical Europe. Still, "the process of European unification stands in opposition to competition between the Nationalists; even now it is set for battle against them, and soon enough it will liberate Europe from them entirely." Croce also maintained that nations were not "natural developments." In the near future, according to him, the people of Europe's various nations would rise to the rank of Europeans, with no artificial barriers separating them. To those who read his vision as nothing more than pure prophecy—"which is forbidden to us and to all men"—Croce replied that it was a call for action and an endeavor to prepare hearts and minds.[13] These and similar voices created the impression that the idea of European unification was fast being realized—an impression that was especially strong during the first Congress of the Pan-European Union in 1926.[14]

During the interwar period, as in the period before 1914, opposing views abounded regarding the character of Europe. The Austrian Jewish writer Robert Musil found himself surrounded by uncertainty and despair and described Europe as "ein babylonisches Narrenhaus" (a Babylonian madhouse).[15] Five years after the Nazis' rise to power, Thomas Mann wrote that Europe's condition was unfortunate, and that the cause was the newfound might of *Massenmensch* (mob mentality); having surfaced during the age of liberalism and socialism, it granted power to those who controlled it. According to Mann, this was a new kind of idealism, superficial and mystical, which would destroy the old humanist idealism. If that idealism were destroyed, he wrote, the word "Europe" would become nothing more than an idea from the past.[16] The German sociologist Georg Simmel claimed that World War I was a madness that had destroyed Europe in the sense of a consistent spiritual creation. However, the danger he foresaw was that after the war, a new type of cosmopolitan internationalism would emerge—lacking nationalistic roots and a unified historical awareness. A new Europe, he declared, was impossible without regard to the deep roots of *Deutschtum*—the German spirit.[17]

How did Jews view Europe, and what did they see in the Europe that existed between the world wars? They had no doubt that, as Arthur Ruppin observed, the fate of European Jews was caught in every historical development, and that even seemingly stable states were threatened by economic and political upheavals. As a result, Hebrew and Yiddish literature and journalism in Eastern Europe followed current events closely even before World War I, and with increased intensity after it. The mood of East European Jewish writers fluctuated between two extremes: a sense of impending catastrophe and hope for a better world.[18] This fluctuation increased greatly after the war: there was no sense that peace in Europe was ensured. In 1919, Nachman Syrkin predicted "eternal war" between the various nations of Europe. According to him, "a terrible hatred" would reign, primarily between Germany and France, "which will exist—which will survive—as long as the society of materialism and competition prevails. This enmity bodes ill for peace between nations, and it is a deep enmity, unfortunately, and not without cause." He added:

> This is no peace, but the birth of a murderous hatred between the nations of central Europe and the Entente Powers . . . Now, the war concluded, this world is even more saturated with danger than before. The Great War merely gave a sharp jolt to the gears of history, helped grind up the remains of the Middle Ages, the empires, the anarchy. But it did not have the power to resolve the differences between nations. It did not have the power to divide the world and its resources fairly among the nations, and only after the Treaty of Versailles is signed, and after the League of Nations is established, will we be sensible of all the bitter desperation of the time.[19]

The pogroms and antisemitism in independent Poland—especially the riots against Jewish residents of Lvov on January 21–23, 1918, in which some seventy Jews were murdered and hundreds more injured[20]—were described as "a single unending mess of riots, spreading from city to city, from station to station, from one train cart to another,"[21] and reinforced fears that the new, nationalistic countries of Eastern Europe would adopt anti-Jewish policies. Some Jews even sounded the alarm and declared that "the threat of extermination" hovered over Poland's Jews, and thus there was no need for Jews to pity the oppressed Polish people—and certainly no need to consider the Poles a nation of freedom fighters and justice seekers. Poland did not deserve to be an independent nation; not since the crusades had Jews faced "a threat like that which is expected from Poland . . . Autonomy for that nation means the destruction of two million of our brothers."[22] The nation of Poland, wrote the newspaper *Hatzfira* on December 5, 1918, "was born with a red stain of blood on its brow."[23] In his 1923 poem, "In the Kingdom of the Cross," Uri Zvi Greenberg described Slavic Europe as a "forest of afflictions" and wrote that a "poisonous gas" would seep into its castles; Europe was a place whose inhabitants dreamed of the destruction of all Jews.²⁴ In 1925, he wrote: "And here I come to a crossroads. I do not believe in our continued existence in the land of the Slavs. I do not believe it is possible to preserve our uniqueness in Europe at all. History teaches this to me in full awareness, to say this day Europe has not accepted the Jews, and cannot bear Jews on her soil, living persons with their own character, who are not Christians."²⁵

In contrast to this catastrophic and apocalyptic vision of Europe as a graveyard, Greenberg also presented a vision of redemption, in which the European Jew would abandon the opera, the museums, the dancing halls, and cafes; exchange his tuxedo, bow tie, and patent-leather shoes for "the flowing Arab *abaya*"; and proclaim that he was turning his back once and for all on Europe, that ailing land. It was admittedly difficult to leave even a land of troubles and a "homeland of grief," but it was necessary to do so because ruin awaited the Jews in Europe. A full revival of the Jewish experience could be achieved only in Palestine. However, Greenberg believed that Zionism would turn the Jewish settlement in Palestine into "a European beacon shining on Damascus . . . [and become] an important political factor and *avant garde* for European Hebrew culture."²⁶

AN EVIL WILL BREAK FORTH FROM GERMANY

Did the intellectual Jewish elite—writers, journalists, and public figures—include any astrologers able, in the mid-nineteenth century or even after World War I, to read the events that would unfold in Europe during the 1920s? And if such astrologers did exist, where did they believe calamity would break out: in the Slavic lands or in Germany?

It was Heinrich Heine, as we have seen, who was exalted as a seer; but in the field of apocalyptic prophecy on the subject of Germany, he was preceded by the writer and thinker Shaul Ascher, in his 1815 *Germanomania*. Ascher—who, until the end of the Napoleonic wars, had been an ardent believer in the universal nature of modern, Christian European culture—believed that reason would instill the spirit of *Weltbürgerlichkeit* and that the European idea of humanity would prevail over national or particularistic differences. He changed his mind after the rise of German *Volkism* and in the wake of the reaction to Napoleon's fall. In his 1815 book, Ascher warned that Germanomania—that is, German nationalism representing the age-old uniqueness of the German race—was instilling a conservative, nationalistic Romanticism that would stand in the way of rational and liberal universalism.²⁷ Ascher further predicted that in order to fan the flames of nationalism, the Germanomanes (or Teutons) would strike at the Jews as a first batch of kindling for the fire: "Fuel has to be gathered in order to maintain the fire of enthusiasm, and our Teutomaniacs wanted to see in the little heap of Jews, a first bundle of twigs to spread the flame of fanaticism."²⁸

Heine's prophecies, however, echoed more strongly; he was a central figure, writing in German—rather than in Hebrew or Yiddish. The nightmarish portrait that he painted in his 1844 poem "Deutschland, Ein Wintermärchen" (Germany, a winter's tale) was treated as a prophecy of what might be expected from a unified Germany—a prophecy that eventually came true:

> It's the future you'll be viewing—
> The future of Germany before your eyes
> Like a billowing fantasm;
> But do not shudder if from the mass
> Exhales a foul miasma! . . .
>
> But the scent of the German futurity
> Was ever so much stronger
> Than anything I ever smelled,
> I could bear it no longer.²⁹

Heine predicted that an independent and unified Germany would give rise to a xenophobic and fanatical nationalism,³⁰ and that if this fanaticism won the struggle for Europe's soul, the Jews would face unprecedented persecution. After the war and the Holocaust, it was said of Heine that he "saw the truth in all its viciousness, heard the rustling of German mysticism, and understood the darkness in that nation's psyche. He tried to warn other nations, and most of all our own—to communicate a true idea of the 'mystical psyche of the Teutonic people.'" According to this description, Heine was "the first European Jew, and perhaps the only one, to grasp the true meaning of the theory of racial superiority . . . He had learned to understand the German nation and to hate it. And indeed he knew very well what Germany's leaders in his time wrote and thought about Europe and the Jews."³¹

Some twenty years after Heine's dismal prophecy, in 1862, Hess asked: "Who can foresee the catastrophes that may befall us as a result of our arrested development?"³² He predicted a "final race war" between the

German race and the Roman Catholic nations.³³ In a pamphlet published in 1863—in which he replied to Abraham Geiger, who described him as a reactionary Romanticist—Hess wrote that Germanness and German culture would never allow Jews to assimilate into the German racial entity.³⁴ Graetz was of a similar mind. He wrote that the Germans were "a lowly, contemptible race" and "a narrow minded and arrogant nation"; it was they who had created the dark world of the Middle Ages and now represented modern barbarity. This opinion was shared by Aharon Aronson, who lived in Palestine. He saw German patriotism as zealotry without moral restraint. In 1910, nearly half a century after Hess and Graetz, he wrote "nothing ... has weakened my cognizance of the threat to civilization posed by the realization of the all-Germanic dream ... What Jew, whether German or Austrian, does not sense the danger that lies in Teutonism?"³⁵

During the run-up to World War II, it was easy to issue retrospective prophesies, as Thomas Mann did through his character Goethe in *Lotte in Weimar* (published in English as *The Beloved Returns*): The Germans' sense of liberty and their love for their homeland could at any minute be transformed into a monster, their nationalism turned into something ominous and terrible. Sometimes, Mann's Goethe said, he was attacked by a paralyzing fear, since sooner or later the Germans' eternal hatred for the Jews was apt to erupt in an awful massacre. In *Doctor Faustus*, which Mann began writing at the height of World War II, the narrator predicts that Germany will once again be ruined because the attempts by Bismarck and other leaders of the Weimar Republic "to normalize Germany in the sense of Europeanizing or 'democratizing' it" had failed.³⁶

The conviction that Nazism was an unavoidable consequence of Germany's *Sonderweg* (special way) in Europe³⁷—as well as a consequence of the age-old demonism inhabiting Germany's soul, an idea that became widely accepted after the Holocaust—was a case of perfect vision in hindsight, or as Kurt Blumenfeld, the leader of the German Zionists, called it, "retrospective prophecy."³⁸ However, these depictions of the nature of German nationalism and the threat it posed did not originate in a vacuum. Even in the 1830s, the historian Leopold von Ranke declared that any significant achievement in Germany after the French Revolution was a result not of imitation of, but of opposition to, French ideas.³⁹ Germany positioned itself against the West as though it rejected—or was pressed to reject—liberal and democratic ideas because they were not German. This outlook was disseminated in later years by spokesmen for the German

Volkist movement. At their head was Julius Langbehn who, in his 1890 bestseller *Rembrandt als Erzieher* (Rembrandt as educator), painted a chilling picture of a degenerate, declining German society that was losing its unique spiritual values; other leaders were Paul de Lagarde and Moller van den Bruck. They and others claimed that Germany did not belong to the West; they rejected the French Revolution's universalist legacy and demanded that Germany distance itself from the materialistic West. Only in this way could the unique collective genius of the German people be expressed.[40] France symbolized the West, its values, and its traits, which stood in contrast to Germany's uniqueness and authenticity.

The majority of German Jews did not reject the idea that German culture had a unique character within the European cultural framework. On the contrary, they adopted the idea enthusiastically, but they saw Germany's culture as one that embodied universal values. On September 16, 1898, Herzl wrote proudly in his diary: "Most Jews these days belong to the German culture."[41] The Jewish elite in both West and East was drawn to the radiant aura of German culture; before and after World War I, that culture symbolized *Weltkultur* (world culture). For example, in his memoirs, the East European *maskil* Abraham Baer Gottlober described Germany, to which he was headed, as "the land of Ashkenaz where lies the treasure of knowledge, in my opinion . . . and the people of the land are all good and righteous."[42] In September 1881, the writer A. S. Friedberg wrote Y. L. Levin that one could not be surprised by Russian antisemitism: Russia was "a country shrouded in fog-like lethargy." Nor was there hope for a Jewish revival in Germany, "the land of study and logic."[43] This positive image no doubt contributed to the acute disappointment that resulted from revelations of German antisemitism. In a series of articles titled "Examples from the World of Truth, or the Education of the Nineteenth Century and Israel's Hopes from Ashkenaz," published in *Hamelitz* in 1896, the author piercingly expressed the dejection of those who believed that "the light has gone from Germany":

> At first we were as though drunk with happiness. In our eyes [Germany] was transformed into Paradise and its people into higher beings. The power of delusive imagination so overwhelmed us that we were misled into believing that an end to suffering was at hand, that soon hatred and jealousy would flee like shadows from the Enlightenment, which would cast its spirit over every living being and unite the people of the world as one . . . And now, this single hope too has

been disappointed ... We stand today before our bitter enemies who never cease to degrade our honor and the honor of our faith, depress them to the lowest depths, and exhibit us in broad daylight in our eternal shame ... This impetuous, bitter vision has now been shattered, at the end of the nineteenth century, in the land of wisdom and science, the forefront of enlightenment—in Germany.[44]

A few years later, in October 1914, Chaim Weizmann wrote that he had fallen captive to Germany's charms and that his admiration was sparked by the German discipline and strength, which stood in stark contrast to lazy, talentless Russia, which was rotten to the core. Compared to Russian antisemitism, German antisemitism was mild and easily borne.[45] Only World War I dampened his enthusiasm for the Germany of "pagan Siegfried," if not for its virtues. In July 1915, he wrote:

I am not an admirer of the German cultural ideals, but I admire the organization and efficiency of Germany ... It is deplorable that this wonderful motor is using itself up now for destructive purposes. I admit that the warlike tendencies have to be destroyed, but the virtues of Germany will remain, blossom out again and if the military cast is destroyed a new and great Germany will arise, which may conquer the world without firing a shot.[46]

The majority of Germany's Jews shared this positive assessment of their country; they cultivated it and expressed steadfast confidence in German values and German justice. As we have seen, they pointed proudly to their integration into Germany's culture and society, cited their contributions to these in almost every field, and believed that the plague of antisemitism would fade away over time, though it might never be cured entirely. Shulamit Volkov sees German Jews' sense of confidence in the success of their integration into German society as hubris on their part.[47] Hubris can certainly be detected in the following speech delivered on January 22, 1919, by Ismar Freund, one of the most respected members of the Berlin community and a director of the Central Association of German Citizens of Jewish Faith. His speech was titled—what else?—"Die Zukunft des Judentums" (The future of the Jews):

Deutschtum [Germanness] as we understand it, Deutschtum as it has developed, the Deutschtum we love with all our hearts is something holy to us, something of an historic importance, is something which represents an intellectual milieu, a cultural element ... We

> hereby declare publicly and with the greatest emphasis . . . we German Jews are conscious of the fact, that we have greatly contributed to what we regard as Deutschtum . . . Ladies and Gentlemen, it is because we know that we have done our share with our life's-blood to build this German essence, because it is part of our innate being, that . . . we are Jewish Germans and therefore German Jews, not only German in the legal sense, or from a political point of view, but because of deep conviction, because we love our German Fatherland . . . out of an inner necessity and because our soul forces and commands us to do so.

A transcript notes that the speech was received with "lively shouts of bravo!"[48]

It was also difficult for German Zionists to conclude that the Jews' hard-won emancipation and integration were in danger, and that the dream of full Jewish integration into the German nation had been shattered. In their agenda of 1932, they declared that Germany's Jews enjoyed excellent social conditions and possessed full civil rights; they were thus entitled and permitted to remain in the country as loyal citizens and good neighbors, and to fight for cultural advancement. At the same time, they had an obligation to help their oppressed coreligionists in Eastern Europe who were in search of a new homeland.[49] On September 16, 1932, Dr. Nahum Goldmann, then a German Zionist leader, declared: "I do not believe we need fear pogroms or a rescission of rights . . . in Czarist Russia the situation was worse . . . While Russian antisemitism endangered the physical existence of the Jews, the greatest danger of German antisemitism is the moral effect of the antisemitic climate."[50] However, Goldmann wrote in his memoirs that "from the first I was one of those—unfortunately a minority—who took the phenomenon of Hitler very seriously." Most German Jews, he wrote, "mindful of their economic and cultural standing in the Weimar Republic, refused to recognize the danger [Hitler] represented"; they saw those who warned about him as "panicky, hysterical alarmists."[51] One person who did issue a warning was the German Jewish writer Jakob Wassermann, who prophesied that a time of darkness unrivalled in a thousand years was at hand.[52] In contrast, on September 20, 1935, the writer Leon Feuchtwanger promised the writer Arnold Zweig that Germany's madness would not last long:

> I do not like to make political prophecies, but through the intensive study of history I have reached the, if I may say so, scientific

conviction that, in the end, reason must triumph over madness and that we cannot consider an eruption of madness such as the one in Germany as something that can last more than a generation. Superstitious as I am, I hope in silence that this time too the German madness won't last longer than the [1914–18] war madness did. And we are already at the end of the third year.[53]

A year later, in 1936, the historian Marvin Lowenthal wrote that within the next few years, Germany must choose between liberty or, "in battlefields too horrible to contemplate," death. However, he added, the fact "that the world, including Jewry, will permit the slow starvation of a million Europeans seems barely credible until we recall how little the world has concerned itself with a million no less starving Polish Jews." German Jews, he continued, "are disappearing from the stage of history." He saw Hitler and Nazism as temporary phenomena—a warp in German history from which they would be expelled in short time.[54] The idea that political nationalism and racial antisemitism were phenomena deeply rooted in German culture, rather than errant outgrowths, was perceived as deriving from Zionist concerns. However, there were also those within the Zionist camp who believed these phenomena would soon die out. Chaim Arlosoroff, for example, who was chairman of the Jewish Agency's political department, believed that the Nazi regime would become reasonable and rational once it was stabilized. In June 1932, Arlosoroff wrote that antisemitism carried at most marginal weight in the Nazi ideology, and that Jews were in far greater danger of assimilation under the Soviet regime and from the collapse of the middle class in the United States, following the financial crisis of 1929. If a new world war broke out within five or ten years, it would be because of Germany's desire to rein in Soviet Russia.[55]

That this was not simply a matter of tragic error or self-delusion on the Jews' part is attested by Thomas Mann's article "The Fall of European Jews," which was published in 1945 in a collection of articles called *The Future of the Jews*—neither the first nor the last book to bear that title. Mann wrote: "Never could a spiritual and philo-European man in Germany be an antisemite." Mann believed that it was a mistake to attribute antisemitism to all Germans, or even to most of them.[56]

Questions such as whether Nazism was a wild, temporary deviation, or whether it was a manifestation of something inherent in German culture—and consequently a threat to Jewish existence in Germany and in Europe as a whole—were frequently raised by Jews only after 1930, particularly after 1933. We will cite here only a few examples of responses written during the 1930s. It is not our intention to judge the authors for their failures as prophets, but rather to examine how they understood the events that took place in the second half of the 1930s against the background of their understanding of the essence of Europe in general, and of Germany in particular. In other words, did they believe that Nazi Germany posed a threat to peace and stability in Europe?

The answer is that most of them feared for the fate of the Jews, but few assumed that Germany would instigate a global war—a war that would determine the fate of Europe and its Jews.

In 1935 some believed that Hitler would soon fall: "The Jews [would] have the last laugh" and would soon witness Germany's financial destruction.[57] In a November 23, 1935, meeting between the Association of German Immigrants in Palestine and the Jewish Agency's directors, Menachem Mendel Ussishkin declared that "there is something positive" in the Nuremberg Laws—namely, that they determined one's eligibility for discrimination on the basis of race rather than religion. Had they discriminated on a religious basis, the result would be the "annihilation of half the Jews in Europe." Ussishkin saw German Jews as a negative model of integration into the surrounding society, one that transformed Germany's Jews into "real Germans in feeling, thought, and disposition."[58] In early 1933, Jabotinsky posed a rhetorical question: "Where is the blind man who believes that Hitler's regime will 'triumph,' that is, that he will turn at least a portion of his promises into reality—except for his decision to destroy the Jews?" Against the Jews, Jabotinsky declared, "there stands an enemy doomed from birth to the shame of failure."[59] (Note that by destruction, Jabotinsky did not mean physical destruction.) About three years later, in January 1936, Jabotinsky expressed his opinion that the Third Reich was just a "banal episode" in the history of Jewish misfortune.[60] Yitzhak Greenbaum—the leader of Poland's Jews, who believed that it was possible to wage an active Jewish war against Germany—declared in the beginning of 1936 that it was Poland's Jews who were headed "toward a new catastrophe in the story of our people, the catastrophe more severe than that of Jews in Germany."[61] However, the agent for this catastrophe, according to Greenbaum, would not be global war or Nazi control of Germany, but conditions in Poland.

The biblical scholar and thinker Yehezkel Kaufmann maintained that the antisemitic revolution in Germany was not due to the theory of racial superiority; instead, antisemitism begat racism and was rooted "in the eternal hatred of the Jews of the Diaspora." He explained:

> Hitler's race theory is certainly not popular belief. A day before the Nationalist Revolution, the people as a whole knew nothing of "Aryans" and "non-Aryans," and probably even today they do not know how these are defined or what these entail. Race theory is the domain of a small number of zealots, who are imposing it on the people . . . Hitler's theory has no popular basis, but with respect to antisemitism specifically, German fascism has served to express genuine popular sentiment.

According to Kaufmann, the danger posed by German fascism, which utilized antisemitism for its own means, was "the economic depletion of the Jews." This would be "a racial lesson of terrifying clarity," with the result that Jews would always be considered aliens in Europe. The popular war against Jews in Germany was in essence a nationalist, economic war, and as a result, the Germans would not allow Jews to live among them as a separate cultural entity. In any case, Kaufmann believed that Hitlerism, "despite its savage tyranny, is not a return to the Middle Ages" and would not revive the ghetto to isolate the Jews. Thus, Kaufmann predicted, the Nazi leadership would enact policies with the purpose of denying Jews their civil rights, pass legislation specifically applicable to them, and turn them into a "national minority."[62] Weizmann also issued words of calm, saying in December 1937 that "the German tragedy is far smaller in scope than the Polish tragedy; it is small enough to overcome, and, moreover, Germany's Jews have greater financial security; they are better able to withstand an attack than the Jews in Poland." He further declared that if several tens of thousands of German Jews immigrated to Palestine, "we shall be able to answer to history that we did as much as could be done."[63] The fate of Poland's Jews was a greater cause for concern. In 1934, Nahum Sokolow, then president of the Zionist Organization, wrote: "Not too long ago, my heart already prophesied the coming of this tragedy. However, we never really felt it as if it were truly palpable."[64]

Other opinions were also heard. In 1924, Chaim Nachman Bialik claimed that there was no more antisemitism in Germany.[65] However, he changed his mind and in May 1933—some five months after Hitler rose to power—wrote to a Viennese friend, the industrialist Max Delfiner, that he had warned many of his friends in Germany about the developing climate, because "who knows what the future holds for our other brethren abroad." In another letter, Bialik wrote: "Now the signs and omens are here. The evil has come even before I thought it would. Would that our brothers had understood what was to come."[66] In January 1934, he wrote to the editorial board of the *Judisk Tidskirt*, the Jewish newspaper in Stockholm, that while he could not predict the future, as far as he could see "the Jews of the Diaspora—the entire Diaspora, and not just in Germany—are on the verge of annihilation." A healthy people should never guess what the future would bring; there was "no divination in Jacob" (Numbers 23:23). What a healthy nation did need, Bialik asserted, was not prophets and seers but open eyes to see and acknowledge the reality of the present.[67] The writer Yehoshua Heschel Yeivin, who belonged to the radical wing of the Revisionist movement, wrote in March 1933 that the Nazi movement had not emerged overnight but had developed over the course of a decade; there was still enough time to study its roots and understand its essence, and to prepare for "the day of destruction and escape it in time." What was taking place in the cultured part of Europe was not "psychosis" or "momentary madness," but a full-scale attack on the Jewish people, "aimed at its destruction and eradication. I mean complete, criminal, material eradication that is taking place and will take place, if not through official pogroms then by devastating any means of economic survival. That is: bringing millions of Jews to a state of chronic hunger and degeneration."[68]

There were, of course, those who interpreted the appearance of antisemitism in Germany differently. In 1934, for example, Professor A. Kolisher, one of the leaders of the Revisionist movement in Europe, published a series of articles entitled "Our Enemy," in which he asserted that the Jews' admiration of German culture blinded them to the barbaric nature of German nationalism and antisemitism. The truth of the matter, he opined, was that Germany was a barbaric country, and it was for this reason that antisemitism could take roots among the masses there, as well as become official policy with the aim of exterminating the Jews (by "extermination," Kolisher meant expulsion of the Jews from German society). The special feature of German antisemitism, Kolisher stated, was the lack of distinction between how the government and the people approached it; he maintained that antisemitism expressed the "soul of Germany at this time."[69] As an anti-Marxist and an avowed anti-Communist, he explained the phenomenon of Nazism as being due to, among other reasons, the triumph of Marxist ideology over liberal values. Nothing could be expected from Germany except horror and terror. In the newspaper *Hazit Haam*, A. Ginsburg wrote that it was impossible to describe Nazism's rise to power as "simple antisemitism. This is not simply a wave of persecution, but a movement to exterminate the Jews. [Hitler] does not want to diminish Jews' rights, but to eliminate them. He does not want to diminish the Jews' power, but to erase them from the face of the earth."[70] In October, 1935, Moshe Shertok (later Sharett), who had succeeded Arlosoroff as head of the Jewish Agency's political department, wrote to David Ben Gurion: "we are clearly facing a new and catastrophic phase of developments there [in Germany]."[71] By "catastrophic," he meant —like many others—an acute crisis, but not a threat to the physical existence of Jews in Germany. Ben Gurion, for example, declared that one of the wealthiest Jewish communities in the world was in danger of witnessing the destruction of all its property, but also that the situation in which German Jews found themselves was likely to place new wind in Zionism's sails.[72]

The Jewish press in Poland was exceptional in its unsparing expressions of apprehension and its depictions of Polish antisemitism as the chief enemy. In a 1935 poem "The Blind Generation," for example, Roman Brandstaetter urged his complacent brothers in Poland to open their eyes and see the disaster that approached.[73] At the same time, the Polish press predicted that Nazi Germany was about to draw Europe into a threatening future. After Kristallnacht, the German threat became tangible; the Germans were described as born murderers,[74] and Germany as a savage beast hiding behind the facade of culture and progress and attempting to return all of Europe to the Middle Ages.[75] Nazism was perceived as a radical expression of German Romanticism, which rejected liberalism, humanism, and democracy.[76]

Only over the course of 1939 did the prediction that a full-scale war was at hand become prevalent, but soothing articles still continued to be published. Thus, for example, after Hitler's speech of January 30, 1939, in which he promised to destroy the Jewish people if war broke out, Y. Gurion, the editor of the Revisionist newspaper *Hamashkif*, wrote that darker threats than this had been made over the past two thousand years of exile. If war broke out, he predicted, it would clear away Hitler's medieval regime.[77] The radical Revisionists' hatred of Britain outweighed their fear of Nazi Germany; one of them wrote at the start of March 1939 that the Nazis were "relative enemies," while the Jews' mortal enemy was Britain.[78] Only in April 1939 did Berl Katznelson dare to announce: "We are on the eve of world war—a world war based on race."[79] From 1933 onward, Katznelson maintained that Germany's Jewish population had been devastated, but to describe this devastation, he used words that in a few years would have a different meaning: one day German Jews woke up and found that they had been "eliminated" from their jobs in the civil service, banks, universities, and the like. When, in 1939, Katznelson warned that Hitler intended to destroy the Jews, what he meant by the word is not at all clear.[80] In contrast, Moshe Beilinson had no trouble declaring—on September 25, 1939, two days before the invasion of Poland—that "German Jews have still not reached the [terrible] condition of Russia's Jews."[81]

Thus pessimists expected that, at worst, Jewish ghettos would return to the heart of an enlightened culture, and Germany's Jews would suffer economic and cultural devastation. There was much talk of dispossession, religious persecution, expulsion, and the destruction the war would bring, but the possibility of organized mass murder was not considered. Even when people wrote about decimation, annihilation, destruction, or eradication, they referred not to physical destruction but to financial and other losses that European Jews could expect from the war. Zionist circles discussed the possibility that the Jews' situation in Europe after the war would not be what it had been before. Even the bleakest prophecies failed to see what was underway in Germany.

Among their followers, there are those who believe the seer's mantle belongs to Zeev Jabotinsky and David Ben Gurion. The claim is that they sounded the alarm in time and were almost alone among their generation in seeing the future: this should establish them as extraordinary individuals who were able to read the signs around them. The poet Uri Zvi Greenberg has also been granted that mantle and has been described as the sole member of his generation to predict the awful fate of Europe's Jews as early as the 1920s. Again, it is not our intention here to judge the prophetic ability demonstrated by these three; it is simply to examine how—if at all—they understood the nature of Nazi Germany within Europe's historical framework.

WHO CRIED WOLF?

In the summer of 1939, after listening to a radio speech by Hitler, Uri Zvi Greenberg warned against the threat of the "brown lava." Hitler, he wrote, would implement his threat to expel Germany's Jews, but after he was finished, the Jews of the world would take little notice of him.[82] In previous years, Greenberg had minimized the importance that should be accorded to Hitler's belligerent policy. "Even the irascible Hitler reins in his German war-lust," he wrote in November 1933; Hitler did not in fact desire war, and there was no reason to frighten Jews with the unlikely prospect of approaching war.[83] In reality, Greenberg continued, Europe did not want to involve itself again in the "atmosphere of gas and blood."[84] In 1939, he repeated this view when he declared that this was no more than a tempest in a teapot: Europe did not want war.[85] Despite this, in a poem published in 1938 that described a vision of a declining British Empire, he wrote "I see the eagles of Amalek from the Rhine / swooping over the spires of Westminster."[86] But this vision, similar to one put forth by Yeats in the same year, stemmed from Greenberg's profound loathing of Britain, and not necessarily from an ability to see the future relating to Nazi Germany's hawkish intentions or military power.[87] The Slavs' "eternal hatred" of the Jews took center stage in Greenberg's apocalyptic and catastrophic worldview. At the same time, his great confidence in Poland's strength and his belief that the interests of Poland and the Zionist movement coincided—with a deep affinity between the two—never waned. Greenberg did not foresee Nazi Germany's rapid conquest of Poland, and in any case, he could not have foreseen the destruction of East European Jewry as a result of Germany's occupation of Poland. As late as May 1939, he wrote that the talk of an "approaching world war" was merely a "paper war" spread by a handful of Jews. Although communism would welcome a world war because it would destroy the old order and hasten a global revolution, European capitalism and governments would not. Only in September 1939 did Greenberg recognize that Hitler is "our common foe," meaning an enemy of the Jews as well as of all Europeans—a "universal Amalek." Ignoring what he had written just a short while before, he claimed that the Jews, and he himself in particular, had demonstrated their spirit of "prophetic power" by being the first to warn the entire world against the Nazi threat:[88] "Alas! I prophesied the truth, and I curse my truth / That in the eyes of my people I appeared as a seer at the wrong time."[89] As an apocalyptic prophet, Greenberg successfully read the signs of the time; but as a political seer, he misread the main historical events. In the late 1930s, it was the preconceived apocalyptic outlook of the future that proved to be far more accurate than any rational predictions.

It is important to note that the Jewish ultra-Orthodox in Eastern Europe fared no better. They viewed modern antisemitism as an inevitable part of Jewish life in the Diaspora, and Nazism as merely another manifestation of that age-old phenomenon. The ultra-Orthodox believed that the Jews would once again be able to ride out the storm. This passive, traditionalist approach, sometimes supported by theodicean arguments, persisted even during the Holocaust. The Zionist movement's catastrophic prophecies concerning the future of European Jewry were perceived by the ultra-Orthodox as no more than propaganda and heretical ideology.

The failure to foresee coming events was also the fate of the Bund, which was the main political and social Jewish force in the interwar period in Poland. Its leaders expressed deep concern about Nazi Germany but interpreted its nature from a Marxist perspective, as a product of capitalism and nationalism. Not one of the leaders foresaw Germany's rapid occupation of Poland. They continued to believe, until the end, that combining Jewish and non-Jewish democratic forces in Poland was the best way to ensure Jewish rights in the Polish homeland. Moreover, the *Bund* was convinced that Zionist pro-emigration propaganda was encouraging Polish antisemitism and thus endangering the Jews of Poland.

Germany held a marginal standing in Jabotinsky's worldview. Although he was a man of culture and had a clear European orientation, he was not particularly enamored of Germany or its culture, and he certainly did not consider German culture as representative of European culture. At times, he acknowledged that "like all of my generation . . . [I am] an admirer and to a certain extent a student of German culture," and that "Germany is a nation with one of the grandest cultures in the world, with a long tradition of order, equal rights, and rule of law";[90] he also appreciated Germany's clean, beautiful cities. Despite that, Germany's culture, literature, and thought appeared only rarely in his writings.[91] In fact, he seldom wrote about Germany until 1933, and he reacted infrequently to the developments that took place in the Weimar Republic. The rise of Hitler and the Nazi party took him entirely by surprise. After reading Hitler's *Mein Kampf*—in which he claimed to find "chapters, or pages, that are quite intelligent"—Jabotinsky concluded that its racist and antisemitic ideology was the sole facet of Nazism that should be taken "seriously." From this appraisal, he inferred that "the German anti-Jewish crusade is the most important and gravest event in the history of recent generations," and he foresaw destruction for Jews around the world if Hitler's regime remained in power.[92] In a similar spirit, the newspaper *Hazit Haam* published an article titled "The Swastika Crusade" on March 10, 1933, which argued that although the Jewish press tended to treat Hitler's words with derision, his threats were real.

At the same time, Jabotinsky ridiculed Nazi Germany's hawkish propaganda and did not believe that it was backed by any substantial power. In June 1933, he even compared the Nazi movement to the Ku Klux Klan and maintained it was a case of "inebriation" that had transformed Germany into a "drunken nation," but the storm would pass; Nazi Germany was not an "iron giant," but an internally weak and unstable state. This seemed to be a perilous time for Jews, since the Nazi example had found favor in the world—"But wait, my friends; sanity will prevail." Most of all, Jabotinsky was convinced that a full-scale European war would not break out again: "Prophecy is a terrible thing . . . If you prophesy you risk being mistaken, but . . . despite the dangers of prophecy I am willing to take the risk: There will not be a war in Europe. Not half a war nor a fourth of one; not between England and Italy nor between any other powers." On April 4, 1939, he still firmly insisted that there was no need to be a prophet in order to understand that a European war was impossible, because the nations of Europe would not be dragged into a massive war in which their civilian populations would also be harmed.[93]

Nor did Jabotinsky see the Nazi party's rise to power as a necessary outcome of the German spirit or of Germany's singular history. In fact, he did not have a conclusive opinion about whether Nazi antisemitism was a pathological outburst uncharacteristic of the German people, or whether it was "a natural phenomenon, a drug buried deep in this nation's blood, whose effects emerge at an appropriate moment."[94] Only at the start of 1940 did he arrive at the conclusion that German antisemitism was "folk antisemitism"—that is, antisemitism nourished by ancient ideas passed from generation to generation and imprinted on the national culture, and which the Nazis transformed into a political instrument. Jabotinsky thus perceived Nazism as an antisemitic movement and was entirely convinced that European civilization had reached such heights of progress that a full-blown European war was impossible. His catastrophic image of a "volcano that will shortly commence to spew its flames of destruction" described the situation of Poland's Jews; it was they, in his opinion, who stood "at the edge of the abyss."[95]

Germany also initially held a marginal place in Ben Gurion's worldview. Nothing in what he said or wrote ever addressed German history or culture, and there is no evidence that he paid close attention to the crises that jarred the foundations of the Weimar Republic, or attempted to predict their outcomes. The Nazis' rise to power changed this situation. In January 1934, after reading *Mein Kampf*, Ben Gurion wrote:

Hitler's rule places the entire Jewish people in danger; Hitlerism is fighting not only the Jews of Germany but the Jews of all the world. Hitler's regime cannot exist for long without war, without a war of vengeance against France, Poland, Czechoslovakia, and the rest of its neighbors . . . or against Soviet Russia, that expansive state . . . Who knows—perhaps only four or five years (if not less) separate us from that awful day.[96]

Thus, in contrast to Jabotinsky, Ben Gurion predicted that the world was in grave danger of a full-blown European war, because Germany intended to go to war against the entire continent: "The war that will break out this time will surpass the previous world war in devastation and horrors."[97] Ben Gurion was also alert to the peril in which such a war would place Europe's Jews, and in June 1939 he declared: "A war might break out that will rain calamity upon us . . . If a world war breaks out . . . it will be Hitler's doing, and first of all he will destroy the Jewish people of Europe."[98]

Ben Gurion was one of the few who predicted the war that was gathering as a result of Nazi Germany's character and purpose.[99] But even if a small number did succeed in predicting the future, the Jews' attempt to decipher Europe's enigmatic soul, their criticism of European civilization, and their distrust and suspicion of Europe all failed to equip them to foresee the emergence of Nazism in the very heart of cultured Europe, or to read Germany's history as "an open book that speaks for itself."[100] This fact would cast a heavy shadow over the attempts to understand Europe and to predict its future in the half-century after World War II.

MANIFOLD EUROPES

Germany—Thought; England—Action; France—Pleasure.
MORRIS WINCHEVSKY,
"A Letter from the Diaspora"[1]

Winchevsky's words echo a widespread motif in European culture: the categorization of Europe's various cultures according to seemingly inherent fundamental traits that determined their unique identities and differentiated among them. One of many examples is the variety of stereotypes that Goethe articulated in his conversations with Eckermann in September 1829. Goethe described the Germans as a people concerned with great ideas and profound philosophical questions, while the English possessed a highly practical intellect and were actively engaged in conquering the world.[2] Nietzsche also devoted more than a few aphorisms to typical German, French, and English traits, particularly in the chapter "Peoples and Fatherlands" in *Beyond Good and Evil*. For example, he wrote: "The German soul is above all manifold, of diverse origins, more put together and superimposed than actually built." Indeed, while industrial England's model seemed fit for admiration and emulation in the eyes of nineteenth-century German liberals, *Volkists* regarded England as a provincial nation of merchants, lacking in depth and soul.[3]

During the nineteenth century, the concept of race was frequently used not only to define ethnic groups and the source of their characteristic traits, but also to define various nations within Europe. Each nation or group of nations was associated with a repertoire of stereotypes meant to denote its individuality and distinctiveness. It was possible to disagree with the validity of these stereotypes—Ahad Haam, for example, described the use of generalizations in characterizing Jews as part of the "European consensus" that created accepted perceptions[4]—but, as we have seen in chapter 4, it was difficult not to employ them.[5] Modern European Jews sometimes spoke of Europe (and European civilization) in general terms, but at the same time, they knew that Europe was not cut from a single cloth.

In *Beyond Good and Evil*, Nietzsche wrote about a general European spirit characterized by boundless curiosity and declared that in Europe there existed a continual movement interweaving the various races and prompting a process of assimilation, even with respect to physiology. He added: "We have found that in all major moral judgments Europe is now of one mind, including even the countries dominated by the influence of Europe."[6] Here Nietzsche was ignoring the age of patriotism and nationalism that emphasized particularistic basic traits, whether real or imagined. Thus, as we have seen, he perceived the German soul as being essentially different from the souls of other European nations. He described it as characterized by a tendency to metaphysical rumination and intense spirituality—an intensity absent among the English, who were mediocre and plebian. Nietzsche considered France a nation exceptional in its noble spiritual culture and traditionalism. In 1815, Christian Friedrich Rühs described the French as a "repellent, withering race."[7] Heine differentiated between the narrow English view of liberty and the broader French perception, which dealt with liberty for all humanity.[8] According to Heine, the French were a social people, while the Englishman's home was his castle; and the Germans were a "speculative nation dreaming of the past and of the future, but not existing in the present."[9] The characters in Thomas Mann's *Doctor Faustus* offer a distinction between the Italian Renaissance (*renascimento*) and the German revival (*Bildungserneuerung*, literally "renewal"): the latter was the German ability to shake off the shackles of a civilization that had lost its vitality. The "young and forward-looking" German spirit was represented by individual and national adolescence; this was a "metaphysical endowment"[10] unique to the Germans.[11] The Russian Slavophiles, as noted, believed that there was an absolute antinomy between the Russian soul and the European soul, represented primarily by France. In French nature and Western nature in general, Dostoevsky wrote, there was no place for human comradeship; instead "what shows up is a principle of individuality, a principle of isolation, of urgent self-preservation, self-interest."[12]

IMAGE, MODEL, AND INFLUENCE

The repertoire of traits and characteristics, of which we have presented only a tiny sample, made its way into Jewish literature. Here is just one example of the writings of the radical Revisionist Jewish thinker Aba Achimeir, who made the following general (and unfounded) observations about the different characteristics of various European nations:

This columnist's generation was educated at the knees of Russian or Ashkenazi [German] culture, and more's the pity. What Russian culture and Ashkenazi culture have in common is that both are the creations of a nation unconcerned with national survival. Russian culture is, at heart, a philanthropic culture. Ashkenazi culture is a culture of individualism, concerned with the individual's worries and joys. Since both peoples feel secure with respect to nationalism, the creators of Russian and Ashkenazi culture did not worry about maintaining a national identity. But if we have absorbed the Russian cosmopolitanism and the Ashkenazi self-centeredness, these are but fatal drugs to us. It is unfortunate, very unfortunate, that our generation has hardly absorbed the Polish culture of the nineteenth century. That is a culture not of humanity, not of the individual, but of the nation. Goethe, Dostoevsky, and Tolstoy have poisoned us—the sons of a nation fighting for its national existence. The great writers and poets of Polish literature would be a healing draught to us, and infuse our very bones.[13]

Images and topoi illustrate how one culture perceives and constructs others, and also how a culture sees itself—or its converse—within another culture. The imagined other culture becomes a model for imitation, a source of inspiration, or a rejected model. These images and topoi are constructed by means of knowledge that takes different forms. During the nineteenth century and part of the twentieth, they were created and disseminated primarily by means of the written word—through literature and the press. The East European Jewish intelligentsia, among others, constructed its image of France and French culture and of England and English culture from such information, which reached it by various means. In any event, we should not ascribe undue power to imagery, although it is an important part of any worldview and although it sometimes serves as a mirror to the observing culture. In many cases, a negative image is born as a means of self-defense against external influence, and this attests to the existence of such an influence more than it attests to success in withstanding it.

The Jews' knowledge and imagery of various European nations dealt with four primary subjects: the soul—that is, the traits attributed to the national character, or the collective mentality and collective national temperament; patterns of government and political culture; spiritual culture—that is, literary and artistic thought and creation; and civilization—namely, material culture, primarily science and technology.

The Russian[14] and German cultures were the two European cultures that, during various periods, influenced modern Jews more than any others. So significant was their influence that it prompted the idea that the Jews had also absorbed and internalized the mentality of the Russian and German peoples. We have chosen here to discuss how France and England were imagined, as well as their cultural influence—not on English or French Jews, but on the Jews of Eastern Europe and on Hebrew society and culture in Palestine. One historian characterized France as a secondary model for the East European Jewish intelligentsia. This is also true, albeit to a lesser extent, with respect to England.[15] Both nations exerted influence by means of thought, literature, and eventually the cinema. Closer acquaintance sometimes altered preconceived images; Chaim Weizmann wrote in February 1905 that "to tell the truth, we had a distorted conception of England and the English,"[16] but acquaintance had changed that conception and created new images. Thus, Weizmann wrote that the English were never in a rush, and had been left behind as a result; and that a dullness of thought in all areas was widespread in England. Only after he became more closely acquainted with England did his opinion about the country and its people evolve.

A few things remain to be said about the concept of influence. One culture's influence upon another may be realized in several ways. It is always dynamic and multilayered; it may be clear or indirect. Influence takes hold in the world of ideas and in the collective habitus. For our purposes here, it suffices to stress that the circumstances under which British culture influenced European Jews differed from the circumstances of its influence on Jews in Palestine, where the latter had a far greater degree of direct contact with the various aspects of that culture.

THE FRENCH SPIRIT AND THE FRENCH MODEL

France's central status in Europe during the nineteenth century aroused a good deal of interest among Jews, and a desire to learn more about it. As if by magic, Paris, the capital and heart of European culture, attracted intellectuals who lived far away and had only heard of its marvels. Jewish literature and the Jewish press attempted to satisfy the desire for knowledge about France. The newspaper *Hamagid*, for instance, published many articles about Paris—for instance, on the 1900 World's Fair in the city, the construction of the Eiffel Tower, and other events that took place in Paris or in France in general. One example of the type of information available to Jewish readers in Eastern Europe is a booklet published in 1814 in Lvov by the rabbi and scholar Shlomo Yehuda Leib Rapoport, titled *Characteristics of Paris, Including a Description of the City (and of the Island Elba)*. Relying on various sources, Rapoport sketched a portrait of the city and the character of its inhabitants. Paris, he asserted, was "the gayest and most elegant city on our entire planet." Another example is a book on Paris by Benyamin Mandelstam. According to Mandelstam, Paris was "the city of cities! All the races and tongues of the world, every exertion of hand and mind." He described its wonders and its darkness:

> I found that Paris, and all its delights, could benefit only those inhabitants who were born there, who have, since birth, been as accustomed to high pleasure as they are to their daily bread, and cannot slake their thirst for new sights. But as for all those who come there from afar, the city drives them away from human morality, for everything there is new to them, and their eyes gaze on without being sated, and they devour every pleasure and every delight . . . and Paris devours their every travail.[17]

The protagonist of a novel by Peretz Smolenskin has a rather different opinion of Paris: he prefers London. Upon arriving in Paris, he writes to his sister:

> Unlike London, all industry and work, this city is ready to burst. Here the tumult of life drowns out the tumult of work and labor in the great streets . . . but my heart does not crave it; I can't endure the clamoring commotion in the streets, and this nation does not capture my heart. The inhabitants here are as unlike the British as the sky is to land. The British man is like a bull straining at his yoke, performing his work gladly.

The French, Smolenskin's protagonist continues, are temperamental and fly rapidly through different moods, while the British are more restrained, yet loyal.[18]

In Jewish literature of the time, French culture—"the French spirit"[19]—represented freedom, permissiveness, and decadence. It was perceived in this way not only by the Orthodox but also by the Jewish intelligentsia in Germany and Eastern Europe. The French tongue, wrote Rabbi Jacob Emden, directly steered its students to "dissipation and obscene language" and at the very least to demonstrations of degeneracy—these being, "as everyone knows . . . the fruit and history of that language."[20] When Samuel

David Luzzatto (known by the acronym Shadal) wished to point out representatives of the empty culture of entertainment in his poem "Derech Eretz or Atheism," he chose several French authors, including Jules Janin, Charles Paul de Kock, and Honoré de Balzac. Germany symbolized decency, while France symbolized untraditional society. In *The Generation of Upheaval*, Shimon Bernfeld described the French intellectual world as beautiful and rich in charm, yet simultaneously clownish, superficial, and devoid of morals and values; it aimed to return man "to his bestial state."[21] This negative attitude is also expressed in Smolenskin's novel, mentioned above, which is set around the time of the Franco-Prussian War. The protagonist writes to his sister that the Jews hang their hopes on France and curse Prussia, which they consider arrogant. But they can expect nothing from France; it is not the nation that brought the world universal values, but rather a land ruled by Catholicism and prejudice. It is true, he continues, that in the past the Jewish people suffered "numerous and terrible injustices" in the German lands, but now things have changed and the Germans are fighting against the Catholics, "our profound enemy."[22] Germany should be judged not by its past but by its future. Ahad Haam regarded France as the clear representative of the decadent spirit of the late nineteenth century; he saw France's attempts to construct a new culture from scratch as futile, a testament to the impossibility of erasing the past. He described reading French literature as not only leading to secularism ("abandoning the faith"), but falling into bad ways.[23]

In October 1897, Herzl repeated this superficial image to the Kaiser and his chancellor—probably in order to win their favor—and added that "those who seek entertainment will always come to France." The chancellor responded: "Yes, cafés and brothels, as they say in Vienna," and the Kaiser declared that the French were "a mad race."[24] Herzl also talked with the French author René Bazin, while sailing from Izmir to Alexandria. In this conversation, he claimed: "mighty literature can disseminate weak ideas throughout the world, . . . but France today has neither great ideas nor a great literature."[25]

This conventional opinion is also expressed in the journalist Elchanan Leib Levinsky's utopian "Masa Leeretz Israel Bishnat 2040." Levinsky writes about a Hebrew teacher and his wife who travel from Russia to spend their honeymoon in Jerusalem and ponder the possibility of arriving there via Paris: "Because today, as in the days of our fathers and mothers, Paris is still the center of life, in the usual sense: the center of hedonism, of dance and fashion, and in general of the good life in the simple sense . . .

Women in particular are drawn to the new Babel."[26] This image of French culture influenced the criticism that emerged regarding the lifestyle and educational system found in the settlements funded by Baron Rothschild. Avraham Shmuel Herschberg—an Orthodox *maskil* and member of Hibbat Zion, a proto-Zionist movement established in the 1880s that promoted Jewish settlement in Palestine, wrote that the baron's sponsorship had brought "the flippant French spirit" to the settlements in Jewish Palestine, and that the schools were educating "wild and immoral Frenchmen, who hate their people and dismiss their Jewish religion."[27]

If this were indeed the prevailing image, we might expect the Jews to keep French culture very much at arm's length. However, on the surface this was not the case. The influence of French culture on the intellectual Jewish elite began at the start of the nineteenth century, when the central topic on the elite's agenda was how to digest the French Revolution, the Napoleonic wars, and their consequences. How these were regarded was influenced by, among other things, the special conditions of Jewish existence in Eastern Europe. The French heritage offered Jews the universal principles of equality and political and civil liberty for the individual—that is, the principles of a democratic or republican regime and the principles of a civil society, including those of separation of church and state and the appearance of a secular society. The French model also offered the principles of national self-determination as well as patriotism and identification with a homeland—a national state.[28]

France could therefore serve as a source of inspiration for various conceptions and models of nationalism, such as republican nationalism, according to which the state is a union of individual parts united, according to their own will, by common law; and integrative nationalism, which emphasizes ethnic and cultural commonality.[29] The principle that nation and state were one and the same presented a great difficulty for Jews in Eastern Europe, who lived in a multinational and multiethnic society and thus preferred enlightened absolutism to democracy, which granted power to the majority. They considered a multinational empire a more comfortable sanctuary than the nation-state. Before World War I, even a radical Jewish movement like the Bund regarded the aspirations to self-rule of various territorial minorities in the Russian Empire—the Poles and Ukrainians—with suspicion and revulsion.[30] However, there were radical *maskilim* who congratulated France for its political culture, primarily for having abolished the Jesuits, overturned the rule of dark faith, and put an end to Catholic antisemitism.[31] France also won praise because it was seen as the begetter of movements that aimed to reform the world. Moses Hess wrote: "England, with its industrial organization, represents the nerve-force of humanity which directs and regulates the alimentary system of mankind; France, that of general motion, namely, the social; Germany discharges the function of thinking." France, he added, effortlessly integrated humanism with nationalism; he described Germany, on the other hand, as Europe's "cogitating brain."[32] Lilienblum wrote that France had not fallen after its defeat by Prussia in 1870 and the rise of the Third Republic: "The Republic will renew its strength, and all who are wise at heart, who cannot find success in the benighted countries, will make their way to France, and there they will gather their strength to fight for truth, to return Man's fate to his own hands; and France's light will yet make its way to all those who dwell in darkness and shadow, under unjust rule and ancient ways of thought. France has not fallen."[33]

Herzl had a rather different opinion of French political culture. His close acquaintance with the French political system inspired a revulsion toward popular politics and a clear preference for the political culture of England. He believed that England's parliamentary regime was significantly preferable to the republican regime in France, which was a fertile ground for extremism and demagoguery. However, this dislike could not prevent the ideas of the French Revolution—namely, a representative democratic government, equality of political and civil rights, and a sovereign public—from becoming fundamental principles in Jewish political thought even before World War I. French thought, particularly the socialist and utopian streams, and French literature such as the French social novel had a great influence on Jewish thinkers, writers, and other creators in Eastern Europe.[34] The output of French culture, in contrast, achieved only secondary standing in the Hebrew cultural marketplace. Out of the hundreds of works translated from Western literature that were published by the Shtibel Publishing House from 1919 to 1939, only some 10 percent were translations of French literature.[35] Similarly, from 1935 to 1939, only 6.1 percent of the 408 films screened in Tel Aviv were in French, compared to 55.8 percent in English and 15.2 percent in German). It is of course difficult to estimate the influence of French literature in translation on Hebrew readers; it is also difficult to determine whether they adopted the behavior of the heroes and heroines of that literature.

In any case, the influence of French culture on the culture of the new Jewish society in Palestine was not limited because of its negative image or because of the fact that France—more accurately Paris, or "Parisian fashion"—symbolized waxing bourgeois tendencies and a desire for luxury; instead, its influence was obstructed due to the absence of effective cultural agents. As a result, French culture's influence on modern Jewish culture was evident mostly in the fields of literature and art, and this was because of the Jewish thinkers, writers, and artists who took up residence in Paris.

"LET US PRAISE ENGLAND"

In *The Travels of Benjamin the Third*, Mendele Mokher Seforim writes about a conversation between the students at the *beit midrash* (house of study) at Tzalmona, where two travelers—Benyamin and Senderl—arrive at the height of the Crimean War (1853–56). The occupants of the *beit midrash* relate fragmented news and rumors about the events taking place in the world outside and extol the glory of Queen Victoria. They also praise England's machines—the steam engine and the train. Indeed, news of England of the Industrial Revolution, the British Empire that ruled the seas and spanned the entire world, had reached even tiny villages in Eastern Europe. England appeared to Jews not only as the opposite of autocratic Russia, but also as the antithesis of pleasure-loving France. Jewish literature made little effort to analyze the French character but attempted to understand the English character in depth, because the latter was considered a central factor in the makeup of England's political culture and methods of government.

England appeared to East European *maskilim* as a positive model of political culture, with its constitutional monarchy and democratic parliament, and its liberal bourgeoisie and respect for tradition.[36] They shared this positive and even reverential perception with various intellectual circles in Europe[37]—and this was well before the birth of the fateful political ties between Zionism and Britain in 1917, and British rule in Palestine. Jewish intellectuals expressed great appreciation for what they regarded as English rationalism, pragmatism, and liberalism. They saw the democratic, parliamentary government as a model and presented it as "an example to all the world":[38] "Yes, dear reader, this legislature is a wonder before the entire world, a sign before many nations to follow its light and to tread its path."[39] England was depicted as a blessed land—the cradle of technological and political progress—despite the great poverty there; and its political and civil culture was considered the highest demonstration of liberty. Kalman Shulman wrote: "Everyone who knows the ways

Manifold Europes

of England is filled with praise for it, and indeed let us praise England, for her government steers straight and true in its doings."[40] The British spirit, wrote Ahad Haam, was one of "liberty, equality, and fellowship."[41] Peretz Smolenskin wrote that unlike the Germans, the British did not wish to impose their worldview upon all other nations. They were a practical people who did not stray toward fantasy and simplistic ideals, because they understood that actions speak louder than words. Their practicality made them the strongest in the world. Smolenskin added:

> [The British people] is one of both thought and action, a people who act but who think before acting . . . These people do not wish to embrace the whole world as do the Ashkenazis [the Germans], nor do they yearn to bring it under their wings and rule over it as do the French; they know that a man's first action must be to look first after his soul, and then after his body, and only then after others, because only in this way can one arrive at the supreme goal of improving the lot of all mankind.[42]

According to Smolenskin, England had not declared war on faith and tradition, and therefore it should be taken as a model for creating improvements and change while maintaining an organic continuity: "and it is our duty to pay attention to this great thing as well, when we wish to launch innovations or reform the Jewish people."[43]

Yet even residence in England was not always enough to instill appreciation for English culture. It was difficult for a Jewish intellectual from Russia to consider it "the cultural capital of the world." In London, Ahad Haam felt "like one who was cast into the great sea and swallowed by its waves—a foreign sapling that, imported from afar, clings to the land here from above in an unnatural way, its roots shallow." As a result, he wrote, he would always feel in England as though he were in "a world that is not mine."[44] Beyond his sensation of being an unwelcome guest, Ahad Haam was impressed by the British codes of behavior—the *Shulhan Arukh* (Jewish legal code) of etiquette, as he put it[45]—and especially by the political culture characterized by self-discipline and ingrained political tradition. He was similarly impressed by the clamor and bustle of the city of London.[46] Despite his distance from English culture, Ahad Haam noted that England in the sixteenth and seventeenth centuries had produced such great spirits as Shakespeare, Bacon, Locke, and Hume, who were "a light before the whole world to this very day."[47] Shakespeare, he wrote, far exceeded Pushkin and Gogol with respect to his overall value to humanity.[48]

As for Herzl, though he was no stranger to British culture, he was impressed most by its parliamentary government, which avoided the flaws of the republican government in France. He was not, however, impressed by England's cultural achievements.[49] Brenner wrote, decisively: "Their modern culture is unimportant, their writing empty and superficial." Still, he added that England had begat such "spiritual" geniuses as Byron, Shelley, Shakespeare, and Carlyle: "and we thank this giant nation, the nation of individual and political freedom, the nation of Locke and Hume, Mill and Darwin."[50] In addition to the contributions of its thinkers to world culture, Brenner found in England a culture worthy of appreciation for its daily life: "It has its good sides too, of course, which a citizen may enjoy: there are many tree gardens, it has peaceful suburbs, it has culture everywhere one goes," and it had "outward political freedom, which cannot be taken lightly at all."[51]

During the first part of Weizmann's stay in England, his impression of English culture was entirely negative. He believed that it was characterized by materialism and lacked poetry and intellectual depth and force. It was inferior to German culture and did not have the abundance of intellectual forces that existed in France:[52] "England is a land of great social contrasts . . . The hypocrisy, querulousness, and shallowness of [English] society are prominently evident . . . Everything here is disguised with a misleading gloss, and internally, why, it is repulsive. England is a land of external 'respectability' that conceals shameful acts, politics, quarrels, private interests—all a great mess."[53] But after a short while, Weizmann changed his mind and became an overt Anglophile. He found that English politics were based on programmatic and realistic thought anchored in empiricism, rather than on formulas or simplistic idealism. "The British genius," he quoted Baron Rothschild, "is its empiricism . . . The Englishman is wary of logical casuistry and written documents," and thus Britain would never sign a constitution. The entire British system was one of oral law.[54]

His Anglophilism convinced Weizmann that England, as he wrote Lord Balfour on November 19, 1917, was a "bulwark of right and justice and of the defence of the weak against the strong."[55] England's decisive role in determining the fate of the Jews, primarily in Palestine, meant that the need to understand the code of English political culture was of the utmost importance.[56] From here arose the urgent need to understand the "British mentality" and their "philosophy of life"—to quote Jabotinsky, who tried, perhaps more than any other Zionist leader, to crack that code. Before and during the British Mandate in Palestine, he devoted numerous articles to this purpose, while claiming that it was impossible to describe a national character: "One can feel it, but not describe it."⁵⁷ According to Jabotinsky's portrayal, the British character was represented by level-headedness, practicality, a businesslike approach, fair play, conservativism, gentlemanliness, and most of all common sense; it had no lofty appetites detached from reality.

Thus the Zionist elite generally acquired a great appreciation for Britain. Even those circles that eventually developed a deep loathing for it and spoke of Britain as "perfidious Albion" could not help admiring various aspects of the British way or recognizing its status as the clear representative of the rational and realistic world. "We are all in favor of the Anglo-Saxon civilization," wrote Aba Achimeir, a radical Revisionist, "but what most represents it is—that the Anglo-Saxon nations are urban nations." According to Achimeir, England symbolized the opposite of the Zionist Socialist ideal, which was an ideal of rural society: "In spite of the old Zionism, Palestine is turning into Manchester, Birmingham, and Liverpool, for the advancement of all Asia. Our fundamental thesis is that the Jewish people are not, at present, an agricultural people. Nor will they be an agricultural people in the future."⁵⁸ At the same time, Achimeir declared that "the age of English culture" was the Elizabethan period, but that "the original spirit of English creativity is weak today, and incomparable to what it was in the time of Shakespeare and Milton."⁵⁹ Thus the Jewish elite in Palestine believed that there was a significant chasm between England—the motherland—and the representatives of British rule in Palestine, with whom the Zionist leadership, and to some extent the public at large, were in close contact.⁶⁰

However, perceptions were not what defined the domain and boundaries of French or British cultural influence on Jewish culture in Palestine. These were decided by the presence and activity of cultural agents, as well as by the affinity for that culture fostered through its literature. In contrast to the sparse activity of French cultural agents in Palestine, the British presence there during the Mandate had a deep influence on how the legislative, judicial, and executive systems were implemented in the Jewish community.⁶¹ The Mandate and knowledge of the English language made the presence of various components of English culture possible. It was even claimed that "precedence must be given to English literature, history, geography, and economics in comparison to [those of] other nations . . . Our students must understand the English spirit and way of life, the qualities and habits of the English man, the way he thinks and reasons."[62] English literature in translation occupied an increasingly central position in the corpus of literature translated into Hebrew: until 1920, scarcely any books had been translated from English, but from 1930 to 1936, ninety-three books were translated from English, out of the 300 translated from various European languages. Not everyone approved of the ever-growing presence of literature translated from English. The author Yaakov Rabinovitz wrote, uneasily, that "the translated works are mostly garbage, or mediocre stock . . . Overnight, our readers of foreign literature have abandoned Dostoevsky in favor of Edgar Wallace."[63]

Thus it might be said that the elites of modern Jewish political culture and of Hebrew culture in Jewish Palestine acquired their ideological and political outlook, and their practical political experience, from Eastern Europe. It was there that they absorbed ideologies and experienced attempts at mending the world, and it was there that they learned the methods of modern political action. However, ultimately the templates of political society and its values were built on the foundations and principles of the British political regime. It is therefore possible to distinguish between, on the one hand, political mentality and political action with respect to political parties—which originated in the political culture of Eastern Europe, in particularly its revolutionary culture—and the principles of formal political behavior on the other.[64]

In concluding this brief examination, we should mention that within the political and cultural discourse in Jewish society in Palestine—and in Israeli society today—England and France do not represent a declining, disintegrating Western culture. The negative heritage of European culture is symbolized primarily by Germany and Eastern Europe, rather than by cultural values associated with England and France. Still, and at times ironically, when Europe is referred to negatively in the public discourse and polemics, that rhetoric relegates both English and French culture to the group of cultures whose traits—which modern Jewish society has taken on and internalized—should be rejected. It would not be a wild conjecture to suppose that most of the opponents of European influence or European culture do not seriously believe that Israeli society should alter itself to expunge these traits.

Manifold Europes

88

I AM IN THE EAST, AND MY HEART IS IN THE WEST

*Judea has always seemed to me like a fragment
of the Occident misplaced in the Orient.*
HEINRICH HEINE,
"Geständnisse" (Confessions)[1]

---

*Come, I will tell you, brothers, that not only our faces are
set to the East; the entire West travels eastward again.*
MORDECHAI ZEEV FEIERBERG,
Whither?[2]

---

*The Jewish people will become part of European
civilization or cease to exist entirely.*
NATHAN BIRNBAUM,
Ost und West (East and West)

On April 26, 1896, Herzl wrote to the Grand Duke Friedrich of Baden: "If it is God's will that we return to our historic fatherland, we should like to do so as representatives of Western civilization, and bring cleanliness, order, and the well-distilled customs of the Occident to this plague-ridden, blighted corner of the Orient. We shall have to do this so as to be able to exist there, and this obligation will educate our people to the extent that they need it."[3]

On September 21, 1898, he repeated: "The return of even the semi-Asiatic Jews under the leadership of thoroughly modern persons must undoubtedly mean the restoration to health of this neglected corner of the Orient." According to him, this restoration would take place because the Jews would bring "civilization and order" with them and thereby alter the history of the region. They would be a "foundation of German culture in the Orient."[4] Germany's patronage of the Zionist movement,

Herzl maintained, would permit Jews to love Germany: "If we should succeed in initiating an organized exodus of the proletarians to be settled, it would engage the interest of the German polity. Actually, it is an element of German culture that would come to the Eastern shores of the Mediterranean."[5]

By "thoroughly modern persons," Herzl was referring to the Jewish elite that had absorbed and internalized German culture. Herzl borrowed the classification of Jews as Asiatic from nineteenth-century anti-Jewish German literature, though he softened it and dubbed them "semi-Asiatic."

Moses Hess predated Herzl in this Zionist version of the white man's burden when he wrote: "It is well understood that we speak of a Jewish settlement in the Orient. We do not, however, mean to imply a total emigration of the Occidental Jews to Palestine. Even after the establishment of a Jewish State, the majority of the Jews who live at present in the civilized Occidental countries will undoubtedly remain where they are."[6]

Hess added that these Jews, "who have only recently broken their way through to culture and have acquired an honorable civic position, will not abandon the valuable acquisition so quickly even if the restoration of Judaea were more than a pious desire."[7] If so, it was not "Asia that [would] regenerate Europe," as Gustave Flaubert wrote, but rather Europe that would "regenerate Asia."[8]

BETWEEN ASIA AND THE ORIENT

Three issues mentioned above pertain to the subject at hand. First, the majority of Europe's Jews are described as semi-Asiatics who would be led by an entirely modern elite, which had absorbed and internalized German culture, and which thus would be an "element of German culture" on the shores of the Mediterranean. Second, the Orient is described as a backward, neglected part of the world. And third, the Jews' return to the land of their forefathers in the Orient was intended to enable them not to shed their Europeanness, but to be European by choice. Not only did European Jews, whom Europe perceived as strangers, not perceive European culture as oppressive and wish to cast it off, but they undertook the mission of disseminating agents of European culture throughout the Orient.

But what was this "Orient"?

The Orient did not know itself as such; it was not aware that it was a single homogeneous entity until the West named and categorized it as the Orient, or the Middle East. The Arab Muslim world knew itself as *Dar al-Islam* (the house of Islam) rather than as the Oriental world or the Arab world. "The Orient" was created as a name and categorization from the Eurocentric point of view, which attributed ontological characteristics that did not originate in religion to the followers of the Muslim faith. It should be noted that in Western literature, the Orient was not only the Muslim world: the name also referred to the Semitic nations of the ancient Near East, the cultures of Mesopotamia (and of ancient Egypt, which was not Semitic) as well as the Jews and Judaism of antiquity. These ancient cultures were described as the diametric opposite of Greco-Roman culture: Semitic culture was pitted against Indo-European (Aryan) culture. Orientalist expertise (*Orientalistik*) meant expertise in the Bible and the ancient Semitic languages, not just in Arabic. At times, the Orient was also divided into the biblical and the nonbiblical Orient.[9] This terminology was accepted in Jewish literature; for example, Simon Dubnow titled the first part of his *History of the Jewish People*, published in 1923, "Orientalische Periode" (The Oriental period). In any case, within the nineteenth century's categorization, the Jewish-Christian and Aryan-Semitic antinomies became more widespread and useful than the antinomy between the Orient and the West.

During the nineteenth century, the East-West antinomy found its way from European literature to Jewish literature, which employed the concept for its own purposes. These two imaginary geocultural regions— Asia and the Orient—also appeared in Jewish literature as denoting two homogeneous human cultural essences. The word "Orient" did not always refer to the (Arab or Ottoman) Muslim Orient; sometimes it meant a mythical, Semitic, or biblical Orient that was born of the imagination—an Orient depicted as a backward region awaiting salvation by the West, or, inversely, as an enlightened region awakened from a long slumber and destined to become the savior and hope of the West.[10]

There is a good deal of irony in the way Jewish columnists made use of the antinomy between the Orient and the West. European Jews, especially those who insisted on being considered Europeans for all intents and purposes, were described by German antisemites as *Orientalisches Fremdlingsvolk* (a foreign Asiatic people), dwelling in and polluting a continent which was not their own.[11] They claimed that the Jews were a nation whose origin lay in the Orient, and that its spirit and culture, which had been defined there, were fundamentally different from the spirit and culture of Europe's Indo-European nations. The Jew was the enemy of humanity (that is, of the West), the French utopian Pierre-Joseph Proudhon wrote in his diary in 1847; therefore it was "necessary to return this race to Asia or to destroy it."[12] By "Asia," he meant Semitic Asia rather than the Indo-European (Aryan) Asia. In Russian, the word *Aziat* (Азиат), which is the source of the common Hebrew pronunciation, was charged with negative connotations and indicated traits such as laziness, ignorance, and degeneration. The term acquired the same meaning in other European languages and made its way from these to Hebrew. The result was that nineteenth-century Hebrew literature contains more than a few scathing references to "idle, unruly Asiatics" and to an Asia "full of dark, rotten spirits."[13] "Asia," according to the writer David Frischman, "was, for us, always a symbol of evil and darkness, of ignorance and trouble, to the extent that we called an evil deed an 'Asian deed.' Asia is the land to which we must arrive as intellectuals in every field and perfect in every science . . . the spirit of the Enlightenment in general flows eternally from East to West."[14] He therefore reasoned that it was necessary to guarantee that immigrants to Palestine would not assimilate with the Arabs, who were "Asians in the full sense of the word."[15] When Itamar Ben Avi, a journalist and the son of Eliezer Ben Yehuda, declared "we are Asiatics," he was not, of course, referring to this "degenerate Asia."

Within Jewish literature, there was a preference for terms such as the "Orient" and "the revival of the Orient" because, unlike the word "Asia," the Russian word for Orient (*Vostok*) was not laden with negative connotations. In addition, there was a widespread fashion of "positive Orientalism"[16] among German intellectual circles at the end of the nineteenth century, and the utopian Orient was not perceived negatively as it was under its Orientalist depiction in Britain and France—a depiction in which the Orient was a frozen, backward world inhabited by a society ruled for centuries by fatalism and fanaticism. Instead, it was considered the wellspring for a soul abundant in creative spirituality.[17] Seemingly, therefore, the call to "return to the Orient" and the description of Arabs as "our brothers by blood, members of the Semitic tribes"[18] attested to the fact that Zionism did not see itself as a colonialist movement attempting to instill its ancient native culture in a new and foreign place, but rather as the result of Jews' bitter disappointment with European culture. The appearance of this positive depiction of the Orient in Zionist discourse seems to express a rejection of the degenerate West as well as a search for an old source of redemption that would inspire a new, complete, and authentic Jewish experience (*Jüdisches Wesen*). In Buber's opinion, for example, only in Palestine could the Jewish people's primordial strength be renewed and expressed to its full extent.[19] The utopian portrait of the Orient as a complete alternative to the West, and the belief that it would revive Europe, were borrowed primarily from the European counterculture that depicted the imaginary Orient as the absolute alternative to European culture and the European character, with its bourgeois values. Since Europe was deeply mired in malaise—materialism, nihilism, decadence, and a Philistine, bourgeois mentality—it was necessary to escape from it to distant lands, even imaginary ones. German *Volkists* and Russian Slavophiles[20] proposed authentic medieval culture and an even earlier mythological past as alternatives. "Civilization," Dostoevsky wrote, "has long since been condemned in the West itself." What Russia needed was primarily "nature"; that is, "nature is needed first of all, then science, then an independent, native, unconstrained life and a faith in one's own national strength."[21] "The monster of civilization," predicted the Slavophile mystic Nikolai Berdyaev, was leading Europe toward destruction.[22]

In contrast to Eduard Gans's call to German Jews to shed their Oriental identity and assimilate into Europe, Martin Buber wrote that the way to salvation and rehabilitation for the Jewish collective "I" was to disconnect itself from Europe, which was sinking into a deep mire. Only then could Jews create an organic, rooted Judaism full of new strength. The utopian, imaginary Orient and its sensory nature were thus perceived by Buber as a cure for the profound schism and fatal illness that modern Western culture inflicted upon Jewish existence. The cure to the ills of the mechanical, atrophying Western culture would be found only outside of Europe, in the Orient. Only there could a complete, healthy, vital, and creative Judaism be reborn.[23] And only there, wrote the poet Uri Zvi Greenberg, could the Jews—an "Oriental handful," whom Europe regarded as "low, Semitic creatures"—give expression to their identity as an organic and territorial racial group. For this reason, Greenberg extolled the pioneers who left behind all of Europe's splendor in order to be "members of the cult of the barefoot and feverish" in Palestine.[24]

In this context, it is impossible not to return to the exhortation that concludes Feierberg's *Whither?*: "If it is true that there is a goal for Israel, then gird yourselves with Torah and its goal, and bring them along to the East . . . but not to Palestine alone, to all the East."[25] Feierberg borrowed the imaginary portrait of the East from Benjamin Disraeli's historical novel *Tancred*;[26] however, he did not clarify what he meant by "the East" or what were the spiritual and cultural traits of this East, which were to be a source of salvation for the Jewish people. Even earlier, on May 18, 1882, the young writer Moshe Aizman published an article in *Hamelitz* titled "Pnei halot ve halot," in which he called for separation from "European civilization with its belief in force and its manifest sins," and for a return to the Orient: "There we will carry the principles of Semitic civilization among the Arab tribes, our relations. And the meaning of a Semitic civilization is wisdom and morality, love of mankind and peace."[27]

Not all intellectuals were enchanted by this exhortation. Lilienblum, for example, considered it a reactionary call to abandon the heritage of the Enlightenment, and warned against the Romantic perception that transformed "Asiatic laziness" and the Arab Orient—the latter, in his opinion, a world of unbearable backwardness—into an ideal.[28] However, even Lilienblum believed that Jews were "alien Asiatics" in Europe and must therefore return to the Orient, since Europe held no answers to the questions of life and religion: "In Europe our faith will not be reformed, and in Europe we have no life . . . The education here is a European one in all respects"—in other words, a corrupting education.[29] However, Lilienblum did not mean to claim that the immigrants to Palestine would leave behind the cultural assets of the West: "The majority of our people will labor mightily to follow in the Europeans' way of life, and will resemble them in all their customs. And why would you bind them under the wings of *Asia's spirit* when she will not succeed, for Asia's spirit will wander and merely pass as a shadow before the spirit of Europe, whose path is one of storms and tempests" (emphasis in the original).[30] Despite this, his words were interpreted as a call to abandon Europeanness, and Y. L. Gordon believed that Lilienblum stood at the head of the camp of those who "revolt against Europe's Enlightenment and say: Let us . . . return to Asia." Gordon described the revolution he underwent from tradition to Enlightenment as a direct result of discovering that he was "a wild Asian . . . in enlightened Europe," but his objection to the idea of a return to Zion derived from his opinion that the Jews had not yet absorbed the values of the European Enlightenment. It was thus too early to speak of a return to the Orient; a premature return would lead to a cultural reaction and the establishment of a dark, unenlightened, Orthodox Jewish state in which, among other things, "on holy days and the Sabbath the [trains] would suddenly cease to run, and the telegraph lines would be silent."[31] Gordon asked: "If we immigrate to Palestine from Europe and do not take with us the yield of its Enlightenment—what do we immigrate for?"[32]

In 1897, the German Jewish statesman Walther Rathenau called upon German Jews to examine themselves in the mirror as a first step toward self-criticism, and to shake off all Asiatic characteristics so that they might be accepted as an inseparable part of the Western experience.[33] In contrast, as noted above, Martin Buber—who, under the influence of Germany's cultural pessimism, transformed himself from a disciple of Romantic nationalism into someone wary of the strengthening of conservative, nationalistic Romanticism and the disintegration of bourgeois, capitalistic society—saw the Orient as an alternative to the atrophying West. Buber described the Orient as a metacultural essence with unique ontological spiritual properties. In his opinion, Europe was eternally in need of a unified organic principle but was unable to generate it itself; hence it required the Orient. However, Buber refrained from calling for an exchange of European culture with Jewish or Chinese culture. Nor did he define the contents and values of the ideal Oriental culture. His call to Jews to return to the East declared only that the Jewish man needed to remove himself from his unnatural environment in Europe in order to achieve salvation of the soul (*Erlösung*) and realize his full human authenticity in his natural place. It is also important to note that there is no Islam in Buber's Asia and Orient; his is the Asia of the prophet Isaiah, Buddha and Laotzu, Jesus and Paul—but not Mohammed.[34] The German Jewish writer Jakob Wassermann also described Jews as Oriental in the sense that they were creative and vigorous and did not yearn to detach themselves from their past, becoming lonely, rootless individualists. The Oriental Jewish man, in the mystical rather than ethnographical sense, was fully realized and confident in his humanity—a serene man, devoid of envy, creative, and free.[35] The Orient—that is, Palestine—was the place where Semitic Jews could detach themselves from divisive forces and create an authentic, or organic, Jewish culture and a modern civilization. Civilization was the jar; Judaism—after the renaissance that would transpire—would be its contents. In the Orient, the contradiction between civilization and culture would be erased, and a perfect harmony would arise between them. In Nathan Birnbaum's vision, a Jewish *Volkstum* would arise in the Orient as a full partner in the great European civilization.[36]

The European Semitic Jew would return to the Orient, which shrank from the spirit of the West, in order to serve it as a teacher and draw it closer to the culture of the West.[37] In a meeting of the Zionist General Council on August 28, 1919, Weizmann said: "Only in Palestine is it possible to achieve our lives' ideal. We live in civilized countries and borrow their culture. This reality has given rise to the fundamental differences between us. They erupt even when we set out to create our own country. Our role now is to erect a bridge between the two worlds, but those crossing this bridge must approach it from both ends."[38]

The myth of the Orient was one thing, reality another. Buber did not call on Germany's Jews to dissociate themselves from Europe; moreover, he wrote that "those who travel to live in Palestine among a Hebrew community . . . will carry German spiritual assets in their very souls."[39] That is, he did not call upon them to abandon the humanist tradition of the West, but simply to leave behind its dark side and the wild overgrowth it sprouted; certainly he did not ask them to leave behind every asset of that culture. In Buber's utopian vision, Jews would assume a central role in the renewal of the world after World War I by serving as mediators between Europe and the Orient. In other words, the Zionist movement had a missionary calling in the Orient. Like Hess, Herzl, and others, Buber was not free of paternalism or a sense of superiority:

> We, who wish to go to Palestine as mediators between Europe and Asia, are not able to appear before the Orient, which is rising from a deep dream, as the messengers of that same West that is soon due to decline, and thus incur its justified suspicion; we were chosen to be messengers to a West that is being recreated, to help our Oriental brothers to establish, through an alliance with this West and by their own efforts, a real society, a life which they did not even know to aspire to until now because of the Oriental effendis and the Western effendis, who prevented them from doing it . . . The matter is in our hands, whether we appear before the Orient's waking eye as agents and hated spies or as beloved teachers and artist-creators.[40]

A vision of a Middle East that underwent a profound process of Europeanization was also put forth by Hans Kohn, a Zionist activist who eventually became a fierce critic of Zionism and a well-known scholar of nationalism. From Jerusalem in 1934 he wrote that despite the fact that Europe was undergoing a difficult crisis, the magic of Europe ensured that a process of Europeanization took place throughout every nation in the Middle East, albeit at varying speeds. The culture of Western Europe had become a universal culture, influencing thought throughout the world and celebrating its victory across the globe. Now members of ancient cultures were stirring from their centuries-long sleep, and a new stage of human development was at hand.[41]

"WE ARE WESTERNERS"

Many Jews expressed fear that the exodus from Europe to the desert, or untamed Asia would result in a painful and intolerable separation from Europe and its culture. In September 1882, Vladimir Zeev Dubnow, a member of the Bilu movement, wrote from Jaffa to his brother Simon—the historian, then living in St. Petersburg—about the cultural deprivation he and his friends experienced because of the lack of newspapers in Palestine. He added, "In short—this is untamed Asia rather than cultured Europe, which becomes more precious to me every day."[42] In early 1910, Dov Ber Borochov wrote to his wife that he did not wish to tie his fate to the "sleepy cultures of the Orient," and that the cultural foundations of his development would suffer if he went to Palestine because it "does not have the libraries I need." If he nonetheless went to Palestine, he added, he would do so because it was better to develop thoughts on virgin ground than to live in an already mature culture.[43]

However, the Jewish migration from Europe to Palestine was generally perceived not as an act that would bring about a complete disengagement from Western culture, but as one that would enable Jewish culture to be reborn by choice. An immigrant may decide which cultural assets he carries with him to sow in the new land, and which assets he relinquishes; he is also freed from the temptations and pressures of the surrounding foreign culture that he leaves. According to this perception, emigration to Palestine offered Jews their only option for acculturation into European culture without risk of assimilation and absorption, because it created the only possibility to selectively transfer Europe to Palestine. Only there could Jews be European and Jewish at the same time. Jews would create the real Europe—Europe as it should be—beyond the borders of that continent.[44]

Statements of this sort were intended, among other things, to assuage concerns about the ramifications of distance and separation from Europe: not only would immigrants to Palestine not find themselves disconnected from European civilization, but they would act as missionaries and agents of that culture in the Orient. "Yes, we are Westerners, in life and in spirit. We can bring the West to the Orient; our strength is drawn from Europe"—these resolute words were written by the essayist Yaacov Rabinovitz in a 1922 article. These words and those he wrote a few years later—in a lengthy comment on his translation of an article by Nikolai Berdyaev[45]—were a reaction to what Rabinovitz saw as mystical and antirational perceptions that expressed a longing for a "new Asiatic culture"—a sort of Jewish Slavophilia that was nourished by the mistaken assumption that "the West was in decline," and by the belief that salvation would come "from the Orient." To speak of "the decline of the West" and of how rationalism and modernity had lost their way, wrote Rabinovitz, was to engage in reactionary eschatology. In effect, revelations of the crisis in Western society and culture were natural, and certainly not evidence of a decline. Rabinovitz ridiculed those who proposed the Orient as an alternative: "One can hate Europe; but he who loves Asia—let him first live in it and know it." Jews not only belonged to Europe, they contributed to its construction:

> The Bible itself proves how Western it is. It traveled to the West and not to the East . . . not only did the Bible go to the West, but we too went with it . . . It is a fact that the Orient neither absorbed nor expelled the Jew, while at the same time the persecution in the West was all in vain: the Jew remained there and his Bible joined the Western hearth . . . The shape of our lives in Palestine is also Western, and the Oriental Jew comes toward us rather than we toward him. By the way, he himself tended more toward France than toward the Arab world.[46]

Rabinovitz also pointed to the disparity between, on the one hand, the call to return to the Orient as a slogan or metaphor that was—in the spirit of conservative ideology and Romanticism—nothing more than a longing for an organic way of life, and, on the other hand, the fact that those who called for a return to the East were strongly influenced by the European heritage and wished to live a typical European lifestyle.

Such declarations of loyalty toward Europe also arrived from Jews who profoundly criticized European society and culture and even described it as unhealthy. This represented an internal critique, not a delight in doomsaying or a bid for divorce. The sharpest critics of Western culture were unwilling to relinquish most of the European assets that European Jews had adopted throughout the nineteenth century. Even feelings of disappointment and disenchantment did not lead them to the conclusion that they must relinquish all of Europe's spiritual and cultural assets and uproot the Europeanness from the Jewish experience. The situation in Palestine appeared different from the traditionalists' perspective: for instance, in Avraham Shmuel Herschberg's report about his journey to Palestine in 1899–1900, he tallied the pianos—ten in all—that he found in settlers' houses in Rishon Letzion and wrote of one of the settlers of Petach-Tikva (a native of his own city, Białystok): "In Białystok this family would have seen several generations pass by before arriving at such a level: Palestine has become a shortcut to European culture." Evidence of "European education" were the books Herschberg found in the settlement's libraries: works by Emile Zola, Alphonse Daudet, Eugene Sue, as well as Russian novels. He wrote: "A native of my city would not see his daughters, even his granddaughters, attending a high school, nor his grandsons learning French." Herschberg criticized what seemed like an attempt to "bring in humanism and Europeanism," but at the same time he claimed that without the infusion of European material culture into Palestine, the Jewish settlers would not be able to rise above the "backward, Asiatic" living conditions of the Arab inhabitants.[47] In contrast, in 1898 the teacher David Yudlevitz expressed his pride in the books found in private homes in the settlement, including books by Ferdinand Lassalle, Charles Darwin, Victor Hugo, Ernest Renan, and Blaise Pascal, and British, Ashkenazi, Russian, and other classics—both in the original texts and in translation.[48] Another settler, Menashe Meirovitz, complained in an 1887 letter about the lack of world literature in the settlement: "We, who are already cut off from European civilization, need [books] in order to rest by reading them and to ponder over them after a day's hard labor. They are the greatest and most honest friends of humanity."[49]

MIMICKING EUROPEAN CULTURE?— EUROPE AS CULTURAL HERITAGE AND ASSET

The return to the Orient—that is, to Palestine—was therefore not meant to uproot Europeanness from the Jewish experience. The accepted opinion was that the Jews had become a European people, and that in Palestine they intended to forge an amalgamation of Jewish and European culture. The urgent question was thus to determine the substance of this new culture, as well as how to create the desired blend of European culture and original Jewish culture (whose essence and substance were themselves a matter of contention). A stormy debate over this question erupted after the 1902 publication of *Altneuland*, Herzl's utopian novel. Ahad Haam wrote a venomous review of *Altneuland*, in which he described Herzl's fictional Jewish society as "blindly aping" European culture. According to him, Herzl promised the Jews that they would achieve in Palestine what they were unable to achieve in Europe. Ahad Haam's primary criticism was aimed at what he saw as the absence of "Jewish and Hebrew character" in Herzl's imagined future society. However, Ahad Haam did not specify which negative European foundations he believed Herzl wished to instill in this society and did not propose an alternative cultural repertoire.[50]

Ahad Haam's argument was justified to some extent. In *The Jewish State*, Herzl wished to reassure those who feared moving away from civilization. He declared that it was possible to transfer a culture from its location and to plant it elsewhere:

> There are English hotels in Egypt and on the mountain peaks of Switzerland, Vienna cafes in South Africa, French theaters in Russia, German operas in America, and the best Bavarian beer in Paris. When we depart from Egypt once again we shall not leave the fleshpots behind.[51]

In a similar spirit, Herzl wrote in his diary on June 7, 1895, that it would be necessary to supply the inhabitants of the Jewish state with *circenses* (mass entertainment): "'German theaters,' 'international theaters,' 'operas,' 'operettas,' 'circuses,' 'concert cafés,' and 'cafés Champs-Élysées.'"[52] The novel *Altneuland* is an ode to the utilization of European technology and science for the purpose of creating an advanced model society. There is almost no sign in the novel of the presence of Jewish culture in the new Jewish society. European culture has full reign: ladies chat about the latest Parisian hats and order their clothes directly from stores on the rue de la Paix; in a party held by the painter Isaacs in his charming Jerusalem villa, which is full of rare art treasures, his daughter, Miriam, sings songs by Schumann, Rubinstein, Wagner, and Gounod—but not songs of Zion—and concludes with the "Lied von Mignon" from Goethe's novel *Wilhelm Meister*: "Kennst du das Land, wo die Zitronen blühen?" (Know'st thou the land where lemon trees bloom).[53] Theater troupes from France and Italy appear in Haifa alongside popular comedies in Yiddish, the biblical play *Moses*, and the opera *Shabtai Tzvi*, but these are not, according to Herzl, the main part of the new Jewish high culture.

Herzl was defended by Nordau, who had pointed out the flaws of European civilization during the nineteenth century and had warned in 1897 that Europe was declining in status.[54] In Herzl's defense, Nordau sang the praises of "Old Europe" and declared that Ahad Haam's suggestion amounted to returning to a state of barbarism that would transform Jewish society into "a wild Asiatic enclave hostile to culture."[55] The Jewish society of the future that Nordau envisioned was a liberal society whose culture would perfectly combine Jewish culture with bourgeois European culture:

> In effect, *Altneuland* is a slice of Europe in Asia. So Herzl has shown us the vision that suits us precisely, the one toward which we strive. We wish that the people returning to its homeland—the Jewish people, once again united and freed from the foreigners' yoke—may remain a cultured people . . . We need not imitate others; we use only our own assets, and we develop them. We have contributed our part to European culture more than we have to our own culture; this culture belongs to us to the same degree that it belongs to the Germans, French, or English. We will not permit a contradiction to be posited between what belongs to us—what is Jewish—and what is European . . . The Jewish people will fully display its uniqueness amid the general European culture.[56]

Nordau also pointed to the internal contradiction buried in the apparent anti-Europeanness voiced by Ahad Haam and several others. According to him, these critics were Europeans despite their outright rejection of Europe's cultural assets and values.[57] Nordau, who had described European culture at the end of the nineteenth century as degenerate, did not believe that the Orient and Asiatic wildness would deliver Jews from the ravages of the decadent West, or East European Jews from the heritage of the ghetto. He came out decisively against those Zionist writers and thinkers who believed that in the Orient, the Jews would be freed from the corruption they inherited from Europe. What Nordau—like Herzl—did believe was that the Jews would bring the West to the Orient; along the way, they would be able to shed all of Europe's ailments and establish a perfect European Jewish society.[58]

The writer Y. C. Brenner responded in a similar manner, though less enthusiastically, to the criticism of Western culture in Hebrew literature. Although it was true, he wrote, that European humanity was faltering, and that it lacked equality:

> What can we do—Europe does not cease to be what she is, even after her treatment of us. That is the truth! Even without her treatment of us she is no symbol of perfection, and even given her treatment of us she is no symbol of depravity. What she has earned and created—not without labor, nor without sacrificed lives—is hers; she is its sovereign, and she lives and lives on as she is able. She is, after all, Europe.[59]

Brenner ridiculed those who claimed that Europe's "spiritual leanings" originated in Judaism and that "Europe, in her ambition to be inclusive—Europe, in following the fundamental line of subjectivity and uniqueness—Europe, in her wish to be elevated to a higher morality—Europe, in her concept of family life—borrowed it all from Israel!"[60]

The most European among the nationalistic Jewish intelligentsia was Zeev Jabotinsky.[61] He described the nineteenth century as a period shaped by an "instinct of the game"—a sort of drive for grand, creative adventure.[62] Twentieth-century Europe had grown apart from the values of the previous century and now adhered to totalitarianism, but this was not necessarily reason to despair of it, and certainly no reason to see the Orient as the alternative to Western culture. In contrast to Buber and the other Zionist Orientalists who were swept along by Buber's opinions and charmed by shallow, exotic Orientalism, Jabotinsky declared: "we, the Jews, have nothing in common with what is known as the 'Orient.'" Like Nordau, he believed that Zionism would extend "Europe's borders to the Euphrates" and clear away all traces of the "Oriental soul" from the memories of the Jews in Palestine, both present and future. Jabotinsky described the Orient as characterized by fatalism and an absence of ethical protest, while Europe, in contrast, was characterized by unending searching, destruction, and reconstruction. The Orient was ruled by tyranny, while Europe had parliamentary democracy, freedom of the press, and public oversight. The Orient was ruled by Islam, which arbitrated every dimension of life, while in Europe, religion had a limited role and did not interfere with cultural and social life. The Orient was "the scarf, the harem, theological fanaticism, patriarchal (that is, despotic) family structure, and, worse yet, a feudal system of tribe and state . . . This 'picturesque' way of life is almost always the sort of existence whose structure must necessarily and mercilessly be changed from top to bottom."[63]

If so, Jabotinsky asked, were the Jews who returned to the Orient not likely to fall into its trap? His answer was that Europe as a geographical concept was not identical to the cultural concept of European. An emigrant from Europe, he wrote—echoing Herzl—took Europe with him everywhere he went. A Jew who emigrated to Palestine would take with him the European tradition that was close to his heart and that had been absorbed into his people's blood for two thousand years; he would continue to cultivate and develop the tradition in Palestine: "We go to Palestine in order to shift Europe's traditional border to the Euphrates,"[64] since "the good of the land demands the replacement of the camel caravan specifically with the train," and "we wish the same for our neighbors in Asia: a living and vital 'Orient' as soon as possible."⁶⁵

Jabotinsky called on the Arab population of the Middle East to "abolish the Orient with haste," but he believed that it would be able to do so only after generations of Western guardianship that would replace the camel caravans with motor vehicles. Only after the Orient "passed through the British school," he declared, would it be able to free itself from the Oriental spirit and be reborn.⁶⁶ And what, Jabotinsky asked, made Jews European in heart and soul? He answered: the fact was that "Europe from a moral point of view is 'ours,'" just as much as it belonged to its nations. Its moral pathos and idea of progress—"the entire gap between two worldviews, which is expressed in the antithesis of two beliefs: the 'Golden Age' and the 'Messiah,' an ideal from the past and an ideal for the future—these traits were given to Europe by us, a long time before our ancestors came to Europe. We brought the Bible with us in a ready form." The Jews made a decisive contribution toward Europe's intellectual development in all areas and were among its primary creators. Western culture was therefore "part and parcel" of Judaism, flesh of its flesh and spirit of its spirit. Consequently, to escape from "Westernness" meant "to deny ourselves." Still, he hastened to add a caveat: his reference was not to Europe as a single entity, but to "moral Europe."

It should be observed that Jabotinsky objected strongly to the essentialist view and maintained that the Orient was "not just a specific stage in cultural development, but a type of development in itself,"⁶⁷ which could undergo change. It was a fact that various Oriental peoples imitated the West in their ways of life: they wore European clothes, established universities, abolished harems, and so forth. Furthermore, Europe was also undergoing similar processes of cultural transformation. No phenomena were particular to a single race; they were particular only to a specific stage in its development.

The radical revisionist Aba Achimeir also declared that the Zionists were by nature Western. "The nation of Israel is a Western nation, or, more precisely, *the* Western Nation, with a definite article!" (emphasis in the original).⁶⁸ This Western orientation was not only the province of the Zionist Right. Chaim Arlosoroff wrote:

> I have a Western, European orientation (the Mediterranean has always been Europe, not Asia). We must not be ashamed of the fact that we wish to ensure that Palestine will look to the West, and not

to the dervishes. Europe has an interest in a European settlement existing here, and not in this land becoming part of Asia.[69]

When Ben Gurion spoke of return to the Orient, he too referred to it as a place rather than an essence. Thus in August 1935, he said at the eighteenth Zionist Congress:

> We are returning to the Orient, but we bring the enlightenment of Western culture to the land [of Palestine], and alongside all of our efforts to once again settle in our Oriental homeland and come into friendly contact with our Oriental neighbors, we will preserve the eternal contact with the centers of Western culture. The Mediterranean Sea will be a bridge to the cultural world of the West—of Europe and America—to the great centers of the Jewish Diaspora.[70]

To Uri Zvi Greenberg, Europe did not symbolize moral values; on the contrary, he described Europe—Slavic Europe, in effect—as a place saturated with pathological hatred for Jews. According to him, Jews were forced to leave because "the land shrieked beneath their feet." But Greenberg could not free himself from his profound affection for Europe, and he described it in two ways: the Jews' natural landscape, at the center of which stood the autochthonous village, characterized by an organic rhythm of life and a direct affinity for nature; and the culture of the modern metropolis. The European experience as described by Greenberg included the following ingredients: buckets and challah; wells and mills; flutes and Ukrainian songs; the ringing of church bells; thatched roofs and red rafters; red apples and cows' bellows; cafes, operas, boulevards, dance halls; museums and libraries; electricity and the steam engine.[71] To abandon this Europe meant abandoning a familiar and formerly beloved world, which the Jews had been forced to hate. Greenberg saw Zionism as a movement established to take "a people born and buried in Europe for centuries upon centuries and move them to the alien Orient," in order to transform them into "a landed people in the Arab sea, like a European lighthouse ... to serve as an important political factor and avant-garde for European-Hebrew culture."[72] The Jews—"lowly Semitic creatures, a handful from the Orient"—came "from Europe to the home of Arab custom, and our vibrant cultural project, which is unique in the Orient, became the avant-garde for European progress and the entry of its government into that desert during the great industrial age."[73] The portrait he proposed of Jewish revival combined ideas from the European school of Romantic and religious conservatism and from the world of modern utopias that found in the steam engine, concrete, and steel the typical expression of the modern world: "If some Messiah is born, we hope he will not rise in the Galilean wilderness but in a Galilean district in which there are electricity, automobiles, hygienic houses, and motor-boats on the Sea of Galilee."[74]

Misgivings and longings for the Europe left behind appear in a chapter of a diary printed in the anthology *Kehiliateinu* (Our community):

> Spiritual Europe—old, ostracized, accursed Europe, in which everyone finds faults—how spacious and lovely she is, and how I yearn for her! After all she is the spirit we inhaled, the marrow of our bones! The Orient, with its depths of wisdom, is shrouded in fog, a sort of region beyond the *Sambatyon*, which may not be approached except on the Sabbath.[75]

At the same time, Europe was described in this anthology as "godforsaken, with paltry culture, thirsting for pleasure," and sentimental.[76] Its cultural assets—theaters, concerts, museums, and libraries—were only its outward expressions.[77] Europe symbolized unacceptable petit bourgeois values: "If an immigrant-pioneer were to import a 'European' suit—he would hide it in his wicker basket or wooden chest. On the street, wearing a blazer was a faux-pas that might suggest the taint of the micro-bourgeoisie on its wearer. Most proscribed and excluded of all was the necktie."[78] Tel Aviv, the new Hebrew city, was characterized by a "childish, pitiable Europeanness."[79] A longing for the organic culture of "a small community full of all that was sacred and hidden in the fog of pure beauty" was expressed in *Kehiliateinu*.[80] Greenberg wrote that the Hashomer Hazair movement (a Socialist Zionist youth movement) dwelled in the Jezreel Valley but "draws water from the wells of Poland and Germany, from Mickiewicz to Freud, and not from here. This is a sign of trouble, a sign that the water of life is not here."[81] That is, he believed that the counterculture of Hashomer Hazair was borrowed from the European counterculture and was not an authentic Jewish culture.[82] If so, even the vision of a future national existence that has been through a socialist revolution was drawn from European wells, albeit from those of the European counterculture. Indeed, for example, in Hashomer Hazair's educational program from the 1940s we read:

> There are good Jews who mourn the destruction of our culture, the process of assimilation which leads to degeneracy and falseness, but

they are unaware of and do not understand the multitude of lies that exists in every other part of life. It is as though the uproar over the decline of Western culture has been silenced in current times; before having tasted the real taste of the West in Eastern Europe, we had already mourned its passing and now it permeates every corner of our lives and our souls, and we adapt, knowingly and unknowingly, to cultural Philistinism and none of us speaks up. Realistic criticism of the social reality, criticism in light of socialism and its revolt against the current regime will provide us with wide-ranging content.

There were those who believed that this counterculture gave birth to a radical wish to destroy every trace of Europeanness. The revolutionary pioneers, wrote Yehoshua Brandstetter, who had emigrated to Palestine in 1909 and was among the first members of Hashomer (Jewish Defense Organization) in Sejera and a member of the Beit Alfa kibbutz, preached against all European traits: "complacency, courtesy, politeness, cleanliness, etc. To such an extent that they no longer need to exercise or learn Hebrew . . . because these are European habits, of which we have no need."[83]

In any event, this romantic period and the almost primeval cries against Europe and bourgeois life were short-lived and marginal. In effect, the accepted position was that the purpose of Jewish settlement in Palestine was not to establish a provincial society similar to the Oriental or primitive East European village. Thus even during the 1880s, members of Bilu declared that Jewish settlement in Palestine needed to be undertaken "in accordance with the latest conclusions of modern science and the latest word of European culture in our generation."[84] The widespread view was that since Palestine was a failed, Oriental land, it would be possible to build it up from the foundations according to modern models of European settlement, and to make it "as organized and neat as European nations"; its settlements would resemble "the pleasant cities in Europe" and display "European organization" and "European manners." Consequently, as soon as the foundations were laid for the new Jewish society, it would be necessary to establish all of the European cultural institutions: theaters, museums, universities, playing fields, scientific centers, and the like.[85] In certain circles, there was admittedly an anti-urban sentiment, fueled by an image of the European city as a sort of hell, but this sentiment was short-lived. Tel Aviv—the modern Jewish city born in 1909 as a suburb of

Jaffa—was described at the start of the 1920s, as we have already seen, as a "bourgeois" city, but it was generally defended with the argument that it was neither Oriental nor Middle Eastern. Instead, it had been constructed from the start as a typical European city, with respect to both its urban structure and its characteristic lifestyle.

Thus immigrants to Palestine saw Europe in several different lights. It was an autochthonous village that followed nature's steady rhythms, was organically embedded in the landscape, and offered a communal existence (*Gemeinschaft*). At the same time, it was also a great urban society, with its lofty cultural (bourgeois) assets and dimly lit backyards. The landscape of lost, faraway Europe gave way to romantic descriptions of Palestine's landscape, which was occasionally depicted as similar to the European landscape—one containing cows and geese—but generally as something different: Palestine was an authentic biblical landscape with dates, figs, and fields of grains, as well as eucalyptus and citrus trees. Time and again, Palestine's landscape was contrasted with that of Europe in order to emphasize the superiority of the former. No region in Europe, for example, had moonlit nights quite like those in Palestine, a hot country where "the sun burns like a ball of fire."[86] Yet even as the landscape was depicted with biblical imagery, the climate was described as healthy, and one to which Jews immigrating from Europe should easily become accustomed.

The call to return to the Orient was sometimes interpreted as a declaration of an existing or desired kinship with the Arab world and as a willingness to adopt Oriental models. However, this was always a case of integrating into the Orient rather than drawing closer to Muslim culture and Islam, and under the influence of European Orientalism, several characteristics were chosen that were considered representative of the Oriental essence.[87] In the art and literature of Jewish Palestine, the Orient was typically depicted in exotic, Oriental colors and only rarely as a complex human and cultural reality. As we will see, the cultural debate in Israel also dealt, in general, with Oriental rather than Muslim culture. The Orient had an influential effect on various aspects of culture in Palestine—dress, architecture, nutrition, and the like—but not on the values of its society or its habitus.

The call to leave Europe and head eastward was not, therefore, a call to abandon Europe. The alternatives that were offered to European culture were taken from a repertoire of models drawn from the world of European thought and from the European reality. The return to the Oriental land of their fathers was not intended to rid Jews of the Europeanness that clung to them, but to enable them to be European Jews by choice. This was considered a necessary condition for the success of the Zionist enterprise and for the creation of a modern, national Hebrew culture. External European characteristics—suits, coffeehouses, the opera, and the like—became cultural norms. Rather than a longing for a utopian Orient, Jews expressed fear of what were described as exilic values, the Levantinization of the society and culture, and the renunciation of their European heritage and its valuable assets.

EUROPEANNESS AND ANTI-EUROPEANNESS IN PALESTINE

> *Decidedly, almost all the development, science, art, civil consciousness, and humanity we have—all of it, all I say, comes from that land of holy wonders! You see, our whole life, from earliest childhood, has been geared to the European mentality.*
>
> FYODOR DOSTOEVSKY,
> *Winter Notes on Summer Impressions*[1]

> *I bring forth Ashkenazi ideas and clothe them in the purity of the Holy Tongue.*
>
> MORDECHAI AHARON GINSBURG,
> *Aviezer*[2]

Culture is, among other things, the set of normative values a society holds. Thus it is important to point out, at the outset of this chapter, that what follows constitutes no sort of value judgment on the contents ascribed to any particular cultural system. As a result, we will do without opaque concepts such as identity, essence, collective character, or collective mentality, whose meaning usually derives from self-awareness and subjective feelings. Although it is essential not to downplay the importance and influence of perceptions, representations, and stereotypes, we will attempt to examine the role of European cultural models and traits in the creation and consolidation of the cultural system of the new Jewish society in Palestine. In other words, we will investigate the status and role of the European heritage within the ensemble of concepts, values, symbols, customs, and practices which formed the cultural system and dominant habitus of Palestine's Jewish society.

We will not attempt to describe the content of the new Jewish (Hebrew) layer of this cultural system—a subject on which there has been much research. In any case, it is important to reemphasize the need to distinguish between rhetorical declarations or ideological expressions of what is desirable and cultural realia, or what we can actually observe. Our interest lies in what can be defined as the European layer of Hebrew culture in Palestine. In other words, we are interested in the role played by the European repertoire in Hebrew culture—a repertoire acquired through processes of transference, adaptation, and innovation. It is important again to note that it is not our intention in this or the following chapter to describe the history of Hebrew culture and the various stages of its development. For such descriptions, we refer the reader to the works cited in our endnotes. Our intention is to provide an overview and a few insights germane to the context of this book.

In using the term "European values," we are not referring to the cultural models perceived as Ashkenazi—that is, to those models that were part of the authentic culture of Ashkenazi Jews and, more precisely, part of Jewish village culture. Within Israel's cultural polemic, the difference between Ashkenazi culture and the European traits of that culture is frequently blurred.[3] It is also important to differentiate between, on the one hand, representations and images of European culture and the symbolic role they played in the public discourse in Jewish society in Palestine since the 1880s, and their actual cultural influence, on the other hand.

Most of those who have written about the Jews' need to leave Europe—including those convinced that the purpose of that departure was, among other reasons, to escape the destructive influence of Europe's immanent ailments, as well as those who believe that the Jewish spirit (*Geist*) could be saved only in Palestine—do not believe that it was necessary or even possible to abandon many of the cultural and material assets that were the fruit of the Jews' Western heritage.

EUROPEANNESS IN HEBREW GARB

On June 8, 1895, Herzl wrote in his diary that the goal of Zionism was to "uproot the [Jewish] centers and transfer them to Palestine. To transplant whole communities in which the Jews feel comfortable."[4] Here Herzl referred, as we have seen, to the organized, planned transfer to Palestine of the high-culture assets of modern Europe's urban, bourgeois world; these included not only values, but lifestyles and institutions. In contrast, one of the authors of the Ramle Platform, the platform of the Poale Tzion party,[5] quoted a line from Horace's *Epistles*: "Those who cross the sea change the sky, not their spirits."[6] The purpose was to clarify that it was not European culture that would be transferred to Palestine, but rather its revolutionary consciousness. This would enable the Jews to establish in a new location a Jewish world built upon the European model of a revolutionary society; revolutionary consciousness could be expressed successfully in Palestine, and the conditions there would not weaken it.

In practice, the process of emigration and the enterprise of constructing a new Jewish society in Palestine were accompanied by both the planned, intentional transfer of a European cultural repertoire and the intensive creation of new cultural components, which were in part a translation of European and traditional Jewish values to the new Hebrew conceptual system. This process of transference was an act of acculturation with no need for or fear of assimilation, because it took place in an autonomous Jewish political community rather than within a largely non-Jewish society. This reality was perceived as releasing Jewish culture from the pressures and temptations of its European cultural environment, and consequently enabling a conscious, deliberate selection of desired traits and models from the latter.[7] Many cultural traits were imported by immigrants as part of their cultural assets and were assimilated into the new cultural system of the *Yishuv*, where they were accepted as self-evident. Their foreign identity inspired neither rejection nor objection, and in most cases, their acceptance was not taken to mean unacceptable imitation. Furthermore, because many of the European immigrants to Palestine had undergone at least some of the processes of modernization and acculturation before leaving Europe, their encounter with its cultural assets did not begin in Palestine; nor was modernization forced upon them by colonial rule or a centralized local authority. For this reason, the combination and amalgamation of originally European traits with authentic Jewish (Hebrew) cultural traits, both old and new, into a single cultural system—a process which, under other circumstances, would be accompanied by difficult conflicts and crises of identity in the host society—did not cause similar problems in the new Jewish society in Palestine. On the contrary, amalgamation and combination were seen as necessary and desirable—and as phenomena that could take place only in Palestine. In Western Europe, Chaim Weizmann wrote, there were Jews who succeeded in enjoying both worlds and combining them harmoniously. Yet others, including him, felt in Europe like guests "overwhelmed with wine at a banquet for strangers." As a result, Palestine was the only place in which it was possible to combine harmoniously "all the good features of the Ghetto" (which he described as a "sewer") and "implant [them] in Palestinian soil" alongside European culture.[8] Only in Palestine, wrote Nachman Syrkin, could "Europeanness in Hebrew garb" emerge, and this was because "Zionism will bring world culture to the Jewish people and create a new Judaism, which will be the historic grafting of the world's loftiest features onto the national characteristics and ancient assets of the Jewish people."[9]

All groups in the Zionist movement agreed that there could be no national revival or return to the homeland without modernization and changes in the social and cultural spheres, in keeping with European models. In an 1895 address to the Rothschild family council (which he recorded in his diary but did not deliver in person), Herzl wrote: "for everyone will take across a piece of the promised land: one in his brain, one with his brawn, and the third through his personal belongings."[10] The imported cultural institutions would satisfy "the longed-for illusion of the old homeland."[11] Thus immigrants would carry with them the cultural assets they had acquired in the modern Western world and would establish all the cultural institutions that were an inseparable part of high European culture. Those institutions did not, and could not, emerge as part of modern Jewish culture in a Europe where Jews were a subculture and an ethnic, national, and religious minority, and where they did not need, and were not able, to establish a full cultural system. In Palestine, on the other hand, an autonomous Jewish society was being built with the declared goal of creating an all-encompassing territorial and national Hebrew Jewish cultural system.[12]

Because of this, it was urgently necessary to select those assets of the overall European cultural repertoire that were considered requisite and appropriate for the new society, and at the same time to impose cultural censorship and reject those traits deemed negative or harmful. Since the construction of this cultural system was accompanied by a series of decisions and rulings, an ideological *Kulturkampf* took place in the *Yishuv* between people who held different outlooks and preferences. The processes through which Jewish Hebrew culture in Palestine was consolidated were accompanied by a permanent and sometimes stormy dispute over the question of what weight and status should be given to the European foundations of Hebrew culture, and what the substance of those foundations should be. Nevertheless, the new Jewish culture was the result not only of planning and initiative,[13] but of uncontrolled importation of traditions, values, and practices. Palestine was a free market for importing cultural merchandise from the West. Immigrants brought with them a variety of

Europe's cultural assets—using their heads, their hands, and the belongings they acquired. As a result, the ability of the cultural elite to tailor the *Yishuv*'s cultural profile to a predetermined model was limited, and the cultural market in Palestine was open to imports from many sources and of many types. Attempts to enforce supervision and censorship over the cultural field were only partially successful. Brenner was thus correct when he cast doubt on the "immigrants'" ability to create "a cultural life and cultural assets" or "European-style intelligence" in a deliberate and organized way.[14] Yet Brenner was overly pessimistic. A hegemonic cultural center with shared values did operate in Palestine; it determined the official norms and ethos of cultural behavior, and it shaped the cultural identity and habitus of Jewish society.

EUROPE IN PALESTINE

"Here in Jaffa, everyone is educated, everyone is intelligent, everyone knows how to behave according to the latest fashion or the custom of Europe's civilized Jews . . . and any passerby in Jaffa's markets will behold real Europeans." So *Havatzelet*, a Jerusalem newspaper, described the modern *Yishuv* in Jaffa in 1891.[15] Mordechai Ben-Hillel Hacohen, one of Tel Aviv's first residents, wrote in his memoirs about the reactions of British soldiers when they arrived in Jaffa's new suburb in December 1917: "'Europe, Europe!' they rejoiced, as though, after floundering in the desert for two years, they had not hoped to find such an orderly city, with its beautiful houses and straight, wide streets, in untamed Asia. The officers and officials were particularly glad to find handsome and well-equipped buildings here in the neighborhood, with infrastructure for plumbing and bathing."[16]

In 1917, Tel Aviv consisted of only a few small neighborhoods, but in comparison with Jaffa, the Oriental city, it had a clearly European personality. It was modeled on the ideal of the modern European suburb. That was how its residents described it, and that was also the impression it left on many of its visitors, who compared it to great European cities such as Berlin, Paris, Vienna, Odessa, Nice, and Cannes: "All of Europe is concentrated here, in this small city." Even those who criticized Tel Aviv compared it not to an Oriental city but to an East European *shtetl*, or warned that the danger it faced was that "its glittering façade will be pseudo-European, but in effect it will become one of the port cities of the Levant."[17]

Besides Tel Aviv, Hebrew settlements in general were described as European—that is, modern—because of their structure and their public institutions. In 1882, the bylaws of Yessod Hamaale's settlers' committee stated that self-rule in the new settlement planned for Upper Galilee would be "in accordance with the local custom of all peoples of Europe in their places of assembly."[18] The settlers, Avraham Shmuel Herschberg wrote, wanted to turn Palestine into a "civilized" country complete with manufactures and industry, and its residents into "cultured people."[19] The Jewish settlement was thus seen as the opposite of the primitive Arab village:[20]

> In the eyes of a man passing through the country ... the settlements will seem a sort of magical sight, as he walks through a great wasteland, climbing hills and descending into valleys, without paved roads, and suddenly the scene changes, and before him lie paved, attractive roads and lovely settlements, splendid in their beautiful buildings, their broad, straight streets, and the vineyards and orchards which surround them, as well as in their steam-powered mills, their hospitals, pharmacies, and bathhouses, aqueducts which deliver water into houses in several settlements, and beautiful synagogues.[21]

Within *Yishuv* society, there was scant objection to the idea of designing the Palestinian landscape and urban and rural settlements according to European models. Nor were there objections to importing material culture and agricultural and industrial technology from Europe.[22] On the contrary, as we have seen, all of these were considered prerequisites for creating a modern society. Importing the traits of modernism was not perceived as a demonstration of Western colonialism, because of their neutral and practical nature—even though in reality they brought about far-reaching changes in the social and cultural systems of Jewish and Arab society.

However, the European model encompassed not only components of modern technology—trains, the telegraph, electricity, industry, etc.—but also the whole of civilized or cultured society. Civilization meant theaters, lending libraries, museums, orchestras, kindergartens, schools, institutions of higher education, journalism, and the like. All of these institutions were meant to satisfy the thirst for culture that arose through the habits of cultural consumption Jews had acquired in their countries of origin. These institutions and others were meant to create a sort of self-sufficient cultural island that did not rely on the backward cultural environment surrounding it, and to provide a civilized standard of living according to the criteria of European high culture.[23] The need to accomplish this led, even in the initial stages of the Jewish society's construction, to the establishment of each of these cultural institutions, in order to form through them the cultural repertoire characteristic of an official national culture.[24]

Technology, means of production, institutions, and the like may be classified as neutral traits of a civilization. Yet the questions at hand were: What about those characteristics classified as cultural traits—that is, those meant to express the particular cultural content, or value culture, of the new society? And what about those contents that determined how the new society defined itself, as well as its normative and symbolic systems? These were essential questions because the official Zionist ideology maintained that national intellectual and cultural creation must express the authentic Hebrew spirit. No wonder, then, that the nature of that spirit in the context of culture and art was the subject of ceaseless debate. Our claim in this matter is that many so-called authentic traits were actually European traits that added Hebrew content. In many cases, this was a matter of reviving a cultural element, considered identical or equivalent to a desirable European element, from Jewish tradition; in other cases, it was an instance of dressing a European element in "authentic" Jewish or Hebrew cloth.

Three spheres of cultural activity originating in Western culture formed an inseparable part of Palestine's new Jewish cultural system: a repertoire of forms of cultural consumption, such as music, cafes, outings at the beach, and cinema; the translation into Hebrew of classic literary works for adults, young adults, and children—including works for the theater and opera—which were often selected based on how well they suited the needs and outlook of the new culture; and the internalization and assimilation of European values into the new Hebrew culture, and their transformation into an inseparable part of it.

IMMIGRANTS AND CULTURES OF ORIGIN

The fact that immigrants brought with them cultural assets that were characteristic of the countries they had left—values, lifestyles, patterns of cultural consumption, and the like—led to the division of Palestine's Jewish culture into subcultures based on countries of origin. Thus, for example, it was claimed that some of the immigrants from Poland during the Fourth Aliyah possessed the habits of a small-time, provincial bourgeoisie,[25] and that others brought with them a type of Romantic and integrative nationalism. According to the prevailing view, German immigrants imported the German bourgeoisie's tradition of *Bildung*: punctuality, discipline, and etiquette, as well as cafes, love of classical music, and more.[26] These "Yekkes" persisted in speaking German; their style of clothing, with its European jackets, was distinctive as well. They crammed their apartments with "stylish and shapely furniture, silver- and crystal-ware, and fine, antique porcelain; they slept on spring mattresses and sat on comfortable couches; and in their crowded rooms they erected full, overflowing bookcases." Merchants who immigrated from Germany "knew how to display their wares in store-front windows with taste and panache."[27] In other words, German immigrants brought with them the habitus of the quasi-European model man and created a sociocultural enclave in Palestinian society. Yet bourgeois immigrants and consumers of high culture hailed from Poland as well, and not every immigrant from Germany was a disciple of its lofty bourgeois and intellectual culture. Moreover, values and institutions that originated in German culture were also imported by immigrants who did not come from Germany, because these were, in reality, general European values.[28]

It is not our intention to downplay the influence of the cultural differences that arose from the various European cultures of origin and from the different habitus from which these immigrants arrived. Nonetheless, it appears that the cultural borders between the various groups that made up Jewish society in Palestine were determined more by ideological and class identification than by culture of origin. In any event, within a short period of time—certainly by the second generation—the differences based on country of origin became blurred and did not greatly influence the nature or substance of cultural consumption. Jews from Russia, Poland, and Germany saw the same plays, attended the same concerts, and read the same literature, even if their preferences may have varied. It is true that stereotypes anchored in culture of origin were preserved and even exaggerated within Palestine's immigrant culture (as was the case in the United States),[29] causing tensions, resentment, and antagonism between the different groups. Yet as far as European Jewish immigrants were concerned, the melting pot of Palestine's reality blurred these differences—especially in the case of the second generation, which was brought up within the Hebrew educational system. The common European cultural background permitted these differences to be minimized, and as a result, all European immigrants became Ashkenazim, or descendants of Europe's culture—and not solely in the eyes of foreign observers.

ANTI-EUROPEANNESS IN PALESTINE

The images of Europe and Western culture in Jewish society in Palestine underwent several processes of construction, deconstruction, and reconstruction after the 1880s. These images were constructed, as we have seen, from generalizations or topoi that acquired a symbolic status. The broadest generalization was built on the foundations of two binary models: the first pitting Europeanness against Jewishness, and the second East against West. Each model adopts the essentialist, ontological understanding by which every well-defined group has its own autarchic worldview, value system, and cultural code. These are internalized by the group and in turn brand it uniquely and determine the range of its behavioral templates. From this point of view, any process of acculturation and cultural adaptation is perceived as coercion, which denies the host culture its heritage and uniqueness and forces it to accept external values foreign to its spirit and heritage.

When this essentialist perception fractures into slogans on the battlefield of cultural debate, each side involved in the polemic enumerates what it considers the positive foundations of Western culture—rationalism, liberalism, democracy, etc.—as well as what it considers the negative foundations of Oriental culture. Similarly, each lists the negative traits of Western culture—fascism and Nazism, colonialism and imperialism, vulgar mass culture, and so on—and also praises the virtues and unique qualities of Oriental culture.[30] This sort of essentialist understanding forms the basis of much of the criticism of the hegemonic system of modern Jewish Hebrew culture in Israel, which, according to some, is merely an imitation of Western culture. In both Jewish Palestine and Israel, this criticism gave rise to several versions of the postcolonial anti-Europeanness that existed both in Europe and outside it.[31]

The anti-European and anti-Western sentiments found in Israeli society consisted—and still consist—of several branches, each of which offers different templates and interpretations of authentic revival based largely on presenting such a revival as an alternative to European Jewish culture.

1. Criticism of what is described as the adoption of the negative manifestations of European society: a capitalistic, bourgeois, and even

hedonistic lifestyle, inappropriate for the realities of Palestine and its pioneering ethos. The city was the antithesis of the pioneering lifestyle; it represented the "illusion of European culture" and even "decadence" —boulevard theaters, cafes, cinemas, and the like. All of these cultural institutions were classified as undesirable, and their adoption or "imitation" was seen as a clear expression of "self-deprecation in the face of Western culture, which has once again brought us into an entanglement of foreign life and values."[32] Adopting European cultural institutions and lifestyles was described as accepting an inferior culture, one that was superficial, nihilistic—even abominable and perverted.

2. Criticism by the Jewish Orthodoxy in Palestine. This was a continuation of the struggle that the Jewish Orthodoxy waged in Europe against the processes of acculturation and secularization, and against the presentation of modern, secular, nationalistic Jewish culture as a full and legitimate alternative to observant Judaism. Western culture— the "culture of Japheth"—was perceived as both an heir to Hellenistic culture and a degenerate secular culture. "We have absolutely no need to learn from Europe's ways," declared Rabbi Zvi Yehuda Kook, "nor even from the civilized [European nations]." He believed it acceptable to adopt Western technology and achievements in medicine, engineering, and the like, but anything that contradicted the Jewish Bible and the unique spirit of Israel must be rejected.[33] Europeanness was usually described as Hellenization, and Western culture was depicted as possessing its negative traits.

3. Criticism from those possessing a nationalist, essentialist, and purist outlook. According to this approach, original culture is an all-encompassing, autarchic *Volkskultur*, and therefore its revival in Palestine must be nourished only from the wells of authentic cultural tradition. This critique sees Hebrew Israeli culture as shallow, superficial, and cosmopolitan—the obvious and inevitable product of drawing from Gentile springs. Leo Strauss makes a more extreme claim, that Jewish Hebrew culture exists only subject to Europe and Europeans, and thus holds the false beliefs that what is good and noble can be found only in Europe, and that Western culture sets the standard in every field:

> From this point of view, there was actually no difference between the nationalists and the assimilated among us. The assimilated aspired to live by the Western lifestyle among the peoples of the West and as an integral part of them; while the

Europeanness in Palestine

nationalists wanted to cast the etiquette, ways of life, opinions, and moral values of the West according to our own national molds.[34]

These words imply that only complete independence from the influence of the Greco-Hellenic-Western mentality, and a return to original Judaism, can save modern Jews from the crisis into which Western civilization has lured them and fully revive the Jewish essence. From this perspective, all Western values—even those perceived as positive, such as the values of Western humanism—are unacceptable. The resurrection of Judaism depends on its ability to dissociate itself decisively from the values of the declining West; Jewish revival is not and cannot be possible in the sphere of Western influence.[35] Accordingly, Jewish nationalism was born as a rejection of the "Europeanization of the people"[36] and is entirely different in its essence from European nationalism. This outlook adopts the distinction between civilization and culture, and from it concludes that it is necessary to separate the assets of Europe's material and technological civilization from its spiritual culture—a distinction drawn from German sociology and philosophy of history. Thus, for example, Fritz Kahn declared in his 1920 book, *The Jews as Race and as Culture*, that in the public sphere, Jews utilized and were surrounded by civilization (trolleys, cars, radios, and so forth), but in private spheres (at home, among their families, or in Jewish company), they lived within a Jewish culture.[37] There is no need to point out that in reality it was difficult to make this distinction, particularly in a reality in which Jews were the dominant actors and aspired to create an all-encompassing Jewish culture. Thus, for example, when the radical Revisionist writer Yehoshua Heschel Yeivin criticized what he described as Ahad Haam's spiritual affinity for "English thoughts and modes of thought," he supported his arguments with none other than Nietzsche's dismissal of Ahad Haam's "English teachers," H. T. Buckle and Herbert Spencer, whom he considered no more than "mediocre thinkers."[38] Brenner pointed out the dichotomy in this outlook in his criticism of H. L. Zuta's *The "Melamed" and the "Teacher,"* in which Zuta, a writer and educator, claimed that Jews must not take lessons from the world on the subject of moral education, since "the wealthy must not return to the starting point"; in other words, Judaism had a rich history of moral education and therefore was not in need of outside instruction. "We have among us," wrote Zuta, "Frenchmen, Germans, and Italians, all of Moses' faith. If we abandon that faith we will become Russian, Turkish, and Arab entirely."[39] All well and good, Brenner wrote mockingly, but how did Zuta's purist call coexist with his own suggestion to study values and standards of behavior from "the Slavic League," which was based on the Pravoslavic religion; from Germany, "which considers religion the goal of patriotism"; and from liberal England, which represented "loyalty and absence of hypocrisy"?[40]

4. Criticism by fringe ideological groups that proposed an alternative, imaginary East—one that would be not Arab Muslim or Jewish, but Hebrew. This critique saw Judaism and Islam as aterritorial cultural religions alien to the authentic, nationalistic character of the ancient Middle East. Jewish cultural foreignness, they claimed, also stemmed from the European character of Palestine's Jewish culture. The following, for example, comes from the platform of a group calling itself "Young Palestine":

> The core of the previous generation belongs to and has remained in Europe. From birth they learned to admire Europe as the capital of the world and as the birthplace of culture. In the Semitic region they were, and have remained, alien in spirit. But the Palestinian generation was raised in Asia, and Asia is its home. We have learned the ancient history of the Semitic lands, which turns our eyes Eastward. We have learned to scorn Europe, which has atrophied in our eyes ... We find this [Arab] reality obvious, and we have no need for complex ideologies from European sources in order to be familiar with it.[41]

In other words, the author called for the creation of an authentic Hebrew Palestinian culture based on ancient foundations, or on the modern existential experience, without relying on either European culture or the culture of the Arab East.

5. Criticism by part of the secular, modern, "Oriental" intelligentsia concerning the influence of various postcolonial and anti-European theories. This criticism conveys discomfort and even cultural rebellion, and carries the torch of the aspiration to revive an authentic, non-European Jewish culture—an "Oriental Jewish culture."[42] From the Oriental intelligentsia's point of view—that of the second and third generation of immigrants from the Muslim world—the European immigrants brought with them shared European assets, and as a result there was no difference between their various European cultures of

origin. In many cases, the subject was not European culture itself, most of whose assets no one intended to reject, but rather Ashkenazi culture—the Jewish culture that was, according to this point of view, imported to Palestine by immigrants from Europe.

At first glance, we have here a thorough rejection of the Western cultural heritage. Yet the perceived foundations of Western culture—belief in the autonomy of the human intellect to interpret the world; belief in individuality; belief in the rule of law; and belief in one's capacity for self-improvement and individual entrepreneurship—are not the real subjects of these critiques. In other instances, it was claimed that the Ashkenazi Jews brought with them negative European values, or adopted them once they were in Palestine;[43] these values were primarily the nationalistic and socialist ideologies and their collective, integrative ethos; the centralized, nationalistic model of government; and the model of a secular nationalistic Judaism. The Oriental intelligentsia described these values as a contradiction to the cultural values and traditions of the East, which are characterized by orientation toward the community, tolerance, and religious and traditional nationalism.[44]

According to the critical, secular Oriental intelligentsia, what Hebrew ideology describes as the combination and merger of the new Jewish spirit and Europeanness—a combination through which modern Jewish Hebrew culture was created—is in fact only a shallow imitation of Western culture; the cultural hegemony of the European immigrants is perceived as based on values extrinsic to Eastern culture. This is a hegemony that turned its back on both the unique character of the natural environment in Palestine (the Orient) and on the unique character of the local (Arab Muslim) culture. Through various methods, this hegemony forced itself upon that part of immigrant society that did not hail from Europe and that had no part in or claim to its assets, and compelled it to exchange its own cultural identity for another. In general, this criticism targets the European heritage, but not America or the Americanization of Israeli culture and society.

Countering the image of the Arab Muslim East as a static world characterized by theocracy, inferiority, and backwardness in all areas—and in contrast to the image of the culture and society of immigrants from the Muslim world—an image which did in fact portray them in a harmful and degrading light—there arose both a positive image of the East and a negative image of the stereotypes of Europe and Ashkenazi culture. This Israeli version of anti-Westernness sometimes involved the rejection of modern values, but in general preference was given to the unique Oriental model of modernism—a modernism not formed, as it was in Europe, within the framework of nationalistic, particularistic societies, nor as part of the process of creating a new sort of Jewish collective.[45] Thus there is no objection here to modernism in itself, but rather a rejection of what is described as arrogance on the part of the European immigrants and of their claim that they alone brought the values of modernism to Palestine.

One prominent result of the cultural unease of the Israeli Oriental intelligentsia was the attempt to formulate an all-encompassing alternative of an authentic Oriental Jewish collective identity,[46] carrying its own values and symbolic assets. This attempt to create opposition to the Ashkenazi Jewish identity (that is, to the European Hebrew culture) led, in many cases, to a need to define Orientalism in integrative essential terms (which were borrowed from the European conceptual framework) and, on the basis of that definition, to note those traits of the Oriental cultural repertoire which were worthy of preservation or revival. The description of Jews from the Muslim world as Arabized Jews, parallel with Europeanized Jews, indicates the choice of an ethnic, cultural definition rather than a religious definition; after all, it was impossible to talk about Muslim Jews.[47] In this way, the description adopts the antinomy between the East and Europe, seeing each as separate, homogeneous cultural and ontological entities. As a result, it is important to note that this portrayal of the East—in which the Ottoman East is seldom mentioned—is not based on the Orientalist image of the East, which was the fruit of European imagination; at the same time, neither is it the East of Arab Muslim culture. Rather, the East in this portrayal is the cultural tradition of the Oriental immigrants. A religious tradition, it developed to a significant extent under the influence of Muslim culture, where the cultural layer of modern secularism was far thinner than it was among European Jews. Thus it is no wonder that when those who adopt this perspective are asked to enumerate the nonreligious templates and traits of the Oriental repertoire—apart from the seemingly ontological characteristics that they ascribe to Orientals—they list, as a rule, its language (Arabic) and (Oriental Arab) literature and music.[48] They do not reject the values and institutions that belong to the European heritage, nor do they attempt to exchange them for the values and institutions of the Muslim heritage.[49] Thus it seems that their protest and revolt is aimed not toward European or Western culture (with the latter including American culture), but toward the values and institutions perceived as symbolically representative of the Ashkenazis' political and socioeconomic hegemony. This is not a question, then, of an all-encompassing alternative model of an Oriental counterculture. Even the sharpest critics of Ashkenazi culture do not propose to reject the central traits of Western culture and uproot them from modern Jewish Israeli culture. It is even possible to say that they claim their modernism is not a result of Western Jews' historical experience, nor the result of the modernization forced upon them by the European immigrants in Palestine, but instead an independent and autonomous creation.

The anti-European literature to which we refer deals, therefore, with representations, and not with cultural realia. In the radical Oriental perception, it is not only Europe that is a single, imagined entity: the East is, too. What was born as the product of European imagination was adopted by those speaking on behalf of Oriental culture in a process of reverse acculturation, in which the negative traits of Oriental culture were replaced by positive ones. While secular Jews of European origin seldom define themselves in terms of ethnic identity, the Oriental cultural elite frequently employs these terms and reinvents its own ethnicity.[50]

The extent to which this description of the culture and society of Jews in the Muslim world is valid, or whether it is a matter of imagined tradition and ethnicity, is not important for our purposes. What is important is the fact that this description ignores many assets of the European repertoire: a liberal civil society, a strong family ethos, and a traditional way of life. The description also ignores the character of Hebrew society, which is based on both the original assets of traditional Judaism and its new interpretation. The description ignores, among other things, the place and contributions of the Hebrew Bible and modern Hebrew literature in the creation of the new society's identity and values.[51] Similarly, it ignores the fact that Palestine's Hebrew culture—in both its self-awareness and the process of its creation and construction—saw both Levantineness and the East European exilic manner as its primary foes. And it ignores the fact that most assets of Hebrew European culture are an inseparable and even obvious part of the cultural experience of immigrants from the Muslim world. Finally, it ignores the fact that every cultural system, including modern ones, is, to some extent, a hybrid, multilayered, and even syncretic system. Though every culture has its own content and values, there is no such thing as an autarchic and exclusive culture;[52] often, a self-concept of exclusivity is the product of reaction to and defense against the other.[53]

AN IMAGINARY EUROPE?

The ambition of Jewish society in Palestine to become a Europe of the Middle East prompted more than a little contempt: Palestine was, after all, nothing more than an Asiatic province. It was a village populated by pathetic Jews clinging with all their might to the hem of Europe's robe—the same Europe that rejected them—and endeavoring to draw nourishment from it in order to create a pale imitation of Europe in the East. Indeed, Jewish immigrants to Palestine from 1882 onward, who had left Europe out of a sense of disappointment and despair, did not wish to give up the cultural assets they had acquired from the continent. Certainly many of them had only a tenuous connection in their country of origin to the assets of official European high culture and were acquainted with it only through intermediaries—primarily literature and cinema. Still, the new Jewish culture formed in Palestine was not a closed one. It was not isolated from European culture, and the latter did not make its way to Palestine only in the minds of immigrants. It also arrived in reality, through the medium of various cultural agents who brought it to Palestine—and not as an imitation, or a pale shadow of the original. As a result, the Israeli cultural experience is pluralistic and even syncretic, and this is also true of the habitus of the majority of the Jewish population. However, the founding kernel of this experience is the hybridization of European and Western values with Jewish and Hebrew ones. This hybridization includes selections from the full range of the European heritage: those seen as representing what is enlightened, noble, and progressive in Europe, as well as those considered representative of its negative qualities.

In the critical literature surveyed above, the East-West antinomy is described as key to the culture war in Israeli society. Thus in Europe, the characterization of Jews as Orientals was an expression of internal cultural colonialism and antisemitism, while at the same time in Israel, the Orient became an instrument of discrimination and oppression in the hands of the very people who had suffered similar treatment, in part by means of that same European characterization. This antinomy is part of the European Jewish immigrants' cultural colonialism.[54] This picture exaggerates the importance of labeling the West European Jews as Orientals in anti-Jewish ideology and modern antisemitism, yet it accurately reflects the perception in Israeli society of Orientals as belonging to a failed group, from a social and political perspective.[55]

The critical literature also suggests a negative image of Israeli society, describing it not as an heir to European culture, but as a society that abandoned the positive values of Western culture and acquired and internalized all of its negative values: "We are residue of all that Europe has tried and abandoned or is abandoning, or is still struggling to abandon with abhorrence and at a great price: nationalism, fascism, colonialism, Orientalism, étatism, state capitalism, the Thatcherist market economy ... We are Europe's leftovers."[56]

The implication is that Israeli society is nothing more than a garbage can for Europe, a clear personification of the universality of evil of European output. Israel, its society, and its culture are presented not only as the waste products of an evil, demonic Europe, but also as the final historical manifestation of this Europe. Israel is also confronted with a new imaginary Europe that is noble and liberal, full of all that is good and devoid of borders, nations, or separate cultural identities—in other words, a Europe that is the fountainhead of universal enlightenment. Yet even in this picture, the alternative is not an imaginary Orient but an imaginary West: a culture that is not arrogant but shaped by the ideal of cosmopolitan humanity,[57] a multicultural and multiethnic civil society (or, in Israeli terms, a multiethnic and binational society) that has no unifying national cultural identity.

Thus the dual portrait of a Europe at once loved and detested, adored and accursed, which took form throughout the course of the nineteenth century, has been revived in an entirely different historical context.

THE UNITED STATES BECOMES THE WEST

During the 1960s, and especially since the 1970s, the State of Israel underwent an accelerated process of Americanization in almost every aspect of life. This process was partly due to the status of the United States as the primary Western power and chief supporter of Israel on the international scene, and to the increasingly close relationship between Israel and the American Jewish community. It was also due to the deep disappointment of the Israeli radical Left in Soviet policies toward Jews in general and toward Israel in particular, and to the profound influence of American values on the world at large. The decline of countries such as Britain and France in the postcolonial era caused them to become temporary allies of Israel, notably in 1956, but from that point on, Israel's political orientation became tied to that of the United States. Even the radical Zionist Left began, toward the end of the 1960s, to consider the United States as an ally and a nation with which Israel shared political values. No longer did the United States represent the reactionary opposition to the world of tomorrow; it became the clear representative of the West, though the many differences between American and West European culture were widely recognized. From the 1960s onward, westernization became synonymous with cultural trends born of American influence, or with imitation of the United States.

After the 1880s, the United States became the primary destination of the mass Jewish emigration from Europe, yet these millions of emigrants had only a vague notion of the particular character of American culture. Before disembarking on American shores, most Jews devoured fragments of information that shaped their overall image of America, as well as a repertoire of stereotypes that chiefly emphasized its suitability for immigration. In general, they judged America in light of the opportunities and risks that awaited them there. In the Russian-language Jewish media, for example, a negative image of America was very common.[58] This negative image was especially pervasive in Orthodox literature, which represented America as an upside-down world whose way of life was entirely different from that of the Old World—that is, Europe. America was represented in this literature as "the Land of Darkness," a "treifene medina" (an unkosher nation), and an inherently materialistic state.[59] The negative image was also widespread in Hebrew journalism and literature, especially among those with radical social perspectives. At the same time, a positive image was established, in which America was perceived as a newborn nation free from the heavy burden of tradition—a "country without a past" and without the burden of a long historical memory, notable for its values and a lifestyle of tolerance, freedom, and progress. In other words, it was a place in which the positive traits of Western civilization achieved their greatest expression and were, in fact, born anew.[60]

Accordingly there were radical *maskilim* in Eastern Europe who pointed to America as a vastly preferable destination for immigrants than Palestine, which was located in the backward East. For example, a popular guide for immigrants that was published in Odessa in 1891 said: "A bit of advice for you: Do not take a moment's rest. Run, do, work, and keep your own good in mind. A final virtue is needed in America—called cheek . . . Do not say, 'I cannot. I do not know.'"[61]

The Hebrew writer David Frischman wrote in 1885 that human history moves toward the West; the torch of enlightenment would shine from now on in America.[62] The historian Simon Dubnow praised America and its constitution, which promised maximal cultural autonomy to every minority:

> I am well aware of the characteristics of American culture which tend to blur the features of Jewish national life rather than help to preserve them. This is true only, however, if immigration and entry are allowed to remain chaotic and unorganized. If the intellectual classes will assume leadership, it will be possible to secure the freedom and opportunity needed for the realization of cultural autonomy. It is not possible, in accordance with the American constitution, to prevent communities from exercising self-government or organizing education in national schools, or setting up some general national organization of Jewry.[63]

The Jewish British writer Israel Zangwill went even further. In a famous 1908 play, he wrote that America not only harbored immigrants of various origins, but, through its melting pot (a term he invented), made them equal partners in a new, humane society:

> Here shall they all unite to build the Republic of Man and the Kingdom of God. Ah, Vera, what is the glory of Rome and Jerusalem where all nations and races come to worship and look back, compared with the glory of America, where all races and nations come to labour and look forward![64]

Only a few adopted the position of the bizarre Jewish American writer Samuel Roth, who issued prophecies of horror. After World War I, in a poem titled "Europe: A Book of America," he declared that "the next future of the world will be in America." In the mid-1920s, however, he foresaw only darkness for America. To Zangwill he wrote:

> I have been too hopeful about America. America will yet prove to be the most ungrateful of all the nations. She will expel us, just as Spain expelled us, just as England expelled us, just as France expelled us . . . America does not yet know what she really is, so her prides are numerous but not concentrated. For things in which she now shows a remarkable interest she will have only a mild curiosity. Passions which have no roots in the ideals of democracy will spring up and find some democratic means of expression. It has been done. It will be done. When she has become conscious of her subconscious character, America will suddenly discover herself to be a sort of glorified

Ku Klux Klan, suspicious of all intruders, especially of Jews . . . I expect to be living when they will be roasting Jews alive on Fifth Avenue.[65]

Jewish society in Palestine existed far away from America, and America was distant from its cultural horizon. Any interest it had in America was focused on American Jews (whom Zionist literature seldom described as living in exile). What Palestine's Jewish society knew about the United States was generally based on history and literature in translation, journalism, and, after the 1930s, the cinema. From these sources, Jews in Palestine learned about American pioneer society, the frontier and the Wild West, African slavery, laissez-faire capitalism, and more; and it was based on these sources that the stereotype—or stereotypes—of America were formed in Palestinian culture. Few Jews there apparently gave much thought to the special nature of American nationalism or found it a model to emulate. During the 1950s, the American melting pot served as a model for the absorption of Jewish immigrants from Muslim countries; but since the 1970s, criticism of the melting pot and its replacement, multiculturalism, have dominated political and cultural thought in Israel.

The new Jewish society in Palestine, then, did not consider American culture one that could—or even should—be emulated and mined as a source of inspiration.[66] Against this background, the words of Chaim Nachman Bialik, regarded as Israel's national poet, diverge from the spirit of the times. In 1926, Bialik made his only journey to America; he remained there for six months. On his return in October of that year, he spoke at length about his impressions of the journey to a large audience in Tel Aviv. Before leaving Palestine, said Bialik, the sum of his knowledge about America consisted of crumbs of impressions. America's negative image was so deeply lodged in his consciousness that he traveled there "out of terror and fear, out of a deep dread—I would say almost a feral dread, or, to alliterate, a feral phobia." What allayed his terror to some extent was the comment addressed to him by one American Jew: "But, America! Oh, America! She is sweeter than honey!" Bialik imagined the unknown America as a land of noise, commotion, and materialism; the negative qualities associated with the concept of business; and spiritual emptiness. Yet the America he discovered was something entirely different: a "new land," in which a new life had been forged and a new type of human being created—one who shook off every bit of the Old World and its old traditions.

Rushing forward, incessantly striving toward the future, without looking back. The American people grows, rising ever higher and marching forward. They move towards the future free of any worry. This is the potential of a cultural, not a savage, nation, confident in its power and unencumbered by any concern about the past.

America, Bialik continued (echoing Tocqueville, with whom he was not familiar), was a place in which men looked not backward but toward the future. It was true that material values held sway in America, but the negative traits responsible belonged to this early period of construction and would be corrected in the future.[67]

It is impossible to know to what extent Bialik's words influenced the image of America in the *Yishuv*. In any case, the dominant Socialist Zionist camp continued to adhere to the image of the United States as a capitalistic, materialistic, and imperialistic nation—certainly not a nation from which to learn the processes of democracy, or a model for the construction of a new Jewish society. Nor did the extreme Zionist Right look to America as a guiding example;[68] it maintained that America's foreign policy in the Middle East was dominated by its interest in oil, especially after the 1940s. All of this changed at the end of the 1960s. After that, parallels were drawn between the American and the Israeli historical experience: both included founding fathers, pioneers, frontiers, an immigration movement, and immigrants from various countries.[69] American influence had made inroads before then, but after the 1960s, that influence became so dominant that products of American culture became an integral part of Israeli society and culture. It would take longer for the image of the United States to change.

The process through which America's image evolved within Jewish society in Israel from 1948 onward calls for a thorough discussion—the proper place for which is not this study.[70] In any case, it is clear that at least since the 1960s, Israeli society entered the American cultural sphere of influence in almost every area, and the Israeli cultural orientation became decidedly American. This does not mean, of course, that the influence of Russian culture—or French, English, and German culture—on various aspects of cultural life in Israel disappeared, but there is no doubt that American cultural influence became dominant. America replaced Europe, against which Jews held a profound grievance. However, it took more than a little time for America's political culture to become a source of inspiration. During the 1950s, among those Israeli politicians and public figures who frequently praised the United States as the leader of the free world (in contrast to the threat posed by the Communist Eastern bloc), few went on to praise American values or the American way of life. The political and public discourse dealt primarily with the political relationship between Israel and the United States, and even more so with the American Jewish community; it dealt very little with the various aspects of American society.[71] All this changed, as we have noted, beginning in the 1970s—a change observable in the increase in the number of books published in Hebrew about various aspects of the general American experience (not only the Jewish American experience), and in the number of American literary works translated into Hebrew. In an era of modern and global culture, the importance of geographical distance faded, and America became a permanent, active presence in almost every aspect of cultural life in Israel.

An unavoidable result of this situation was that America became the symbol of Western culture. Now, when representatives of anti-Western sentiments in Israeli culture wished to point to a lenient, corrupt, untraditional, and materialistic culture—a culture that is thoroughly negative and a threat to authentic Jewish values—the source of danger they indicated was American, rather than European, culture. From their perspective, Israel's importation of the American dream was better described as a nightmare. The changes in Jewish attitudes toward Europe from the nineteenth century to World War II and the Holocaust also occurred in attitudes toward America during the latter half of the twentieth century. America was at once glorious and accursed—depending on the beholder's political and cultural orientation.

The political conflict between the United States and several countries of Western Europe—a conflict that became increasingly acute at the end of the twentieth century and the start of the twenty-first—carved a gulf of sorts between America and Europe, and it sharpened the essential differences between them. Spokesmen of both the European Right and the European Left renewed the longstanding motif of a profound difference between the so-called Old and New Worlds, and this motif was adopted in various Israeli circles. This inspired a debate in Israel on whether Western values were more truly represented by America or by Old Europe, now revived and beginning to put on new clothing. Was it possible to see Europe's tyrannical regimes—and the Holocaust—as a drastic but temporary deviation from its exalted values, or was Europe continuing to reveal not only its intrinsic antisemitism but also weakness, feebleness, and acquiescence, particularly to the perceived Muslim threat? Was Europe, at the end of the twentieth century, once again becoming an atrophied and unhealthy culture? Was Europe betraying its American ally, who had liberated it from the tyrannical Nazi regime? Or was Europe—unlike the United States—learning from its own history that the use of military and economic measures to impose its values on the rest of the world was inappropriate and harmful, constituting the sort of imperialism that had no place in a postcolonial world? The clash between Europe and the United States began to be perceived as a clash between two civilizations in which Israel had to take a stand. Over the last decade, various circles in Israeli society have shown signs of returning to the negative image of America that predominated from the 1940s to the 1960s. America was no longer a model of efficiency and progress, of political freedom and civil rights, but the last remaining imperialist nation—a nation that polluted the universe; inundated the world with mindless cultural products; represented unrestrained, profit-chasing capitalistic imperialism; and displayed strong currents of narrow, zealous, evangelical fundamentalism. In short, a spirit of hatred toward America and what it represented began to take hold in Israel. It is no wonder that Ziauddin Sardar and Merryl Wyn Davies's *Why Do People Hate America?* was translated into Hebrew in 2006, by a publishing company of radical social tendencies. What is called Occidentalism was now no longer aimed at countries with a recent colonial past, but at the United States. Andrei S. Markovits's *Uncouth Nation: Why Europe Dislikes America*[72] is an attempt to describe the phenomena of European anti-Americanism and anti-Americanization, which target all aspects of the American experience, not just American foreign policy. This opposition is expressed through both protests and criticism, and through hatred and loathing. In Markovits's opinion, this attitude is the domain not only of the intelligentsia in Western Europe—on both Left and Right, each group for its own reasons—but also of many segments of the public. Moreover, Markovits does not consider this simply a fashion or a passing phenomenon; he traces its roots to the very birth of the United States. It appears to us, however, that Markovits conflates various types of criticisms and perceptions and does not balance them with a parallel corpus of expressions that might reveal a positive approach to America (for example, in his discussion of anti-Americanism in France, Tocqueville is not mentioned). It seems that even a partial survey of mutual perceptions on both sides of the Atlantic would reveal many ambivalent exchanges and relationships—and, of course, many generalizations and stereotypes.[73]

Which way the winds blow in the near future will depend more than a little on the development of political and cultural trends in Israel, as well as on the results of the United States' foreign policy. For our purposes, most important is the fact that in the contemporary historical and cultural consciousness of Israeli society—particularly during the last generation—there exist two stereotypes of the West, each of which excites both positive and negative images. No less important is the fact that criticism of America draws liberally on concepts and opinions that originate in the United States' self-criticism, just as the Jewish criticism of Western Europe in the nineteenth and twentieth centuries drew on both the conservative European *Kulturpessimismus* and Europe's revolutionary radicalism. Furthermore, in the case of America, just as in the case of Europe, negative attitudes toward American policy and decisive rejection of American cultural values are not sufficient to cancel either the influence of American culture or its massive presence in Israeli culture—not even its presence in the culture, or habitus, of those who hold it in a negative light and warn others to keep away from it.

ISRAEL AS WESTERN

Is Israel, then, a Western nation? This question was addressed not long ago by the sociologist Sammy Smooha in an article titled "Is Israel Western?" The subtext of the article is directed toward those who congratulate themselves that Israel, despite its geographic location, is a Western country and not, Heaven forbid, Oriental; it attempts to demonstrate that Israel does not meet the criteria of Westernness. Smooha proposes a distinction between modernity and Westernness: the processes of modernization have a universal character, while Westernness is expressed in ten principal attributes that are common to Western European countries and provide them with a uniform character. The properties Smooha lists relate to national characteristics (for example, Western countries have fixed borders and a low birth rate; religion and the military do not occupy a central position; and theirs is a civic nationalism). Consequently, even though Israel sees itself as part of the Western world and as possessing a Western character, that is not the case—which illustrates how difficult it is to export the Western model in its entirety to non-European nations.[74] Smooha, of course, uses as his comprehensive model Europe after World War II. And indeed, Israel's geopolitical situation is different from that of European nations, as is the makeup of its population. The Jewish tradition's position and role in Israeli culture and society are unlike the position of the Christian tradition—Catholic or Protestant—in European society. Nonetheless, if we consider, for example, an important criterion such as quality of life, we find that the quality of life in Israel is similar to that of Western European countries. The United Nation's Human Development Index of 2006, which reports data from 2004, finds Israel ranked twenty-third in the world with respect to life expectancy, gross national product, level of education, and human health. Ahead of it on the index are the Western European countries, as well as Canada, Australia, Japan, and the United States. The other Middle Eastern countries trail Israel significantly (Kuwait, for instance, is thirty-third). Most importantly, Smooha maintains that although the Israeli lifestyle is becoming increasingly European, it remains distinct. However, the measure of Westernness he proposes—which includes television viewing, use of cellular phones, and the like as primary cultural traits—ignores a long and important list of cultural traits that form an inseparable part of the culture and lifestyle of Jewish society in Palestine. The reason for this is, apparently, that these cultural elements are so deeply internalized in Israeli society that they are self-evident, and their European origin has been forgotten.

EUROPE, OLD OR NEW?

Europe on the Brink was the name of a special program aired on Kol Israel's *Reshet Bet* radio channel on February 2 and March 3, 2004. According to the program, Europe stood on the brink of "antisemitism, Islamic terror, incitement against the State of Israel, and the precarious conditions of Jews in European communities." In other words, Europe was depicted here from a Jewish and Israeli perspective. Once again, a portrait emerged of Europe as a decadent, superficial, vacuous, and materialistic culture. This was Old Europe, where—behind a facade of enlightenment, rational intellect, tolerance, and liberalism—the destructive forces of nationalism, racism, human-rights violations, aggressive imperialism, and of course antisemitism were and had always been present, the latter a fatal, incurable illness. The question was by what right had Europe placed itself at the head of the international moral order, dispensed advice, and judged and sentenced others for their crimes. It was, after all, a continent where during the 200 years from the French Revolution and Napoleon to the civil war in the former Yugoslavia, many tens of millions—or even more—had been killed, slaughtered, and murdered. Were these horrors atoned for by the fact that Europe had created lofty cultural assets now consumed by the entire civilized world?[1] Overall, Europe was simply deluding itself—and tempting others to accept the delusion—that it was now a new world that had managed to shed all the evils of its past.

Some of the motifs of this image of Europe are common to the Jewish critique and the general anti-Western position, including the picture presented by extremist conservative groups in Europe itself and in the United States. An example is the nightmarish vision put forth by Patrick Buchanan, the right-wing presidential candidate, in his 2002 book *The Death of the West: How Dying Populations and Immigrant Invasions Imperil Our Country and Civilization*.[2] According to his vision, Western Europe is a dying society that has lost its will to live, and whose economic prosperity is fragile. In contrast to critiques issuing from these circles, the criticism from Israel and the Jewish world is generally devoid of schadenfreude or the anticipation of aging Europe's inevitable decline. Concern for Europe's future is frequently expressed, as is the hope that it will extricate itself from its state of decline and return to its senses and its status as the pinnacle of culture.

It is probably for this reason that conflicting responses were expressed within the Israeli discourse to the rejection of the European constitution in May 2005. Some considered the rejection merely a delay caused by social and economic problems in certain countries, arguing that there was a solid foundation for the existence of a Europe without borders. However, others believed that the causes for the rejection were a profound fear of change, a manifestation of popular nationalistic sentiments that refused to accept the bureaucratic vision of politicians, and racism. Some believed that what they considered a revival of European nationalism legitimized Jewish nationalism in Palestine; the rejection of the constitution was incontrovertible evidence that the age of nationalism was still alive. Europe, however, knows how to beguile its would-be prophets. In any case, we should not rush to evaluate Europe's future according to political upheavals while ignoring long-term trends.[3]

Apocalyptic descriptions of Europe in the present, and of its future destiny, are almost nonexistent in the Jewish public discourse from the end of World War II to nearly the last quarter of the twentieth century. Occasionally, a prophecy appeared of Europe's decline, in the spirit of the pessimistic prophets prior to World War II; there were also expressions of sweeping hatred for the West and all it represented,[4] similar to sentiments expressed in the anti-Western literature of the postcolonial world. These prophecies arose, in general, as part of an attempt to formulate a historiosophical doctrine on which to base an essentialist ideology for the revival of an original, ideal Jewish culture diametrically opposed to Europe. In contrast to the vision of a Europe in decline, an eschatological vision was presented of the revival of a modern, authentic Judaism in Palestine. This vision stemmed from a recognition of the immense influence of European culture on modern Jewish culture, and from the desire to escape the former. One example of this attitude is the bleak picture drawn by Eliezer Livneh, previously a prominent ideologue for the Mapai party and, during the period in which he wrote *Israel and the Crisis of Western Civilization*, a central ideologue for the Movement for Greater Israel. Livneh described a satiated, materialistic Western civilization that was decadent and dying, devoid of spirituality and unable to be saved from the inherent crisis it faced.[5] He concluded that Jews and Judaism had no future if they could not free themselves from the "fanatical devotion to the universal future of Western humanism."[6]

This pessimistic picture of Europe's decline returned to the forefront of the Jewish and Israeli public discourse during the end of the twentieth century and the beginning of the twenty-first—just as an opposite, optimistic picture of Europe emerged, in which religious wars and the polarization between nationalism and full-scale European revolution had disappeared decisively, and in which totalitarian regimes had passed away.[7] Just as it seemed that Europe was at last beginning to achieve the Erasmian ideal of a common identity,[8] it began to be portrayed in the Jewish and Israeli public discourse once again as an accursed—or at least untrustworthy—Europe.

Does this portrayal depict and judge reality from a limited point of view, or is it possible that this time—having learned from the experiences of the not-too-distant past—the Jewish seismograph has succeeded in detecting signals that others have failed to sense?

BETWEEN GERMANY AND SOVIET RUSSIA

According to the poet Uri Zvi Greenberg, Europe remained "Europe of the cross" even after the Holocaust. He did not distinguish, for example, between Poland and Germany, or between Germans and Slavs: all were part of Christianity—"our eternal enemy"—and it was from Christianity that they drew their hatred and their thirst for Jewish blood. As a result they were not "human," but bestial. Greenberg's decisive conclusion was that "the spirit of Europe is a deathly poison"; behind European philosophy and art there flowed, and would always flow, the "dark blood" of murderers.[9] However, in the Israeli public discourse, Europe after World War II and the Holocaust was generally not portrayed as a dying continent, nor was it considered homogeneous. There were three main reasons for this. First, it was impossible to consider, for instance, England and the Soviet Union—two of the nations that had fought and defeated Nazi Germany—as part of the same demonic culture that had given birth to Nazism. Second, the cold war and the division of Europe into two blocs—West and East—led to a different approach toward each of them, determined according to various and sometimes extreme ideologies and political orientations. The third reason—Jews' affinity toward Western culture and its values and assets—was too profound to allow them to uproot it entirely.

It was Germany, of course, that represented Europe's demonic side; not, however, the whole of Europe. The perception that Germany was a special case distinguished it from the other European nations, including those that had cooperated with Nazi Germany and those considered organically antisemitic. After World War II, the public discourse in Israel returned to the question of the organic nature of Germany and the Germans, but this time with far greater intensity and force. This discourse attempted to decipher the German code and determine whether Nazism was an inevitable result of the unique nature of the collective German personality and of its particular historical path (*Sonderweg*) in the context of European history. A common claim within this discourse was that Nazism was a uniquely German phenomenon that came into being as the result of the profound mythological layer embedded within the innermost soul of every German and of the unique spiritual tendencies ingrained in the German people. These inevitably led to racist antisemitism, and to the murder of the Jewish people.[10]

A series of antisemitic events that took place in Germany after 1945, as well as what was seen as a revival of neo-Nazi elements, only strengthened the claim that the German character was fundamentally bestial, and that this bestial foundation was destined to re-erupt during a time of crisis, again aimed first and foremost against the Jews. This outlook, primarily during the 1950s, reinforced Germany's image as a nationalistic state that was militaristic and antisemitic by nature—a nature that would never change, and toward which hatred was an Israeli duty. Representatives from both sides of the ideological and political fence expressed this claim in response to the decision of the United States, Britain, and France to reinstate a German army in the Federal Republic. Yaacov Hazan, one of the leaders of Mapam, declared in a Knesset debate in November 1954 that a neo-Nazi army was being raised in West Germany that threatened the destruction of the world and thus of Israel. According to him, this was a preliminary step toward a third world war. A representative of the Zionist Left, Yitzhak Ben-Aharon, declared that "Adenauer's Germany is a thin, transparent guise of an old man masking [the reality of] renewed neo-Nazism," while a representative of the Communist Party, Shmuel Mikonis, maintained that this was a revival of German militarism and constituted a "terrible danger to the nations of Europe and all humanity." According to him, Israel's government was increasing its "cooperation with West Germany's Nazi government." The Right also warned against German armament, but for different reasons. Arieh Altman, one of the leaders of the Herut movement, declared that "an armed Germany will fight side by side with Russia against the West," since "the German people should be considered a threat, as Nietzsche once said."[11] Foreign Minister Moshe Sharett's response was that "all the doomsday prophecies on this matter [the ties with West Germany] have been proven entirely false for now."[12] These claims were also raised during the debate about Israel's arms deal with Germany in June 1959. Once more, Mikonis maintained that "the regime in West Germany today is founded on the same dark forces and the same murderous militaristic trends that characterized Hitler's regime." Adenauer's Germany, he declared, was paving the way for yet another edition of the Third Reich.[13]

It should be noted that the radical and pro-Soviet Israeli Left did not object to the creation of an army in East Germany. Its stance derived from its pro-Soviet orientation and not from an essentialist perception regarding the unalterable German nature. Within the Israeli Left, in contrast to the Right, it was not an essentialist outlook that determined the attitude toward Germany after 1945, but rather the tension between historical memory, an international political orientation, and pragmatic questions of economic and political policy. In any case, the cries that German militarism would soon awake were sounded in vain. Officially, Israel did not view West Germany's new economic and political status with trepidation. Likewise, the official position of Israel, and public opinion there, expressed almost no concern regarding the unification of the two Germanies at the end of 1990 and did not describe that unification as paving the way toward a Teutonic revival. On the contrary, they welcomed the collapse of Communist, anti-Israeli East Germany.

The question of whether West Germany was different than Nazi Germany came again to the forefront of Israeli public discourse following the reparations agreement in 1951–53, the German involvement in the arming of the Arab world, and the establishment of diplomatic relations between Germany and Israel in 1965. Again, many attempted to answer the questions of whether German culture was indeed the progenitor of Nazi Germany,[14] and whether the Germans were a nation of murders. In any case, the validity of concepts such as collective spirit and national character was examined. For example, two 1967 books dealt with the question of whether West Germany was different—whether it had been able to internalize liberal and democratic values and to escape the tendency toward extreme nationalism that was imprinted on German society. The first of these books, *The Other Germany*, was written by the journalist Vera

Elyashiv; the second, *A Land Haunted by Its Past: The New Germany*, was written by the journalist and historian Amos Elon.[15] In her book, Elyashiv asked: "Should we treat the Nazi regime as a German illness, or was it a human plague that just happened to break out in Germany? And if it was a German illness—is Germany now inoculated against it, or is it more susceptible than other nations?"[16] Her answer was: "I did not find a new Germany, but an almost random mixture of old and new . . . The 'sick man of Europe' is not found today on the shores of the Bosporus, but on the banks of the Rhine."[17] Amos Elon's response to the same question was: "It is admittedly a new Germany, but at times it is desperately difficult to discern its true nature."[18]

After 1945, several waves of neo-Nazi and antisemitic incidents and events occurred in Germany. The outbursts of this sort that broke out in 1992, after Germany's unification, were interpreted as evidence that in the absence of a liberal and democratic tradition in Germany, militant nationalism was apt to reemerge; in any case, unification would alter Europe's internal balance, the spiritual map of Germany, and the whole of Europe for the worse.[19] It is impossible to disagree with Moshe Zimmermann's opinion that the ambivalent attitude toward Germany was a permanent condition: "The average Israeli is trapped between two forces, two drives—on the one hand, adaptation to the new Europe, in which Germany is a central player, and on the other hand, the search for collective identity, inseparable from the memory of the Holocaust."[20]

Another issue that occupied the Israeli government and public opinion was the attitude toward German culture. On the level of principle, the question was whether it was possible to differentiate between Germany's great cultural heritage—that of Goethe and Schiller, Beethoven and Brahms—and the factors and phenomena that gave rise to Nazism.[21] On the practical level, the question was whether it was necessary or appropriate to import German cultural products (in particular, translations of German literature) and to create cultural ties with West Germany. In 1949, Gershom Schocken, *Haaretz*'s publisher and editor, who was then serving as a member of the Knesset for the Progressive Party, proposed a law that would ban most contact between Israelis and Germany and would define the special circumstances under which such contact would be allowed. In 1987, Schocken wrote: "reality trumped the memory of the Holocaust."[22] Over time, an attempt was made to differentiate between utilitarian political and economic ties and cultural ties,[23] as well as between formal, political ties and individual connections.[24] But cultural ties—both private and official—flourished from the end of the 1970s onward. Hatred of Germany and the Germans declined, and the debate about whether Richard Wagner's music should be performed became the last trace of that hatred.[25]

On the opposite pole of Europe from Germany were the Soviet Union and the Communist bloc nations. For the radical Zionist Left (Mapam and Ahdut Haavoda), the East—the Soviet Union and communism—represented the positive values of the new European culture, seen as the complete opposite of the values of the bourgeois, capitalistic, reactionist, and degenerate society found in the West, especially the United States. The Zionist Left, with its orientation toward the Soviet Union, saw Soviet culture as progressive—the preferred and desired model for a collectivist, mobilized, and centralized society that does not idolize selfish individualism and materialism. From this point of view, the Messiah had arrived in Eastern Europe, and there a new society and new humanity had arisen. The persecution of Jews in Stalinist Russia, the imprisonment of tens of thousands of Jews in gulags, the Doctors' Plot, and the Prague trials cast almost no shadow on this image of the Soviet Union as "the world of tomorrow"—until the twentieth Congress of the Communist party in February 1956.[26]

In addition to this political orientation toward the Soviet Union and its political and social ideology, the Soviet cultural models had a large influence on Hebrew culture during the Yishuv period and particularly, during the 1950s, on well-defined segments of Israeli society, mainly those belonging to the "Marxist Left," and, among other things, on the choice of translated literature and imported art.[27] However, in the end, the Leftist anti-Western ideology was unable to prevent Israeli society from becoming increasingly bourgeois or the increasing Americanization of its culture.

In contrast, from the beginning of the 1950s to the start of the 1990s, some Israelis warned that the Jews of the Soviet Union were facing death because of the official antisemitic policy. This apocalyptic picture turned out to be baseless. There is, of course, great irony in the fact that there were those who feared the breakup of the Soviet Union—whose antisemitic policies and refusal to allow Jews to emigrate were protested by Jewish organizations and the State of Israel—because they believed that in this new reality, traditional antisemitism would rear its head and no central authority would exist to fight it.

FRANCE AND THE RETURN TO THE DREYFUS TRIAL

At the end of the twentieth century and the beginning of the twenty-first, France was the symbol of accursed Europe. This image was the result of a long chain of antisemitic events whose motives and severity, and the danger they posed to French Jews, are a matter of dispute.[28] (On July 8, 2004, the French president Jacques Chirac also admitted that antisemitism and racism, including Islamophobia, were a threat to French unity.[29])

The sources and causes of antisemitism in France are controversial: is it traditional antisemitism, or does it stem from opposition to Zionism, or criticism of Israeli policies on the Palestinian question? Does that criticism arise from and serve as justification for an antisemitic position, or is the criticism legitimate? Is this antisemitism French—whether it issues from the Left, the Right, or both camps—or was it imported to France by its six million Muslim immigrants, estimated to be 10 percent of the population? And, in the latter case, is the antisemitism a reaction to the Mideast conflict, or the result of the crisis brought about by the Muslim population's integration into the French Republic and its values? In any case, the antisemitic incidents in France stirred fear because they were at odds with the political and cultural tradition that France symbolizes. Thus it is no wonder that the public discourse focused on the fact that France was the spiritual birthplace of modern antisemitism,[30] while ignoring republican France's struggle against that antisemitism.

One of the paradoxes of this situation is that to some, the sins of Israel and its supporters, Jews around the world, appeared not necessarily as an expression of absolute evil inherent to Jews, but as a manifestation of the European ghosts, such as ethnoreligious nationalism, racism, and colonialism, that infected Zionism and Israeli society.[31] Another paradox is the fact that some French Jews responded to evidence of antisemitism by presenting Jews as the authentic representatives of French secularism and culture—a noble cultural heritage betrayed by liberal or leftist antisemites. Others saw it as a return of the old theological anti-Judaism in new clothes. In contrast were those who claimed it was a matter of anti-Zionism or anti-Israeli sentiment, stemming from the fact that, as they saw it, the State of Israel was not acting according to Europe's exalted universal values, but had inherited the destructive worldview of the anti-Enlightenment. Their conclusion was that the only way to wipe out antisemitism as a European phenomenon was not to complete the destruction of the Jewish presence in Europe, but to model Israel's political and cultural character on the European values of enlightenment and civil society.

In any case, the shock and fear regarding demonstrations of antisemitism in France and the future of the Jewish community there and in other Western European nations[32] arise not only from concern for the welfare of Jews in those countries, but also from the fear that Europe has not rid itself of its ghosts—and that this is not a question of ghosts alone.[33]

Thus we see both fear that Europe might cease to be Europe, and that it might revert to its European nature.

FROM A "JEWISH CENTURY" TO A "MUSLIM CENTURY"?

At the end of the nineteenth century, Friedrich Nietzsche wrote in *The Dawn of Day* that the twentieth century would be the one that would determine the fate of the Jews in Europe. Nietzsche, of course, never imagined through what terrible events that fate would be decided.

At the close of the twentieth century, predictions began to emerge that the following century would be the Muslim century or the century of Islam, and that Muslims would determine the fate of Europe and were likely to become its masters. Such prophecies increased steadily at the start of the twenty-first century, and the question came almost to the forefront of the political and public debates in which Europe—and the rest of the world—was engaged. These prophecies rely on what is perceived as the rising strength of radical Islam, but they are primarily due to the increase in the number of immigrants from Muslim countries who have settled in Western Europe. The size of this immigrant population in the European Union during the first decade of the twenty-first century is estimated at 4 percent of the overall population of the region, in contrast to that area's Jewish population in 1939, which is estimated to have been 0.7 percent.[34]

It is important to recall that the phrase "Muslim population" refers to a varied group: there are many differences between immigrants from Pakistan or Turkey, and immigrants from North Africa or the Middle East. Still, all of these groups are frequently subject to sweeping generalizations. The generalizations arise in part from the belief that "Islam has a universal history of its own and does not belong in the universal history of Europeans," as the German philosopher Ernst Troeltsch wrote.[35] From this point of view, there is no validity to the claim that, in comparison to Islam's intellectual influence on medieval Europe (primarily Spain) and its contributions to Europe's development, the Muslim world in the twenty-first century has no intellectual assets to contribute to the West. On the contrary, although Islam did not have much influence on Europe's religious development during the Middle Ages, it was still considered a military and even existential threat; the main threat Islam is thought to pose in the twenty-first century is a religious one.

Thus, as we have written in the introduction, a nightmare vision has begun to spread in Europe according to which the millions of Muslim immigrants are new barbarians, camped not beyond the city walls but within the city itself. All this is an outcome of the fact that in previous centuries, Europe had sent tens of millions of migrants to other continents; now it finds itself filled with migrants from those same countries in Asia and Africa, whose presence counters the decline in European birthrates. In just a short time, the warnings say, France will find itself struggling to preserve its French identity,[36] London will become Londonistan,[37] Germany will turn into Mecca,[38] and Europe itself will become a Muslim colony. According to these prophecies, we are currently witnessing the twilight of Europe's existence as a historical and cultural entity.[39]

The fact that this new wave of prophecy also flows from Jewish pens is not surprising. What is surprising is that their essays are invited to lead the charge in demanding that Europe reassert itself in order to save itself before it is too late. These writers make such statements, no doubt, out of concern for the fate of the Jews in Western Europe, as well as for the fate of Israel; however, it is impossible to shake the historical irony that clings to this phenomenon, in which it is the Jews, of all people, who prod Europe to save itself from Muslim encroachment—when it was Europe that, in the twentieth century, declared war against the Jewish people, which it described as an Asiatic, Semitic, and foreign race encroaching on a culture that was not its own, and even attempting to control it from within. The irony is that the warning cries against Europe's Islamization fundamentally resemble the anti-Jewish literature that was published in the nineteenth century to fight the *verjudung* (Judaization) of Europe.

We are confronted with a play of historical irony acted by Christians and Jews who consider themselves partners in the struggle against radical Islam in the name of the shared values of Judeo-Christian civilization —or, in other words, of Western culture.[40] Indeed, a fascinating historical metamorphosis has occurred. In the Middle Ages, particularly during the Crusades, the Christian anti-Jewish literature found similarities between Muslims—the external foe—and Jews, the enemy from within. Both were infidels; both had negative and even demonic inherent traits attributed to them.[41] Later, thinking of the Jews' role in the translation of Greek philosophical works into Latin, the American Jewish historian Ismar Schorsch wrote: "Paradoxically the contact with Islam had made Judaism part of the Western world."[42] At the same time, in the twenty-first century, there appears to be no connection between European Islamophobia and European antisemitism; on the contrary, the hostility between Jews and Muslims created a complete separation between them in the European consciousness. Yet, the Muslim presence in Europe is perceived to be one of the primary factors feeding the new antisemitism in Europe. In other words, Islam is a new source for the tradition of inherent antisemitism in Europe.

Are we then faced with a phenomenon that confirms Claude Lévi-Strauss's statement that "it is not the resemblance, but the differences which resemble each other"?[43] Is there any similarity between the Jewish and Muslim cases that might lead us to claim that Muslims are Europe's new Jews—a foreign, threatening other?[44] It is impossible not to notice the similarity between the old descriptions of Jews who migrated from Eastern and Central Europe to Western Europe, carrying the Middle Ages with them, and the descriptions of Muslim immigrants today. There are also nearly identical descriptions expressing wonder at how much like average Europeans past Jewish immigrants and present Muslim immigrants seemed.

However, the profound difference is not only that Muslims have a sizeable home front of Muslim nations, or that radical Islam has an ideological position regarding the sinking of the degenerate West and the Islamic mission to conquer it both physically and spiritually, and impose Islam on Europe. It should be noted that such a perception of the extension of *Dar al-Islam* (the Islamic world) to the West is both similar to and entirely different from the belief of the liberal Jewish minority in nineteenth-century Germany that the Jewish people had a mission to disseminate the idea of ethical monotheism, as well as many Jews' participation in radical movements that aimed to change the face of Europe. Instead, the great difference lies in the nature of Europe. Before World War II, there were Jews in Europe who wished to differentiate themselves from European society, and to preserve autonomous and separate communal frameworks; in contrast, other Jews searched for different methods of integration in

European culture and society, with some success. At the same time, there were Jews who tried, and in large measure succeeded, to consolidate a new model and new formula for an aterritorial national existence. The Muslim nationalist perception today is roughly similar to that nationalist perception of a nation without need for specific territory; however, while Judaism is the faith of a single people, Islam is the faith of many, and this idea is the basis for a broad concept of integration. Moreover, there is no Muslim concept of exile or diaspora; nor has there been any sort of Muslim Zionism—a call for an organized return to Muslim lands.

Yet another difference exists. It is accepted in the scholarship of this field that modern antisemitism was, among other things, a reaction to Jews' emancipation and integration in Christian European society. Jews were perceived not only as foreign and different, but as guileful—as a people capable of masquerading as Europeans despite their fundamental and essential difference.[45] In other words, modern antisemitism was not aimed against Orthodox Jews, who were distinguishable from the general European population not only by their religion but by their dress and lifestyle. Instead, it was aimed at those whose external differences from their European counterparts were blurred or even absent. The question in this context is whether Islamophobia is aimed only at Muslims who maintain a distinctive lifestyle and dress, and even emphasize their differences, or whether it also applies to Muslims who have become secularized and undergone the process of assimilation.

In Europe during the latter half of the twentieth century, the beliefs in *Volk*—in what is often called "race, blood, and soil"—diminished considerably. Religious influence weakened, and Europe became in large part an overtly secular continent. In contrast, the principle of multiculturalism grew in strength and reinforces an awareness of guilt relating to Europe's misdeeds in the age of colonialism and imperialism. On the one hand, this reality simplifies the processes of integration and acculturation that new immigrants face in Europe; on the other hand, though, it encourages not acculturation and integration, but rather maintains individuality and even self-segregation. It should also be noted that, in contrast to Jews, Muslims lack the centuries-old experience of life in exile under a non-Muslim rule—and certainly not as part of a non-Muslim, secular society. It is clear that their theological, ideological, and practical efforts at expressing their new reality have only just begun. In any case, in today's secular European society, Muslims are the most conspicuous religious element, and the mosque has replaced the church as the religious institution that attracts the masses. It is thus no wonder that there are those who see European liberalism—the ideology of multiculturalism that is opposed to any expression of Eurocentrism—and the idea that the Muslim world was no less Europe's victim than were the Jews as the causes of Europe's political weakness in its approach to the Muslim world, as well as its weakness with respect to the so-called Islamic invasion of Europe (they ignore the sizable contribution of religion to European antisemitism). The calls for Europe to defend its identity do not necessarily demand a defense of the principles of the Enlightenment, but rather a return to nationalism's Romantic idealism.

Like the Jews, Europe's heterogeneous Muslim population observes various patterns of existence within European society, develops different existential ideologies, and essentially proposes similar solutions. We might therefore say that the Jewish experience in Europe could shed light on the nature of the Muslim experience there; however, the Jewish experience cannot predict the twists and turns of the Muslim century, or where the latter will lead Europe and its Muslim population. All that can be said is that in the twenty-first century, the Muslim Question has inherited the place of the Jewish Question as a European problem—a problem that will affect not only the situation of European Muslims, but also the various moods and streams of thought that will lead to various opinions of the meaning of European identity.

Will Europe, then, become Muslim or post-Western, as some doomsayers and skeptics prophesy? Predictions regarding Muslims and Islam form a rich and complex repertoire that has not always proven itself. Prophecies of decline and revival do not emerge one after the other, imitating the swing of a pendulum; rather, they appear side by side. Europe's Muslim population will not form a single nation; it will branch out into different streams, each with its own outlook and its own way of life.

CONCLUSION

BETWEEN REAL EUROPE AND THE EUROPEAN SPIRIT

Is it possible to write a single history of the Jews in Europe—a Jewish history? Or is it possible to write several histories of the Jews in Europe—a history of Jewish communities interwoven with the histories of various nations?[1] The answer is that both are possible. Jews had a separate history within various European nations, which formed part of those nations' own histories; they also had a shared history as an ethnic and religious minority throughout Europe that underwent similar processes and faced similar obstacles. There is no contradiction between the internal history of a minority as an autarchic culture, in which immanent and unique changes take place, and the history of a minority that experiences changes under the influence of the majority culture. Jews were the only minority to inhabit all of the European nations; as such, they were exposed both to particular cultures and to the general European culture. It is these facts that make Jewish culture in Europe unique as a historical development and that are responsible for the uniqueness of that minority's response patterns and perspective. Our claim has been that despite the unique character of the various national European cultures in which Jews lived, and by which they were influenced, the Jewish elite was thoroughly familiar with Europe's overarching cultural background and absorbed a significant part of it. The Jews in Europe were therefore, to one extent or another, European Jews.

This common background is clearly expressed by the fact that over the course of the nineteenth and twentieth centuries, much of what is sometimes labeled the product of Western culture evolved into a set of universal values and ways of thought whose European origins are frequently obscured; critics of European culture have often used it as a basis for attack. As for the Jews, Europe served them as a reservoir of models and cultural traits that many considered worth adopting and internalizing into modern Jewish culture. Every modern Jewish culture was born in

Europe. It was impossible not to be influenced by Europe while living in it; it was impossible not to transfer its cultural patterns to Palestine.

In December 1923, David Ben Gurion wrote on his way back to Palestine after a visit in Moscow:

> Europe—the continent of profound contrasts and contradictions ... The continent of blinding light and blinding darkness; the lofty aspirations for liberty and justice, and the lean, ugly reality; the continent of revolution and market speculation ... the holy suffering and unclean corporation, the addiction and the bribery ... the idealism and greed, the changing values and the old tyrannies of tradition, the worship of work and the false idols ... and the lights and the shadows are intertwined, grasping and relying one on the other. And no one knows where sanctity ends and impurity begins: which is a relic of the past, and which the seed of the future? ... And great are the obstacles before a new world and a new society; who will emerge victorious?"[2]

Ben Gurion, of course, was writing not about Europe but about the Soviet Union six years after the Russian Revolution. We have replaced "the Soviet Union" with "Europe" and substituted "continent" for "land." It seems possible to apply Ben Gurion's words—which echo the opening lines of Dickens's *Tale of Two Cities*—to Europe as a whole. Our inspiration here comes from Winston Churchill's words about the future of the European continent, particularly Western Europe and about the lights and shadows intertwined there—that is, about the tragic duality Europe embodies. In a speech delivered in Zurich on September 19, 1946, Churchill described Europe as "this noble continent," "the fountain of Christian faith and Christian ethics," and added:

> [Europe] is the origin of most of the culture, arts, philosophy, and science, both of ancient and modern times. If Europe were once united in the sharing of its common inheritance, there would be no limit to [its] happiness ... Yet it is from Europe that have sprung that series of frightful nationalistic quarrels, originated by the Teutonic peoples, which ... wreck the peace and mar the prospects of all mankind.[3]

Today we would find Churchill's view Eurocentric, but Churchill excelled in describing Europe's duality and offering the continent a path to redemption in the spirit of Erasmian utopianism. In contrast, it cannot easily be said that Israel—officially or unofficially—has followed the reemergence of the idea of European unification with any great interest, especially as the idea seemed as distant from reality as it had been in the past. We have found few recent echoes of Churchill's September 1946 speech, in which he declared the need to recreate the "European family" and a "united Europe,"[4] nor of the European Union's advisory council meeting in Strasbourg in 1949. The State of Israel was occupied with its own relationships with various nations in Western Europe and was less interested in the unification movement's slow, if steady, consolidation. Ben Gurion was aware of the difficulty of predicting what future might be born from the mess of contrasts he described, and he maintained that the difficulties of prophecy had accompanied the Jews for the past two centuries. Indeed, they had failed to foresee the results of the monstrous element of Europe's character, and later had failed to predict its inevitable decline. Postwar Europe surprised them once more. It is possible that the fact that the State of Israel exists in the condition in which many European nations found themselves before and after World War I, and is similarly mired in a struggle over territorial sovereignty, is what has caused many Israeli observers to follow the unification process with distrust, to ignore the revolutionary change that the entire continent has experienced since the 1990s, and to emphasize specifically what appears to them as failure and regression.

The main expectation they had of Europe was that after the Holocaust it would cleanse itself of antisemitism and even demonstrate a pro-Israel stance. The disappointment that this has not always been the case has led to more than a few Europhobic declarations. Until the 1990s, hatred of Europe and what it symbolized was directed at Germany and the nations of the Communist bloc.

Since the 1990s, Western Europe has often been the target of loathing and has come to symbolize the whole of Europe. One of the manifestations of this situation is the support of Israel and the American Jewish community for the United States in its conflict with the nations of Western Europe—a political conflict that has also taken the form of cultural polarization.[5] In the presence of anti-Western trends developing vigorously in the postcolonial world, the slings and arrows of criticism and hatred have been turned on the United States, and it has become an unambiguous symbol of Western culture.[6] Europe's antagonism toward the United States and American culture is deeply rooted, as we have seen in chapter 9; in recent years, it has surfaced anew. According to William

Hitchcock, "Europe and America after September 11, 2001, are turning to an ugly rivalry."[7] This antagonism joins claims about the decline of America that are heard in the United States itself, as well as the radical Muslim perception that speaks of the necessary and inevitable decline of the United States.[8] However, it appears that the prophecies of a growing chasm between the United States and Europe are based on events during the second Bush presidency. These forecasts attempt to construct a deterministic historical schema on the basis of a short time frame. Changes in government—both in the United States and in Europe—as well as other influential events may alter the picture considerably. Anti-Europeanism will likely remain a substratum of European politics and culture; still, it appears to us that this movement will not cause Europe, or the European Union, to turn its back on its partnership with the United States, or to position itself as a foe.

From the Jewish point of view, the position expressed by the writer David Frischman at the start of the twentieth century has been reinforced: "America was our symbol of good and of light, of learning and of freedom."[9] This was not always the prevailing image of the United States in the Jewish consciousness. In parts of the Zionist Left, America was depicted during the 1940s and 1950s as a clear embodiment of materialism, aggressive and destructive capitalism, and cultural vapidness and superficiality. However, the more Europe's luster faded, and the more Israel's dependence on the United States increased, and its connection to and affinity with the American Jewish community became central and decisive factors in the nation's existence, the more its criticism of America faded. In former colonies around the world, as well as in various circles in Europe, the United States acquired a demonic image as the unrestrained heir of nineteenth-century European imperialism; at the same time, in the eyes of a large portion of the Israeli public, it became the standard-bearer for Westernness and Western values.

Attitudes are one thing, affinity another. Jewish affinity toward European culture was necessarily and essentially different from that of other nations in the postcolonial world. Jews were a minority in Europe; they were, in fact, the only minority whose population extended throughout Europe—if by minority we mean not a group living on the edges of European culture, but one living in its midst, both in various European societies and in Europe as a whole. At times these two allegiances conflicted, but in many cases they complemented one another. In any case, there was no inherent contradiction between them. The Jews were also not a society that lived under European colonial rule. As a result, Europe continues—even after most of its Jewish population has emigrated or was murdered[10]—to cast its spell on them and to be a source of concern.[11]

In Jewish Palestine, Western culture was given new content and a new role to play. It symbolized not itself, but the culture that its emigrants took with them. The antinomy between East and West became anchored in the social and cultural experience in Israel. This antinomy, which is originally European, transformed complex entities into simplified ones. It applies an essentialist perspective in order to define these two entities and to characterize their contents; and to create, by their means, generalized and static antinomies with regard to Israeli culture and society. These static images ignore the dynamic nature of culture—particularly that of cultures undergoing stages of transition and reconstruction.

The fact that Jews continue to debate the questions of Europe's future—how to relate to it, and how to appreciate it—and that they think and live according to cultural patterns and values that emerged from Europe demonstrates the extent to which Europe and its Western culture continue to be central to the Jewish experience. The world of Jews living outside Europe is not Eurocentric, but Europe plays an important part in it. For Jews at the start of the twenty-first century, Europe remains—just as it was during the nineteenth and twentieth centuries—glorious and accursed.[12]

"Can we uproot our Europeanness?" This was, as we have seen, a rhetorical question posed by Graetz. More than a century later, the relevant question is no longer whether the fact that most Jews no longer live in Europe will enable them to uproot it—or even whether they should—but what that Europeanness represents, what parts are worth preserving, and which parts need uprooting.

INTRODUCTION

1. See, recently, Vital, *A People Apart*; Gartner, *History of the Jews in Modern Times*; Webber, *Jewish Identities in the New Europe*.

2. Often we are referring to a concrete idea when we discuss concepts such as Europe, Western culture, the Orient, and Oriental nature. "Western culture" here generally refers to European culture rather than American culture. For a useful survey of the current literature on this topic, see Delanty's review essay "Conceptions of Europe." (We deal with this topic in greater detail in chapter 1.) The questions of when the United States of America began to represent the West to the Jews, and what differences they observed between the Old West (Europe) and the New West (America), are the subject of a separate discussion (see chapter 9).

3. In H. Graetz, *The Structure of Jewish History and Other Essays*, 194 and 196.

4. Zeev Jabotinsky, "The Orient," *Razsviet* (Dawn), September 26, 1926.

5. Y. Shavit, "Vladimir Zeev Jabotinsky" (in French).

6. Lilienblum, *Autobiographical Writings*, 2:196 (in Hebrew; unless otherwise noted, all translations from Hebrew are our own).

7. Berdichevsky, "Transvaluation of Values," 29 (in Hebrew).

8. This argument, as we shall see, was revived in Slezkine's *The Jewish Century*.

9. See Buruma and Margalit, *Occidentalism*; and Carrier, *Occidentalism*. See also chapter 9.

10. See Stråth, *Europe and the Other and Europe as the Other*. Theodore H. Von Laue writes that the "European minority" created and molded the system of globalization: for example, nation-states struggling against Western hegemony do this by means of tools and concepts taken from the West. See Von Laue, *The World Revolution of Westernization*, 3–34.

11. In fact, the awareness of decline began long before World War I. See Orluc, "Decline or Renaissance." Her article also deals with the difference between the constructs "Europe" and "the Occident."

12. See Heschel, "Jewish Studies as Counterhistory."

13. *Kehiliateinu*, 1922, 145 (in Hebrew).

14. Uri Zvi Greenberg, "Vision of Europe."

15. See volume 81 of the periodical *Eretz Aheret* (September–October 2003), dedicated to the subject: "A Letter to Europe: The Continent through Israeli Eyes."

16. On the economic links between Europe and Israel, see Monin, *The European Union and Israel*.

17. A report by the European Monitoring Centre on Racism and Xenophobia (now the EU Agency for Fundamental Rights) in March 2004 stated that there has been a rise in known occurrences of antisemitism in a large number of European nations; the report attributed responsibility to white males of European origin and to fundamentalist Muslims. The report was criticized on the ground that it intentionally ignored the role of Muslim organizations in Europe in antisemitic occurrences (*Haaretz*, April 1, 2004). The irony here is clear: part of the Jewish reaction perceives cases of antisemitism not as the result of a deeply rooted phenomenon in ancient European society, but primarily as the result of demographic changes in Europe—that is, the result of the heavy Muslim immigration to several Western nations. On this topic, see the conclusion of this book.

18. See, for example, the controversy in the wake of the poet Natan Zach's comments that "the values that have provided some basis for faith in mankind's future are the values of nineteenth-century European liberalism . . . We should not see the Holocaust, which lasted twelve years overall, as the most important chapter in European history" (literary supplement to *Maariv Sifrut*, September 13, 1988, in Hebrew).

1. EUROPE DISCOVERS ITSELF, JEWS DISCOVER EUROPE

1. Nietzsche, *Beyond Good and Evil*, 170.
2. Herder, *Reflections on the Philosophy of the History of Mankind*, 15.
3. Book 1, chap. 6.1, 122.
4. An example is Ephorus's *Europa*, a book from the fourteenth century B.C. that has been lost but is known from books 3–11 of Strabo's *Geographies*. During the second century B.C., Agatharchides of Cnidus wrote his *History of Europe*, which treated events from 323 B.C. on. The term "Europe," meaning Greece and its surroundings, expanded during the Middle Ages to refer to the Roman West, in contrast to the Greek East—that is, Byzantium, or the realm of non-European Christianity. The deep antinomy between the *imperium orientale* and the *imperium occidentale* thus came into place in medieval times. See J. Fischer, *Oriens, Occidense, Europa*; Wintle, "Europe's Image"; Khan, *The Birth of the European Identity*; Ullmann, *The Carolingian Renaissance and the Idea of Kingship*, 138–46.
5. See Schmidt, "Jewish Representations of the Inhabited Earth during the Hellenistic and Roman Periods."
6. It is important to stress that the concept "Europe" appeared as early as during the papacies of Gregory the Great (590–604) and Boniface IV (608–15), and then and during the Carolingian period, the term meant the region in which Christianity reigned. See Ullmann, *The Carolingian Renaissance*, 135–66. Against this background, it is easy to understand why Heine declared that European civilization began when "die allzu vollblütigen barbarischen Leiber . . . christlich vergeistigt [wurden]" (coarse barbarians . . . were refined through Christianization; Heine, *Die romantische Schule: Erstes Buch*, in *Sämtliche Schriften*, 9:17).

7. See Bisaha, *Creating East and West*, 86. The pope, of course, was aware that Europe was not really cohesive or united. We should mention that the idea of European superiority was due not only to arrogance, but also to the desire of making "disintegrated" Europe more unified in order to better contend with the Ottoman threat. It should also be noted that the Ottoman Empire is not usually considered part of the East that must be defended against the Orientalist image given it by the West—perhaps because the Ottomans were not Arabs, and perhaps because the Muslim Ottoman Empire ruled over parts of the West for hundreds of years.

8. See Kumar, "The Idea of Europe." On the known process in which the inhabitants of Western Europe spread throughout the rest of the continent—into the north, the Balkans, and the South—see Wright, *The Geographic Lore of the Crusades*, 312–22.

9. William Penn, for example, wrote his "Essay towards the Present and Future Peace of Europe" in 1693.

10. Rousseau, *Considérations sur le gouvernement de Pologne* (Thoughts on the government of Poland), 347.

11. Quoted in Hay, *Europe*, 123.

12. We relied here on the rapidly growing body of literature on this subject. See Hay, *Europe*; Bartlett, *The Making of Europe*; den Boer, "Europe to 1914"; Burke, "Did Europe Exist Before 1700?"; Cowling, *Conceptions of Europe in Renaissance France*; Cuisenier (ed.), *Europe as a Cultural Area*; Chabod, *Der Europagedanke*; Darnton, "A Euro State of Mind"; Gollwitzer, *Europabild und Europagedanke* and "Zur Wortgeschichte und Sinndeutung von 'Europa'"; Hale, "The Renaissance Idea of Europe"; Heater, *The Idea of European Unity*; Littlejohns and Soncini, *Myths of Europe*; Lively, "The Europe of the Enlightenment"; Mikkeli, *Europe as an Idea and as an Identity*; Pagden, *The Idea of Europe*; Parker, "Europe: How Far?"; Pegg, *The Evolution of the European Idea*; Reinhard, *Lebensformen Europas*; Schmidt, "The Establishment of 'Europe' as a Political Expression"; Wilson and van der Dussen, *The History of the Idea of Europe*; Wintle, *Culture and Identity in Europe*. For a recent critical survey of the definitions of Europe, Eurocentrism, Western culture, and Western civilization, as well as the various efforts to write European history or "Eurohistory," see Davies, *Europe*. His conclusion is: "In the end, therefore, intellectual definitions raise more questions than they answer. It is the same with European history as with a camel. The practical approach is not to try and define it, but to describe it." An interesting travel book, searching for the "misty term 'Europe'" is Mak, *In Europe*.

13. Novalis, "Die Christenheit oder Europa." This essay was written in 1799 but not published until in 1826. See Littlejohns, "Everlasting Peace and Medieval Europe." In his 1761 *Le cosmopolite, ou, Le citoyen du monde* (The cosmopolitan, or the citizen of the world), Louis Charles Fougeret de Monbron described the sense of being at home experienced by eighteenth-century travelers in Europe. The concept of *Weltbürger*, of course, refers to a citizen of all Europe, rather than the literal meaning of a citizen of the entire world.

14. See Malkin, *Ethnicity and Identity in Ancient Greece* (in Hebrew). We note here that the "cosmopolitanism" that Margaret C. Jacob finds in Europe during the early modern period is really several different manifestations of cross-Europeanism which preceded the French Revolution and the Napoleonic wars. This cross-Europeanism was a sense of belonging that spanned political and religious boundaries, as well as a flow of ideas across the same borders. See Jacob, *Strangers Nowhere in the World*.

15. *History of Civilization in Europe*, translated by William Hazlitt.

16. Nietzsche, *Beyond Good and Evil*, 115. On Nietzsche's attitude toward Jews (and Europe), see Passerni, "The Last Identification"; Brinker, "Nietzsche and the Jews"; and Gorel, "Nietzsche contra Wagner on the Jews."

17. Nietzsche, *Human, All-Too-Human*, 346–48.

18. Ortega y Gasset, *The Revolt of the Masses*, 194. See Medin, "José Ortega y Gasset and the Spaniards."

19. Hayden White wrote that "Europe is of course a mystification. For 'Europe' has never existed anywhere except in discourse, which is to say in the talk and writing of visionaries and scoundrels." See White, "The Discourse of Europe and the Search for European Identity," 67. However, Europe is a region distinguished by the search for any shared identity, and this fact alone has differentiated it from other regions, at least until the mid-twentieth century.

20. In his 1748 *The Spirit of the Laws*, Montesquieu differentiated between the nations of Southern Europe and the nations of the north. Nature, he said, gave "laziness" to the north, while it endowed southern countries with "industry and activity" (Montesquieu, *The Spirit of the Laws*, 332).

21. See Y. Shavit and D. Mendelson, "The Discovery of Italy and the 'South' in Western Literature" (in Hebrew). See also Payne, "The Concept of 'Southern Europe' and Political Development." Heine ("Italien: Reise von München nach Genua," in *Sämtliche Werke* 5:224) quoted a tourist: "Wenn Europa der Kopf der Welt sei, so sei Italien das Diebesorgan dieses Kopfes" (If Europe is the brain of the world, then Italy is the organ thief of the brain).

22. On the generally negative image of Greece in travel literature from the seventeenth and eighteenth centuries, see S. Said, "The Mirage of Greek Continuity." The wheel turned after the eighteenth century: during the fifteenth century, Italy's city-states perceived the "northern countries" (France and Germany) as barbarian; while beginning in the eighteenth century, "Western Europe"—that is, Europe north of the Alps—considered Italy as a place with a glorious past but an almost primitive present.

23. See Wolff, *Inventing Eastern Europe*, 3. On the subject of the Balkans as a geographical, ethnological, and historio-cultural construct, see Todorova, *Imagining the Balkans*. She writes: "As in the case of the Orient, the Balkans have served as a repository of negative characteristics against which a positive and self-congratulatory image of the 'European' and the 'West' had been constructed" (188). In this case as well, the measure of the move from Asiatic-ness, Orientalism,

or provinciality to belonging in Europe is primarily a question of whether the Balkan countries share an important part of what is known as European values, and may therefore be seen as civilized and Europeanized states (and cultures). Rabbi Dr. Mordechai Ehrenpreis, a native of Lvov who served as chief rabbi of Bulgaria's Jews in the years 1900–1914, and was later appointed chief rabbi of Sweden's Jews, attested to the attitude of Western Jews toward Balkan Jews when he wrote about his move from Berlin, where he studied, to Sofia: "This decision of mine, to leave a cultured, European place and assign myself to the much-maligned East, seemed to me a sort of intellectual suicide, diving into the chaotic darkness of the unknown. We, who were educated in the centers of European culture, have for the most part grown away from an arrogant perception of ourselves, to a greater or lesser extent; though, as for me, I have discovered that it is completely unfounded." At the same time, however, Ehrenpreis distinguished between Bulgaria's Sephardi Jews and the Ashkenazi Jews, who "became European" (Ehrenpreis, *Between East and West*, 84–85, in Hebrew). Regarding Poland as a "European country," Andrzej Walicki writes that "a majority of Western historians, referring to the socio-economic theory of modernization, conceive of nineteenth-century Poland as a backward East-European country," while Marx and Engels "took into account historical heritage and political culture," and "always treated Poland as part and parcel of Europe, and as an eastern outpost of the West." This outlook, writes Walicki, is an antidote to the "prevalent indifference towards the history of those European nations which, as a result of political divisions, do not belong to the contemporary 'West' and, because of this, are treated by many people, often unconsciously, as not belonging to Europe as well" (Walicki, *Philosophy and Romantic Nationalism*, 391). After Poland and other East European nations joined the European Union, this perception certainly died out.

24. See Penrose, *Travel and Discovery in the Renaissance*. On Europe's influence on the rest of the world, see the thirty-one-volume series *An Expanding World: The European Impact on World History, 1450–1800*, edited by A. J. R. Russell-Wood.

25. See Goody, *The East in the West*, 1–10.

26. Johnson, *The History of Rasselas*, 22–23.

27. Quoted in Lewis, *What Went Wrong? The Clash between Islam and Modernity in the Middle East*, 76.

28. Nietzsche, *Beyond Good and Evil*, 178–79.

29. On this subject see Geary, *The Myth of Nations*. Nietzsche and Ortega y Gasset predated the research literature that sees nationalism as a modern phenomenon. Thus, for example, Eric Hobsbawm writes that "nations do not make states and nationalism but the other way around" (Hobsbawm, *Nations and Nationalism since 1780*, 10). On the other hand, Ernest Gellner writes that "nationalism is not the awakening of nations to self-consciousness; it invents nations where they do not exist" (Gellner, *Thought and Change*, 168). For another opinion on a much earlier development of European nationalistic consciousness, see Hastings, *The Construction of Nationhood*; and Greenfeld, *Nationalism*.

30. Ortega y Gasset, *The Revolt of the Masses*, 194

31. The common religious foundation was also, as we know, both a catalyst and a background for the religious division of the Reformation.

32. See Grab, *Napoleon and the Transformation of Europe*.

33. In 1855, Shimshon Halevi Bloch's *Shvilei Olam* was published in Lvov. This was the second book written in Hebrew devoted to the description of Europe. A sequel of sorts is Abraham Mendel Moher's *Shvilei Olam*, which was published in Lvov in 1856 and printed in many editions up to the end of the nineteenth century. In her memoirs, the Jewish merchant Glikl of Hameln (1691–1719) recalls events that took place in many of the nations of Europe, and describes various Jewish journeys across the continent. However, nowhere in the work does she use the word "Europe." See Davis, "Glikl bas Juda Leib."

34. Shulman, *Sefer Divrei Yemei Olam*, 4:6–7.

35. Quoted in Etkes, "'Compulsory Enlightenment' as a Crossroads in the History of the Haskalah Movement in Russia" (in Hebrew).

36. During the Hundred Days, Napoleon proposed a grand European federal system; later, during his exile on Saint Helena, he wrote of a great European family. Had he completed his conquest of the continent, he would have united Europe under a single law, with a single court, single currency, and so on; and he predicted that such a union would occur eventually. Needless to say, Napoleon's vision was of a Europe united under French hegemony, flying the banner of enlightenment and progress. After the Napoleonic wars and the restoration of the French monarchy, and during the rest of the nineteenth century, intellectuals of various nations returned to Napoleon's idea and found the United States a model fit for emulation. Starting from the assumption that nations are not an eternal construction, but the outcome of consensus (a perpetual referendum), Ernest Renan concluded in 1881 that a similar consensus could give birth to European union (confederation). See Elie Barnavi, "The Idea of Europe" (in Hebrew).

37. Mendelssohn, "An einen Mann von Stande."

38. Mevorach, *Napoleon and His Era*, 58–78 (in Hebrew).

39. Quoted in Feiner, *The Jewish Enlightenment*, 312. See also Lesser, *Chronik der Gesellschaft der Freunde*, 8–10.

40. Quoted in Mendes-Flohr, *Modern Jewish Studies*, 64–85 (in Hebrew). See also Rubaschoff, "Erstlinge der Entjudung."

41. Y. L. Gordon, *The Letters of Y. L. Gordon*, 1:90 (in Hebrew).

42. Herder, *Reflections on the Philosophy of the History of Mankind*, 15. See Low, *Jews in the Eyes of the Germans*, 78.

43. Quoted in Livneh-Freudenthal, "The Verein für Kultur and Wissenschaft der Juden 1819–1824," 351 (in Hebrew). See also Meyer, *The Origins of the Modern Jew*, 167–68. Meyer writes that Gans initially spoke of "total embodiment" (*einverleiben*), and later of the merging (*aufgehen*) of the Jewish world in the European world (*untergehen*), but he did not refer to extinction.

44. Zunz, "Zur Geschichte und Literatur," *Gesammelte Schriften*, 1:41–42.

Hamutal Bar-Yosef writes that the intellectual Jews' "cosmopolitan" awareness was formed in the mid-nineteenth century specifically in czarist Russia rather than in the nations of Western Europe, where the Jewish intellectuals identified strongly with the local nationalistic culture. At least in the context of German culture, it is true that the concept of cosmopolitanism was not in use, but when the term "Europe" was used—even when Europe was considered synonymous with Germany—the meaning involved a wider cultural framework than the German framework alone. See Bar-Yosef, "Zionism and the Jewish Cosmopolitan" (in Hebrew).

45. Yehuda Leib Margaliot, an Orthodox rabbi and former *maskil*, quoted in Feiner, *The Jewish Enlightenment*, 387.

46. Toward the end of the nineteenth century, a new claim was added: Jews were not only capable of integrating into modern European society, and of making important contributions to it in different fields, but in fact they were the creators of Europe. It was they who had given Europe the Bible, of which the New Testament was a descendant, and in doing so, they had endowed barbaric Europe with their worldview and values. "The Jews," Heinrich Heine wrote, "gave Europe the modern principle [*das moderne Prinzip*]" ("Shakespeare's Mädchen und Frauen," in Heine, *Sämtliche Werke*, 10:227).

47. See chapter 4.

48. Goldstein, "Wir und Europa." We will return to this subject in greater detail in chapter 4.

49. See Ehrenpreis, *Between East and West*, 244 (in Hebrew).

50. Quoted in *Kehiliateinu*, 1922, 277.

51. Quoted in Y. Shavit, "Window on the World," 8 (in Hebrew).

52. Quoted in J. Katz, "A State within a State," 40 (in Hebrew).

53. Quoted in Low, *Jews in the Eyes of the Germans*, 361.

54. Reprinted in Lilienblum, *The Writings of M. L. Lilienblum* [in Hebrew], 4:32–33.

2. THE GLORIOUS NINETEENTH CENTURY— EUROPE AS PROMISED LAND

1. Reprinted in Yehuda Leib Levin, *Zikhronot vehegyonot*, edited by Yehuda Slutsky (Jerusalem: Mosad Bialik, 1968), 140.

2. Page 49.

3. See Heilbronner, "Fin-de-siècle from the Bottom-Up" (in Hebrew). Walter Laqueur emphasizes that *fin de siècle* was a term whose negative meaning acquired great popularity in France at the close of the nineteenth century; its popularity declined in France in 1905–6, while the term remained in use in Germany and Russia until World War I. Laqueur also points out that the concept of *fin de siècle* appeared in European literature as early as the 1830s. No less significantly, he also notes that alongside the global pessimism and doomsday prophecies of *fin de globe*

and *Weltende*, there was a widespread consensus that the nineteenth century was an extraordinary one in terms of its accomplishments; it was the golden age of *la belle époque*. See Laqueur, "Fin-de-siècle."

4. Quoted in Wheen, *Karl Marx*, 201.

5. Hugo, "The United States of Europe" (1845 speech, translated into English and published by the World Peace Foundation in Boston in 1914).

6. On the move at the start of the modern era to the current method of defining centuries, see Borst, *The Ordering of Time*. A few other works were extremely helpful in writing this chapter: Y. Shavit, "The 'Glorious Century' Or the 'Cursed Century'"; Feiner, "Post-Haskalah at the End of the 19th Century" (in Hebrew); Werses, "Awake, My People" (in Hebrew); Govrin, "At the Threshold of the Twentieth Century"; Bar-Yosef, "Fin-de-Siècle in Russia and Its Consequences for Zionism" and *Decadent Trends in Hebrew Literature* (both in Hebrew).

7. In Herzl, *Philosophische Erzälungen*, 111–18. Indeed, in his earlier work, such as the short story "Der Sohn" (The son; ibid., 121–33), Herzl expressed an unmistakable spirit of cultural despair, which Carl E. Schorske calls the "personal frustration and aesthetic despair of the typical fin-de-siècle intellectual" and Michael Stanislawski terms "an antibourgeois aesthetic." However, even though Herzl was critical of bourgeois society at the end of the century, he wanted to elevate rather than destroy it. See Schorske, *Fin-de-Siècle Vienna*, 9; Stanislawski, *Zionism and the Fin de Siècle*, 6.

8. Quoted in Mosse, *German Jews Beyond Judaism*, 3.

9. Eduard Gans, "A Society to Further Jewish Integration" (1822), in Mendes-Flohr and Reinharz, *The Jew in the Modern World*, 215–19. See also Livneh-Freudenthal, "The Verein für Kultur and Wissenschaft der Juden (1819–1824)" (in Hebrew).

10. Zunz, *Die Gottesdienstlichen Vorträge der Juden historisch entwickelt* (Jewish sermons and their historical evolution), 448–81.

11. Lilienblum, *Derekh Tshuva*, 83 (in Hebrew).

12. Quoted in Doron, *The Zionist Thought of Nathan Birnbaum*, 198 (in Hebrew).

13. See R. Cohen, "The Rhetoric of Jewish Emancipation and the Vision of the Future" (in Hebrew); Feiner, "Inventing the Modern Era" (in Hebrew); and Gay, *The Enlightenment*, 56–125.

14. Untitled poem by Moses Ensheim of Metz, *Hameassef*, October–November 1790, 32–35.

15. Werses, "The French Revolution through the Viewpoint of Hebrew Literature" (in Hebrew); Feiner, "'Rebellious French' and 'Jewish Freedom'" (in Hebrew).

16. Shulman, *Sefer Divrei Yemei Olam*, 4:7 (in Hebrew).

17. Yaakov Shmuel Bik of Brody, a *maskil* who became an admirer of Hasidism, quoted in Feiner, "'Rebellious French' and 'Jewish Freedom,'" 218–19. Criticism of this sort had already been heard in France during the revolution. Rousseau anticipated the nineteenth-century fear of science when he wrote: "Science,

beautiful and sublime as it is, is not made for man . . . he has too limited a mind to make great progress in it, and too much passion in his heart not to make bad use of it." Condorcet also believed that social progress would be far slower than the advancement of the physical sciences. See Vyverberg, *Historical Pessimism in the French Enlightenment*, 61–72. In this context, of course, it is impossible not to mention Voltaire's *Candide* (1759) and *L'Ingénu* (1767). See also McMahon, *Enemies of the Enlightenment*; C. Frankel, *The Faith of Reason*; and Bowler, *The Invention of Progress*.

18. Shulman, *Sefer Divrei Yemei Olam*, 2:77–78.

19. "The Sins of Youth," in Lilienblum, *Autobiographical Writings*, 1:193–94. See also 2:147 (in Hebrew).

20. Shulman, *Sefer Divrei Yemei Olam*, 7:9.

21. Ibid., 57.

22. Ibid., 36.

23. Ibid., 9:99–100. The Russian Jewish *maskil* Moshe Bazilovsky wrote in *Words of Wisdom or the Belief in Natural Science*: "Europe is in the most successful and perfect part of the world. While Europe weathered many storms on the road to such perfection, Europe was not prevented from achieving a high level of excellence and morality. Although not all countries in Europe reached such heights, Russia is not counted among them, owing to the blessed enterprise of Peter the Great" (in Hebrew, 21). Alexander II's reforms during the 1870s included the modernization of the government bureaucracy and the judicial system, construction of railways, and the expansion of the higher educational system. Such expressions of awe at the process of Russia's modernization during the age of Alexander II resemble, for example, those of Mikhail Pogorin on Russia's modernization and Europeanization in the days of Peter the Great. Pogorin wrote that Peter had introduced Russia not only to Western technology, but also to secular institutions of higher education, etiquette, European dress, and the like. See Walicki, *The Slavophile Controversy*, 52.

24. Hay, *Europe*, 124–27.

25. Fuenn, *Nidchei Israel*, 1:15.

26. Luria, *Omer Basade*.

27. Quoted in Bacon, "An Anthem Reconsidered" 55; see also Stanislawski, *For Whom Do I Toil?* 50.

28. Quoted in Shulman, *Sefer Divrei Yemei Olam*, 4:19–20.

29. Y. L. Gordon, *The Letters of Y. L. Gordon*, 1:314 (in Hebrew).

30. Berdichevsky, *Ginzei Micha Yosef*, 4:15–16.

31. On the Jewish reaction to the Damascus Affair, see J. Frankel, *The Damascus Affair*. On the influence of the Revolution of 1848 and Jewish responses to it, see Baron, "The Impact of the Revolution of 1848 on Jewish Emancipation."

32. Quoted in Volkov, *Germans, Jews, and Antisemites*, 28.

33. "Nationality Now and in the Future," in Dubnow, *Nationalism and History*, 174.

34. J. Wolff, "Eine Jahrhundert-Betrachtung," *Der Israelit*, 40 (103), December 28, 1899, 3027–29.

35. J. Kohn, "Zur Jahrhundertwende," *Allgemeine Zeitung des Judentums*, 64 (7), February 16, 1900, 76–78.

36. Quoted in Pulzer, "The Return of Old Hatreds," 216.

37. Moritz Lazarus, *Was heisst national?* 49.

38. See Bury, *The Idea of Progress*; and Briggs, *The Nineteenth Century*.

39. On enthusiasm for science and technology in Germany and England at the end of the century, see Rieger, *Technology and the Culture of Modernity in Britain and Germany*. The *Haskalah* saw science and technology as tools for expanding knowledge about various phenomena in the existing physical universe that were evidence of God's greatness, as well as about the natural laws He established. In contrast, during the nineteenth century, technology and science were perceived as tools that allowed man and society to exploit nature for their own uses, as well as to alter the world as it was created. On Jews' perception of knowledge from the end of the eighteenth century to the 1920s—in particular, as evident in texts aimed at young readers—see Kogman, "The Creation of Images of Knowledge in Texts for Children and Young Adults Published During the Haskalah Period."

40. See Feiner, *Haskalah and History*, 274–340; and Y. Shavit, "The Works of Henry Thomas Buckle and Their Application by the *Maskilim* of Eastern Europe" and "Window on the World" (both in Hebrew).

41. Zvi Hermann Shapira, "Hahamin Hizaharu Bedivreihem" (O wise men, speak with care), *Mimizrah umimaarav*, 1 (supplement), 1893–94, 3–20. Shapira was the first to propose the establishment of the Jewish National Fund.

42. Nahum Sokolow, "Divrei Hayamim: Al Miftan Hamea [At the threshold of the century]," *Hatzfira*, no. 2 (1900): 1–2.

43. Nachman Syrkin, "Al Miftan Meat Haesrim." The Hebrew press in Palestine also published articles and news stories about scientific and technological advancements toward the end of the century. Following the invention of the stethoscope, Eliezer Ben-Yehuda wrote: "Tales more wonderful than any past generation's are now becoming reality; what were once hallucinations have taken on form and stand proudly before us. Scarcely a day passes without hearing about some new invention which once even the most farfetched imaginations could not have thought achievable." See Ben-Yehuda, "The Wonders of Science," *Hazvi*, March 12, 1879. A year earlier, on February 2, 1878, *Hatzfira* reported "new and wonderful inventions arriving one after the other at a breakneck pace in recent days. Such tidings and revelations can never have been imagined by the sages of yore; they will be greeted with wonder and amazement by all." Less than two years had passed since the newspaper marveled at the invention of the typewriter and telephone, and now it marveled at Edison's invention of the phonograph: "indeed, this machine is enough to strike any man dumb with wonder."

44. Herzl, *The Jewish State*, 36 (in English).

45. Herzl, "Das Automobil," *Neue Freie Presse*, August 6, 1899.

46. Around the same time, inspired by an automobile showroom, the royalist journalist Léon Daudet—one of the heads of *Action Française* and son of Alphonse Daudet, the writer, he and Herzl met several times in Paris—wrote that "the automobile is war." Herzl describes the automobile as follows: "The Cleveland car seems to be the last word as of today. It operates on storage batteries which, it is true, have to be recharged every 100 kilometers . . . This gave me a further idea, that of developing mutualism" (*The Complete Diaries of Theodor Herzl*, 3:851–52).

47. Herzl, *Philosophische Erzählungen*, 25–40. Jules Verne dealt with this subject in two books: *Five Weeks in a Balloon* (1869) and *The Clipper of the Clouds* (1886). Herzl also addressed the subject in an article published in the *Neue Freie Presse* in December 1891: "The dreamer hopes that technological progress will come to heal the injuries that it itself has caused. When he sees how the idle pastime of flash photography suddenly sparks astronomical discoveries and deepens our ability to study how birds fly—advancements that might one day lead to the invention of a navigable airship—naturally he believes he may assume that some simple, wonderful method will be discovered by chance by which technology will forge peace between capital and labor. In the meantime we must try to do it with the instruments of practical politics." (By "practical politics," Herzl probably meant social legislation.) In a June 29, 1900, *feuilleton* titled "Zeppelin und Kress," Herzl again wrote with awe of the pioneers of aviation, including Wilhelm Kress, an engineer who experimented with flying machines that resembled airplanes and helicopters. It should be noted that the first zeppelin flight was conducted in 1900; the Wright brothers' first flight took place in December 1903. See Gross, "Herzl's Economic Conception" (in Hebrew).

48. Moses Mendelssohn was already concerned with this question; in December 1783, after the Montgolfier brothers' invention of the manned hot-air balloon during the same year, he wrote: "The discovery [of the hot-air balloon] will probably lead to great revolutions. Whether they will be for the good of human society nobody will as yet dare to decide. But who will on this account hesitate to promote progress? The discovery of eternal truths is, as such, good; it is for Providence to take care of them in the right direction" (quoted in Altmann, *Moses Mendelssohn*, 661). Herzl's story has echoes in *Altneuland*, in which Herzl describes the nineteenth century's utopian visions as "lovely dreams, or, if you like—lovely airships." Indeed, as Herzl himself wrote to Max Nordau in June 1896, some chose to interpret the story as an allegory for the Zionist idea.

49. Herzl, "Wahlbilder aus Frankreich," *Neue Freie Presse*, August 17, 1893.

50. Herzl, *The Complete Diaries of Theodor Herzl*, 1:45. For a broad discussion of Herzl's social and economic views and their origins, see Zilbersheid, "Herzl's Social and Economic Vision" (in Hebrew); and Gross, "Herzl's Economic Conception."

51. Herzl, *The Complete Diaries of Theodor Herzl*, 2:527. See also Yaacov Shavit, "Science, Technology, and the 'New Jew,'" *Haaretz*, July 8, 2004.

52. Herzl, *The Complete Diaries of Theodor Herzl*, 2:26.

53. Ibid., 1:114.

54. Herzl, *Zionist Lectures and Articles*, 1:25 (in Hebrew).

55. Herzl, *Altneuland*. The novel abounds with declarations in this vein: "it was this cultured and despairing Jewish youth which had brought the greatest blessing to Palestine by its technological application of the latest scientific discoveries" (120).

56. Herzl, "Zionismus," in *Theodor Herzl's Zionistiche Schriften*, edited by Leon Kellner (Berlin: Judischer Verlag, 1899), 119–33.

57. Herzl, *Complete Diaries*.

58. See Weber, *France*.

59. Herzl, *Altneuland*, 52.

60. See Oved, "Nineteenth-Century Utopias and *Altneuland*" (in Hebrew).

61. Wallace concluded his book as follows: "The flowing tide is with us . . . And as this century has witnessed a material and intellectual advance wholly unprecedented in the history of human progress, so the coming century will reap the full fruition of that advance, in a moral and social upheaval of an equally new and unprecedented kind" (*The Wonderful Century*, 381).

62. See Gould, "Second-Guessing the Future."

63. Herzl, *The Complete Diaries of Theodor Herzl*, 1:43 and 181. Herzl returns to this theme in *Altneuland*: "Never before have great cities been built so quickly and so splendidly, because never before were the technical facilities so abundant" (53). On February 1, 1896, Herzl wrote with amusement that he had been nicknamed the Jewish Jules Verne. Note that in several of his later books, Verne displayed a sense of pessimism regarding the influence of technology and science on humanity; for example, see *Paris au XXe Siècle* (Paris in the twentieth century), which was not published until 1994. Verne did not predict future inventions; instead, he followed the scientific developments of his own day. See Clamen, *Jules Verne et les Sciences*; and Martin, *The Mask of the Prophet*. On the myriad inventions of the second half of the nineteenth century, many of which were never successfully implemented, see de Vries, *Victorian Inventions*. On optimistic forecasts in the United States, see Gutfeld, "Back to the Future—American Leaders Forecast the Year 2000 from the Vantage of 1892" (in Hebrew). Between 1833 (when John Adolphus Etzler's *The Paradise Within the Reach of All Men* was published) and 1933, twenty-five American technological utopias were published that had been influenced by European utopian literature. See H. Segal, *Technological Utopianism in American Culture*, 56–77. On science and technology's place in Zionist utopias, see Elboim-Dror, *Yesterday's Tomorrow*, 160–66 (in Hebrew).

64. Quoted in Laskov, *Documents on the History of Hibbat-Zion and the Settlement of Eretz-Israel*, 1:367 (in Hebrew).

65. Buber, "If Herzl Were Still Alive," 205 (in Hebrew).

66. See Halevy, "Max Nordau"; and Geller, "The Conventional Lies and Paradoxes of Jewish Assimilation."

67. Nordau, *Paradoxes*, 331.

68. Ibid., 339.

69. See, for example, the Russian Slavophile Vladimir Soloviev (1853–1990) in his 1899 "Tale of the Antichrist," in which he predicts a European invasion by the "yellow races" during the twentieth century. Quoted in Walicki, *A History of Russian Thought from the Enlightenment to Marxism*, 390–91.

70. See Volkov, *The Rise of Popular Antimodernism in Germany*.

71. See Sternhell, "Reflections on the Turns of Centuries" (in Hebrew).

72. Jabotinsky, "The Elders' Rebellion," 231 (in Hebrew).

3. THE ACCURSED CENTURY—
EUROPE AS AN AILING CULTURE

1. Dostoevsky, *Notes from Underground*, trans. Richard Pevear and Larissa Volokhonsky (New York: Alfred A. Knopf, 1993), 8.

2. What Pevear and Volokhonsky translate as "unfortunate century," Constance Garnett renders as "unhappy century" (4). Dostoevsky presents those members of the Russian intelligentsia who did not believe in knowledge, science, and technology—in short, the products of the human intellect. He contrasted nationalism with cosmopolitanism and perceived learning and science as contaminated by "Europeanness"; Europe here represented an abstract, imaginary kingdom invented by human imagination. Tidings that the West was ill and near to death traveled eastward to Russia and found an echo there as early as the first half of the nineteenth century. Thus, for example, the Slavophiles quoted an 1840 article in *Revue des deux mondes* (Review of the two worlds), as proof that "the West itself [is] aware of its sickness" (quoted in Walicki, *The Slavophile Controversy*, 50). In 1905, the Zionist-Socialist thinker Dov (Ber) Borochov wrote in a similar vein: "We do not trust progress: We know that its devotees have exaggerated its value to no end. After all, progress advances technology, science, perhaps even the fine arts; certainly it advances hysteria and prostitution: but there is no room yet to talk about the moral progress of the nations" (*Works*, 1:2–3).

3. Chekhov, *The Duel and Other Stories*, 3.

4. See Walicki, *The Slavophile Controversy*; Von Laue, *The World Revolution of Westernization*, 35–49; and Greenfeld, *Nationalism: Five Roads to Modernity*, 223–74. According to Greenfeld, the Russian intelligentsia proposed three defenses against Western superiority: to imitate the West and resemble it; to see the West as an unsuitable model for Russia; and to highlight the superiority of Russia and the Russian soul over the West. See also Bar-Yosef, "Fin-de-Siècle in Russia and Its Consequences for Zionism" (in Hebrew).

5. See Tuchman, *The Proud Tower*, 55. How different the spirit of Kipling's poem is from the spirit of Alfred, Lord Tennyson's 1885 poem "Hands All Round," about the British Empire: "To all the loyal hearts who long / To keep our English Empire whole! / To all our noble sons, the strong / New England of the Southern Pole! /

To England under Indian skies" (Tennyson, *Tiresias and Other Poems*, 195–97). See also Buckley, *The Triumph of Time*. On the pessimistic mood in the last quarter of the nineteenth century, see Jeffrey Paul von Ara, *Progress and Pessimism: Religion, Politics, and History in Late Nineteenth Century Britain* (Cambridge, Mass.: Harvard University Press, 1985).

6. See Stern, *The Politics of Cultural Despair*; and Schorske, *Fin-de-Siècle Vienna*. See the chapter "The War against the West" in Kohn, *The Mind of Germany*, 93–98. Regarding the despondent mood in Britain—among other things a result of comparisons with dynamic Germany's achievements—see Heilbronner, "Fin-de-siècle from the Bottom-Up" (in Hebrew). On the German context, see also Dana Arieli-Horowitz, "Political Degeneration from the Fin-de-Siècle to Nazism" (in Hebrew).

7. See Friedländer, "The Nineteenth Century and the End of Mankind" (in Hebrew); Friedländer, "Themes of Decline and End in Nineteenth-Century Western Civilization"; and Herman, *The Idea of Decline in Western History*.

8. There is a difference between profound criticism and pessimism, and in fact pessimism did not dominate American consciousness at the end of the century. See Gutfeld, "Back to the Future—American Leaders Forecast the Year 2000 from the Vantage Point of 1892" (in Hebrew).

9. See Huizinga, *The Waning of the Middle Ages*. See also Sluchovsky, "Eschatological Anxieties."

10. Quoted in Weber, *France*, 9.

11. Nordau, *Degeneration* (New York: D. Appleton and Co., 1895), 1. The Zionist leader and writer Zeev Jabotinsky disagreed with most of Nordau's assessments in *Degeneration*, and in a 1926 piece titled "L'Amérique à un métre," one of Jabotinsky's characters observes that "this was a decade when that word [*fin de siècle*] was on the tongue of every man who knew how to read and write, when the thinkers' world nearly split into two camps . . . If it was even a 'literary fashion,' few other fashions were as prevalent; it sparked as great a fervor as Romanticism in its time. That word encompassed a gigantic, sweeping rainbow of moods and yearnings." Those moods were politically influential as well. See Jabotinsky, *Al Sifrut Veomanut*, 188.

12. See Gilman, *Decadence*; Chamberlin and Gilman, *Degeneration*; Swart, *The Sense of Decadence in Nineteenth-Century France*; Carter, *The Idea of Decadence in French Literature*; Teich and Porter, *Fin de Siècle and Its Legacy*; and M. Harrington, *The Accidental Century*.

13. In a 1929 article, D. H. Lawrence ("Pornography and Obscenity") described the nineteenth century in England as a barren century laden with obsequiousness and lies—a century that had tried to annihilate humanity.

14. Auerbach's critique "Europa: Chronik der gebildeten Welt, 1838" is quoted in Sorkin, "The Invisible Community," 103–4.

15. Yehuda Leib Levin, "The End of the Century." This series of articles was published in *Hamelitz* on April 28, May 6, and May 30, 1899.

16. See Stern, *The Politics of Cultural Despair*; Dana Arieli-Horowitz, "Political Degeneration from the Fin-de-Siècle to Nazism."

17. Luzzatto, "Derech Eretz or Atheism" (in Hebrew). See Y. Shavit, *Athens in Jerusalem*, 154–67; and Feiner, "A Critique of Modernity," 145–65 (in Hebrew).

18. Yehuda Leib Levin, "Sheelot Hazman" (Questions of our time), *Hashachar* 9, 1878, 133–34.

19. Levin, letter to the editor, *Hamagid*, no. 13, 1883.

20. Hamutal Bar-Yosef writes that Feierberg was influenced by the Russian symbolists' neo-mysticism ("Fin-de-Siècle in Russia and Its Consequences for Zionism," 178–79; in Hebrew).

21. Mordecai Zeev Feierberg, *Whither?* translated by Ira Eisenstein (London: Abelard-Schuman, 1959), 123–24.

22. Graetz, *The Structure of Jewish History and Other Essays*, 196–99. See also Michael, *Heinrich Graetz*, 178–79.

23. Eisler, in Elboim-Dror, *Yesterday's Tomorrow*, 25.

24. Ibid., 25–27. However, at the close of the novel, Avner, the protagonist and now the king of "New Judea," requests his son and heir to bring him a sack of earth from Europe "that on my death my head may rest on the soil of my native land" (35). See also Avineri, "Edmund Eisler's Zionist Utopia."

25. Bernfeld, "Toward the End of the Nineteenth Century" (in Hebrew).

26. See Y. Shavit, "The Works of Henry Thomas Buckle and Their Application by the *Maskilim* of Eastern Europe"; and Fuchs, *Henry Thomas Buckle* (in German).

27. "Luach Achiasaf" (A review), *Hashiloach*, 4, June–November 1898, 557–58.

28. Lilienblum, *Derekh Tshuva*, 42, 45, 48.

29. In Elboim-Dror, *Yesterday's Tomorrow*, 55–73.

30. Levinsky, "Thoughts and Deeds," *Hashiloach* 7, 1901, 183–90.

31. Dubnow, "Autonomism, the Basis of Nationalism," in *Nationalism and History*, 131.

32. Quoted in Werses, "On the Threshold of the Twentieth Century," 52–53 (in Hebrew). Levinsky was writing against the backdrop of the Second Boer War in South Africa (1899–1902) and the Boxer Rebellion in China (1898–1901).

33. "A Glance into the Future," in Nordau, *Paradoxes*, 333–43.

34. Ahad Haam, *The Letters of Ahad Haam*, 5:30 (in Hebrew).

35. Ibid., 57.

36. Ben Gurion, *The Letters of David Ben Gurion*, 1:245 (in Hebrew).

37. See Teveth, *Kinat David* 1:262–63.

38. Weizmann, *The Letters and Papers of Chaim Weizmann*, series A: *Letters*, 4:451.

39. Borochov, *The Letters of B. Borochov*, 614–15 (in Hebrew).

40. Quoted in Schechtman, *Rebel and Statesman*, 1:198.

41. Jabotinsky, *Letters*, 1:33 (in Hebrew).

42. Jabotinsky, *Autobiography*, 92 (in Hebrew).

43. Zweig, *The World of Yesterday*, 192–99.

4. THE EMERGENCE OF THE MODERN EUROPEAN JEW

1. Dostoevsky, *Winter Notes on Summer Impressions*, 8.

2. Nietzsche, *Beyond Good and Evil*, 185. Nietzsche continues: "and above all one thing that is both of the best and of the worst: the grand style in morality, the terribleness and majesty of infinite demands, infinite meaning, the whole romanticism and sublimity of moral questionabilities—hence precisely the most attractive, captious, and choicest part of those plays of color and seductions to life in whose afterglow the sky of our European culture, its evening sky, is burning now—perhaps burning itself out. We artists among the spectators and philosophers are grateful for this to the Jews."

3. Y. L. Gordon, "A Vial of Perfume," Feuilleton No. 7, in *The Works of Yehuda Leib Gordon: Prose*, 198 (in Hebrew).

4. Quoted in Druyanow, *Pinsker and His Times*, 156 (in Hebrew).

5. Nietzsche, *The Dawn of Day*, 210–14. See also S. Gilman, "Heine, Nietzsche and the Idea of the Jew"; Simon, "Nietzsche on Judaism and Europe"; Yovel, "Nietzsche and the Jews"; and Low, *Jews in the Eyes of the Germans*, 377–88.

6. Werner Sombart claimed in *The Jews and Modern Capitalism* that Jews were responsible for defining Europe's economic development and were its chief entrepreneurs. See Mendes-Flohr, "Werner Sombart."

7. Wistrich, "Radical Antisemitism in France and Germany" (in Hebrew).

8. Drumont, *La France Juive*. Drumont was preceded by the utopian socialist Alfonse Toussenel in his 1845 book, *Les Juifs, rois de l'époque: histoire de la féodalité financière* (The Jews, kings of the age: a history of financial feudalism). See Nolte, *Three Faces of Fascism*, 48–53.

9. See Opalski and Bartal, *Poles and Jews*, 27. On the depiction of Jews in Polish literature, see also Segel, *Strangers in Our Midst*; and Gutman, "Jews—Poles—Antisemitism" (in Hebrew).

10. Jacob Katz ("A State within a State"; in Hebrew) has shown that the antisemitic slogan that Jews were "a state within a state" could exist only after the emergence of the concept of citizenship—and, furthermore, after the rise of the nation-state. See also Volkov, *Germans, Jews, and Antisemites*, 67–155; and Aschheim, "The Jews Within." Yuri Slezkine's *The Jewish Century* puts forth the claim that the Jews had shaped nineteenth-century Europe by acting as "Mercurian" nomads: "mobile, clever, articulate, occupationally flexible and good at being [strangers]," they had ushered in modernity (30). This is once again, in a new guise, the myth of the pivotal Jewish role in the creation of modern Europe.

11. On the transformations of the term "Jewish Question," see Toury, "The Jewish Question"; and Talmon, *The Myth of the Nation and Vision of Revolution*.

12. Similar processes that took place outside of Europe, including within Jewish societies in the Muslim East, are called "Westernization" because the West came to those places from the outside. In any case, Westernization is always a part of modernization—that is, the process of change experienced by traditional

societies—whether it occurs through the adoption of Western values or through their rejection and the attempt to create new, supposedly authentic values in their place.

13. On the extent to which the process of urbanization contributed to assimilation, see Lowenstein, "Was Urbanization Harmful to Jewish Tradition and Identity in Germany?"

14. Graetz, "The Significance of Judaism for the Present and the Future," 6. On the activities of the Alliance Israélite Universelle in Mediterranean countries with the purpose of disseminating Western influence, see Rodrigue, *Images of Sephardi and Eastern Jewries in Transition*. The AIU's goal was to "bring a ray of Western civilization into communities which have degenerated as a result of centuries of oppression and ignorance" (73) and, more specifically, to disseminate "French customs, mentality, and character" (31). Although the AIU highlighted many evils that the West had inflicted upon the Orient, it had no doubt of the West's superiority in all aspects of life. According to the AIU, Rodrigue writes, "Westernization was the path of progress, the only means for the 'regeneration' of the 'degenerate' Eastern Jew" (73).

15. See Oz, *A Tale of Love and Darkness*, 58. Oz invokes Milan Kundera's observation that the Jews were the cosmopolitan factor that forged the spiritual unity of Central Europe (*Mitteleuropa*) and endowed its cities, great and small, with a European quality. See Kundera, "The Tragedy of Central Europe."

16. Zweig, *The World of Yesterday*, 20–21.

17. For a useful summary of the literature on this subject, see Shimoni, Pereg, and Mikulincer, *Psychological Aspects of Identity Formation and Their Implications for Understanding the Concept of Jewish Identity* (in Hebrew); Ben-Rafael, *Jewish Identities* (in Hebrew); and S. Herman, *Jewish Identity* (in Hebrew).

18. Kroeber, "Reality Culture and Value Culture." Norbert Elias defined "habitus" as a "second nature" emerging from educational and socializing processes, rather than as a revelation of static, essential, qualitative traits. These traits are determined by social codes that vary from group to group within a particular population: not all British citizens, for example, exhibit the trait of British gentlemanliness. At the same time, Elias also wrote of traditions and cultural components that characterize a given people as a whole. See Elias, *The Germans*. Pierre Bourdieu defined "habitus" as a system of various schemes of action, perception, and thought internalized by means of socialization into a more or less accepted code of conduct in different situations. See Gisèle Sapiro's introduction to the Hebrew translation by Avner Lahav of Bourdieu, *Questions de sociologie* (Tel Aviv: Resling, 2005, 10–11); and Algazi, "Studying Learned Nature" (in Hebrew).

19. Quoted in Toury, *Prolegomena to the Entrance of Jews into German Citizenry*, 81 (in Hebrew). Fifty years before Lessing wrote, an anonymous Christian visiting Berlin in the 1780s recorded this portrait of the Jewish community in that city: "They are no longer stiff-necked, cowardly, and coarse as the members of their nation used to be . . . The hairstyles of many are similar to those of the Christians

and their mode of dress is no different from ours . . . They are developing good taste and a liking for poetry as they begin to read more journals and attend the theater . . . When the weather is fine, one can see them strolling in groups through the Tiergarten Park or along Unter den Linden Boulevard" (quoted in Feiner, *The Jewish Enlightenment*, 258). What stands out in this description is not necessarily the rapid integration of Jewish Berliners into German bourgeois society, but the fact that it is a description of a minority that expresses admiration of the fact that a small, Jewish group was successful in adopting the behavioral patterns of its bourgeois environment—despite its dissimilar and even alien character.

20. Harshav, "The Revival of Palestine and the Modern Jewish Revolution," 9 (in Hebrew).

21. On the creation of tradition in Jewish Orthodoxy, see Silber, "The Emergence of Ultra-Orthodoxy."

22. The case of English Jews is unusual in that they did not require ideology to justify their integration into English society. See Endelman, "The Englishness of Jewish Modernity in England."

23. See Kaznelson, *Juden im deutschen Kulturbereich*; Joseph Jacobs, *Jewish Contribution to Civilization: An Estimate* (Philadelphia: Conat, 1919); Louis Finkelstein, ed. *The Jews: Their Role in Civilization*, 2nd ed. (New York: Schocken, 1974), 305–35; J. Katz, "German Culture and the Jews"; Graupe, *The Rise of Modern Judaism*; Mendes-Flohr, "New Trends in Jewish Thought"; and Reinharz, *Fatherland or Promised Land*, 84–86. For a short summary of the evolution of the concept of "contribution," see Y. Shavit, "From Admission Ticket to Contribution."

24. Acculturation is a process in which cultural layers are actively transferred from one group to another. The American Jewish sociologist Milton M. Gordon proposed a distinction between several different fields and patterns of assimilation and acculturation, among them cultural, or behavioral, assimilation; structural assimilation; assimilation as a result of intermarriage; and civic assimilation. See M. Gordon, *Assimilation in American Life*, 60–83. See also Kazal, "Revisiting Assimilation"; and Toury, "The Jewish Question." There is of course truth in the claim that Europe's Jews took different paths (and a different pace) in their journey from tradition to modernity and assimilation into modern culture and secular states. See Endelman, *The Jews of Georgian England*, 6. However, the subject at hand is not the path but the result. There were also, of course, different forms and ranges of assimilation patterns that were also related to the identity of the assimilated, as well as to the nature of the states into which they were integrated; however, this assimilation resulted in similar patterns in most cases. It is also worth mentioning Paul C. P. Siu's distinction between the "marginal man" and the "sojourner." The latter clings to the culture of his own ethnic group, in contrast to the bicultural complex of the former. Even when the sojourner makes adjustments to his new environment, he never fully becomes a part of it. As a result, he is characterized by multiple identities (and identity crises). See Siu, "The Sojourner."

25. See Bartal, "Non-Jews in Hebrew and Yiddish Literature in Eastern Europe, 1856–1914" (in Hebrew).

26. For the development of the concept of national character, see Barker, *National Character and the Factors in Its Formation*.

27. *Reshit Limudim* was a textbook on European geography; two further editions were published in 1797 and 1820. The book was later printed in several expanded editions, the last of which was published in Lvov in 1869. Louis Moréri's *Le Grand dictionnaire historique, ou le mélange curieux de l'histoire sacrée et profane* (The great historical dictionary, or anthology of sacred and secular history) described the traits of various European peoples as follows: "The French are polite, skillful, generous, but hasty and inconsistent; the Germans are sincere, good workers, but heavy, and too much addicted to wine; the Italians are agreeable, sensitive, and soft-spoken, but jealous and treacherous; the Spaniards are secretive, cautious, but blustering . . . the English are brave to the point of recklessness, but haughty, scornful, and almost truculently proud" (quoted in Hazard, *European Thought in the Eighteenth Century*, 447). The work was updated frequently—some twenty editions were published before 1758—and it was translated into English, German, Italian, Dutch, and Spanish.

28. Herzl, in *Stenographisches Protokoll der Verhandlungen des II. Zionisten-Congresses* (Vienna: Verlag des Vereines "Erez Israel," 1898), 10. See also chapter 7.

29. See Brenner, *Marketing Identities*.

30. R. Cohen, "Urban Visibility and Biblical Visions," 733.

31. See Bartal, "The Image of Germany and German Jewry in East European Jewish Society during the 19th Century."

32. Y. L. Gordon, "Al Nahar Kvar" (On the Kevar River), in *The Works of Yehuda Leib Gordon: Prose*, 287 (in Hebrew). See also Kurzweil, "The Image of the Western Jew in Hebrew Literature" (in Hebrew).

33. Jellinek, "Ein Zwiegespräch," 76. The article by Jellinek appeared in *Neuezeit*, March 31, 1882 and was reprinted in Druyanow, *Pinsker and His Times*, 149–59.

34. Dubnow, *Divrei Yemei Am Olam* 8:46 (in Hebrew). In this spirit, Jehuda Reinharz wrote that "Western culture clearly consisted of the French language and culture in France, the German language and culture in Germany, and the Russian language and culture in Russia. Accordingly, if Jews wished to be modern, or Western, they needed to become German, French, or Russian, in language and in culture" (Reinharz, "Jewish National Autonomy," 252). Y. L. Gordon wrote on the same subject: "The Jews of France and Germany, England and Italy, try very hard to be Frenchmen and Germans, Englishmen and Italians, and to cease to be Jews. They adopt their country's language and customs, and bear their country's happiness and endure all its woes as their own. They have forgotten their origins and the bonds that bind them to their brethren in other lands" ("A Vial of Perfume," Feuilleton No. 7, in *The Works of Yehuda Leib Gordon: Prose*, 141; in Hebrew).

35. Quoted in Doron, *The Zionist Thought of Nathan Birnbaum*, 95 (in Hebrew). In contrast to Western Jews, Birnbaum maintained, the Jews of Eastern Europe would not be able to produce a high level of civilization.

36. Birnbaum, *Die Assimilationsucht*, 1, 4–16.

37. Leni Westfahl (later Leni Yahil), who organized Mapai activities among immigrants from Central Europe to Palestine beginning in September 1941, quoted in Gelber, *New Homeland* 236 (in Hebrew).

38. Ahad Haam, *The Letters of Ahad Haam*, 4:201 (in Hebrew).

39. Quoted in Kleiner, *From Nationalism to Universalism*, 76–77.

40. Mendele Mokher Seforim, *The Collected Works of Mendele Mokher Seforim*, 386 (in Hebrew).

41. Quoted in Meyer, *The Origins of the Modern Jew*, 139.

42. A proclamation published (in Hebrew) by the Polish rebels during the 1836 rebellion claimed that in the new Poland, the regime would not distinguish between its citizens on the basis of religion or ethnicity, but "only by [their] homeland." Quoted in Bartal, *The Jews of Eastern Europe*, 88.

43. See Hermann, "Fatherland."

44. Mendele Mokher Seforim, *Fathers and Sons* (in Hebrew). This quote comes from the 1862 and 1868 versions of the text and does not appear in later versions; cited in Bartal, "Non-Jews in Hebrew and Yiddish Literature," 83.

45. Hissin, *Memories and Letters of an Early Pioneer*, 25–26, 48 (in Hebrew).

46. Quoted in Engel, "A Young Galician Jew on the Anti-Jewish Boycott in Congress Poland, 1913," 29–55 (in Hebrew).

47. See Ben-Sasson, "Poland and Poles in the Eyes of Polish Jews during the Second World War" (in Hebrew).

48. Herschberg, *In Oriental Lands*, 65–66 (in Hebrew).

49. "The Jews as a Spiritual (Cultural-Historical) Nationality in the Midst of Political Nations," in Dubnow, *Nationalism and History*, 110.

50. J. Wolff, "Eine Jahrhundert-Betrachtung," *Der Israelit*, 40 (108), December 28, 1899, 3027–29.

51. See Volkov, *Germans, Jews, and Antisemites*, 170–201. The book *Juden im Deutschen Kulturbereich: Ein Sammelwerk*, edited by Siegmund Kaznelson, includes a thousand-page survey of the Jewish contributions to all areas of life in Germany. It was scheduled to be published in Berlin in 1934, but the Nazi censor banned it. See Y. Shavit, "From Admission Ticket to Contribution," as well as the other chapters in J. Cohen and R. Cohen, *The Jewish Contribution to Civilization*.

52. On this topic, see Lowenstein, "Jewish Participation in German Culture"; and "The Publication of Moritz Goldstein's 'The German-Jewish Parnassus' Sparks a Debate over Assimilation, German Culture, and the 'Jewish Spirit'"; and "German History and German Jewry." Moritz Goldstein maintained that the German people would find insufferable a situation in which their cultural assets rested in Jewish hands. See also Botstein, *Judentum und Modernität*.

53. According to Norbert Elias, the Germans' national pride and self-esteem led them to emphasize their accomplishments in science, literature, philosophy, music, and art—German *Kultur*, in short. See Elias, *The Germans*, 323.

54. Quoted in Low, *Jews in the Eyes of the Germans*, 61.

55. Shulman, *Sefer Divrei Yemei Olam*, 4:13–16.

56. Y. L. Gordon, *The Letters of Y. L. Gordon*, 1:90 (in Hebrew).

57. Levinsohn, *Sefer Ahiyah Shiloni Hahozeh*. The book was written as a reaction to another book, written by a British missionary, but the publication of Levinsohn's work was delayed by censorship.

58. Geiger, "Über den Austritt aus den Judenthume," 65–66.

59. "Shakespeare's Mädchen und Frauen," in Heine, *Sämtliche Werke*, 10:227. Moses Hess believed that European culture was permeated by so many Jewish elements that it was impossible to separate the two: without Jewish contributions, European culture did not exist. See Avineri, *Moses Hess*, 174.

60. H. Graetz, "Correspondence," in *The Structure of Jewish History and Other Essays*, 256.

61. Ibid., 220.

62. Herzl, *The Complete Diaries of Theodor Herzl*, 1:28.

63. Dubnow, "The Jews as a Spiritual (Cultural-Historical) Nationality," in Dubnow, *Nationalism and History*, 100–115.

64. Ruppin, *The Sociology of the Jews*, 1:36–41 (in German). See also Volkov, *Germans, Jews, and Antisemites*, 224–47; and Y. Shavit, "From Admission Ticket to Contribution."

65. See Miri Paz's interview with the Jewish French philosopher André Glucksman in *Davar*, November 29, 1991, 20.

66. Eran and Shavit, "Chanukka und 'die verlockenden Sirenen,'" 158.

67. See Feiner, "The Pseudo-Enlightenment and the Question of Jewish Modernization."

68. Y. L. Gordon, *The Works of Yehuda Leib Gordon: Prose*, 223 (in Hebrew).

69. This is an allusion to two Talmudic sayings: "It is that you should not follow their customs in matters that are established by law for them, for example, going to their theaters, circuses, and playing fields" (Neusner, *Sifra in Perspective*, 3:78), and "it is forbidden on grounds of idolatry [to go into gentiles' amphitheaters] . . . He who goes to a stadium or a camp to see the performances of sorcerers and enchanters or of various kinds of clowns, mimics, buffoons, and the like . . . he who sits in an amphitheater [e.g., where gladiators are fighting], lo, this one is guilty of bloodshed" (*Tosefta: Abodah Zarah*, translated by Jacob Neusner, New York: Ktav 1981, 316–17).

70. Y. L. Gordon, *The Works of Yehuda Leib Gordon: Prose*, 259–60 (in Hebrew).

71. Mendele Mokher Seforim, *Fathers and Sons*, 19 (in Hebrew).

72. Lilienblum, *The Letters of Moshe Leib Lilienblum to Yehuda Leib Gordon*, 132 (in Hebrew).

73. Ibid., 201.

74. "Shakespeare's Mädchen und Frauen," in Heine, *Sämtliche Schriften*, 10: 257–58.

75. Mann, *Doctor Faustus*, 391.

76. Quoted in Meyer, *German-Jewish History in Modern Times*, 2:234. See also Riesser, *Börne und die Juden*, 21.

77. Lazarus, *Was heisst national?* 23–30.

78. See Rotenstreich, "Hermann Cohen"; Reinharz, *Fatherland or Promised Land*, 21–22; Brumlik, "Zur Zweideutigkeit deutsch-jüdischen Geistes"; and Mendes-Flohr, "New Trends in Jewish Thought."

79. Klatzkin, "Germanness and Jewishness," 68 (in Hebrew).

80. Quoted in M. Brenner, *The Renaissance of Jewish Culture in Weimar Germany*, 90.

81. Buber, "Toward the End of the German-Jewish Symbiosis" 392 (in Hebrew).

82. Geiger, "Über den Austritt aus den Judenthume," 67–87 (in Hebrew).

83. Quoted in A. Gordon, "In Palestine, in a Foreign Land," 96 (in Hebrew). See also Miron, *German Jews in Israel* (in Hebrew).

84. Mendes-Flohr, "In the Shadow of the World War," 18.

85. See M. Breuer, *Modernity Within Tradition*.

86. Hess, *The Revival of Israel*, 164.

87. Jacobowski, *Werther, der Jude*. As well as writing poetry and prose in which he expressed the loneliness of Jews in German society, Jacobowski belonged to a group of activists against antisemitism (the Verein zur Abwehr des Antisemitismus). His novel achieved great popularity. See Elon, *The Pity of It All*, 231–32.

88. "The poem was reprinted in 1966 (Jacobowski, "Dank"). Many thanks to Professor Sabine von Mering for her assistance in locating this item.

89. Quoted in Mendes-Flohr, "Jewish Cultural Life under National-Socialist Rule," 283. See also the autobiography of the revolutionary playwright Ernst Toller, *I Was a German*.

90. See Liptzin, *Germany's Stepchildren*. In contrast to Jacobowski, Stephen Zweig represents the Jewish man of letters who wishes to identify not with the national culture, but with the ideal of a nationless, humanist Europe; his fate, however, is similarly tragic.

91. See S. Gilman, *Jewish Self-Hatred*.

92. Quoted in Liptzin, *Germany's Stepchildren*, 144. See also Volkov, *Germans, Jews, and Antisemites*, 35–36; Bachrach, "Walther Rathenau." The *Allgemeine Zeitung des Judentums* (66 [1902]: 402–4) described Rathenau's outlook as "semitischer Antisemitismus" (Semitic antisemitism).

93. Quoted in Pulzer, "Legal Equality and Public Life," 162.

94. Franz Oppenheimer, "Stammesbewusstsein und Volksbewusstein," *Jüdische Rundschau* 15, no. 8 (February 25, 1910): 86–89.

95. See Richard Huldschiner, "Stammesbewusstsein—Volksbewusststein," *Die Welt* 14, no. 9 (1910): 185–86.

96. See Ernst Müller, "Nationales Bewusstsein und nationales Sein," *Die Welt*

14, no. 10 (1910): 207–9. On the various definitions of Jews as a separate group in Germany and czarist Russia, see van Rahden, "Circumstantial Ethnic Belonging in Contrast to Identity Defined by 'Milieu'" (in Hebrew); and Nathans, *Beyond the Pale*, 73.

97. See S. Gilman, "Max Nordau, Sigmund Freud, and the Question of Conversion."

98. See Azuléos, *L'entrée en bourgeoise des juif allemands*.

99. Quoted in Gombrich, *In Search of Cultural History*, 9.

100. See, for example, Reinharz, *Fatherland or Promised Land*; and M. Brenner, *The Renaissance of Jewish Culture in Weimar Germany*, 131–34.

101. Quoted in Doron, *The Zionist Thought of Nathan Birnbaum*, 193.

102. See Lowenstein, "The Beginning of Integration," 159–71; and Richarz, "Jewish Women in the Family and Public Sphere."

103. Buber, "Toward the End of the German-Jewish Symbiosis," 295 (in Hebrew).

104. "In Reproach of the Myth of German-Jewish Dialogue," in Scholem, *Devarim Bego*, 114–17. See also "Jews and Germans" in Scholem, *Devarim Bego*, 96–113. For another perspective, see Bach, *The German Jew*, 169–250.

105. Quoted in Slutsky, *The Russian-Jewish Press in the Nineteenth Century*, 40 (in Hebrew). The special character of the Jewish population in Odessa—a pluralistic, cultured, and free port city in the so-called New Russia—especially in contrast to the Jewish population in the Pale of Settlement, gave rise as early as 1841 to the description of the city as "alien to the Jewish spirit," and to the claims that the Jews who lived there "try to fully resemble Europeans." Quoted in Yossi Goldstein, "The Migration of Jews to the New Russia and the Socioeconomic Revolution They Underwent in the Nineteenth Century" (in Hebrew).

106. See Nathans, *Beyond the Pale*.

107. Quoted in J. Frankel, *Prophecy and Politics*, 87.

108. Rabinowich, "Russian Must Be Our Mother Tongue," quoted in Mendes-Flohr and Reinharz, *The Jew in the Modern World: A Documentary History*, 400. According to the 1891 population census, 32 percent of all Jewish men in the Russian Empire spoke Yiddish, and 17.5 percent of Jewish women were able to read Russian. See Stampfer, "Literacy among East European Jewry in the Modern Period."

109. See the description and analysis of this phenomenon in Nathans, *Beyond the Pale*.

110. Druyanow, "On the Agenda: 2. Vilna," (in Hebrew). In a survey conducted in 1904–5 at a Jewish library in Poltava, in southern Russia, some 65 percent of the respondents read only Russian.

111. See Bar-Yosef, "Zionism and the Jewish Cosmopolitan."

112. "On Jews and Russian Literature" (1908), in Jabotinsky, *Al Sifrut Veomanut*, 61–68 (in Hebrew).

113. See Mintz, "The Place of the Jewish Workers' Movement in the Politization of the Jewish People."

114. Friedman, "On Jewish Public Life in Poland," *Kuntres*, October 12, 1926, 14–15 (in Hebrew).

115. For an extensive description of the process of Polonization, see Heller, *On the Edge of Destruction*, 211–32. The acculturation of Polish Jews accelerated between the two world wars. On Jewish economic, societal, and cultural contributions, see Lichten, "Notes on the Assimilation and Acculturation of Jews in Poland." On Jewish participation in Polish culture in the nineteenth century, see Bartal, *The Jews of Eastern Europe*, 82–89. See also Weeks, *From Assimilation to Antisemitism*.

116. D. Cohen, *Chesed Neurim*, 180. A firsthand and masterly description of Polish Jewry in 1924 can be found in a 1925 travel book by Alfred Döblin. He wrote that Polish Jews were a "nation" in every respect: they had "their own costumes, their own language, religion, manners, norm, and national feelings and consciousness" (Döblin, *Journey to Poland*, 50).

117. "Once Upon a Time," in Jabotinsky, *Al Sifrut Veomanut*, 339–44.

118. There are many theoretical debates proposing various definitions of modernization, as well as various descriptions of the processes of modernization of Jews in various countries. On the latter topic, see, among others, Eisenstadt, *Modernization*; Wagner, *A Sociology of Modernity*; J. Katz, *Toward Modernity*; and G. Cohen, "German Jewry as a Mirror of Modernity."

119. See Toury, "Emancipation and Assimilation"; and S. Cohen, *American Modernity and Jewish Identity*. On the tension between borrowing and adopting, on the one hand, neutral cultural traits, and on the other hand, concepts, values, and norms, in the context of Muslim society in the modern era, see Bernard Lewis, *What Went Wrong? Western Impact and Middle Eastern Response*; and Huntington, *The Clash of Civilizations and the Remaking of World Order*.

120. It is worth noting that cultural transmission indicates the manner in which a cultural repertoire travels from place to place, and from society to society. Acculturation refers to the process of welcoming and absorption of this repertoire in the absorbing society. The processes through which one culture borrows from another are universal, but, as we have seen, in the context of relations between minority and majority cultures, this is a matter of acculturation.

121. See Chadwick, *The Secularization of the European Mind in the 19th Century*, 17.

122. There is no basis for the claim that German Jews were attracted to German culture because of its demonic and unrestrained nature, with the goal of extricating themselves from the burden of Judaism's stifling norms. See Rivka Shechter, "The Enchanting German Demon," *Maariv*, literary supplement, April 12, 1991, 4 (in Hebrew).

123. See Mosse, *German Jews beyond Judaism*.

124. Eliezer Schweid, *Judaism and the Solitary Jew* (in Hebrew).

125. I. Breuer, "Der Begriff des Wunders im Judentum."

126. In 1933, some 57 percent of Jewish students in Germany studied in public

schools. See Walk, *The Education of the Jewish Child in Nazi Germany* (in Hebrew). See also Elias, *The Civilizing Process*.

127. See the comprehensive description in Kaplan, *Jewish Daily Life in Germany*.

128. On the new perceptions of history and historical time, see Arieli, "New Horizons in the Historiography of the Eighteenth and Nineteenth Centuries" (in Hebrew). Arieli writes that the change that occurred in the perception of man's history and place in the universe was a revolutionary turning point in the self-understanding of the non-Jewish intelligentsia, as well as in the understanding of Jewish history and in the approach to the Wissenschaft des Judentums among Zunz's generation. See also "Breakthrough into the Past: The Verein für Kultur und Wissenschaft der Juden," in Schorsch, *From Text to Context*, 205–32.

129. In Buber, *Correspondence*, 1:352 (in Hebrew).

130. See Volkov, *Germans, Jews, and Antisemites*, 159–201; and M. Brenner, *The Renaissance of Jewish Culture in Weimar Germany*. Regarding the case of Poland's Jews, see Hertz, *The Jews in Polish Culture*.

131. In Jakob Wassermann's novel, *Der Fall Maurizius* (The Maurizius affair), when the Jewish intellectual Gregor Waremme—who hides his Jewishness under the name Georg Warschauer and writes books about the German spirit and the Germans' universal mission to rule over a unified Europe—is forced into exile in the United States, he longs for Europe, which he believes had followed him into exile. In the United States, "he had begun to understand what Europe really meant to him. It stood not only for his own past, but for the past of three hundred million men, together with what he knew of it, and carried with him in his blood; not only the particular region which had produced him, but also the image and outline of all the countries between the North Sea and the Mediterranean, their atmosphere, their history, their development, not merely in connection with this, that, or the other town in which he had stayed, but with hundreds of others, and in them, the churches, the palaces, the mansions, the works of art, the libraries, and all the traces their great men had left behind them. Was there a single event in his life with which the memories of several generations were not linked up, memories born at the same time as himself? Europe was—the idea was inconceivable and filled him with awe—a single whole that had existed for thousands of years: Pericles and Nostradamus, Theodoric and Voltaire, Ovid and Erasmus, Archimedes and Gauss, Calderon and Dürer, Phidias and Mozart, Petrarch and Napoleon, Galileo and Nietzsche, a countless host of radiant spirits, and another host, equally innumerable, of demons, light always finding its counterpart in an equal mass of darkness, but shining bright in the midst of it, creating a vase of gold from the black dross around—catastrophes, noble inspirations, revolutions, eras of darkness, manners and fashions, the common weal, its fluctuations, its interrelations, its gradual evolution; the Mind, such was Europe." Quoted in Hazard, *European Thought in the Eighteenth Century*, 495–96.

132. See, among others, J. Frankel, "Assimilation and Ethnicity in Nineteenth

Century Europe" (in Hebrew); Volkov, *Germans, Jews, and Antisemites*; Schatzker, *Jewish Youth in Germany* (in Hebrew); Klein, "Assimilation and Dissimilation"; Gotzmann, *Eigenheit und Einheit*; and Mandel, "Assimilation and Cultural Exchange in Modern Jewish History." Zionism was the radical expression of this reconstruction and was seen by its internal detractors as a *Rückwatschelei* (step backward) toward an ancient and irrelevant past.

133. See Barth, "Introduction." According to Barth, ethnic groups define their identities as a foundation for give-and-take between them and other ethnic groups. This negotiation is thus carried out not from a position of weakness, but as a dialogue and exchange born of self-awareness and self-confidence.

134. In the epilogue to *Jewish Daily Life in Germany*, Marion A. Kaplan, the volume's editor, wrote: "Did Jews seamlessly fuse with other Germans? No. Nor did most ever want to do so. The latter is a major finding of our research. Jews bridged two worlds in the modern era" (380). The book presents a detailed portrait of the various aspects of this duality and its development in various layers of Jewish society in Germany. In our present chapter, we have attempted to claim that, beyond declarations and definitions, it is necessary to pay attention to the various practical details of life. These give far better expression to the new shape of Jewish life than do declarations of loyalty or identity. Consequently, what matters is not whether Jews wanted to fuse with the Germans, but whether their patterns of daily behavior brought this fusion about. This is true, of course, not only with respect to Germany's Jews.

135. See Pulzer, *What about the Jewish Non-intellectuals in Germany?* And see, for example, Arthur Ruppin's biography by Goren, *Arthur Ruppin, 18–25* (in Hebrew). Indeed, the "English Lady" asked Graetz: "What will become of Judaism? Will it be preserved only by the poor and uneducated among our people?" ("Correspondence," in H. Graetz, *The Structure of Jewish History and Other Essays*, 194).

5. ANTISEMITISM AS AN INCURABLE EUROPEAN DISEASE

1. *Razsvet*, October 9, 1881, quoted in J. Frankel, *Prophecy and Politics*, 86–87.
2. For a critique of the view that emphasizes the continuous aspect of antisemitism, see Volkov, *Germans, Jews, and Antisemites*, 67–90. However, it is necessary to distinguish between changes in the causes and nature of antisemitism and the continuity of the phenomenon itself.
3. *Lutezia*, in Heine, *Sämtliche Werke*, 11:216.
4. The Damascus Affair is explored in detail in J. Frankel, *The Damascus Affair*.
5. Hess, *The Revival of Israel*, 70–71.
6. Ibid., 73.
7. Quoted in J. Frankel, *The Damascus Affair*, 246.
8. Quoted in Bartal, *The Jews of Eastern Europe*, 134–42.
9. See Markish, "Lev Levanda between Assimilation and Palestinophilia."

10. Quoted in Meyer, *Response to Modernity*, 291–92.

11. Herzl, *The Complete Diaries of Theodor Herzl*, 1:171.

12. Quoted in Meyer, *Without Wissenschaft There Is no Judaism*, 27–29.

13. Pulzer, *Jews and the German State*, 37. See also Schorsch, *Jewish Reactions to German Anti-Semitism*; and Meyer, "The Great Debate on Anti-Semitism."

14. "The Ethics of Nationalism" (May 1899), in Dubnow, *Nationalism and History*, 116–30, and "The Moral of Stormy Days" (1905), in ibid., 200–214.

15. Dubnow wrote: "Do not put your trust in Amalek, neither Amalek's government nor its people, because the Old Russia is bound to reappear in every Russia that is to come!" ("The Moral of Stormy Days," 205).

16. Ibid., 200–14.

17. "On Jews and Russian Literature," in Jabotinsky, *Al Sifrut Veomanut*, 79 (in Hebrew).

18. Herzl, "Die Woche" (The week), *Die Welt*, July 9, 1897. See also Herzl, "The Opinions of Mr. Claude Montefiore," *Die Welt*, May 6, 1898.

19. Herzl, *Altneuland*, 65.

20. Herzl, *The Complete Diaries of Theodor Herzl*, 1:131–32.

21. "On the Question of Zionist Theory," in Borochov, *Works*, 1:1–17.

22. See Wistrich, "Radical Antisemitism in France and Germany" (in Hebrew).

23. Nietzsche, *Beyond Good and Evil*, 251.

24. Weizmann, *The Letters and Papers of Chaim Weizmann*, series A: *Letters*, 6:187. In December 1913, Weizmann told Lord Balfour that "we believe that Germans of the Mosaic faith are an undesirable, demoralising phenomenon," but that "we totally disagree with Wagner and Chamberlain as to the diagnosis and the prognosis . . . after all, these Jews have taken part in building Germany and contributing to her greatness" (ibid., 7:81).

25. Nahum Sokolow, *Hamagid*, March 17, 1880.

26. Wechsler, *Ein Wort der Mahnung an Israel* (Würzburg: 1881), 98.

27. Quoted in Laskov, *Documents on the History of Hibbat-Zion and the Settlement of Eretz Israel*, 1:332 (in Hebrew).

28. Leon Pinsker, *Autoemancipation!*

29. Quoted in Druyanow, *Pinsker and His Times*, 158–59 (in Hebrew).

30. See Slutsky, *The Russian-Jewish Press in the Nineteenth Century*, 148 (in Hebrew).

31. Quoted in Druyanow, *Writings on the History of the Hibbat Zion Movement and the Jewish Settlement in Palestine*, 1:349–51 (in Hebrew).

32. Syrkin, "The Jewish Question and the Socialist Jewish State" (1898), in *The Collected Works of Nachman Syrkin*, 3–59 (in Hebrew).

33. In Greek mythology, Scylla and Charybdis were two sea monsters that lived in caves on either side of the Strait of Messina and abducted seafarers.

34. Jabotinsky, "Pogroms in Berlin," *Razsvet*, November 11, 1923 (in Russian).

35. "Once Upon a Time. . .," in Jabotinsky, *Al Sifrut Veomanut*, 339–44 (in Hebrew).

36. Remba, *Jabotinsky to the World and His People*, 2:159–60 (in Hebrew).
37. Jabotinsky, *The Jewish Warfront*, 60–65.
38. Uri Zvi Greenberg, *Sadna De'ara* (Jerusalem, 1925), 4.
39. Sokolow, "A Journey to Poland in 1934," 319 (in Hebrew).
40. Ibid., 321.
41. Ibid., 326.
42. Uri Zvi Greenberg, "In Malchus fun Tzelm," 463.
43. See Efron, *Defenders of the Race*. On the influence of the idea of race on Jewish thinkers and doctors, see Falk, *Zionism and the Biology of the Jews* (in Hebrew).
44. Quoted in Stiftel, "Nahum Sokolow."
45. Mendele Mokher Seforim, "Shem and Japheth on the Train," 26. The story was published in Hebrew in 1890, and in Yiddish in 1910.
46. Vladimir Harcabi, "From the Days of the Flood." Harcabi omits what follows in the quote: "there is neither male nor female: for ye are all one in Christ Jesus." See Nathans, *Beyond the Pale*, 242–43.
47. Moses Lilienblum, "Derekh Tshuva," in *Autobiographical Writings*, 2:196 (in Hebrew).
48. Lilienblum, *The Letters of Moshe Leib Lilienblum to Yehuda Leib Gordon*, 200 [in Hebrew]. And see Shavit, *Athens in Jerusalem*, 38–39.
49. Lilienblum, "The General Jewish Question and Eretz-Israel," *Razsvet*, October 9, 1881, 160.
50. Lilienblum, *On the Revival of Israel in the Land of Its Fathers* (in Hebrew). See also Y. Shavit, *Athens in Jerusalem*, 188–219.
51. Quoted in M. Breuer, "The Reaction of German Orthodoxy to Antisemitism," 208 (in Hebrew).
52. See, for example, the words of Jakob Friedrich Fries, a professor of philosophy in Heidelberg, in *Über die Gefährdung des Wohlstandes und des Charakters der Deutschen durch die Juden*. On Fries's and similar proposals, see Low, *Jews in the Eyes of the Germans*, 111.
53. See Almog, "Jews as a Disease," in *Nationalism, Zionism, and Antisemitism*, 243–61 (in Hebrew).
54. Quoted in M. Breuer, "The Reaction of German Orthodoxy to Antisemitism," 189 (in Hebrew).
55. Herzl, "Mauschel," *Die Welt*, 51, October 1897.
56. Herzl, *The Complete Diaries of Theodor Herzl*, 1:231.
57. Ibid., 69. See also Shmuel Almog, "Between Zionism and Antisemitism," in *Nationalism, Zionism, and Antisemitism*, 221–41.
58. Weizmann, *The Letters and Papers of Chaim Weizmann*, series A: *Letters*, 7:81–82.
59. Jabotinsky, "A Philosophical Night," *Hazit Haam*, June 6, 1933.
60. "The Destruction of the Soul," in Kaufmann, *In the Throes of Time*, 257–74 (in Hebrew). See also T. Lessing, *Der jüdische Selbsthass*.

6. OLD EUROPE OR NEW EUROPE?

1. Nietzsche, *The Dawn of Day*, 210–11.
2. Musil, *Der Mann ohne Eigenschaften*.
3. Among these, we note Albert Demangeon's 1920 *Le déclin d'Europe*. Even a radical thinker like Alexander Herzen—a "science worshipper" and not a Slavophile, but one who believed that Russia had a role to play as *Kulturträger* (cultural agent) in the Orient—predicted disaster for Europe as early as the nineteenth century. In 1851, he wrote that Europe was "approaching a terrible cataclysm," and that any attempts to stem the tide would succeed only in the short term. See Herzen, *From the Other Shore*, 167.
4. See K. Fischer, *History and Prophecy*.
5. See A. Harrington, "Ernst Troeltsch's Concept of Europe."
6. Samuel Roth, *Europe: A Book for America* (New York: Boni and Liveright, 1919), 3. Six years later, Roth prophesied the expulsion of Jews from the United States and the rebirth of the East through some cataclysmic, messianic event: "The bones of Europe will move with a faint shudder of decay. There will dwell over every European city, like a cloud, the yellow atmosphere of an insidious canker. It will be terrible to look on . . . I have been too hopeful about America. America will yet prove to be the most ungrateful of all nations. She will expel us, just as Spain expelled us, just as England expelled us, just as France expelled us . . . But we still have a century or so in America. Salvation, then, will come from the East." Another example of esoteric literature that dealt not with the decline of the West, like literature following World War I, but rather with its destruction, is Lewis Spencer's *Will Europe Follow Atlantis?* Spencer belonged to a group that obsessively attempted to prove that the lost continent of Atlantis and its civilization were not merely myths but had actually existed in the Atlantic Ocean; he published many essays on the topic. In 1942, Atlantis's history offered an apocalyptic vision that saw Europe—wicked as Sodom—suffering a similar fate. Europe's great sin was that under the Nazi regime it had forgotten God. But Europe could escape the fate of the sinful: "Tried in the fires of war and suffering, Great Britain shall emerge from them mighty for peace and all its works, and shall pursue her illustrious destiny as the standard-bearer of world-freedom and justice" (157). After the cataclysm, "civilization will not fail in Europe, as many believe. But it will be a new species of culture, a growth straining to the light of the future rather than one which draws its nourishment from the fetid exhalations of the past" (162).
7. Thomas Mann described Germany's reaction to the war that had loomed over Europe for many years before finally exploding in a mad frenzy: "In our Germany its effect is undeniably and preeminently enthusiasm, and from a world-stagnation that could go no longer: as a hope for the future, an appeal to duty and manhood, in short as a holiday for heroes." See Mann, *Doctor Faustus*, 290. Mann believed that "Germany's defeat signaled the end of an era defined by bourgeois

humanism and there was a sense that life was deteriorating—an extreme feeling that emerged fourteen years after the turn of the century and had lain at the bottom of the panic, the awful sense of destiny . . . No wonder the disintegration of defeat increased this feeling to its highest pitch" (340).

8. Greenberg, *Mefisto* (in Yiddish).

9. See Lindenbaum, "Uri Zvi Greenberg's *Mefisto*" (in Hebrew).

10. In 1938, Angell came out against the British government's conciliatory approach to Nazi Germany and published another book, *Peace with the Dictators*.

11. A second edition was published in 1920.

12. See Peter Bugge, "The Nation of Supreme"; and Ortega y Gasset, *The Revolt of the Masses*, 144–45.

13. Croce, *The History of Europe in the Nineteenth Century*, 351–62. As noted, Croce did not consider his vision to be an act of prophecy, "which is forbidden to us and to everyone for the simple reason that it would be vain, but a suggestion of what paths moral consciousness and the observation of the present may outline for those who in their guiding concept and in their interpretation of the events of the nineteenth century agree with the narrative given of them in this history" (362).

14. The Polish Jewish violinist Bronisław Huberman (1882–1947), who founded the Palestine Orchestra in 1936, is numbered among the supporters of this idea. In 1925, he published *Mein Weg zu Paneuropa* (My path to pan-Europe). There is an extensive literature on the history of proposals to unify Europe after World War II. Among others, see Morgan, "A Vague and Puzzling Idealism"; and Pegg, *The Evolution of the European Idea*. Proposals for a Pax Europeana were put forth in the eighteenth century and thereafter by figures such as the Duc du Sully, the Abbé de Saint-Pierre (in his *Project for Settling an Everlasting Peace in Europe*, 1712–13), and the Comte de Saint-Simon, who proposed a federalist scheme in *The Reorganization of the European Community* (1814).

15. Musil, "Das hilflose Europa oder Reise vom Hundersten ins Tausendste."

16. Mann, *Achtung, Europa!* 73–80.

17. Simmel, "Die Idee Europa."

18. See Noverstern, *The Lure of Twilight* (in Hebrew) and *Yaavdu Shamaim Vaaretz*.

19. Syrkin, "Letters from Europe," *Kuntres* 7, Sept. 1919: 5–8 (in Hebrew).

20. See Mendelsohn, *Zionism in Poland*, 89. See also Konrad Zielinski, "Polish-Jewish Relations in the Kingdom of Poland during the First World War," *European Journal of Jewish Studies* 2, no. 2: 269–82.

21. "A Long Letter to Federevsky," *Kuntres* 7, Sept. 1919: 7–8 (in Hebrew).

22. Syrkin, "In the Press," ibid., 8–12 (in Hebrew).

23. Yehoshua Thon, *Hatzfira*, December 5, 1918, 2–4.

24. Uri Zvi Greenberg, "In Malchus fun Tzelm" (in Yiddish).

25. Greenberg, "At Closing-Time" (in Hebrew).

26. Greenberg, "The Downfall of Jewry in Poland," 20–21 (in Hebrew).

27. See M. Graetz, "The Formation of the New Jewish Consciousness in the Time of Mendelssohn's Disciple Shaul Ascher" (in Hebrew).

28. Quoted in Meyer, *The Origins of the Modern Jew*, 142.

29. In Heine, *The Complete Poems of Heinrich Heine*, 532.

30. See Tauber, "Envisioning the 20th Century."

31. Gabriel Talfir, "Enemy No. 1," *Gazit*, 5–6, 1943, 1–2 (in Hebrew).

32. Hess, *The Revival of Israel*, 232.

33. Ibid., 224–27.

34. Quoted in Etinger, "Judaism and the History of the Jews in Graetz's Worldview," 1:106–8 (in Hebrew). It is important to point out that Herzl was not concerned by, let alone afraid of, Germany's growing power. On the contrary, he praised the "genius" of Kaiser Wilhelm II and described him as a "splendid ruler" from whom one could expect great accomplishments (see Herzl, "Zionismus," in *Theodor Herzl's Zionistiche Schriften*, edited by Leon Kellner [Berlin: Jüdischer Verlag, 1899], 119–33). He described the kaiser's policy as expanding and aggrandizing Germany, but doing so very cautiously. Ignoring the kaiser's avowed antisemitism, Herzl saw Germany's elevated status as a catalyst for fulfilling the Zionist agenda.

35. Quoted in Livneh, *Aharon Aaronson*, 188–89 (in Hebrew).

36. Mann, *Doctor Faustus*, 373.

37. For a discussion on this subject, see Zimmermann, *Germany's Singular History* (in Hebrew).

38. Blumenfeld, *Erlebte Judenfrage*, 183.

39. See Iggers, *The German Conception of History*, 74.

40. See Stern, *The Politics of Cultural Despair*; and Pulzer, "The Return of Old Hatreds" and "The Response to Antisemitism." We have seen that the attitude toward the West and the attempts to define its character also occupied a large number of Jewish thinkers and writers in Eastern Europe. Among them, we mention Ivan Kireevsky, author of "The Character of European Civilization and Its Approach toward Russian Civilization" (1852), and Nicolai Danilevsky, author of "Russia and Europe" (1869). See Walicki, *The Slavophile Controversy*, 121–78 and 503–8; and Dukes, *Russia and Europe*, 1.

41. Herzl, *The Complete Diaries of Theodor Herzl*, 2:543.

42. Gottlober, *Memories and Travels*, 246 (in Hebrew). Gottlober wrote that he had "told an acquaintance that I was thinking of leaving the country [Russia] in order to seek wisdom in Germany. For the streets of Germany, in my opinion, are paved with wisdom . . . and its citizens are all good and decent people, welcoming seekers after knowledge, and providing for all their needs." On Russian and Jewish students in Germany, see Weill, *Étudiants russes en Allemagne*; and Williams, *Culture in Exile*.

43. Quoted in Druyanow, *Writings on the History of the Hibbat Zion Movement and the Jewish Settlement in Palestine*, 2–3 (in Hebrew).

44. Yehuda Leib Vintz, *Hamelitz*, March 7, 1896, 1.

45. Weizmann, *The Letters and Papers of Chaim Weizmann*, series A: *Letters*, 7:66. See Reinharz, *Chaim Weizmann*, 401.

46. Weizmann, *The Letters and Papers of Chaim Weizmann*, series A: *Letters*, 7:219.

47. Volkov, *Germans, Jews, and Antisemites*, 22–32.

48. Quoted in Reinharz, "The Response of the Centralverein deutscher Staatsbürger jüdischen Glaubens to Antisemitism in the Weimar Republic," 85–110 (in Hebrew).

49. See Reinharz, "Ideology and Structure in German Zionism 1882–1933."

50. *Jüdische Rundschau*, September 16, 1932.

51. Goldmann, *The Autobiography of Nahum Goldmann*, 127.

52. Wassermann, *Josef Kerkhovens dritte Existenz*.

53. Quoted in Friedländer, *Nazi Germany and the Jews*, 1:171.

54. Lowenthal, *The Jews of Germany*, 21.

55. Tzahor, "Chaim Arlosoroff and His Attitude towards the Rise of Nazism."

56. Quoted in Lynx, *The Future of the Jews*, 14–15.

57. Arieh Altmann, "October: The German Version," *Hayarden*, November 29, 1935 (in Hebrew).

58. Quoted in Yossi Goldstein, *Ussishkin's Biography*, 2:137 (in Hebrew).

59. Jabotinsky, "Not Until It's Over!" 193 (in Hebrew).

60. Zeev Jabotinsky, "This Too Is a Yellow Patch," *Hayarden*, January 13, 1936 (in Hebrew).

61. Greenbaum, *The Wars of the Jews of Poland*, 347 (in Hebrew).

62. "The Antisemitic Revolution in Germany," in Kaufmann, *In the Throes of Time*, 221–25 (in Hebrew).

63. Weizmann, *Speeches*, 4:848 (in Hebrew).

64. Sokolow, *Journey to Poland*, 320–21 (in Hebrew).

65. See Sheva, *O Seer, Go, Flee Away*, 222 (in Hebrew).

66. Bialik, *The Letters of C. N. Bialik*, 5:222 and 224 (in Hebrew).

67. Ibid., 307.

68. Y. H. Yeivin, "When Shall We Be Wise," *Hazit Haam*, March 17, 1933 (in Hebrew).

69. Kolisher, *Betar: Yarkhon lesheelat hahayim, hamada, vehasifrut* 2, no. 7 (January–February 1934), 206–18, 304–21.

70. A. Ginsburg, *Hazit Haam*, June 30, 1933 (in Hebrew).

71. Quoted in Gelber, "The Zionist Leadership's Response to the Nuremberg Laws," 59. See also "The Reaction of the Zionist Movement and the Yishuv to the Nazis 'Rise to Power.'"

72. Ben Gurion, *Memoirs*, 1:675 and 2:520–21 (in Hebrew).

73. Quoted in N. Cohen, *Books, Authors, and Newspapers*, 279 (in Hebrew).

74. Ibid.

75. Aharon Zeitlin, "Back to the Forest," *Undzer Expres*, March 24, 1933 (in Yiddish).

76. Itzik Manger, "Hitler or Heine," *Moment*, April 28, 1933 (in Yiddish).

77. Y. Gurion, "The Seven Days: Hitler's Speech," *Hamashkif*, February 3, 1939 (in Hebrew).

78. M. A. Perlmutter, "'Heil Hitler' in Hebrew Jerusalem," *Hayom*, March 1, 1939 (in Hebrew).

79. Quoted in Shapira, "The Conception of Time in the Partition Controversy," in *Visions in Conflict*, 307–24 (in Hebrew).

80. See Tubin, "Berl Katznelson before the Holocaust" (in Hebrew). There seems to be a fair amount of forced interpretation in the way Tubin analyzes Katznelson's terminology.

81. Quoted in Yifat Weiss, "The Transfer Agreement and the Boycott Movement: A Jewish Dilemma on the Eve of the Holocaust," *Yad Vashem Studies* 26 (1998): 126 (in Hebrew).

82. Uri Zvi Greenberg, "When Amalek Spoke," *Der Moment*, May 2, 1939 (in Yiddish).

83. Uri Zvi Greenberg, "The War within Our People," *Hayarden*, November 10, 1933 (in Hebrew).

84. Uri Zvi Greenberg, "The Last Chapter of the World War," *Hayarden*, October 24, 1934 (in Hebrew).

85. Uri Zvi Greenberg, "I Did Not Keep My Vineyard," *Hamashkif*, March 24, 1939 (in Hebrew).

86. Uri Zvi Greenberg, "Yehuda Today, Yehuda Tomorrow," *Hayarden*, July 30, 1938 (in Hebrew). Regarding the fear in Britain during the 1930s of German aerial raids, see Bialer, *The Shadow of the Bomber*, 46–48.

87. See Y. Shavit, "Eschatology and Politics" (in Hebrew).

88. Uri Zvi Greenberg, "Our Common Enemy," *Hamashkif*, September 13, 1939 (in Hebrew).

89. "Beboi Cheshbon: Hameshorer veimo baam," in Greenberg, *Rehovot Hanahar*, 85 (in Hebrew).

90. Jabotinsky, *Doar Hayom*, May 3, 1935, and *Der Moment*, April 14, 1933.

91. In 1936, Jabotinsky translated a section of Goethe's *Faust* that was published in *Metzuda*, the organ of Beitar (a Zionist youth movement) in Warsaw.

92. Quoted in Yaacov Shavit and Liat Shtayer-Livni, "Who Cried Wolf? How did Zeev Jabotinsky Understand the Nature and Intentions of Nazi Germany?" (in Hebrew).

93. Ibid.

94. Jabotinsky, "Not until It's Over!" *Doar Hayom*, May 3, 1935 (in Hebrew).

95. See Y. Shavit and Shtayer-Livni, "Who Cried Wolf?" See also Jacob Katz, "The Holocaust—Was It Predictable?" (in Hebrew; published in English as "Was the Holocaust Predictable?" *Commentary* 59, May 5, 1975, 41–48); and Nedava, "Predicting Historical Events and Sensing the Holocaust" (in Hebrew).

96. Ben Gurion, *Memoirs*, 2:11 (in Hebrew).

97. Ibid.

98. See Teveth, *Kinat David*, 1:437–38, and *Ben-Gurion and the Holocaust*.

99. See Teveth, *Ben-Gurion and the Holocaust* and "A-Historiographical Non-Historiographical Historiography" (in Hebrew).

100. Nedava, "Predicting Historical Events and Sensing the Holocaust."

7. MANIFOLD EUROPES

1. Morris Winchevsky, "A Letter from the Diaspora," *Hakol*, 27 (4), 1879. Winchevsky (1856–1930)—also known as Benzion Novakhovitsh and Leopold Benedict—was a socialist columnist born near Kovno, who lived in London for many years. See Klausner, *A History of Modern Hebrew Literature*, 6:307–50 (in Hebrew).

2. Goethe, "Während aber die Deutschen sich mit Auflösung philosophischer Probleme quälen," 371.

3. Nietzsche, *Beyond Good and Evil*, 244.

4. "Half a Consolation," in Ahad Haam, *Al Parashat Derakhim*, 1:123–27 (in Hebrew).

5. See Peabody, *National Characteristics*; Firchow, *The Death of the German Cousin*; and O'Sullivan, *Friends and Foes*. O'Sullivan writes, correctly, that the question is not why stereotypes appear, but in what context they appear (71–91) and, of course, how they are used.

6. Nietzsche, *Beyond Good and Evil*, 115.

7. Rühs, *Historische Entwicklung des Einflusses Frankreichs*.

8. Heine, "French Affairs," 14.

9. "Englische Fragmente," in Heine, *Sämtliche Schriften*, 2:533–36.

10. Mann, *Doctor Faustus*, 116.

11. On stereotypes of Germany and the Germans found in English literature, see, among others, O'Sullivan, *Friends and Foes*; Boerner, "National Images and Their Place in Literary Research"; Buchanan and Cantril, *How Nations See Each Other*; and Peabody, *National Characteristics*. An example of how Germany and Germans were represented in popular English literature can be found in Jerome K. Jerome's *Three Men on the Bummel* (1900) and *Diary of a Pilgrimage* (1891).

12. Dostoevsky, *Winter Notes on Summer Impressions*, 48. The writer Dennis Fonvisin wrote in letters from abroad that in France, money was God, but that no other nation on earth was as full of invention in all fields of craft and art—a gift that carried an unfortunate influence on the nation's morality (quoted in Greenfeld, *Nationalism*, 253). Isaiah Berlin wrote that the Russian intelligentsia had adopted "German romantic rhetoric about the unexhausted forces of the Germans and the unexpended German language with its pristine purity and the young, unwearied German nation, directed as it was against the 'impure,' Latinised, decadent western nations" (Berlin, "The Birth of the Russian Intelligentsia," 120). In contrast, in a 1916 article, "Qassim Amin," the Egyptian intellectual Muhammad Hussein Haykal wrote about the French sense of family and their subtle, polished way of thought, which gave rise to a broad philosophy that left no question

of morality, religion, or faith unexamined. See Bashkin, Kozma, and Gershoni, *Sculpting Culture in Egypt*, 112–13 (in Hebrew). Indeed, it is interesting to compare the impressions of East European Jewish men of letters who arrived in France from the mid-nineteenth century onward with the impressions of the Egyptian sheik Rifa'ah Rafi' at-Tahtāwi, as described in his 1843 book *Takhlis al-Ibriz fi Talkhis Baris* (The extraction of gold in a summary of Paris). At-Tahtāwi spent five years in Paris (1826–31), where he was sent by Muhammad 'Ali to absorb new ideas. His book is a riveting account of the influence of the lifestyle and values of French society and culture on a religious Muslim intellectual. See Abu-Lughod, *Arab Rediscovery of Europe*, 71–76; Lewis, *The Muslim Discovery of Europe*, 219–20 and 291–94; and Rustow, *Politics and Westernization in the Near East*, 28–65.

13. Aba Achimeir, "Poles in Palestine," *Hamashkif*, January 24, 1941 (in Hebrew).

14. We should distinguish here between Russian culture and the Jewish experience in Russia from the end of the nineteenth century to the 1917 revolution. Jewish immigrants with a radical worldview absorbed and internalized concepts and methods from the revolutionary movements in Russia and brought them to Palestine. However, these were not characteristic Russian traits, though a subset of Russian literature became a spiritual home for and reservoir of models of human behavior. See D. Segal, "The Impact of Russian Literature and Culture on the Emergence of the Jewish Liberation Movement," 1–16. A scholar of the influence of Russian political culture on the second and third *aliyot* (waves of immigration) describes the Russian foundation of the kibbutz movement during the 1950s and 1960s by pointing out the presence of Russian words, Russian literature in translation, and songs of Russian origin in kibbutzim (see Galili, "The Soviet Experience of Zionism"). In fact, many immigrants from Russia were not thoroughly versed in Russian culture.

15. Bartal, "An 'Alternative Model'" (in Hebrew).

16. Weizmann, *The Letters and Papers of Chaim Weizmann*, series A: *Letters*, 4:72.

17. Mandelstam, *Paris*, 92. See Levi, "Discovering Metropolis" (in Hebrew).

18. Smolenskin, *Hatoeh Bedarkei Hahayim*, part 4, 9–11.

19. See Y. Shavit, "The 'Spirit of France' and the 'French Culture' in the Jewish Yishuv in Eretz Israel" (in Hebrew; or an expanded version of this article, "L'esprit français et la culture française dans le yishuv en Erets-Israel," *REEH: Revue Européenne des Études Hébraïques*, 6 [2002]: 9–39); and Weber, "Stereotypes of France."

20. See Benzion Dinur, *Historical Writings*, vol. 1 (Jerusalem: Mosad Bialik, 1972), 239–37.

21. Bernfeld, *The Generation of Upheaval*, 12–13 (in Hebrew).

22. Smolenskin, *Hatoeh Bedarkei Hahayim*, part 4, 22–24.

23. Pierre Loti's novel *Les Désenchantées* (The disillusioned, 1906), translated into Hebrew by A. A. Kabak in 1929, tells of young women in a Turkish harem

caught in a deep spiritual crisis after reading European (primarily French) literature, and of youths in Istanbul who believed that "they had reached the heights of civilization by virtue of their Parisian dress" (259).

24. Herzl, *The Complete Diaries of Theodor Herzl*, 2:133.

25. Ibid., 136.

26. In Elboim-Dror, *Yesterday's Tomorrow*, 55.

27. Herschberg, *The Way of the New Yishuv in Eretz-Israel*, 14, 25 (in Hebrew). It should be noted that the intention of the Alliance Israélite Universelle was to disseminate the European way, but in reality European culture was identified with "French customs, mentality, and character." See Rodrigue, *Images of Sephardi and Eastern Jewries in Transition*, 31.

28. See Kolatt, "The Reflection of the French Revolution in the Jewish National Movement" (in Hebrew).

29. See Bell, *The Cult of the Nation in France*.

30. See Mintz, "The Place of the Jewish Workers' Movement in the Politicization of the Jewish People" (in Hebrew).

31. See Straus, "France and the French People in Y. L. Gordon's Works."

32. Hess, *The Revival of Israel*, 76.

33. Lilienblum, *An Autobiography*, 2:78 (in Hebrew).

34. See Shaanan, *Studies on the Literature of the Haskalah and the Influence of French Literature* (in Hebrew).

35. See Amichay-Michlin, *The Love of A. J. Shtibel*, 445–55 (in Hebrew).

36. See Y. Shavit, "First Encounters."

37. See Buruma, *Voltaire's Coconuts*. England was depicted as a country that melded political liberty with economic prosperity and burgeoning intellectual growth; in particular, it excelled in the practical sciences and rational behavior. On England as a model for Russian intellectuals, see Greenfeld, *Nationalism*, 156–58. As a counterpoint to these impressions, it is worth mentioning the satirical and critical depiction of England as John Bull, the typical Englishman John Arbuthnot presented in 1712 in his political satires; as Colonel Blimp in Sir David Low's caricatures in the 1920s and 1930s; and as Colonel Bramble in André Maurois's *Les silences du colonel Bramble* (1918). Regarding the components of the characteristic and typical identity attributed to the British, and the changes these underwent, see Paxman, *The English*.

38. *Hamagid*, February 28, 1874.

39. Ibid., July 10, 1862.

40. Shulman, *Sefer Divrei Yemei Olam*, 5:49 (in Hebrew).

41. "Higia hashaa" (The hour has arrived), in Ahad Haam, *Al Parashat Derakhim*, 4:389.

42. Smolenskin, "Am Olam" (An eternal people), 138 (in Hebrew).

43. Smolenskin, "Am Olam," 22–23.

44. Ahad Haam, *The Letters of Ahad Haam*, 4:99 (in Hebrew).

45. Ibid., 7:101 (in Hebrew).

46. Ibid., 4:103 (in Hebrew).

47. "Tehiyat haruah" (The spirit reborn), in Ahad Haam, *Al Parashat Derakhim*, 2:178 (in Hebrew).

48. "Hahinuch haleumi" (National education), in Ahad Haam, *Al Parashat Derakhim*, 4:136 (in Hebrew).

49. Regarding Herzl's relationship to England, see Beller, "Herzl's Anglophilia."

50. "Leregel haknisa," in Y. C. Brenner, *The Complete Works of Y. C. Brenner*, 2:157 (in Hebrew).

51. Ibid., 10 and 168.

52. Weizmann, *The Letters and Papers of Chaim Weizmann*, series A: *Letters*, 4:168–70.

53. Ibid., 95.

54. Freundlich and Yogev, *The Minutes of the Zionist General Council*, 1:197 (in Hebrew). Weizmann himself maintained that the difference between England and Germany lay in the fact that "in Germany everything is top-down: the government dictates policy, which then passes through countless bureaucrats until it finally reaches the masses down below. In England, policy is the result of thousands of ideas and ways of thought that originate with the people." See Weizmann, *The Letters and Papers of Chaim Weizmann*, series A: *Letters*, 7:219. In the end, however, England had, more than any other nation, "the best human material in the world." Europe was a *Kulturträger* for its colonies, but "only to a certain degree."

55. Weizmann, *The Letters and Papers of Chaim Weizmann*, series A: *Letters*, 7:8.

56. Among the books published in Palestine on the subject of England, we note Renier, *The English: Are They Human?* Originally published in London in 1931, it was published by Williams and Norgate in Hebrew in 1940 in a translation by Y. L. Baruch.

57. Jabotinsky, "The Englishman" (in Hebrew). See also Jabotinsky, "Public School Boys" (translated from Russian into Hebrew).

58. "Halom Anu Nasanu," in Achimeir, *Revolutionary Zionism*, 153–54. See also Y. Shavit, "My Heart Is in the East" (in Hebrew).

59. "Nes Hanuka Baavar Ubahove," in Achimeir, *Revolutionary Zionism*, 255.

60. See Bentwich, *Haanglim*, 11. David Raziel, the commander of the Irgun (the National Military Organization) in Palestine, wrote to the head of Britain's Criminal Investigation Department on December 29, 1938, that his depiction as an enemy of Great Britain was inaccurate: English was the only European language he commanded, and his education, steeped in English influence, had naturally led him to a love of English culture. See Alfassi, *Irgun Tzvai Leumi* [National Military Organization], 1:433–35. There is a claim that the letter has been forged, supposedly by Raziel's opponents, in an attempt to portray him as pro-British. The hatred of Britain peaked in early 1944, and the educational backgrounds of those who expressed it (such as Menachem Begin) did not incorporate elements of English culture. In the end, few disagreed with Ben Gurion's assessment in

1946, against the background of the Yishuv's bitter confrontation with England, that "there are two Englands": the England represented by British imperialism and the British policies in Palestine, and the England that was "British democracy on its own soil, with its lofty political and institutional and intellectual culture, with its... decency, honesty, tolerance, liberty, all shining exemplars. Much—not necessarily all—of the political, public, and spiritual glory of the British people lies in its own land." See Ben Gurion, *Towards the End of the Mandate*, 387–88.

61. See Reuveni, *The Administration of Palestine under the British Mandate 1920–1948*, 227–37 (in Hebrew). On how the British judicial approach influenced the "Yekke" judges of Israel's Supreme Court, and on their Anglophilism—an example of the admiration of Israeli liberals who hail from Germany for the British ideal of liberty and the British judicial system—see Salzberger and Oz-Zalzberger, "The Hidden German Origins of the Israeli Supreme Court" (in Hebrew).

62. A. Riger, *Hahinuch haivri beeretz Israel*. 1:24.

63. Rabinovitz, "Al Maamadenu Hatarbuti." On Israel's relationship with Britain during the war of independence and the first decade of Israeli statehood, see, most recently, Bar-On, *Of All the Kingdoms* (in Hebrew).

64. See Avineri, "The Presence of Eastern and Central Europe in the Culture and Politics of Contemporary Israel"; and Galili, "The Soviet Experience of Zionism." See also "The Labor Movement in Palestine and the October Revolution in the 1920s," "The Trumpeldor Labor Battalion," and "Characteristics of the Shift to the Left," in Shapira, *Visions of Conflict*, 188–257 (in Hebrew).

8. I AM IN THE EAST, AND MY HEART IS IN THE WEST

1. Heine, "Confessions," 337.
2. Mordecai Zeev Feierberg, *Whither?* translated by Ira Eisenstein (London: Abelard-Schuman, 1959), 124.
3. Herzl, *The Complete Diaries of Theodor Herzl*, 1:343.
4. Ibid., 2:671.
5. Ibid., 670.
6. Hess, *The Revival of Israel*, 260.
7. Ibid., 261.
8. Flaubert, *Bouvard et Pécuchet*, 282–83.
9. See, for example, Marchand, "German Orientalism and the Decline of the West"; and Kalmar, "Jesus Did Not Wear a Turban." We should add here that non-Arab nations, such as the Turks and Persians, were included in the concept of the Orient.
10. Edward Said's *Orientalism* does not address either the perception of the ancient Orient or the positive aspects of the Orient in European literature. It is worth remembering that the word "Orient" also refers to the Far East—to Persia and India. See Schwab, *The Oriental Renaissance*. China is not the subject of that work, even though it was perceived as an ancient civilization rich in achievements,

and even though since the eighteenth century, some scholars have noted that specific foundations of Chinese culture (as understood by the West) are analogous to elements of one or another European culture; others, in contrast, have described Chinese civilization as different from that of the West and believed it could provide lessons concerning the foundations of culture and government. See Guy, *The French Image of China before and after Voltaire*; Rose, "China as a Symbol of Reaction in Germany; Maverick, *China, A Model for Europe*; and Clarke, *Oriental Enlightenment*. In the eighth volume of Dubnow's *History of the Jewish People*, only a brief paragraph is devoted to Jews outside Europe. Dubnow wrote that the Muslim world was enveloped in the darkness of night, and that Asia was the old mother of Europe, who had seemingly drifted to sleep under the weight of her many centuries.

11. See Bachrach, *Racism*, 95–109 (in Hebrew).

12. Quoted in Wistrich, "Radical Antisemitism in France and Germany" (in Hebrew).

13. See Y. Shavit, "Shall a Nation Dwell Alone?" (in Hebrew).

14. Frischman, *Early Works*, 136 (in Hebrew). In January 1888, L. Plaskow wrote to M. M. Ussishkin: "We have no chance of establishing a homeland in the land of our fathers, and therefore [we need] a modest settlement of tens of thousands of families, which will make Palestine a sort of miniature Europe, part of today's Europe, that has wound up in the Orient; and moreover, it will be a European center for Asia." See Laskov, *Documents on the History of Hibbat-Zion and the Settlement of Eretz Israel*, 6:69 (in Hebrew).

15. See also Zevulun Leib Barit, a Lithuanian rabbi, in his letter of support for the Hibbat Zion, in Slutzky, *Shivat Zion*, 110.

16. See Mendes-Flohr, "Fin-de-siècle Orientalism and the Aesthetics of Jewish Self-Affirmation" (in Hebrew).

17. Among those who disseminated this idea was Duke Alexander Graf von Keyserling (1880–1946), in particular in his popular 1914 book, *Das Reisetagbuch eines Philosophen* (The travel diary of a philosopher). See Rohr, *Graf Keyserling's magische Geschichtsphilosophie*.

18. Quoted in Laskov, *Documents on the History of Hibbat-Zion and the Settlement of Eretz Israel*, 1:258 (in Hebrew).

19. See Tal, "Myth and Solidarity in the Zionist Thought and Activity of Martin Buber" (in Hebrew).

20. See, for example, the essays "The Character of European Civilization and Its Attitude toward Russian Civilization" (1852), by Ivan Kireevsky, and "Russia and Europe" (1869), by Nicolai Danilevsky. Konstantin Serge Aksakor considered the West an entirely negative region, full of violence, hatred, and cosmopolitanism—all rooted in the weakness of its nationalism. On these writers, see Walicki, *The Slavophile Controversy* 92–114 and 238–83.

21. Dostoevsky, *Winter Notes on Summer Impressions*, 64.

22. Nikolai Berdyaev, "The Cultural Crisis in Light of Historical Philosophy," 89–98 (in Hebrew). Yaakov Rabinovitz—the editor of the journal that published

the article, *Hedim*—wrote that this was a reactionary Russian philosophical idealism that arose as a reaction to Marxism. However, he wrote, "we will not flee to the desert" (116–17). See also Maor, "Nikolai Berdyaev and the Jewish People" (in Hebrew).

23. Buber, "The Spirit of the Orient and Judaism."

24. Uri Zvi Greenberg, *Yerushalayim Shel Mata*, 50–58.

25. Feierberg, *Whither?* 125.

26. Disraeli, *Tancred, or the New Crusade* (London: Henry Wiburn, 1847). See Werses, "Nachman's Last Speech" (in Hebrew); and Rozen, "Pedigree Remembered, Reconsidered, Invented."

27. Quoted in J. Frankel, *Prophecy and Politics*, 83–84.

28. Moshe Leib Lilienblum, "'Ezrat Sofrim [Writers' Gallery]': A Letter to the Publisher," *Hamelitz*, 22, June 1882, 436.

29. Lilienblum, *The Letters of Moshe Leib Lilienblum to Yehuda Leib Gordon*, 198–203 (in Hebrew).

30. Lilienblum, *The Writings of M. L. Lilienblum*, 1:50 (in Hebrew).

31. Quoted in Feiner, "Y. L. Gordon as Anti-Clerical and Warrior in the Jewish 'Culture War'" (in Hebrew).

32. Y. L. Gordon, *The Letters of Y. L. Gordon*, 2:114 (in Hebrew).

33. Hartenau, "Höre Israel!" To a nationalist German antisemite such as, for example, Ernst Jünger, Rathenau remained outside of the *Volkskörper* (racial body) of the Germanic *Volk*, and his desire to be considered German reflected—specifically because he was "seemingly similar" to the Germans—the great threat that "racially pure" Germans faced from the "assimilating Jews." See Friedländer, "Europe's Inner Demons."

34. Buber, "The Spirit of the Orient and Judaism." In the 1912 version of this article, Buber wrote about the alliance between Germany and the Jews as a sort of universal mission, but this passage was removed from the editions published after World War II. See Mendes-Flohr, "Between German and Jewish: Christians and Jews."

35. Wassermann, "Der Jude als Orientale."

36. Quoted in Doron, *The Zionist Thought of Nathan Birnbaum*, 196–98 (in Hebrew).

37. Quoted in ibid., 55.

38. Freundlich and Yogev, *The Minutes of the Zionist General Council*, 200 (in Hebrew).

39. Buber, *Die Stunde und die Erkenntnis*, 91–92.

40. Buber, "In später Stunde," 5. The Jews, added the writer Moshe Smilansky—who belonged to the "bourgeois" sector in the *Yishuv*, the modern Jewish community in Palestine—"are the only European element that can bring European progress to the Arab-Turkish lands without, in so doing, harming the needs and hopes of the Oriental nations, as other European elements might" ("Maaseinu," 137). However, Jews had no need to fear assimilation in the Arab environment

because the Jewish immigrants formed an elite group that could not assimilate into Arab culture, which occupied a lower status. But Smilansky profoundly criticized the fact that few settlers in the *Yishuv* learned Arabic or were acquainted with Arab culture, even though "Jews and Arabs are closely related in race and blood" (125–38).

41. Kohn, *Die Europäisierung des Orients*. See the chapter "Wege der Europäisierung" (Paths to Europeanization), 259–340.

42. Quoted in Laskov, *Documents on the History of Hibbat-Zion and the Settlement of Eretz Israel*, 1:504 (in Hebrew).

43. Borochov, *The Letters of B. Borochov*, 326–27 (in Hebrew).

44. See Almog, *Zionism and History*, 141–64.

45. Rabinovitz, "The Crisis of Culture as Seen through the Philosophy of History," 89–98 (in Hebrew).

46. Rabinovitz, "On the Orient and the West" (in Hebrew).

47. Herschberg, *In Oriental Lands*, 187 (in Hebrew).

48. Quoted in Schidorsky, *Libraries and Books in Late Ottoman Palestine*, 45.

49. Quoted in ibid., 47.

50. Quoted in Y. Shavit, "Ahad Ha-'Am and Hebrew National Culture."

51. Herzl, *The Jewish State*, 120 (in Hebrew). Herzl also wished to reassure Jews who spoke a variety of languages (in particular, apparently, German), writing: "Let every man retain the language in which his thoughts are at home . . . In the new country we shall remain what we are now, just as we shall never cease to think with melancholy affection of those native lands from which we have been driven away" (134–35).

52. Herzl, *The Complete Diaries of Theodor Herzl*, 1:40.

53. Herzl, *Altneuland*, 196. For Hebrew versions of the lyrics, in which the lemon tree was replaced by a pomegranate tree, see Y. Shavit, "The Scent of the Lemon Tree" (in Hebrew).

54. Max Nordau, "Das Jahr 1896 in der Weltgeschichte," *Neue Freie Presse*, January 1, 1897.

55. Nordau, *Zionist Writings: Lectures and Essays*, 2:110–19 (in Hebrew). The article "Achad Haam über Altneuland" was published on March 13, 1903, in *Die Welt*. See Laskov, "Altneuland."

56. Nordau, *Zionist Writings*, 2:110–19.

57. See Schulte, "Max Nordau" (in Hebrew).

58. See Wistrich, *Laboratory for World Destruction*, 61–84 and 85–132 (in Hebrew).

59. Y. C. Brenner, *The Complete Works of Y. C. Brenner*, 2:145 (in Hebrew).

60. Ibid., 45.

61. See Y. Shavit, "Vladimir Zeev Jabotinsky" (in French).

62. Jabotinsky, "The Elders' Rebellion" (in Hebrew).

63. Zeev Jabotinsky, "The Orient," *Razsviet* (Dawn), September 26, 1926, and "The Picturesque Orient," *Razsviet*, February 7, 1932 (both translated into Hebrew).

64. "The Arabesque Fashion," in Jabotinsky, *Al Sifrut Veomanut*, 213–22.

65. Zeev Jabotinsky, "The Orient," *Razsviet* (Dawn), September 26, 1926.

66. Ibid.

67. Jabotinsky, "The Orient."

68. "We, the Westerners," in Achimeir, *Revolutionary Zionism*, 168–72 (in Hebrew).

69. Quoted in Yaacov Goldstein, *The Path to Hegemony*, 93 (in Hebrew).

70. Ben Gurion, *Memoirs*, 2:402 (in Hebrew).

71. Uri Zvi Greenberg, *Yerushalayim Shel Mata* (Earthly Jerusalem).

72. Uri Zvi Greenberg, "Beli Shadai" (Without God), in *Sadan* 1–2 (1925): 18.

73. Uri Zvi Greenberg, "Al Heter Histori vedemama metzuva" (On historical license and imposed silence), in *Sadna De'ara* (Jerusalem: 1925), 18.

74. Greenberg, *Klapei Tishim Vetisha*, 33.

75. *Kehiliateinu*, 1922, 136–37.

76. Ibid., 181.

77. Ibid., 178. One of the contributors to the anthology asked: "Is it possible to give up the thousands of possibilities of culture—is it possible to give up one's shining impressions of life in the European city, of the wide world, which teems with unknown wonders—and all this to realize our idea in Palestine?" (68).

78. Quoted in Erez, *The Third Aliyah*, 2:602 (in Hebrew).

79. Ibid., 130.

80. Ibid., 214.

81. Uri Zvi Greenberg, "Manifesto lebitui" (A manifesto for expression), in *Sadan*, 1–2 (1925): 1 (in Hebrew).

82. See Margalit, "Hashomer Hazair," 17–52; and Peled, *The "New Man" of Zionist Revolution* (in Hebrew).

83. Quoted in Zeira, "Trembling, But Not Because of the Cold" (in Hebrew).

84. Quoted in Laskov, *Documents on the History of Hibbat-Zion and the Settlement of Eretz Israel*, 1:367 (in Hebrew).

85. Berl Katznelson, "Toward the Coming Days" (1919), in Katznelson, *The Works of Berl Katznelson*, Tel Aviv: 1944, 1:85–86 (in Hebrew). See also Zeev Jabotinsky, "Work and Mood," *Hadashot Haaretz*, January 27, 1919.

86. Lunz, "A Journey into Philistia," 165 (in Hebrew).

87. See Rubinstein, *The Zionist Dream Revisited*, 65–77 (in Hebrew); and Manor, "Orientalism and Jewish National Art," 142–61.

9. EUROPEANNESS AND ANTI-EUROPEANNESS IN PALESTINE

1. Dostoevsky, *Winter Notes on Summer Impressions*, 8–9.

2. Ginsburg, *Aviezer*, 66 (in Hebrew).

3. There is a great deal of irony in the claim that the European immigrants imposed Ashkenazi culture and hegemony on Palestine. The name Ashkenaz was

given to Germany in the eleventh century. By the fourteenth century, the Jewish communities in northern France, Germany, and the Slavic countries were already known as Ashkenazi communities. The Polish Ashkenazi world began to coalesce in the tenth century, and from the fifteenth to seventeenth centuries, there was a turning point in Poland's Jewish population that resulted in the reorganization of the Polish Jewish community's legal system and the end of its dependence on German scholars. Poland then became "Ashkenaz," and the Jews of Poland now represented the typical "Ashkenazi" Jew. (On the history of Polish Jewry, see Reiner, "On the Roots of the Urban Jewish Community in Poland in the Modern Period," in Hebrew) In practice, within the Israeli cultural polemic, the word "Ashkenazi" is used to mean European, even though in the past, many of the creators of Hebrew culture associated Ashkenazi culture with the *shtetl* and its Yiddish culture.

4. Herzl, *The Complete Diaries of Theodor Herzl* 1:41. Translation modified by the authors.

5. At the Ramle Convention, held on October 7–9, 1906. The Poale Tzion party is a socialist Zionist party.

6. Slutsky, *Poalei-Tzion in Eretz-Israel 1905–1919 (Documents)*, 23 (in Hebrew).

7. See Even-Zohar, "The Emergence and Crystallization of Local and Native Hebrew Culture in Eretz-Israel"; and Y. Shavit, "The Status of Culture in the Process of Creating a National Society in Eretz-Israel: Basic Attitudes and Concepts."

8. Weizmann, *The Letters and Papers of Chaim Weizmann*, series A: *Letters*, 5:325–27.

9. Syrkin, "From Outside into the Tent," in *The Collected Works of Nachman Syrkin*, 134–72 (in Hebrew).

10. Herzl, *The Complete Diaries of Theodor Herzl*, 1:181.

11. Ibid., 2:738. On October 27, 1898, Herzl wrote his impressions of Alexandria in his diary: "Alexandria shows how a clever European administration can draw a habitable, comfortable city even out of the hottest soil" (ibid.).

12. On the process of constructing the Hebrew culture's institutional system, see Z. Shavit, *The History of the Jewish Community in Eretz-Israel since 1882* (in Hebrew).

13. On the concept of cultural planning, see Even-Zohar, "Cultural Planning."

14. "In Life and In Literature," in Y. C. Brenner, *The Complete Works of Y. C. Brenner*, 2:60 (in Hebrew). See also Y. Shavit, "The *Yishuv* between National Regeneration of Culture and Cultural Generation of the Nation," 141–57 (in Hebrew).

15. Quoted in Ben-Arieh and Bartal, *The History of Eretz Israel*, 183 (in Hebrew).

16. Hacohen, *War of the Nations*, 2:775 (in Hebrew).

17. See Y. Shavit and Gideon Biger, *The History of Tel Aviv*. In September 1942, the socialist newspaper *Davar* lamented that all the ills of European civilization, characteristically symbolized by Paris, adhered to Tel Aviv primarily because of its flourishing nightlife during World War II: "We wanted to build a city of peace and

rest for our ailing spirit [and instead] we have gone and built a tiny Paris in the Middle East. We have transferred all of Europe's glorious civilization to Allenby St. and the beach."

18. Quoted in Y. Shavit, "Regulations of the First Colonies" (in Hebrew).

19. Herschberg, *The Way of the New Yishuv in Eretz-Israel*, 110 and 116 (in Hebrew).

20. Many Western travelers pointed out the backwardness of Arab agriculture. Henry Baker Tristram, for example, wrote in his travel diary for 1863–64: "Is it matter for surprise, that under such a wretched system, or rather absence of system, the land should have gone back from its ancient fertility?" (Tristram, *The Land of Israel*, 592). See also Eyal, "Between East and West," 201–23 (in Hebrew).

21. Herschberg, *The Way of the New Yishuv in Eretz-Israel*, 27 (in Hebrew).

22. S. Katz, "The First Furrow" and "On the Technological History of Palestine in the Late Ottoman Period" (both in Hebrew). On the different models of Jewish settlement, see Penslar, *Zionism and Technocracy*; and Troen, *Imagining Zion*.

23. See Y. Shavit, "The Status of Culture in the Process of Creating a National Society in Eretz-Israel" (in Hebrew). In his review of the July 1923 premiere of Verdi's *La Traviata* in Tel Aviv's Eden Hall, the critic Gershon Hanoch wrote: "Maybe the West is sinking, maybe it's not; but in the meantime, until it does sink, how much magic lies in store for us, for all of us, in these secular pleasures, and in the fact that there is such a thing as 'opera—Hebrew opera'" (Hanoch, *Hapoel Hazair*, August 3, 1923).

24. Nurit Gertz claims that at the time of the Israeli War of Independence, the Europe-Asia antimony was commonly accepted, with Europe representing the civilized Jewish community and uncivilized Asia representing the Arabs. However, it seems that the contrast of the developed *Yishuv* with backward Arab society usually highlighted the active, dynamic nature of Jewish society, "which makes the wilderness bloom," and not necessarily its Western or European character. See Gertz, *Myth in Israeli Culture*, 29–35.

25. See Ben-Porat, *The Bourgeoisie*, 59–100 (in Hebrew). In Israel Zarhi's 1941 novella *Malon Orhim* (The guesthouse), the cultural opposition between Polish and German immigrants is almost caricatured. The guesthouse, established in Jerusalem by a German immigrant couple, hosts mostly other German immigrants, who become uncomfortable upon the arrival of a couple who had lived in Germany for twenty-five years yet were still *Ostjuden* (East European Jews), unable to shed their foreign manners. According to one "civilized" German Jew, the table manners and eating habits displayed by this couple are "an utterly unbearable abomination." This guest, a former judge who considers the Nazis an insult to the honor of the German people, commits suicide along with his wife. The owners of the pension furnish the dining room with furniture they brought from Germany: a substantial dining table, armchairs, a grandfather clock, and the like. This furniture is what gives them a feeling of being in the "homeland" while they are in "foreign lands" (i.e., Palestine).

26. See Sela-Sheffy, "The *Yekes* in the Legal Field and Bourgeois Culture in Pre-Israel British Palestine" (in Hebrew).

27. Rabau, *I Am a Tel-Avivi*, 102–3 (in Hebrew).

28. Sheffi, "Anatomy of Rejection," 217–34 (in Hebrew). In a review of Yoav Gelber's *New Homeland: Immigration and Absorption of Central European Jews 1933–1948*, Henry Wassermann claims that the German immigrants were unable to withstand the pressure of their host environment and maintain their identity and cultural unity. There might be an assumption buried here, to the effect that immigrants from other European countries such as Russia and Poland had a less profound cultural identity and therefore found it easy to cast off. See Wassermann, "Here 'Yekkeness' is Shed Successfully and Responsibly," *Haaretz Literary Supplement*, June 8, 1990. As noted, we distinguish between the *Yekkes*' German habitus and their claims about their attitude toward Germany and ambivalent attitude toward German culture. On this, see Miron, *German Jews in Israel* (in Hebrew). Poles were the largest immigrant group: from 1919 to 1939, there were some 130,000 Polish immigrants, about 44 percent of the total number of immigrants during that period. Polish immigrants were not a homogeneous group. Furthermore, in contrast with the immigrants from Germany, the Polish *aliyah* did not document itself very thoroughly; as a result, it is difficult to establish how much affinity this group had for Polish culture—the country, its language, and its literature. In other words, it is hard to know to what extent these immigrants were Polish, to what extent theirs was actually a Jewish culture, and how many had already been educated in the new Hebrew culture while they were in Poland, which would have eased their integration into Palestine. Critics of the Polish *aliyah*, primarily after 1924, depicted it as a petit bourgeois immigration with a traditional, provincial, and exilic character, which had difficulty adapting its way of life. This, of course, was a gross generalization. In any case, many Polish immigrants faced financial, social, and cultural difficulties in the process of integration and expressed their yearning for genteel Europe. For more, see Yunas-Dinovitz, "Between Integration and Detachment" (in Hebrew).

29. See Berrol, "Germans versus Russians."

30. Claims from the Romantic school can be recognized in postmodernist criticism of the Enlightenment. See Liedman, *The Postmodernist Critique of the Project of Enlightenment*; and Saul, *Voltaire's Bastards*.

31. On anti-Europeanness, see Buruma and Margalit, *Occidentalism: The West in the Eyes of its Enemies*; and Carrier, *Occidentalism: Images of the West*. On the decline of Eurocentrism, which claims that Europe represents universal human history while recognizing that European values influenced the values and worldviews of non-European societies, which adopted them—and on the attempt to escape this worldview so as to understand the historical processes that took place in these societies—see Chakrabarty, *Provincializing Europe*. On this subject in Japan, see, for example, Tanaka, *Japan's Orient*. The relationship between Western orientation and anti-Westernness became polarized in the Arab world as well. The

most radical pro-Western stance was expressed by the Egyptian Coptic intellectual Salama Musa (1887–1958); this earned him the title "enemy of the Arabs and of Islam." In his 1927 *Alyoum w Algad* (Today and tomorrow), Musa describes Napoleon as the first Westerner to import European civilization to Egypt and deliver it from "the nightmare whose name is the Orient." The Egyptians, he wrote, were part of the West (during the Greco-Roman-Byzantine period) for over a thousand years and must rejoin the West in heart and soul and tailor their worldview, society, and lifestyle to the European model (quoted in Perlmann, "The Education of Salama Musa"). See also Badawi, "The Lamp of Umm Hashim"; and Tutungi, "Tawfiq al-Hakim and the West." Another spokesman for the Western orientation in nationalist Egyptian thought was the doctor Muhammed Sharat, who wrote in 1930 that "any [medical] examination of blood confirms that modern Egypt is not African or Asian but European: i.e., belonging to the people who live around the Mediterranean Sea" (quoted in Gershoni and Jankowski, *Egypt, Islam and the Arabs*, 115). In contrast, Sayyid Qutb, the spiritual leader of the Muslim Brotherhood in Egypt (who was hanged by the Nasserite regime in 1966), spent two years in the United States (1949–50) and there developed radical anti-Western ideas. A book of his published posthumously in Saudi Arabia in 1985 greatly influenced the development of the pan-Islamic anti-American ideology in the following years, with Al Qaeda at its forefront. See Tripp, "Sayyid Qutb"; and Calvert, "The World Is an Undutiful Boy!" Antiwesternism was already evident in the writings of spokesmen for integrative nationalism in Egypt (that is, a complete integration of the various pillars of Egyptian identity) during the second quarter of the twentieth century. They perceived the West as a satanical reality that brought destruction upon Egyptianness—both through the West's influence from afar and through its presence in Egypt; the chief representative of this stream of thought was Ahman Husayn. See Gershoni, *Egypt between Distinctiveness and Unity*, 172–73 (in Hebrew). The same polarization of views took place in the late Ottoman period and in modern Turkey between those who favored a "Westernization project" and claimed that "the secret for making Turkey fully European lies in reflecting Europeanness in Turkish," and that Western civilization should be adopted in its entirety; and those who supported a Turkish (later, Turkish Islamic) renaissance but did not object to adopting Western technology and science, distinguishing between civilization (*medeniyet*) and culture (*hars*). See Tunaya, *Westernization Movement in Turkish Political Life* (in Turkish).

32. See Fichman, "Popular Culture" 6 (in Hebrew).

33. See Kook, "As the Civilized among Them" (in Hebrew).

34. Strauss, "Progress or Return?"

35. See Ben-Yosef, *The Townlet* (in Hebrew).

36. See Buber, *Between a People and its Land*, 13 (in Hebrew).

37. See M. Brenner, *The Renaissance of Jewish Culture in Weimar Germany*, 46–48.

38. Yeivin, "The Foreign Legion Comes Home" (1947–48; in Hebrew).

39. Zuta, *The "Melamed" and the "Teacher,"* 20 (in Hebrew).

40. "From the Notebook," in Y. C. Brenner, *The Complete Works of Y. C. Brenner*, 2:137 (in Hebrew). In Brenner's lengthy story "From Both Sides" (1912), the author writes mockingly about the trend in Hebrew literature wherein writers who were radicals during their youth, and used to praise the West, change their colors in their old age and discover that "Europe is a young and naive child; how great our national entity is in contrast . . . and invariably some of them further add some nonsense about 'the revival of the Orient' . . . What foolishness!" (Brenner, *The Complete Works of Y. C. Brenner*, 1:325; in Hebrew). For more on this story, see Brinker, *Narrative, Art, and Social Thought in Y. H. Brenner's Work*, 65–114 (in Hebrew).

41. Avneri, *War or Peace in the Semitic Lands*, 9 (in Hebrew).

42. The classification of Jews who lived in Islamic countries as "Oriental" appeared during the nineteenth century as part of the West-East antinomy. Consequently, the Sephardi Jews were the first to be Orientalized, followed by the Jews inhabiting most of the Muslim world. See Schroeter, "Orientalism and the Jews of the Mediterranean."

43. On this subject, see, among others, Smooha, "Jewish Ethnicity in Israel; Tsur, *A Torn Community*; Shenhav, *The Arab-Jews*; Chetrit, *The Mizrahi Struggle in Israel*; and Kimmerling, *Immigrants, Settlers, Natives*. On the wide gulf between the study of Orientalism as a collection of essential traits and the study of the story of the Jews in Muslim lands as a heterogeneous and varying phenomenon, see Frenkel, "The Historiography of the Jews in Muslim Countries in the Middle Ages" (in Hebrew); and Barnai, "The Jews of Muslim Countries in Modern Times and the 'Jerusalem School of History'" (in Hebrew). It is fitting to mention the fact that in the discussion of the Muslim Orient, the role of the Ottoman Empire (the Muslim empire that ruled over the Middle East and part of Europe for some 500 years) is generally omitted.

44. See E. Cohen, *The Moroccans* (in Hebrew).

45. S. Fischer, "Two Patterns of Modernization" (in Hebrew). Some researchers of East European Jewish culture also wish to regard its modernization not as a process that took place under the influence of the West, but as an autonomous process resulting from the special circumstances of East European history. East European cultures also wished to present their modernization as an intrinsic and autarchic development. On Poland, for example, see Walicki, *Philosophy and Romantic Nationalism*, 11–30.

46. See the writer Sami Michael's pointed critique of this perception, in "There Are Those Who Wish to Keep Us in the Bathtub Known as 'The Culture of the Orient'" (in Hebrew).

47. The comparison to Arab Christians is not relevant, because Arab Christians are included in the same ethnic group as Arab Muslims.

48. On the importance attributed to music in the search for African-American authenticity, see Gilroy, *The Black Atlantic*, 72–110. On Oriental music, see Flam,

"Representation of the East in Hebrew Songs" (in Hebrew); and Halper, Seroussi, and Squires-Kidron, "Musica Mizrahit." A survey conducted in 1995 found that 59.3 percent of Jewish Israelis of North African or Middle Eastern heritage prefer to integrate into Western (European and American) culture. The response of spokesmen of this heritage to Eastern culture is not surprising: they saw the results of the survey as proof for their claim that the "Ashkenazis" had succeeded in "imposing" their cultural orientation on Jews of Eastern origin. See *Maariv*, March 9, 1995, 10 (in Hebrew).

49. See Lissak, "'Critical' Sociologists and 'Establishment' Sociologists in an Israeli Academic Community" (in Hebrew). It is important to point out that the radical Oriental intelligentsia does not represent the entire intelligentsia of the immigrants from the Muslim world. Other groups sought ways to integrate specific Jewish traditions with knowledge of Muslim culture, Hebrew identity, and modernization. See Efron, "In Search of Identity" (in Hebrew).

50. See Gans, "Symbolic Ethnicity."

51. See Even-Zohar, "Who's Afraid of Hebrew Culture?" (in Hebrew).

52. See Gilroy, *The Black Atlantic*. See also Calderon, *Multiculturalism versus Pluralism in Israel*, 200 (in Hebrew); and *Haaretz*, special supplement, "Israel: A Western or Oriental Nation?" September 31, 1985.

53. The concept of multiculturalism is an American import, but there are many types of multiculturalism. Multiculturalism in Switzerland, for example, is different from the multiculturalism found in the Indian subcontinent. Moreover, the image of a homogeneous Hebrew Jewish culture applies neither to the *Yishuv* nor to Israel as a state. Another possibility for weakening the longing for Europe was the "Mediterranean option"—that is, defining Israeli society and culture as belonging to the Mediterranean region and possessing a Mediterranean character. In this case as well, the European nature of society and culture was perceived as artificial—European dreams—as opposed to the reality: a society settled in the Mediterranean region, inspired by its natural environment, and possessing characteristics of Mediterranean society and people. The State of Israel is not a European mirage but a Mediterranean society. It is important to note that central norms of social and cultural life are left unmentioned in the repertoire of supposedly Mediterranean traits. It is also unclear whether Mediterraneanness refers to a specific localism, a geohistorical region, a detachment from Europe (that is, the Mediterranean is separate from Mediterranean Europe), or an alternative to the concept of Orientalism. For a useful summary of the Mediterranean outlook, see Nocke, "Yam Tikhoniut."

54. See Raz-Krakotzkin, "The Zionist Return to the West and the Mizrahi Jewish Perspective" and "A Few Comments on Orientalism, Jewish Studies and Israeli Society" (in Hebrew).

55. The result of this perception was that activities aimed at modernizing immigrants from the Muslim world in accordance with modern Western values (e.g., standards of health and personal hygiene) were considered patronizing and op-

pressive; any process of acculturation was perceived as "pedagogy for the purpose of creating cultural inferiority and perpetuating it in the name of cultural cultivation," rather than as an effort to abolish that inferiority. See Hinasky, "Eyes Wide Shut" (in Hebrew). See also Rozin, "Term of Disgust" (in Hebrew); and Hirsch, "We Are Here to Bring the West" (in Hebrew).

56. Ofir and Azulai, "One Hundred Years since the First Zionist Congress" (in Hebrew). According to this perspective, there is now no trace in Israel of European values as described in the article "Our Renewal," by Jacques Derrida and Jürgen Habermas: "Christianity and capitalism, science and technology, Roman law and the Code Napoléon, the bourgeois urban way of life, democracy and human rights, and secularization of state and society have spread across other continents, so these achievements are no longer specifically European" (Derrida and Habermas, "Our Renewal").

57. See Sternhell, "Reflections on the Turns of Centuries" (in Hebrew).

58. Zabarenko, "The Negative Image of America in the Russian-Language Jewish Press."

59. See Blondheim, "The Orthodox Rabbinate Discovers America" (in Hebrew).

60. See Bartal, "Heavenly America" (in Hebrew); Feingold, *Haskalah Literature Discovers America*, 104–91 (in Hebrew); and Richman, *The Image of America in the European Hebrew Periodicals of the Nineteenth Century*. Heine wrote that when all of Europe became one giant prison, a "single hole" would still be found for escape: America. And, "Heaven be praised, that hole is larger than the prison" ("Italien: Reise von München nach Genua," in *Sämtliche Werke*). On the other hand, Heine also wrote: "Or should I go to America, to this incredible prison of freedom, where the unseen chains would hurt me even more than those visible here at home, where the most despicable of all tyrants, the mob, rules so brutally! You know how I think about this damn land, which I once loved, when I did not really know it" ("Ludwig Börne: Eine Denkschrift," in Heine, *Sämtliche Werke*, 11:35).

61. Quoted in Rischin, *The Promised City*, 25.

62. Quoted in Klausner, *A History of Modern Hebrew Literature*, 4:281.

63. "A Historical Question: The Question of Emigration," in Dubnow, *Nationalism and History*, 197–99.

64. Zangwill, *The Melting Pot*, 102–3. To Moses Hess, America symbolized "the general regenerating power by means of which all elements of the historical people will be assimilated into one" (Hess, *The Revival of Israel*, 124).

65. Roth, *Now and Forever*, 138–40.

66. Alon Gan attributes this lack of interest on the part of Palestinian Jewish society, at least until the 1960s, to the essential difference between Jewish nationalism and American nationalism, with the latter's emphasis on universal values. He also investigates the agents of change responsible for the shift in attitudes toward America since the 1960s, but there is room for much more investigation in this area. See Gan, "Israel and American Jewry Relations" (in Hebrew).

67. Bialik, "On America."

68. Zeev Jabotinsky is, perhaps, the only non-American Zionist leader who wrote enthusiastically in praise of America. In a 1926 piece, he had one of his characters, a visitor from the United States, say that Americans are depicted as "a middling and prosaic nation," but in fact the typical American is a "democratic pioneer," and American culture is a democratic culture, free of the class divisions found in Europe. There is also no basis for the idea that America is a nation lacking in culture; on the contrary, there is a great cultural flowering, and most importantly, it abounds in vitality. See Jabotinsky, *Al Sifrut Veomanut*, 195. Jabotinsky also had the American visitor prophesy that in the near future, America would become Europe's instructor in the matter of social ethics. In an article in 1936, Jabotinsky wrote that America is the "great child, the giant child of humanity's old age." See Jabotinsky, "Land of Mighty Longing," *Hayarden*, March 22, 1935. In 1940, during his last stay in the United States, Jabotinsky wrote that the United States is the "land of the future," in which an amalgamation had developed of "the best streams of White humanity . . . Never before has such a combination been seen." In the New Deal, Jabotinsky found an example of socialist reform policy worthy of emulation. It was therefore America that would take the torch of a moral and just world from Europe. See Jabotinsky, "According to the Librarian," *Hamashkif*, April 22, 1940. However, he wrote nothing about the American system of government or American political culture.

69. See, for example, Elon, *The Israelis*.

70. See Smooha, "Is Israel Western?" (in Hebrew).

71. Public discussion in Israel of the elements and essence of Americanism was paltry in comparison to the discourse on what composed Europeanness. For the most part, discussion of America seems to have been built on impressionistic reactions. For example, after a three-month visit to the United States in 1969, the writer Benyamin Tamuz "discovered" Americans' "noble qualities": kindheartedness and generosity toward others. He also concluded that America had prematurely reached old age and lived with a consciousness that its power was past its prime (this, in 1969!). Furthermore, in contrast to prevailing opinion, he found that the country most responsible for the flourishing of mass culture was also the country that would return high culture to its former glory, and that America would be granted "the status of an Athens." See Tamuz, "The American Circle," *Haaretz Literary Supplement*, October 24, 1969, 23 (in Hebrew). There is a wide gulf between this optimistic report and Yitzhak Laor's poem, published in the *Haaretz Literary Supplement* on February 21, 2002, and titled "The Newest Testament," in which the United States is described as a murderous and bloodthirsty empire. Tamuz's opinion, of course, is at the opposite extreme to the common image of American culture as shallow and lacking in tradition. Such an opinion was expressed by, for example, the great Swiss cultural historian Jakob Burckhardt, when he wrote that a large part of the American public had, to a great extent, given up on "spiritual continuity" with European culture "and wish to share in the enjoyment of art and poetry merely as forms of luxury"; furthermore, in the

United States, "everything turns into big business." See Burckhardt, *Reflections on History*, 64 and 176.

72. Markovits, *Uncouth Nation*.

73. On the perception of the United States as a challenge to which a response would foster a sense of unity within Europe, see Servan-Schreiber, *The American Challenge*.

74. Sammy Smooha, "Is Israel Western?"

10. EUROPE, OLD OR NEW?

1. See A. B. Yehoshua, "Zeus, Europe, and the Children," *Maariv*, Books and Culture section, January 10, 1992 (in Hebrew). See also Gerstenfeld, *European-Israeli Relations* and *Israel and Europe: An Expanding Abyss?*

2. There are also European predictions of America's inevitable decline. See Todd, *After the Empire*. Some voices in the Israeli discourse in the early twenty-first century emphasize the seemingly growing strength of isolationist nationalist movements.

3. On the European Union and its future, see chapter 1. See also, among others, Smith and Stirk, *Making the New Europe*; Wintle, *Culture and Identity in Europe*; Shore, *Building Europe*; Holmes, *Integral Europe*; Rumford, *The European Union*; and Calleo, *Rethinking Europe's Future*. It is also important to note that the claim that the ethnonationalist mentality is in decline is not well-founded. On the contrary, various parts of Europe have seen a revival of ethnonationalism; the most recent example is Kosovo's declaration of independence in March 2008.

4. See Ben-Gal, *When Dining with the Devil* (in Hebrew).

5. Livneh, *Israel and the Crisis of Western Civilization* (in Hebrew). In a review of the book, Yeshayahu Leibowitz maintained that there was no conflict between "Israel" and "Western civilization," because "Israeli" traits were in effect "bad copies or dismal imitations of values, aspirations, and trends of [Western] civilization" (which, according to Livneh, was in a state of degeneration). See Leibowitz, "The State of Israel Inculcates Assimilation," *Haaretz*, September 17, 1972 (in Hebrew).

6. See also Moshe Ben-Yosef, "Another Perspective (Or: The Decline of the West in Zionism)," *Kivunim*, August 1984, 91–96 (in Hebrew).

7. See Talmon, *The Myth of the Nation and the Vision of Revolution*.

8. According to a 2004 survey conducted in EU nations, about two-thirds of the respondents reported that they felt ties to Europe; 57 percent wanted Europe to be part of their identity; and 41 percent said their identity remained entirely nationalist. The shared European background was expressed in a high rate of mobility among the various EU nations, as well as in shared values and institutions such as democracy, social security, quality of life, and the like. Over the past nineteen years, the Erasmus Mundus educational program has enabled some 1.2 million students to study in universities outside their own countries; some have dubbed this the "Erasmus generation."

9. "The Terror in Full: Behold the Gentile," in Greenberg, *Rehovot Hanahar*, 169–77 (in Hebrew).

10. See J. P. Tedeschi, "The Myth of the Jews and the Myth of the Germans" (in Hebrew); Shoham, *Valhalla, Calvary and Auschwitz*; and Shechter, *Auschwitz, Faust-Kingdom*. See also "Israelis' Way to the Holocaust: A Footnote as Alibi—The Goldhagen Debate" and "The Chameleon and the Phoenix: Germany in Israel's Eyes," in Zimmermann, *German Past—Israeli Memory*, 196–279 (both in Hebrew).

11. Quoted in Ben Gurion, *The Restored State of Israel*, 1:463–64 (in Hebrew).

12. Quoted in Sharett, *Moshe Sharett and the German Reparations Controversy* (in Hebrew), 430–48.

13. Quoted in Ben Gurion, *The Restored State of Israel*, 2:579–80 (in Hebrew). On Mapam's orientation and internal debates regarding its attitude toward the Soviet Union, as well as the changes the party experienced over the course of Israel's first decade, see Zur, "A Difficult Divorce" (in Hebrew); and Gan, "Followers to Germany?" (in Hebrew). Gan writes, justifiably, about the "disappointed love" of HaKibbutz Hameuchad's leadership for the Soviet Union, and about their "disappointed hate" for Germany. See also Kafkafi, *Truth or Faith*, 192–206 (in Hebrew).

14. See Thomas Mann's lecture "Germany and the Germans," delivered on May 29, 1945.

15. See also Binyamin Tammuz's series of articles in *Haaretz* in January 1967.

16. Elyashiv, *The Other Germany*, 17 (in Hebrew).

17. Ibid., 191.

18. Elon, *A Nation Haunted by Its Past*, 92 (in Hebrew).

19. Shlomo Avineri, "History's Lesson and the Two Germanies," *Haaretz*, November 13, 1992 (in Hebrew). See also Shafer, *Ambiguous Relation*; Flanagan, "Trying to Square a Triangle of Interests."

20. "The Chameleon and the Phoenix: Germany in Israel's Eyes," in Zimmermann, *German Past—Israeli Memory*, 276 (in Hebrew).

21. See Witzthum, "Germany in Israel" (in Hebrew); and Sheffi, "Anatomy of Rejection" (in Hebrew).

22. Gershom Schocken, *Politika*, January 21, 1987, 27–29 (in Hebrew).

23. Weitz, "Between the Poet and the Diplomat," "The Path to the 'Other Germany,'" and "Political and Ideological Conflicts" (all in Hebrew).

24. See Ben Elishar, "The Nationalist Camp and the President's Visit to Germany" (in Hebrew).

25. See Sheffi, *The Ring of Myths* (in Hebrew). For evidence for the close ties between Israel and Germany in the realms of culture, science, and higher education, see the German Foreign Office's January 2005 publication on events held to mark forty years since the establishment of diplomatic relations between Israel and Germany, as well as *Deutschland*, a pamphlet marking the event.

26. It can be said that the horrors of Stalinism and the Soviet concentration camps have had almost no hold on the collective memory of Israel (or the West). See Applebaum, *Gulag*.

27. See Kafkafi, *Truth or Faith*, 192–206 (in Hebrew).

28. See Faber, Schoeps, and Stawski, *Neu-alter Judenhass*; *The Face of the Holocaust: Antisemitism in the Third Millennium*, The Tel Yitzchak Institute for Holocaust Education, 2004 (in Hebrew); and "A New Jewish Order: On Modern Antisemitism," *Haaretz* Passover supplement, April 5, 2004. According to a survey conducted on August 2004, France had seen a 170 percent rise in antisemitic incidents during that year thus far, compared to the whole of 2003. See *Haaretz*, August 29, 2004, 11a (in Hebrew). On perceptions of the nature of antisemitism in various countries, see Shapira, "Israeli Perceptions of Anti-Semitism and Anti-Zionism."

29. *Haaretz*, July 9, 2004.

30. See Schor, *L'antisémitisme en France dans l'entre-deux-guerres*.

31. See Finkielkraut, *Au nom de l'autre*.

32. See Trigano, "Is There a Future for French Jewry?"

33. See Wistrich, *European Anti-Semitism Reinvents Itself*. For a survey of Israel's relations with Europe since 1948, see Sachar, *Israel and Europe*.

34. See Della Pergola, *World Jewry beyond 2000*, 13.

35. Quoted in A. Harrington, "Ernst Troeltsch's Concept of Europe," 486.

36. Barnavi, *Les religions meurtrières*.

37. See Phillips, *Londonistan*; Husain, *The Islamist*; Laqueur, *The Last Days of Europe*; and Bowen, *Why the French Don't Like Headscarves*.

38. "Mekka Deutschland: Die stille Islamisierung," *Der Spiegel*, March 26, 2007. See also "Wie gefährlich ist der Islam?" *Stern*, September 12, 2007; Tibi, *Der Islam und Deutschland*.

39. See Fallaci, *The Force of Reason*.

40. See, for example, an article by George Milbradt, minister-president of Saxony, in *Maariv*, April 4, 2007.

41. See J. Cohen, "The Eastern Connection" (in Hebrew).

42. "The Myth of Sephardic Supremacy," in Schorsch, *From Text to Context*, 88.

43. Lévi-Strauss, *The Raw and the Cooked*, 77.

44. See U. Shavit, "A Fifth Column in the West?"

45. See Friedländer, "Europe's Inner Demons."

CONCLUSION: BETWEEN "REAL EUROPE" AND THE "EUROPEAN SPIRIT"

1. See Volkov, "Jews among the Nations" (in Hebrew). See also Beck, *The Jews in European History*; and Dan Diner, "Geschichte der Juden-Paradigms einer europischen Geschichtsschzeibung," in *Gedachtnizeiten uber judische und andere Geschichten* (Munich: Beck, 2003), 246–60. For new insights on the history of the Jews in Europe and its historiography, see J. Cohen and Rosman, *Rethinking European Jewish History*.

2. Ben Gurion, *Memoirs*, 1:267–68 (in Hebrew).

3. Quoted in Best, *Churchill*, 286.

4. Quoted in ibid., 283–84.

5. On anti-Americanism in Germany, see Diner, *America in the Eyes of the Germans*. On anti-Americanism in France, see Todd, *After the Empire*. Todd predicts that Europe's liberation from American hegemony and the threat of the American social model will occur in the near future. For an opposite view, see Revel, *Anti-Americanism*.

6. The description of the rift between Western Europe and the United States has lent itself to great exaggerations, which read the conflict as a return to the state of cultural antagonism that existed between the two during the nineteenth century and until World War I; the result is that the West will turn against itself. See Kupchan, "The End of the West." It is impossible not to point out that along with the calls for divorce from the West, there is an expectation that the West will be a source of aid to ailing nations in Africa and Asia—as well as criticism that it is not doing enough on their behalf.

7. Hitchcock, *The Struggle for Europe*, 445.

8. On predictions of America's decline, see Huntington, "The U.S."

9. Frischman, *Early Works*, 2:493 (in Hebrew).

10. The highest concentrations of Jews in Europe are in France (about 500,000), Britain (about 300,000), Russia (about 235,000), and Germany (115,000). See *Haaretz*, July 21, 2005, 3A. See also Wasserstein, *Vanishing Diaspora*. On Jewish culture in the postwar periods see Grubu, *Virtually Jewish*. For an example of an unconvincing attempt to formulate a universal European Jewish identity, see Pinto, "The Third Pillar?"

11. The nearly obsessive attention paid to the question of the bond between Jews and Europe is reflected, for example, in two articles that appeared in 1997. In the first of these, Benjamin Gross's "The Jews and the 'European Question,'" (*Makor Rishon*, July 20, 2007), the author claims that the revival of antisemitism in modern Europe is the clear result of the continued perception of Jews as other—not, this time, as other in the sense of a religious national minority within Europe, but in the sense of a nationalist Jewish state in a Muslim Arab Middle East. Gross regards modern Europe as an empty, metaphysically superficial entity—different, of course, from Judaism. In order to be saved and redeemed, Europe must therefore learn from Judaism and the Jews, then and now a people possessed of religious and metaphysical awareness. The second article, Avraham Burg's "The New Jewish Paradox" (*Haaretz*, September 10, 2007) makes the opposite claim: Jewish nationalism in Israel has lost the humanist universalist dimension of Judaism, and only by reviving this dimension will it be able to serve as a bridge between the clashing civilizations of Christianity and Islam. Should the West fail to accept this dimension from Judaism, its decline is assured. Conversely, if the floundering West does adopt it, a golden age will arise. Both articles express a sense of Jewish superiority and even of a missionary utopia.

12. After the publication of the Hebrew version of this book, *Haaretz* ran an

interview with the writer Aharon Appelfeld, a Holocaust survivor. Appelfeld said that the Jewish intelligentsia in Eastern Europe saw itself as European, but that this Europeanness was not found in Palestine: "Modern Europe was built by Jews, and they contributed to what is beautiful in Europe. They contributed to humanism, to the liberal movements, to philanthropy, to literature, painting, music. Europe is not some anti-Jewish thing. When we say Europeanness, in some sense we also mean a certain type of Jewishness, because this Europeanness was created by Jews, among others . . . Most Jews lived in Europe for 2,000 years. Europe shaped them and they shaped Europe. So you are talking about a symbiotic Jewish-European foundation. You can't escape it." See Dror Mishani, "Between Rechavia and Mea Shearim," *Haaretz*, September 22, 2006 (in Hebrew).

BIBLIOGRAPHY

For many works published in the early twentieth century or before, the bibliographic information includes place of publication but not the publisher.

Abu-Lughod, Ibrahim. *Arab Rediscovery of Europe: A Study in Cultural Encounters*. Princeton, N.J.: Princeton University Press, 1963.
Achimeir, Aba. *Revolutionary Zionism* [in Hebrew]. Tel Aviv: Vaad Lehotsaat Kitve Ahimeir, 1965–66.
Ahad Haam [Asher Zvi Hirsch Ginsberg]. *Al Parashat Derakhim* [in Hebrew]. 2nd ed. Berlin: Judische Verlag, 1930.
———. *The Letters of Ahad Haam* [in Hebrew]. Edited by Aryeh Simon. 5 vols. New and expanded ed. Tel Aviv: 1956–59.
Alfassi, I., ed. *Irgun Tzvai Leumi* [National Military Organization]: *Collection of Archival Sources and Documents, April 1937–April 1941*. Tel Aviv: Jabotinsky Institute, 1990.
Algazi, Gadi. "Studying Learned Nature: The Shaping of the Concept of Habitus in Bourdieu's Work [in Hebrew]." *Israeli Sociology* 4, no. 2 (2002): 401–10.
Almog, Shmuel. *Nationalism, Zionism, and Antisemitism: Essays and Studies*. Jerusalem: Hasifriyah Haziyonit, 1992.
———. *Zionism and History: The Rise of a New Jewish Consciousness*. Translated by Ina Friedman. New York: St. Martin's, 1987.
Altmann, Alexander. *Moses Mendelssohn: A Biographical Study*. Philadelphia: Jewish Publication Society of America, 1973.
Amichay-Michlin, Dania. *The Love of A. J. Shtibel* [in Hebrew]. Jerusalem: Mosad Bialik, 2000.
Applebaum, Anne. *Gulag: A History*. New York: Doubleday, 2003.
Arieli, Yehoshua. "New Horizons in the Historiography of the Eighteenth and Nineteenth Centuries [in Hebrew]." In Arieli, *History and Politics*, 34–63. Tel Aviv: Am Oved, 1992.
Arieli-Horowitz, Dana. "Political Degeneration from the Fin-de-Siècle to Nazism [in Hebrew]." In *Fins de Siècle: End of Ages*, edited by Yosef Kaplan, 291–316. Jerusalem: Merkaz Zalman Shazar, 2005.
Aschheim, Steven E. "'The Jews Within': The Myth of 'Judaization' in Germany." In *The Jewish Response to German Culture: From the Enlightenment to the Second World War*, edited by Jehuda Reinharz and W. Schatzberg, 212–41. Hanover, N.H.: University Press of New England, 1985.
Avineri, Shlomo. "Edmund Eisler's Zionist Utopia." *Midstream* 31, no. 2 (1985): 50–53.

———. *Moses Hess: Prophet of Communism and Zionism*. New York: New York University Press, 1968.

———. "The Presence of Eastern and Central Europe in the Culture and Politics of Contemporary Israel." *East European Politics and Societies* 2 (Spring 1996): 163–73.

Avneri, Uri. *War or Peace in the Semitic Lands* [in Hebrew]. Tel Aviv: Sifriyat Maavak, 1947.

Azuléos, Daniel. *L'entrée en bourgeoise des juif allemands, ou le paradigme libéral (1800–1933)*. Paris: Presses de L'université Paris-Sorbonne, 2005.

Bach, H. I. *The German Jew: A Synthesis of Judaism and Western Civilization*. Oxford: Littman Library of Jewish Civilization, 1984.

Bachrach, Zvi. *Racism: The Tool of Politics—From Monism towards Nazism* [in Hebrew]. Jerusalem: Magnes, 1985.

———. "Walther Rathenau: His Judaism and His Attitude towards Zionism." In *European Jews and Jewish Europeans between the Two World Wars*, edited by Raya Cohen, 223–30. Tel Aviv: Tel Aviv University Press, 2004.

Bacon, Gershon. "An Anthem Reconsidered: On Text and Subtext in Yehuda Leib Gordon's 'Awake, My People.'" *Prooftext* 15 (1995): 185–94.

Badawi, M. "The Lamp of Umm Hashim: The Egyptian Intellectual between East and West." *Journal of Arabic Literature* 1 (1970): 145–61.

Barkai, Abraham, and Paul R. Mendes-Flohr, eds. *German-Jewish History in Modern Times*. Vol. 4: *Renewal and Destruction, 1918–1945*. New York: Columbia University Press, 1998.

Barker, Ernest. *National Character and the Factors in Its Formation*. 2nd ed. London: Methuen, 1939.

Barnai, Jacob. "The Jews of Muslim Countries in Modern Times and the 'Jerusalem School of History' [in Hebrew]." *Peamim* (Summer 2002): 83–115.

Barnavi, Élie. "The Idea of Europe [in Hebrew]." *Zmanim* 43: 5–17.

———. *Les religions meurtrières*. Paris: Flammarion, 2006.

Bar-On, Mordechai. *Of All the Kingdoms: Israel's Relations with the United Kingdom during the First Decade after the End of the British Mandate in Palestine, 1948–1958* [in Hebrew]. Jerusalem: Yad Ben Zvi, 2006.

Baron, Salo Wittmayer. "The Impact of the Revolution of 1848 on Jewish Emancipation." *Jewish Social Studies* 11 (1949): 195–248.

Bartal, Israel. "An 'Alternative Model': France as a Source of Influence for the Modernization of East European Jewry (1772–1863) [in Hebrew]." In *The French Revolution and Its Impact*, edited by Richard I. Cohen, 271–85. Jerusalem: Merkaz Zalman Shazar, 1991.

———. "Heavenly America: The U.S.A. as an Ideal Model for 19th-Century East-European Jews [in Hebrew]." In *Following Columbus: America 1492-1992*, edited by Miriam Eliac-Feldon, 511–22. Jerusalem: Merkaz Zalman Shazar, 1996.

———. "The Image of Germany and German Jewry in East European Jewish Society during the 19th Century." In *Danzig, between East and West: Aspects of Modern Jewish History*, edited by Isador Twersky, 3–17. Cambridge, Mass.: Harvard University Press, 1985.

———. *The Jews of Eastern Europe, 1772–1881*. Translated by Chaya Naor. Philadelphia: University of Pennsylvania Press, 2002.

———. "Non-Jews in Hebrew and Yiddish Literature in Eastern Europe, 1856–1914 [in Hebrew]." Ph.D. diss., Hebrew University, 1980.

Barth, F. Introduction. In *Ethnic Groups and Boundaries: The Social Organization of Culture Difference*, edited by F. Barth, 9–38. Boston: Little, Brown, 1969.

Bartlett, Robert. *The Making of Europe: Conquest, Colonization and Culture Change, 950–1350*. Princeton, N.J.: Princeton University Press, 1993.

Bar-Yosef, Hamutal. *Decadent Trends in Hebrew Literature: Bialik, Berdichevski, Brenner* [in Hebrew]. Beersheba, Israel: Ben-Gurion University of the Negev Press, 1997.

———. "Fin-de-Siècle in Russia and Its Consequences for Zionism [in Hebrew]." In *Fins de Siècle: End of Ages*, edited by Yosef Kaplan, 173–84. Jerusalem: Merkaz Zalman Shazar, 2005.

———. "Zionism and the Jewish Cosmopolitan [in Hebrew]." In *The Age of Zionism*, edited by Anita Shapira, Jehuda Reinharz, and Jay Harris, 127–43. Jerusalem: Merkaz Zalman Shazar, 2000.

Bashkin, Orit, Liat Kozma, and Israel Gershoni, eds. *Sculpting Culture in Egypt: Cultural Planning, National Identity and Social Change 1890–1939* [in Hebrew]. Tel Aviv: Ramot, 1999.

Bazilovsky, Moshe. *Words of Wisdom or the Belief in Natural Science* [in Hebrew]. Zhitomir, Russia: 1869.

Beck, Wolfgang, ed. *The Jews in European History*. Cincinnati, Ohio: Hebrew Union College Press, 1994.

Bell, David A. *The Cult of the Nation in France: Inventing Nationalism, 1680–1800*. Cambridge, Mass.: Harvard University Press, 2003.

Beller, Steven. "Herzl's Anglophilia." In *Theodor Herzl and the Origins of Zionism*, edited by Ritchie Robertson and Edward Timms, 54–61. Austrian Studies 3. Edinburgh: Edinburgh University Press, 1997.

Ben Elishar, Eliyahu. "The Nationalist Camp and the President's Visit to Germany [in Hebrew]." *Hauma* 58 (1987): 362–462.

Ben Gurion, David. *The Letters of David Ben Gurion* [in Hebrew]. Edited and annotated by Yehuda Erez. Vol. 1. Tel Aviv: Am Oved, 1971.

———. *Memoirs* [in Hebrew]. Edited by Gershon Rivlin. 2 vols. Tel Aviv: Am Oved, 1971–72.

———. *The Restored State of Israel* [in Hebrew]. Tel Aviv: Am Oved, 1969.

———. *Towards the End of the Mandate: Memoirs (June 1946–March 1947)*. 2nd ed. Tel Aviv: Am Oved, 1993.

Ben-Arieh, Yehoshua, and Israel Bartal, eds. *The History of Eretz Israel: The Last Phase of Ottoman Rule (1799–1917)* [in Hebrew]. Jerusalem: Keter, 1983.

Ben-Gal, Eli. *When Dining with the Devil* [in Hebrew]. Tel Aviv: Am Oved, 1989.

Ben-Porat, Amir. *The Bourgeoisie: The History of the Israeli Bourgeoisie* [in Hebrew]. Jerusalem: Magnes, 1999.

Ben-Rafael, Eliezer. *Jewish Identities: Fifty Intellectuals Answer Ben-Gurion* [in Hebrew]. Beersheba, Israel: Ben-Gurion University of the Negev Press, 2001.

Ben-Sasson, Havi. "Poland and Poles in the Eyes of Polish Jews during the Second World War [in Hebrew]." Ph.D. diss., Hebrew University, 2005.

Bentwich, Norman. *Haanglim* [The English]. Tel Aviv: 1937.

Ben-Yosef, Moshe. "Another Perspective (Or: The Decline of the West in Zionism) [in Hebrew]." *Kivunim* (August 1984): 91–96.

———. *The Townlet: On Zionism, Within Quotes and Without* [in Hebrew]. Tel Aviv: Alef, 1986.

Berdichevsky, Michah Yosef. *Ginzei Micha Yosef* [The archives of M. Y. Berdichevsky]. Edited by Avner Holzman. Vol. 4. Holon, Israel: Holon Municipality, 1990.

———. "Transvaluation of Values [in Hebrew]." In *The Works of M. Y. Berdichevsky (Bin Gorion)*. Tel Aviv: Dvir, 1964.

Berdyaev, Nikolai. "The Cultural Crisis in Light of Historical Philosophy [in Hebrew]." *Hedim* 4 (May 1926): 89–98.

Berezin, Mabel and Martin Schain, eds. *Europe without Borders: Remaking Territory, Citizenship, and Identity in a Transnational Age*. Baltimore, Md.: Johns Hopkins University Press, 2003.

Berlin, Isaiah. "The Birth of the Russian Intelligentsia." In *Russian Thinkers*, edited by H. Hardy and Aileen Kelly, 114–35. London: Hogarth, 1978.

Bernfeld, Shimon. *The Generation of Upheaval* [in Hebrew]. Warsaw: Achisaf, 1897.

———. "Toward the End of the Nineteenth Century [in Hebrew]." *Luach Achiasaf* 6 (1898): 23–42.

Berrol, S. "Germans versus Russians: An Update." *American Jewish History* 73, no. 2 (1983): 142–57.

Best, Geoffrey. *Churchill: A Study in Greatness*. London: Hambledon and London, 2001.

Bialer, Uri. *The Shadow of the Bomber: The Fear of Air Attack and British Politics, 1932–1939*. London: Royal Historical Society, 1980.

Bialik, Chaim Nachman. *The Letters of C. N. Bialik* [in Hebrew]. Edited by P. Lachover. 5 vols. Tel Aviv: Dvir, 1937–39.

———. "On America." In Bialik, *Devarim She Beal Pe*, 1:93–106. Tel Aviv: Dvir, 1932.

Birnbaum, Nathan. *Die Assimilationsucht: Ein Wort an die sogenannten Deutschen, Slaven, Magyaren etc. mosaischer Confession von einem Studenten jüdischer Nationalität*. Vienna: 1882.

Bisaha, Nancy. *Creating East and West: Renaissance Humanists and the Ottoman Turks*. Philadelphia: University of Pennsylvania Press, 2006.

Blondheim, Menahem. "The Orthodox Rabbinate Discovers America: The Geography of the Mind [in Hebrew]." In *Following Columbus: America 1492–1992*, edited by Miriam Eliac-Feldon, 438–51. Jerusalem: Merkaz Zalman Shazar, 1996.

Blumenfeld, Kurt. *Erlebte Judenfrage: Ein Vierteljahrhundert deutscher Zionismus*. Edited by Hans Tramer. Stuttgart: Deutsche Verlags-Anstalt, 1962.

Boerner, Peter. "National Images and Their Place in Literary Research: Germany as Seen by Eighteenth-Century French and English Audiences." *Monatschrifte* 76, no. 4 (1975): 358–70.

Borochov, Dov Ber. *The Letters of B. Borochov, 1897–1917* [in Hebrew]. Edited by Matityahu Mintz and Zvia Balshan. Tel Aviv: Am Oved, 1989.

———. *Works*. Translated by M. Avidov. Tel Aviv: Hakibbutz Hameuhad, 1955.

Borst, Arno. *The Ordering of Time: From Ancient Computus to Modern Computers*. Chicago: University of Chicago Press, 1993.

Botstein, Leon. *Judentum und Modernität: Essays zur Rolle der Juden in der deutschen und österreichischen Kultur 1848–1938*. Vienna: Böhlau, 1991.

Bowen, John R. *Why the French Don't Like Headscarves: Islam, the State, and Public Space*. Princeton, N.J.: Princeton University Press, 2007.

Bowler, Peter J. *The Invention of Progress: The Victorians and the Past*. Oxford: Basil Blackwell, 1989.

Brenner, David A. *Marketing Identities: The Invention of Jewish Ethnicity in Ost und West*. Detroit, Mich.: Wayne State University Press, 1998.

Brenner, Michael. *The Renaissance of Jewish Culture in Weimar Germany*. New Haven, Conn: Yale University Press, 1996.

Brenner, Y. C. *The Complete Works of Y. C. Brenner* [in Hebrew]. Tel Aviv: Kibbutz Hameuhad and Dvir, 1955–60.

Breuer, Isaac. "Der Begriff des Wunders im Judentum." *Doresh Tov Leamo*, 1916.

Breuer, Mordechai. *Modernity within Tradition: The Social History of Orthodox Jewry in Imperial Germany*. Translated by Elizabeth Petuchowski. New York: Columbia University Press, 1992.

———. "The Reaction of German Orthodoxy to Antisemitism [in Hebrew]." In *Between Israel and the Nations*, edited by Shmuel Almog et al., 185–213. Jerusalem: Merkaz Zalman Shazar, 1987.

Briggs, Asa, ed. *The Nineteenth Century: The Contradictions of Progress*. London: McGraw-Hill, 1970.

Brinker, Menahem. *Narrative, Art, and Social Thought in Y. H. Brenner's Work* [in Hebrew]. Tel Aviv: Am Oved, 1990.

———. "Nietzsche and the Jews." In *Nietzsche, Godfather of Fascism? On the Uses and Abuses of a Philosophy*, edited by Jacob Golomb and Robert S. Wistrich, 107–25. Princeton, N.J.: Princeton University Press, 2002.

Brumlik, Micha. "Zur Zweideutigkeit deutsch-jüdischen Geistes: Hermann Cohen." In *Judentum im deutschen Sprachraum*, edited by Karl E. Grozinger, 371–81. Frankfurt: Suhrkamp, 1991.

Buber, Martin. *Between a People and Its Land: The Principles of the Birth of an Idea* [in Hebrew]. 2nd ed. Jerusalem: Schocken, 1984.

———. *Correspondence* [in Hebrew]. Edited by Greta Schraeder. Translated by Yehoshua Amir and Gavriel Shtern. Vol. 1. Jerusalem: Mosad Bialik, 1982.

———. "If Herzl Were Still Alive [in Hebrew]." In *Hope for the Present Hour*, 204–7. Tel Aviv: Am Oved, 1992.

———. "In später Stunde." *Der Jude* 1 (1920–21).

———. "The Spirit of the Orient and Judaism." Reprinted in Buber, *On Judaism*, edited by Nahum N. Glatzer and translated by Eva Jospe, 56–78. New York: Schocken, 1962.

———. *Die Stunde und die Erkenntnis*. Berlin: Schocken, 1936.

———. "Toward the End of the German-Jewish Symbiosis [in Hebrew]." In Buber, *Israel and the World: Essays in a Time of Crisis*, 293–95. Jerusalem: Schocken, 1961.

Buchanan, William, and Hadley Cantril. *How Nations See Each Other: A Study in Public Opinion*. Westport, Conn.: Greenwood, 1972.

Buckley, Jerome H. *The Triumph of Time: A Study of the Victorian Concepts of Time, Progress and Decadence*. Cambridge, Mass.: Belknap Press of Harvard University Press, 1966.

Bugge, Peter. "The Nation of Supreme: The Idea of Europe 1914–1945." In *The History of the Idea of Europe*, edited by K. Wilson and J. van der Dussen, 83–106. London: Routledge, 1995.

Burckhardt, Jakob. *Reflections on History*. Translated by M. D. Hottinger. London: Allen and Unwin, 1943.

Burke, P. "Did Europe Exist Before 1700?" *History of European Ideas* 1 (1980): 21–29.

Buruma, Ian. *Voltaire's Coconuts, or Anglomania in Europe*. New York: Vintage, 2000.

——— and Avishai Margalit. *Occidentalism: The West in the Eyes of Its Enemies*. New York: Penguin, 2004.

Bury, J. B. *The Idea of Progress: An Inquiry into Its Origins and Growth*. Reprint ed. New York: Dover, 1960.

Calderon, Nissim. *Multiculturalism versus Pluralism in Israel* [in Hebrew]. Haifa: Haifa University Press, 2000.

Calleo, David. *Rethinking Europe's Future*. Princeton, N.J.: Princeton University Press, 2001.

Calvert, John. "'The World Is an Undutiful Boy!': Sayyid Qutb's American Experience." *Islam and Christian-Muslim Relations* 11, no. 1 (2000): 86–103.

Carrier, James G., ed. *Occidentalism: Images of the West*. Oxford: Clarendon Press of Oxford University Press, 1995.

Carter, Alfred E. *The Idea of Decadence in French Literature, 1830–1900*. Toronto: University of Toronto Press, 1958.

Chabod, F. *Der Europagedänke: von Alexander dem Grossen bis Zar Alexander I*. Translated from the Italian. Stuttgart: Urban Bücher, 1963.

Chadwick, Owen. *The Secularization of the European Mind in the 19th Century.* New York: Cambridge University Press, 1975.

Chakrabarty, Dipesh. *Provincializing Europe: Postcolonial Thought and Historical Difference.* Princeton, N.J.: Princeton University Press, 2000.

Chamberlin, J. E., and R. L. Gilman, eds. *Degeneration: The Dark Side of Progress.* New York: Columbia University Press, 1985.

Chekhov, Anton P. *The Duel and Other Stories.* Translated by Constance Garnett. Paperback ed. New York: Modern Library, 2003.

Chetrit, Sami Shalom. *The Mizrahi Struggle in Israel: Between Oppression and Liberation, Identification and Alternative 1948–2003.* Tel Aviv: Am Oved, 2004.

Clamen, Michel. *Jules Verne et les Sciences: Cent ans après.* Paris: Belin pour la Science, 2005.

Clarke, J. J. *Oriental Enlightenment: The Encounter between Asian and Western Thought.* London: Routledge, 1997.

Cohen, David. *Chesed Neurim.* Tel Aviv: Am Oved, 1955–56.

Cohen, Eitan. *The Moroccans: The Negative of the Ashkenazim* [in Hebrew]. Tel Aviv: Resling, 2002.

Cohen, Gershon D. "German Jewry as a Mirror of Modernity." *Leo Baeck Institute Year Book* 20 (1975): ix–xxxi.

Cohen, Jeremy. "The Eastern Connection: Muslim Factors in the Christian Polemic against Jews in the 12th Century [in Hebrew]." In *Daniel Carpi Jubilee,* 59–72. Tel Aviv: Tel Aviv University Press, 1996.

——— and Richard I. Cohen, eds. *The Jewish Contribution to Civilization: Reassessing an Idea.* Oxford: Littman Library of Jewish Civilization, 2008.

Cohen, Jeremy, and Moshe Rosman, eds. *Rethinking European Jewish History.* Oxford: Littman Library of Jewish Civilization, 2009.

Cohen, Nathan. *Books, Authors, and Newspapers: The Jewish Cultural Center in Warsaw, 1918–1942* [in Hebrew]. Jerusalem: Magnes, 2003.

Cohen, Richard I. "The Rhetoric of Jewish Emancipation and the Vision of the Future [in Hebrew]." In *The French Revolution and Its Impact,* edited by Richard I. Cohen, 145–70. Jerusalem: Merkaz Zalman Shazar, 1991.

———. "Urban Visibility and Biblical Visions: Jewish Culture in Western and Central Europe." In *Cultures of the Jews: A New History,* edited by David Biale, 762–84. New York: Schocken, 2003.

Cohen, Steven M. *American Modernity and Jewish Identity.* New York: Tavistock, 1983.

Cowling, David, ed. *Conceptions of Europe in Renaissance France.* Amsterdam: Faux Titre, 2006.

Croce, Benedetto. *The History of Europe in the Nineteenth Century.* 2nd ed. Translated by Henry Furst. London: Allen and Unwin, 1939.

Cuisenier, J., ed. *Europe as a Cultural Area.* The Hague: Mouton, 1979.

Darnton, Robert. "A Euro State of Mind." *New York Review of Books,* February 28, 2002, 30–32.

Davies, Norman. *Europe: A History*. New York: Harper Perennial, 1998.
Davis, Natalie Zemon. "Glikl bas Juda Leib: Ein jüdisches, ein europäisches Leben." In *Die Hamburger Kauffrau Glikl. Jüdische Existenz in der Frühen Neuzeit*, edited by Monika Richarz, 27–48. Hamburg: Christians, 2001.
de Vries, Leonard. *Victorian Inventions*. London: John Murray, 1971.
Delanty, Gerard. "Conceptions of Europe: A Review of Recent Trends." *The European Journal of Social Theory* 6, no. 4 (2003): 471–88.
Della Pergola, Sergio. *World Jewry beyond 2000: The Demographic Prospects*. Oxford: Oxford Centre for Hebrew and Jewish Studies, 1999.
den Boer, Pim. "Europe to 1914: The Making of an Idea." In *The History of the Idea of Europe*, edited by K. Wilson and J. van der Dussen, 1:13–78. London: Routledge, 1995.
Derrida, Jacques, and Jürgen Habermas. "Our Renewal." *Kulturchronik* 4, no. 21 (2003): 22–26.
Diner, Dan. *America in the Eyes of the Germans: An Essay on Anti-Americanism*. Translated by Allison Brown. Princeton, N.J.: Markus Weiner, 1996.
Döblin, Alfred. *Journey to Poland*. Edited by Heinz Graber. Translated by Joachim Neugroschel. New York: Paragon House, 1991.
Doron, Joachim. *The Zionist Thought of Nathan Birnbaum* [in Hebrew]. Jerusalem: Hasifriyah Haziyonit, 1988.
Dostoevsky, Fyodor. *Notes from the Underground*. Translated by Constance Garnett. Reprint ed. New York: Dover, 1992.
———. *Winter Notes on Summer Impressions*. Translated by David Patterson. Evanston, Ill.: Northwestern University Press, 1988.
Drumont, Eduard. *La France Juive: Essai d'histoire contemporaine*. Paris: C. Marpon and E. Flammarion, 1886.
Druyanow, Alter. "On the Agenda: 2. Vilna [in Hebrew]." *Haolam* 1 (1911): 5–7.
———. *Pinsker and His Times* [in Hebrew]. Jerusalem: R. Mas, 1953.
———, ed. *Writings on the History of the Hibbat Zion Movement and the Jewish Settlement in Palestine* [in Hebrew]. 4 vols. Odessa, Russia: 1918–19.
Dubnow, Simon. *Divrei Yemei Am Olam*. 5th ed. Vol. 8. Tel Aviv: Dvir, 1950.
———. *Nationalism and History: Essays on Old and New Judaism*. Edited by Koppel S. Pinson. Philadelphia: Jewish Publication Society, 1958.
Dukes, Paul, ed. *Russia and Europe*. London: Collins and Brown, 1991.
Efron, John M. *Defenders of the Race: Jewish Doctors and Race Science in Fin-de-Siècle Europe*. New Haven, Conn.: Yale University Press, 1994.
Efron, Yonit. "In Search of Identity: A Historic Perspective on Jewish Israeli Intellectuals from Iraq and Egypt [in Hebrew]." Ph.D. diss., Tel Aviv University, 2005.
Ehrenpreis, Mordechai. *Between East and West* [in Hebrew]. Tel Aviv: Am Oved, 1986.
Eisenstadt, Shmuel N. *Modernization: Protest and Change*. Englewood Cliffs, N.J.: Prentice-Hall, 1966.

Elboim-Dror, Rachel. *Yesterday's Tomorrow* [in Hebrew]. Vol. 2: *A Selection from Zionist Utopias*. Jerusalem: Yad Ben Zvi, 1993.

Elias, Norbert. *The Civilizing Process: The History of Manners, State Formation and Civilization*. Translated by Edmund Jephcott. Vol. 2: *State Formation and Civilization*. Oxford: Blackwell, 1982.

———. *The Germans: Power Struggles and the Development of Habitus in the Nineteenth and Twentieth Centuries*. Edited by Michael Schröter. Translated by Eric Dunning and Stephen Mennell. New York: Columbia University Press, 1996.

Elon, Amos. *The Israelis: Founders and Sons*. New York: Holt, Rinehart and Winston, 1971.

———. *A Nation Haunted by Its Past* [in Hebrew]. Jerusalem: Schocken, 1967.

———. *The Pity of It All: A History of the Jews in Germany, 1743–1933*. New York: Metropolitan Books, 2002.

Elyashiv, Vera. *The Other Germany* [in Hebrew]. Tel Aviv: Am Hasefer, 1967.

Endelman, Todd M. "The Englishness of Jewish Modernity in England." In *Toward Modernity: The European Jewish Model*, edited by Jacob Katz, 225–46. New Brunswick, N.J.: Transaction, 1987.

———. *The Jews of Georgian England, 1714–1830: Tradition and Change in a Liberal Society*. Philadelphia: Jewish Publication Society, 1979.

Engel, David. "A Young Galician Jew on the Anti-Jewish Boycott in Congress Poland, 1913: From the Writings of the Young Salo Baron [in Hebrew]." *Gal-Ed* 19:29–55.

Eran, Mordechai, and Yaacov Shavit. "Chanukka und 'die verlockenden Sirenen': Der Diskurs über die kulturellen Grenzen in der jüdischen Presse Deutschlands im 19. Jahrhundert." *Trumah* 16 (Winter 2006): 151–72.

Erez, Yehuda, ed. *The Third Aliyah* [in Hebrew]. Vol. 2. Tel Aviv: Am Oved, 1964.

Etkes, Immanuel. "'Compulsory Enlightenment' as a Crossroads in the History of the Haskalah Movement in Russia [in Hebrew]." In *The East European Jewish Enlightenment*, edited by Immanuel Etkes, 167–77. Jerusalem: Merkaz Zalman Shazar, 1993.

Ettinger, Shmuel. "Judaism and the History of the Jews in Graetz's Worldview [in Hebrew]." In *Studies in Modern Jewish History*, vol. 1: *History and Historians*, edited by Shmuel Almog and Dov Kulka, 87–116. Jerusalem: Merkaz Zalman Shazar, 1992.

Even-Zohar, Itamar. "Culture Planning." In *Papers in Cultural Research* 2005; available online at http://www.tau.ac.il/~itamarez/works/books/ez-cr2004-toc.htm.

———. "The Emergence and Crystallization of Local and Native Hebrew Culture in Eretz-Israel, 1882–1948." *Cathedra* 16 (July 1980): 165–89.

———. "Who's Afraid of Hebrew Culture? [in Hebrew]." In *Aheret: Studies on the Past, Future, and Present*, edited by Aharon Amir, Amir Or, and Guy Maayan, 38–50. Jerusalem: Karmel, 2002.

Eyal, Gil. "Between East and West: Discourse on the 'Arab Village' in Israel [in Hebrew]." In *Coloniality and the Postcolonial Condition: Implications for Israeli Society*, edited by Yehouda Shenhav, 201–23. Tel Aviv: Hakibbutz Hameuhad, 2004.

Faber, Klaus, Julius H. Schoeps, and Sascha Stawski, eds. *Neu-alter Judenhass: Antisemitismus, arabisch-israelischer Konflikt und europäische Politik*. Berlin: Verlag für Berlin-Brandenburg, 2006.

Falk, Raphael. *Zionism and the Biology of the Jews* [in Hebrew]. Tel Aviv: Resling, 2006.

Fallaci, Oriana. *The Force of Reason*. New York: Rizzoli International, 2006.

Feiner, Shmuel. "A Critique of Modernity: S. D. Luzzatto and the Anti-Haskalah [in Hebrew]." In *Italy: Samuel David Luzzatto: The Bicentennial of His Birth*, edited by R. Bonfil, Y. Gottlieb, and H. Kasher, 145–65. Jerusalem: Magnes, 2004.

——— . *Haskalah and History: The Emergence of a Modern Jewish Historical Consciousness*. Translated by Chaya Naor and Sondra Silverston. Oxford: Littman Library of Jewish Civilization, 2002.

——— . "Inventing the Modern Era: On the Rhetoric and Self-Awareness of the Haskalah [in Hebrew]." *Dapim Lemehkar Basifrut* 2 (1997–98): 9–28.

——— . *The Jewish Enlightenment*. Translated by Chaya Naor. Philadelphia: University of Pennsylvania Press, 2004.

——— . "Post-Haskalah at the End of the 19th Century [in Hebrew]." In *Fins de Siècle: End of Ages*, edited by Yosef Kaplan, 251–89. Jerusalem: Merkaz Zalman Shazar, 2005.

——— . "The Pseudo-Enlightenment and the Question of Jewish Modernization." *Jewish Social Studies* 3, no. 1 (1996): 62–88.

——— . "'Rebellious French' and 'Jewish Freedom': The French Revolution in the East European Haskalah's Image of the Past [in Hebrew]." In *The French Revolution and Its Impact*, edited by Richard I. Cohen, 215–47. Jerusalem: Merkaz Zalman Shazar, 1991.

——— . "Y. L. Gordon as Anti-Clerical and Warrior in the Jewish 'Culture War' [in Hebrew]." In *Sadan: Studies in Hebrew Literature—The Life and Works of Y. L. Gordon*, edited by Ziva Shamir, 221–29. Tel Aviv: Tel Aviv University Press, 1998.

Feingold, Ben-Ami. "Haskalah Literature Discovers America," in *Between History and Literature*, edited by M. Oron [in Hebrew], 91–104. Tel Aviv: 1983.

Fichman, Yaacov. "Popular Culture [in Hebrew]." *Tarbut* 2, no. 8 (June 1923).

Finkielkraut, Alain. *Au nom de l'autre: Réflexions sur l'antisémitisme qui vient*. Paris: Gallimard, 2003.

Firchow, Peter Edgerly. *The Death of the German Cousin: Variations on a Literary Stereotype, 1890–1920*. Lewisburg, Pa.: Bucknell University Press, 1986.

Fischer, J. *Oriens, Occidense, Europa: Begriff und Gedanke Europa in der Späten Antike und im frühen Mittelalter*. Wiesbaden, Germany: Franz Steiner, 1957.

Fischer, Klaus P. *History and Prophecy: Oswald Spengler and the Decline of the West*. New York: P. Lang, 1989.

Fischer, Shlomo. "Two Patterns of Modernization: On the Ethnic Problem in Israel [in Hebrew]." *Theory and Criticism* 1 (Summer 1991): 1–22.

Flam, Gila. "Representation of the East in Hebrew Songs [in Hebrew]." In *The Challenge of Independence: Ideological and Cultural Aspects of Israel's First Decade*, edited by Mordechai Bar-On, 248–61. Jerusalem: Yad Ben Zvi, 1999.

Flanagan, Tanja G. "Trying to Square a Triangle of Interests: Germany, Jews and the State of Israel." In *Occasional Papers on Jewish Civilization, Israel and the Diaspora*, edited by Yossi Shein, 25–84. Washington: Georgetown University Press, 2005.

Flaubert, Gustave. *Bouvard et Pécuchet* [1880]. Paris: Maxi-Livres, 2005.

Frankel, Charles. *The Faith of Reason: The Idea of Progress in the French Enlightenment*. New York: King's Crown, 1948.

Frankel, Jonathan. "Assimilation and Ethnicity in Nineteenth Century Europe: Towards a New Historiography [in Hebrew]." In *Jewish Nationalism and Politics: New Perspectives*, edited by Jehuda Reinharz, Gideon Shimoni, and Yosef Salmon, 23–65. Jerusalem: Merkaz Zalman Shazar, 1996.

———. *The Damascus Affair: "Ritual Murder," Politics, and the Jews in 1840*. New York: Cambridge University Press, 1997.

———. Prophecy and Politics: Socialism, Nationalism, and the Russian Jews, 1862–1917. Paperback ed. Cambridge: Cambridge University Press, 1984.

Frenkel, Miriam. "The Historiography of the Jews in Muslim Countries in the Middle Ages: Landmarks and Prospects [in Hebrew]." *Peamim* 92 (Summer 2002): 23–61.

Freundlich, Yehoshua, and Gedalia Yogev, eds. *The Minutes of the Zionist General Council* [in Hebrew]. Vol. 1. Tel Aviv: Hakibbutz Hameuhad, 1975.

Friedländer, Saul. "'Europe's Inner Demons': The 'Other' as Threat in Early Twentieth-Century European Culture." In *Demonizing the Other: Antisemitism, Racism, and Xenophobia*, edited by Robert S. Wistrich, 210–21. Amsterdam: Harwood Academic Publisher, 1999.

———. *Nazi Germany and the Jews*. Vol. 1: *The Years of Persecution, 1933–1939*. New York: Harper Collins, 1997.

———. "The Nineteenth Century and the End of Mankind [in Hebrew]." *Zmanim* 2 (Winter 1980): 16–25.

———. "Themes of Decline and End in Nineteenth-Century Western Civilization." In *Visions of the Apocalypse: End or Rebirth?* edited by Saul Friedländer, Gerald Holton, Eugene Skolnikoff, and Leo Marx, 83–103. New York: Holmes and Meier, 1985.

Fries, Jakob Friedrich. *Über die Gefährdung des Wohlstandes und des Charakters der Deutschen durch die Juden*. 1816.

Frischman, David. *Early Works* [in Hebrew]. Vol. 2. Warsaw: 1914.

Fuchs, Eckhardt. *Henry Thomas Buckle: Geschichtsschreibung und Positivismus in*

England und Deutschland. Leipzig, Germany: Leipziger Universitätsverlag, 1994.

Fuenn, Shmuel Joseph. *Nidchei Israel*. Vilna, Poland: 1850–51.

Gan, Alon. "Followers to Germany? Cracks in the Glass House [in Hebrew]." *Israel: Studies in Zionism and the State of Israel* 9 (2006): 109–42.

———. "Israel and American Jewry Relations: The Israeli Perspective [in Hebrew]." *Iyunim Bitkumat Israel* 8 (1998): 8–32.

Galili, Ziva. "The Soviet Experience of Zionism: Importing Soviet Political Culture to Palestine." *The Journal of Israeli History* 24, no. 1 (March 2005): 1–33.

Gans, Herbert J. "Symbolic Ethnicity: The Future of Ethnic Groups and Cultures in America." In *On the Making of Americans: Essays in Honor of David Reisman*, edited by Herbert J. Gans, 193–220. Philadelphia: University of Pennsylvania Press, 1979.

Gartner, Lloyd P. *History of the Jews in Modern Times*. Oxford: Oxford University Press, 2001.

Gay, Peter. *The Enlightenment: An Interpretation—The Science of Freedom*. New York: Norton, 1977.

Geary, Patrick J. *The Myth of Nations: The Medieval Origins of Europe*. Princeton, N.J.: Princeton University Press, 2002.

Geiger, Abraham. Über den Austritt aus den Judenthume: Ein augfefundener Briefwechsel [in Hebrew]." In *Abraham Geiger: Selected Writings on Religious Reform*, edited by Michael A. Meyer, 67–87. Jerusalem: Merkaz Zalman Shazar, 1979.

Gelber, Yoav. *New Homeland: Immigration and Absorption of Central European Jews 1933–1948* [in Hebrew]. Jerusalem: Yad Ben Zvi, 1990.

———. "The Reaction of the Zionist Movement and the Yishuv to the Nazis 'Rise to Power.'" *Yad Vashem Studies* 18 (1987): 41–101.

———. "The Zionist Leadership's Response to the Nuremberg Laws [in Hebrew]." *Dapim Leheker Hashoah*, 1989: 49–79.

Geller, Jay. "The Conventional Lies and Paradoxes of Jewish Assimilation: Max Nordau's Zionist Answer to the Jewish Question." *Jewish Social Studies* 1, no. 3 (1995): 130–60.

Gellner, Ernest. *Thought and Change*. Chicago: University of Chicago Press, 1964.

Gershoni, Israel. *Egypt between Distinctiveness and Unity: The Search for National Identity 1919–1948* [in Hebrew]. Tel Aviv: Hakibbutz Hameuhad, 1980.

——— and James P. Jankowski. *Egypt, Islam and the Arabs: The Search for Egyptian Nationhood, 1900–1930*. New York: Oxford University Press, 1986.

Gerstenfeld, Manfred. *European-Israeli Relations: Between Confusion and Change*. Jerusalem: Jerusalem Center for Public Affairs, 2006.

———, ed. *Israel and Europe: An Expanding Abyss?* Jerusalem: Jerusalem Center for Public Affairs, 2005.

Gertz, Nurit. *Myth in Israeli Culture: Captives of a Dream*. London: Vallentine Mitchell, 2000.

Gilman, Richard. *Decadence: The Strange Life of an Epithet*. New York: Farrar, Straus and Giroux, 1979.

Gilman, Sander L. "Heine, Nietzsche and the Idea of the Jew." In *Nietzsche and Jewish Culture*, edited by Jacob Golomb, 76–100. London: Routledge, 1997.

———. *Jewish Self-Hatred*. Baltimore, Md.: Johns Hopkins University Press, 1990.

———. "Max Nordau, Sigmund Freud, and the Question of Conversion." *Southern Humanities Review* 27, no. 1 (1993): 1–25.

Gilroy, Paul. *The Black Atlantic: Modernity and Double Consciousness*. Cambridge, Mass.: Harvard University Press, 1993.

Ginsburg, Mordechai Aharon. *Aviezer* [in Hebrew]. Vilna, Poland: 1824.

Goethe, Johann Wolfgang von. *Gedenkausgabe der Werke, Briefe, Gespräche*. Edited by Ernst Beutler. Vol. 24: *Gespräche mit Eckermann*. Zürich: Artemis, 1949.

Goldmann, Nahum. *The Autobiography of Nahum Goldmann: Sixty Years of Jewish Life*. Translated by Helen Sebba. New York: Holt, Rinehart and Winston, 1970.

Goldstein, Moritz. "Wir und Europa." In *Vom Judentum: Ein Sammelbuch*, 2:195–209. Prague: Verein jüdischer Hochschüler Bar Kochba, 1913.

Goldstein, Yaacov. *The Path to Hegemony: Mapai—The Consolidation of Its Policy, 1930–1936* [in Hebrew]. Tel Aviv: Am Oved, 1980.

Goldstein, Yossi. "The Migration of Jews to the New Russia and the Socioeconomic Revolution They Underwent in the Nineteenth Century [in Hebrew]." *Shvut*, n.s., 12, no. 28 (2004–5): 7–29.

———. *Ussishkin's Biography* [in Hebrew]. Vol. 2: *Eretz Israel, 1919–1941*. Jerusalem: Magnes, 2001.

Gollwitzer, Heinz. *Europabild und Europagedanke: Beiträge zur deutschen Geistesgeschichte des 18. und 19. Jahrhunderts*. Munich: Beck, 1951.

———. "Zur Wortgeschichte und Sinndeutung von 'Europa.'" *Saeculum ii*, 1964: 161–71.

Gombrich, E. H. *In Search of Cultural History*. Oxford: Clarendon Press of Oxford University Press, 1969.

Goody, Jack. *The East in the West*. Cambridge: Cambridge University Press, 1998.

Gordon, Adi. "In Palestine, in a Foreign Land." In *The Orient: A German-Language Weekly between German Exile and Aliyah* [in Hebrew]. Jerusalem: Magnes, 2004.

Gordon, Milton M. *Assimilation in American Life: The Role of Race, Religion, and National Origins*. New York: Oxford University Press, 1964.

Gordon, Y. L. *The Letters of Y. L. Gordon* [in Hebrew]. Edited by Yitzchak Yaacov Weissberg. 2 vols. Warsaw: 1893–94.

———. *The Works of Yehuda Leib Gordon: Prose* [in Hebrew]. Tel Aviv: Dvir, 1960.

Goren, Yaacov. *Arthur Ruppin: His Life and Works* [in Hebrew]. Tel Aviv: Yad Tabenkin, 2005.

Gottlober, Abraham Baer. *Memories and Travels* [in Hebrew]. Edited by Reuven Goldberg. Jerusalem: Mosad Bialik, 1967.

Gotzmann, Andreas. *Eigenheit und Einheit: Modernisierungdiskurse des deutschen Judentums der Emanzipationszeit*. Leiden, the Netherlands: Brill, 2002.

Gould, Stephen Jay. "Second-Guessing the Future." In Gould, *The Lying Stones of Marrakech: Penultimate Reflections in Natural History*, 201–16. New York: Harmony, 2000.

Govrin, Nurit. "At the Threshold of the Twentieth Century." *Sadan* 4 (2000): 27–35.

Grab, Alexander. *Napoleon and the Transformation of Europe*. New York: Palgrave Macmillan, 2003.

Graetz, Heinrich. "The Significance of Judaism for the Present and the Future." *The Jewish Quarterly Review* 1 (1889–1890).

———. *The Structure of Jewish History and Other Essays*. Translated, edited, and introduced by Ismar Schorsch. New York: Jewish Theological Seminary of America, 1975.

Graetz, Michael. "The Formation of the New Jewish Consciousness in the Time of Mendelssohn's Disciple Shaul Ascher [in Hebrew]." In *Studies in the History of the Jewish People and the Land of Israel*, edited by Uriel Rappoport, 4:219–37. Haifa: University of Haifa Press, 1978.

Graupe, Heinz Mosche. *The Rise of Modern Judaism: An Intellectual History of German Jewry 1650–1942*. Translated by John Robinson. Huntington, N.Y.: R. E. Krieger, 1978.

Greenbaum, Yitzhak. *The Wars of the Jews of Poland, 1913–1940* [in Hebrew]. Tel Aviv: Hotzaat Haverim, 1941.

Greenberg, Uri Zvi. "At Closing-Time [in Hebrew]." *Sadan*, 1925.

———. "The Downfall of Jewry in Poland [in Hebrew]." *Sadan*, November–December 1924, 20.

———. "In Malchus fun Tzelm [In the kingdom of the cross]." In *Gezamlte Verk*, 2:457–72. Jerusalem: Magnes, 1979.

———. *Klapei Tishim Vetisha* [Against ninety-nine]. Tel Aviv: Sadan, 1927.

———. *Mefisto* [in Yiddish]. Warsaw: Literatur-fund baym fareyn fun yiddisher literatn un zhurnalistn in Varshe, 1922.

———. *Rehovot Hanahar* [in Hebrew]. Jerusalem: 1951.

———. "Vision of Europe." In *Hagavrut Haolah: Collected Works*, vol. 1: *Poetry*, part 1, 141–42. Jerusalem: 1990.

———. *Yerushalayim Shel Mata*. Tel Aviv: Hedim, 1924.

Greenfeld, Liah. *Nationalism: Five Roads to Modernity*. Cambridge, Mass.: Harvard University Press, 1992.

Gross, Nachum T. "Herzl's Economic Conception [in Hebrew]." In Gross, *Not by Spirit Alone: Studies in the Economic History of Modern Palestine and Israel*, 89–102. Jerusalem: Magnes, 1999.

Grubu, R. E. *Virtually Jewish: Reinventing Jewish Culture in Europe*. Berkeley: University of California Press, 2002.

Guizot, François. *History of Civilization in Europe*. Translated by William Hazlitt. London: Penguin, 1997.

Gutfeld, Arnon. "Back to the Future: American Leaders Forecast the Year 2000 from the Vantage of 1892 [in Hebrew]." In *Fins de Siècle: End of Ages*, edited by Yosef Kaplan, 317–41. Jerusalem: Merkaz Zalman Shazar, 2005.

Gutman, Israel. "Jews—Poles—Antisemitism [in Hebrew]." In *The Broken Chain: Polish Jewry through the Ages*, edited by Israel Bartal and Israel Gutman, vol. 2: *Society, Culture, Nationalism*, 605–39. Jerusalem: Merkaz Zalman Shazar, 2001.

Guy, B. *The French Image of China before and after Voltaire*. Geneva: Delices, 1963.

Hacohen, Mordechai Ben-Hillel. *War of the Nations: An Eretz Israel Diary* [in Hebrew]. Vol. 2. Jerusalem: Yad Ben Zvi, 1985.

Hale, J. "The Renaissance Idea of Europe." In *European Identity and the Search for Legitimacy*, edited by S. Garcia, 46–63. London: Eleni Nakou Foundation, 1993.

Halevy, Moshe. "Max Nordau: His Zionist Thought and His Work in the Zionist Movement [in Hebrew]." Ph.D. diss., Tel Aviv University, 1988.

Halper, Jeff, Edwin Seroussi, and Pamela Squires-Kidron. "Musica Mizrahit: Ethnicity and Class Culture in Israel." *Popular Music* 8, no. 2 (1989): 131–41.

Harrington, Austin. "Ernst Troeltsch's Concept of Europe." *European Journal of Social Theory* 7, no. 4 (2004): 479–98.

Harrington, Michael. *The Accidental Century*. New York: Macmillan, 1965.

Harshav, Benjamin. "The Revival of Palestine and the Modern Jewish Revolution [in Hebrew]." In *Perspectives on Culture and Society in Eretz-Israel*, edited by Nurit Gertz, 7–31. Tel Aviv: Open University Press, 1988.

Hartenau, W. [Walther Rathenau]. "Höre Israel!" In *Deutschtum und Judentum: Ein Disput unter Juden aus Deutschland*, edited by Christoph Schulte, 29–39. Stuttgart: 1993.

Hastings, Adrian. *The Construction of Nationhood: Ethnicity, Religion and Nationalism*. Cambridge: Cambridge University Press, 1997.

Hay, Denys. *Europe: The Emergence of an Idea*. 2nd ed. Edinburgh: Edinburgh University Press, 1968.

Hazard, Paul. *European Thought in the Eighteenth Century, from Montesquieu to Lessing*. Translated by J. Lewis May. New Haven, Conn.: Yale University Press, 1954.

Heater, D. *The Idea of European Unity*. Leicester, England: Leicester University Press, 1992.

Heilbronner, Oded. "Fin-de-siècle from the Bottom-Up: Images of Popular Culture in Germany and England at the End of the 20th Century [in Hebrew]." In *Fins de Siècle: End of Ages*, edited by Yosef Kaplan, 227–50. Jerusalem: Merkaz Zalman Shazar, 2005.

Heine, Heinrich. "Confessions." In *Prose and Poetry*, translated by Ernest Rhys, 337. London: Dent, 1934.

———. *The Complete Poems of Heinrich Heine: A Modern English Version.* Translated by Hal Draper. Cambridge, Mass.: Suhrkamp, 1982.

———. "French Affairs." In *The Works of Heinrich Heine*, translated by Charles Godfrey Leland, vol. 7. London: 1891–1905.

———. *Sämtliche Schriften*, edited by Klaus Briegel. Munich: Carl Hanser, 1968–76.

———. *Sämtliche Werke*. Revised and annotated by Gotthard Erler. 14 vols. Munich: Kindler, 1964.

Heller, Celia. *On the Edge of Destruction: Jews of Poland between the Two World Wars.* New York: Schocken, 1980.

Herder, Johann Gottfried. *Reflections on the Philosophy of the History of Mankind.* Abridged and edited by Frank E. Manuel. Translated by T. O. Churchill. Chicago: University of Chicago Press, 1968.

Herman, Arthur. *The Idea of Decline in Western History.* New York: Free Press, 1997.

Herman, Simon N. *Jewish Identity: A Social, Psychological Perspective* [in Hebrew]. Tel Aviv: Am Oved, 1979.

Hermann, Hans Peter. "Fatherland: Patriotism and Nationalism in the Eighteenth Century." In *Heimat, Nation, Vaterland: The German Sense of Belonging*, edited by James Steakely and Jost Herman, 1–24. New York: P. Lang, 1996.

Herschberg, Avraham Shmuel. *In Oriental Lands* [in Hebrew]. Reprint ed. Jerusalem: Yad Ben Zvi, 1977.

———. *The Way of the New Yishuv in Eretz-Israel* [in Hebrew]. Reprint ed. Jerusalem: Yad Ben Zvi, 1979.

Hertz, Alexander. *The Jews in Polish Culture.* Translated by Richard Lourie. Evanston, Ill.: Northwestern University Press, 1988.

Herzen, Alexander. *From the Other Shore.* Translated by M. Budbery. London: Weidenfeld and Nicolson, 1956.

Herzl, Theodor. *Altneuland.* Translated into English by Paula Arnold. Haifa: Haifa Publishing, 1960.

———. *The Complete Diaries of Theodor Herzl.* Edited by Raphael Patai. Translated by Harry Zohn. 5 vols. New York: Herzl Press, 1960.

———. *The Jewish State: An Attempt at a Modern Solution of the Jewish Question* [in Hebrew]. Translated by Berl Yocker. Tel Aviv: N. Newman, 1956.

———. *Philosophische Erzählungen.* Berlin: B. Harz, 1919.

———. *Theodor Herzl's Zionistische Schriften.* Edited by Leon Kellner. Berlin-Charlottenburg: Judischer Verlag, 1905.

———. *Zionist Lectures and Articles* [in Hebrew]. Vol. 1: *1895–1899.* 2nd ed. Jerusalem: Hasifriyah Haziyonit, 1976.

Heschel, Susannah. "Jewish Studies as Counterhistory." In *Insider/Outsider: American Jews and Multiculturalism*, edited by David Biale, Michael Galchinski, and Susannah Heschel, 105–15. Berkeley: University of California Press, 1998.

Hess, Jonathan M. *German Jews and the Claim of Modernity*. New Haven: Yale University Press, 2002.

Hess, Moses. *The Revival of Israel: Rome and Jerusalem, the Last Nationalist Question*. Translated by Meyer Waxman. Lincoln: University of Nebraska Press, 1995.

Hinasky, Sarah. "Eyes Wide Shut: On the Spread of Albinism in Israeli Childcare [in Hebrew]." In *The Arab-Jews: Nationalism, Religion, and Ethnicity*, edited by Yehuda Shenhav, 257–84. Tel Aviv: Am Oved, 2003.

Hirsch, Dafna. "'We Are Here to Bring the West': Hygiene Education within the Jewish Community of Palestine during the British Mandate [in Hebrew]." Ph.D. diss., Tel Aviv University, 2006.

Hissin, Haim. *Memories and Letters of an Early Pioneer* [in Hebrew]. Edited and translated by Shulamit Laskov. Jerusalem: Yad Ben Zvi, 1990.

Hitchcock, William I. *The Struggle for Europe: The Turbulent History of a Divided Continent, 1945 to the Present*. New York: Doubleday, 2003.

Hobsbawm, Eric. *Nations and Nationalism since 1780: Programme, Myth, Reality*. Cambridge: Cambridge University Press, 1990.

Holmes, Douglas R. *Integral Europe: Fast-Capitalism, Multiculturalism, Neofascism*. Princeton, N.J.: Princeton University Press, 2000.

Huizinga, Johan. *The Waning of the Middle Ages*. Translated by F. Hopman. Harmondsworth, England: Penguin, 1972.

Huntington, Samuel P. *The Clash of Civilizations and the Remaking of World Order*. New York: Simon and Schuster, 1996.

———. "The U.S.: Decline or Renewal." *Foreign Affairs* 67, no. 2 (Winter 1988–89): 76–96.

Husain, Ed. *The Islamist*. London: Penguin, 2007.

Iggers, George G. *The German Conception of History: The National Tradition of Historical Thought from Herder to the Present*. Rev. ed. Middletown, Conn: Wesleyan University Press, 1968.

Jabotinsky, Zeev. *Al Sifrut Veomanut* [On literature and art]. Edited by M. Atar Etinger. Jerusalem: E. Jabotinsky, 1948.

———. *Autobiography* [in Hebrew]. Tel Aviv: E. Jabotinsky, 1936.

———. "The Elders' Rebellion [in Hebrew]." In Jabotinsky, *Uma Vehevra*, edited by Yosef Or and Hananyah Raykhman, 225–36. Jerusalem: E. Jabotinsky, 1949–50.

———. "The Englishman [in Hebrew]." Reprinted in *Zionist Revisionism: Towards a Turning-Point*, edited by Yosef Nedava, 166–77. Tel Aviv: Hotsaat Makhon Jabotinsky, 1986.

———. *The Jewish War Front*. London: Allen and Unwin, 1940.

———. *Letters* [in Hebrew]. Vol. 1: *May 1898–July 1914*. Edited by Daniel Carpi. Tel Aviv: Makhon Jabotinsky beYisrael, 1995.

———. "Not until It's Over! [in Hebrew]." *Doar Hayom*, May 3, 1935.

———. "Public School Boys [translated into Hebrew]." 1932. Reprinted in *Zionist*

Revisionism: Towards a Turning-Point, edited by Yosef Nedava, 92–101. Tel Aviv: Hotsaat Makhon Jabotinsky, 1986.

Jacob, Margaret C. *Strangers Nowhere in the World: The Rise of Cosmopolitanism in Early Modern Europe*. Philadelphia: University of Pennsylvania Press, 2006.

Jacobowski, Ludwig. "Dank [Thanks]." In *Ludwig Jacobowski, Die ungeteilte Melodie*, edited by Fred B. Stern, 53. Basel: Zbinden, 1966.

———. *Werther, der Jude*. Berlin: Verlag Berlin-Wien, 1892.

Jellinek, Adolf. "Ein Zwiegespräch." In Jellinek, *Aus der Zeit: Tagesfragen und Tagesbegebenheiten*. Budapest: Sam Markus, 1886.

Johnson, Samuel. *The History of Rasselas, Prince of Abyssinia*. Introduction and notes by Michael Irwin. Ware, England: Wordsworth Editions, 2000.

Kafkafi, Eyal. *Truth or Faith: Yitzhak Tabenkin as Mentor of Hakibbutz Hameuhad* [in Hebrew]. Jerusalem: Yad Ben Zvi, 1992.

Kalmar, Ivan Davidson. "Jesus Did Not Wear a Turban: Orientalism, the Jews, and Christian Art." In *Orientalism and the Jews*, edited by Ivan Davidson Kalmar and Derek J. Penslar, 3–31. Waltham, Mass.: Brandeis University Press, 2005.

Kaplan, Marion A., ed. *Jewish Daily Life in Germany, 1618–1945*. Oxford: Oxford University Press, 2005.

Kaplan, Yosef, ed. *Fins de Siècle: End of Ages* [in Hebrew]. Jerusalem: Merkaz Zalman Shazar, 2005.

Katz, Jacob. "German Culture and the Jews." In *The Jewish Response to German Culture: From the Enlightenment to the Second World War*, edited by Jehuda Reinharz and W. Schatzberg, 85–99. Hanover, N.H.: University Press of New England, 1985.

———. "'A State within a State': The History of an Antisemitic Slogan [in Hebrew]." *Proceedings of the Israel Academy of Science and Humanities* 4, no. 3 (1971): 29–58.

———, ed. *Toward Modernity: The European Jewish Model*. New Brunswick, N.J.: Rutgers University Press, 1987.

Katz, Shaul. "The First Furrow: Ideology, Settlement, and Agriculture in Petah-Tikva in its First Decade (1878–1888) [in Hebrew]." *Cathedra* 23 (April 1982): 124–57.

———. "On the Technological History of Palestine in the Late Ottoman Period: Three Case Studies [in Hebrew]." In *The Second Aliyah*, edited by Israel Bartal, Zeev Tsahor, and Yehoshua Kaniel, 189–212. Jerusalem: Yad Ben Zvi, 1997.

Kaufmann, Yehezkel. *In the Throes of Time*. Tel Aviv: Dvir, 1936.

Kazal, Russell A. "Revisiting Assimilation: The Rise, Fall, and Reappraisal of a Concept in American Ethnic History." *American Historical Review* 100 (1995): 437–71.

Kaznelson, Siegmund. *Juden im deutschen Kulturbereich: Ein Sammelwerk*. 2nd ed. Berlin: Jüdischer Verlag, 1959.

Kehiliateinu, 1922: Contemplation, Misgivings, and Yearnings of the Pioneers [in

Hebrew]. Introduction and notes by Muki Tzur. Jerusalem: Yad Ben Zvi, 1989.
Khan, H. A., ed. *The Birth of the European Identity: The Europe-Asia Contrast in Greek Thought 490–322 B.C.* Nottingham, England: Nottingham University Press, 1994.
Kimmerling, Baruch. *Immigrants, Settlers, Natives: The Israeli State and Society between Cultural Pluralism and Cultural Wars.* Tel Aviv: Am Oved, 2004.
Klatzkin, Jakob. "Germanness and Jewishness [in Hebrew]." *Hatekufah* 11 (1921): 493–502.
Klausner, Yosef. *A History of Modern Hebrew Literature* [in Hebrew]. 10 vols. Jerusalem: Ahiassaf, 1960–62.
Klein, Dennis. "Assimilation and Dissimilation: Peter Gay's Freud, Jews and Other Germans: Masters and Victims in Modernist Culture." *New German Critique* (Winter 1980): 151–65.
Kleiner, Israel. *From Nationalism to Universalism: Vladimir (Zeev) Jabotinsky and the Ukrainian Question.* Edmonton, Alberta: Canadian Institute of Ukrainian Studies Press, 2000.
Kogman, Tal. "The Creation of Images of Knowledge in Texts for Children and Young Adults Published during the Haskalah Period [in Hebrew]." Ph.D. diss., Tel Aviv University, 2000.
Kohn, Hans. *Die Europäisierung des Orients* [The Europeanization of the East]. Berlin: Schocken, 1934.
———. *The Mind of Germany: The Education of a Nation.* New York: Scribner, 1960.
Kolatt, Israel. "The Reflection of the French Revolution in the Jewish National Movement [in Hebrew]." In *The French Revolution and Its Impact*, edited by Richard I. Cohen, 287–315. Jerusalem: Merkaz Zalman Shazar, 1991.
Kook, Zvi Yehuda. "As the Civilized among Them [in Hebrew]." In Kook, *Lenetivot Israel* [The ways of Israel], 136–37. Jerusalem: Mossad Harav Kook, 1989.
Kroeber, A. L. "Reality Culture and Value Culture." In Kroeber, *The Nature of Culture*, 152–66. Chicago: University of Chicago Press, 1952.
Kumar, Krishan. "The Idea of Europe: Cultural Legacies, Transnational Imagining, and the Nation-State." In *Europe without Borders: Remapping Territory, Citizenship, and Identity in a Transnational Age*, edited by N. Berezin and M. Schain, 33–50. Baltimore, Md.: Johns Hopkins University Press, 2003.
Kundera, Milan. "The Tragedy of Central Europe." *New York Review of Books*, April 26, 1984, 33–38.
Kupchan, Charles A. "The End of the West." *Atlantic Monthly*, December 2002.
Kurzweil, Baruch. "The Image of the Western Jew in Hebrew Literature [in Hebrew]." In *Chapters in the German Jewish Heritage: Essays*, edited by A. Tarshish and Y. Ginat, 170–89. Jerusalem: Leo Baeck Institute, 1975.
Laqueur, Walter. "Fin-de-siècle: Once More with Feeling." *The Journal of Contemporary History* 31, no. 1 (January 1996): 5–47.

———. *The Last Days of Europe: Epitaph for an Old Continent*. New York: St. Martin's, 2007.

Laskov, Shulamit. "Altneuland." *Zionism* 15 (1990): 35–53.

———, ed. *Documents on the History of Hibbat-Zion and the Settlement of Eretz Israel* [in Hebrew]. 7 vols. Tel Aviv: Tel Aviv University, 1982–93.

Lawrence, D. H. "Pornography and Obscenity." In Lawrence, *Late Essays and Articles*, 233–53. Edited by James T. Boulton. Cambridge: Cambridge University Press, 2004.

Lazarus, Moritz. *Was heisst national?* Berlin: Dümmlers Verlagsbuchhandlung, 1879.

Lesser, Ludwig. *Chronik der Gesellschaft der Freunde*. Berlin: 1842.

Lessing, Theodor. *Der jüdische Selbsthass*. Berlin: Jüdischer Verlag, 1930.

Levi, Oded Mende. "Discovering Metropolis: Benyamin Mandelstam's Travels in the Big City [in Hebrew]." In *Perspectives on Modern Hebrew Literature in Honor of Professor Nurit Govrin*, edited by Avner Holzman, 293–305. Tel Aviv: Tel Aviv University Press, 2005.

Levinsohn, Isaac Baer. *Sefer Ahiyah Shiloni Hahozeh*. 1839.

Lévi-Strauss, Claude. *The Raw and the Cooked*. Translated by John and Doreen Weightman. New York: Harper and Row, 1969.

Lewis, Bernard. *The Muslim Discovery of Europe*. New York: Norton, 1982.

———. *What Went Wrong? The Clash between Islam and Modernity in the Middle East*. New York: Oxford University Press, 2002.

———. *What Went Wrong? Western Impact and Middle Eastern Response*. Oxford: Oxford University Press, 2002.

Lichten, Joseph. "Notes on the Assimilation and Acculturation of Jews in Poland, 1863–1943." In *The Jews in Poland*, edited by Chimen Abramsky, Maciej Jachimczyk, and Antony Polonsky, 106–29. New York: Blackwell, 1986.

Liedman, Sven-Eric, ed. *The Postmodernist Critique of the Project of Enlightenment*. Poznan Studies 58. Amsterdam: Rodopi, 1997.

Lilienblum, Moshe Leib. *Autobiographical Writings* [in Hebrew]. Edited by Shlomo Breiman. 3 vols. Jerusalem: Mosad Bialik, 1970.

———. *Derekh Tshuva* [The way of return]. Warsaw: 1898–99.

———. *The Letters of Moshe Leib Lilienblum to Yehuda Leib Gordon* [in Hebrew]. Edited by Shlomo Breiman. Jerusalem: Magnes, 1968.

———. *On the Revival of Israel in the Land of Its Fathers* [in Hebrew]. 1882.

———. *The Writings of M. L. Lilienblum* [in Hebrew]. Edited by Shlomo Breiman. 4 vols. Kraków, Poland: 1912–13.

Lindau, Baruch. *Reshit Limudim*. Berlin, 1788.

Lindenbaum, Shalom. "Uri Zvi Greenberg's *Mefisto*: Awareness as an Expression of Metaphysical Despair [in Hebrew]." *Nativ* 4 (September 1988): 64–76.

Liptzin, Solomon. *Germany's Stepchildren*. Philadelphia: Jewish Publication Society of America, 1944.

Lissak, Moshe. "'Critical' Sociologists and 'Establishment' Sociologists in an Israeli Academic Community: Ideological Struggles or an Academic Discourse? [in Hebrew]." *Iyunim Bitkumat Israel* 6 (1996): 66–98.

Littlejohns, Richard. "Everlasting Peace and Medieval Europe: Romantic Myth-Making in Novalis' *Europa*." In *Myths of Europe*, edited by Richard Littlejohns and Sara Soncini, 171–81. Amsterdam: Rodopi, 2007.

———, and Sara Soncini, eds. *Myths of Europe*. Amsterdam: Rodopi, 2007.

Lively, J. "The Europe of the Enlightenment." *History of European Ideas* 1 (1980): 91–102.

Livneh, Eliezer. *Aharon Aaronson: The Man and His Time* [in Hebrew]. Jerusalem: Mosad Bialik, 1969.

———. *Israel and the Crisis of Western Civilization* [in Hebrew]. Jerusalem: Schocken, 1972.

Livneh-Freudenthal, Rachel. "The Verein für Kultur and Wissenschaft der Juden 1819–1824 [in Hebrew]." Ph.D. diss., Tel Aviv University, 1996.

Low, Alfred D. *Jews in the Eyes of the Germans: From the Enlightenment to Imperial Germany*. Philadelphia: Institute for the Study of Human Issues, 1979.

Lowenstein, Steven M. "The Beginning of Integration, 1780–1870." In *Jewish Daily Life in Germany, 1618–1945*, edited by Marion A. Kaplan, 159–71. Oxford: Oxford University Press, 2005.

———. "German History and German Jewry: Boundaries, Junctions and Interdependence." *Leo Baeck Institute Year Book* 43 (1998): 315–22.

———. "Jewish Participation in German Culture." In *German-Jewish History in Modern Times*, vol. 3: *Integration in Dispute, 1871–1918*, edited by Steven M. Lowenstein et al., 305–35. New York: Columbia University Press, 1997.

———. "The Publication of Moritz Goldstein's 'The German-Jewish Parnassus' Sparks a Debate over Assimilation, German Culture, and the 'Jewish Spirit.'" In *The Yale Companion to Jewish Writing and Thought in German Culture 1096–1996*, edited by Sander L. Gilman and Jack Zipes, 299–305. New Haven, Conn.: Yale University Press, 1997.

———. "Was Urbanization Harmful to Jewish Tradition and Identity in Germany?" In *People of the City: Jews and the Urban Challenge*, edited by Ezra Mendelsohn, 80–96. New York: Oxford University Press, 1999.

Lowenthal, Marvin. *The Jews of Germany: A Story of Sixteen Centuries*. Philadelphia: Jewish Publication Society of America, 1936.

Lunz, Avraham. "A Journey into Philistia [in Hebrew]." *Ivri Anochi* (Brody), October 1874.

Luria, David ben Aharon. *Omer Basade*. Vilna, Poland: 1853.

Luzzatto, Shmuel David. "Derech Eretz or Atheism: A Poem by Shadal to His Generation [in Hebrew]." In Luzzatto, *Selected Writings*, edited by M. E. Artom, 2:41–73. Jerusalem: Mosad Bialik, 1976.

Lynx, J. J., ed. *The Future of the Jews*. London: Drummond, 1945.

Mak, Geert. *In Europe: Travels through the Twentieth Century*. Translated by S. Garrett. London: Pantheon, 2007.

Malkin, Irad. *Ethnicity and Identity in Ancient Greece* [in Hebrew]. Tel Aviv: 2003.

Mandel, Maud. "Assimilation and Cultural Exchange in Modern Jewish History." In *Rethinking European Jewish History*, edited by Jeremy Cohen and Moshe Rosman, 72–92. Oxford: Littman Library of Jewish Civilization, 2009.

Mandelstam, Benyamin. *Paris: Reflections and Observations on this Gay City . . . as I Saw and Observed Them during My Stay There in 1874*. Warsaw: 1875.

Mann, Thomas. *Achtung, Europa! Aufsätze zur Zeit*. Stockholm: Bermann-Fischer, 1938, 73–93.

———. *Doctor Faustus*. Translated by H. T. Lowe-Porter. New York: Knopf, 1948.

———. "Germany and the Germans." In *Essays*, vol. 2, ed. H. Kurzke, 281–98. Frankfurt am Main: Fischer Taschenbuch Verlag, 1977.

Manor, Dalia. "Orientalism and Jewish National Art: The Case of Bezalel." In *Orientalism and the Jews*, edited by Ivan Davidson Kalmar and Derek J. Penslar, 142–61. Waltham, Mass.: Brandeis University Press, 2005.

Maor, Yitzhak. "Nikolai Berdyaev and the Jewish People [in Hebrew]." *Molad* 18 (May 1960): 211–19.

Marchand, Suzanne. "German Orientalism and the Decline of the West." *Proceedings of the American Philosophical Society* 145, no. 4 (December 2001): 465–73.

Margalit, Elkana. "Hashomer Hazair": From Youth Community to Revolutionary Marxism (1923–1936) [in Hebrew]. Tel Aviv: Hakibbutz Hameuhad, 1971.

Markish, Simon. "Lev Levanda between Assimilation and Palestinophilia [in Hebrew]." *Shvut*, n.s., 4, no. 2 (1991): 1–52.

Markovits, Andrei S. *Uncouth Nation: Why Europe Dislikes America*. Princeton, N.J.: Princeton University Press, 2007.

Martin, Andrew. *The Mask of the Prophet: The Extraordinary Fictions of Jules Verne*. Oxford: Oxford University Press, 1990.

Maverick, Lewis A. *China, a Model for Europe*. San Antonio, Tex.: Paul Anderson, 1946.

McMahon, Darrin M. *Enemies of the Enlightenment: The French Counter-Enlightenment and the Making of Modernity*. Oxford: Oxford University Press, 2002.

Medin, Tzvi. "José Ortega y Gasset and the Spaniards: On Interpretations of His Work." In *Outside the Bullring: Spain in the Twentieth Century*, edited by Raanan Rein and Tamar Groves, 187–203. Tel Aviv: Ramot, 2005.

Mendele Mokher Seforim [Shalom Yaakov Rabinovitch]. *The Collected Works of Mendele Mokher Seforim* [in Hebrew]. Tel Aviv: Dvir, 1953–54.

———. *Fathers and Sons* [in Hebrew]. Odessa: 1867–68.

———. "Shem and Japheth on the Train." Translated by Walter Lever. In *Modern Hebrew Literature*, edited by Robert Alter. New York: Behrman, 1975.

Mendelsohn, Ezra. *Zionism in Poland: The Formative Years, 1915–1926*. New Haven, Conn.: Yale University Press, 1981.

Mendelssohn, Moses. "An einen Mann von Stande." In *Gesammelte Schriften*, edited by G. B. Mendelssohn, 5:492–94. Reprint ed. Hildesheim, Germany: Georg Olm, 1972.

Mendes-Flohr, Paul R. "Between German and Jewish: Christians and Jews." In *German-Jewish History in Modern Times*, vol. 4: *Renewal and Destruction, 1918–1945*, edited by Abraham Barkai and Paul R. Mendes-Flohr, 153–63. New York: Columbia University Press, 1998.

———. "Fin-de-siècle Orientalism and the Aesthetics of Jewish Self-Affirmation [in Hebrew]." *Jerusalem Studies in Jewish Thought* 3, no. 4 (1983–84): 623–72.

———. "In the Shadow of the World War." In *German-Jewish History in Modern Times*, vol. 4: *Renewal and Destruction, 1918–1945*, edited by Abraham Barkai and Paul R. Mendes-Flohr, 7–30. New York: Columbia University Press, 1998.

———. "Jewish Cultural Life under National-Socialist Rule." In *German-Jewish History in Modern Times*, vol. 4: *Renewal and Destruction, 1918–1945*, edited by Abraham Barkai and Paul R. Mendes-Flohr, 283–312. New York: Columbia University Press, 1998.

———. "New Trends in Jewish Thought." In *German-Jewish History in Modern Times*, vol. 3: *Integration in Dispute: 1871–1918*, edited by Steven M. Lowenstein et al., 336–59. New York: Columbia University Press, 1997.

———. "Werner Sombart: The Jews and Modern Capitalism: An Analysis of Its Ideological Premises." *Leo Baeck Institute Year Book* 21 (1976): 97–107.

———, ed. *The Wisdom of Israel: Historical and Philosophical Perspectives* [in Hebrew]. Jerusalem: Merkaz Zalman Shazar, 1979.

———and Jehuda Reinharz, eds. *The Jew in the Modern World*. New York: Oxford University Press, 1980.

———, eds. *The Jew in the Modern World: A Documentary History*. New York: Oxford University Press, 1995.

Mevorach, Baruch, comp. *Napoleon and His Era: Hebrew Records and Testimonies by Napoleon's Contemporaries* [in Hebrew]. Jerusalem: Mosad Bialik 1968.

Meyer, Michael A., ed. *German-Jewish History in Modern Times*. 4 vols. New York: Columbia University Press, 1996–98.

———. "The Great Debate on Anti-Semitism: Jewish Reaction to New Hostility in Germany 1879–1881." *Leo Baeck Institute Year Book* 11 (1966): 137–70.

———. *The Origins of the Modern Jew: Jewish Identity and European Culture in Germany 1749–1824*. Detroit, Mich.: Wayne State University Press, 1967.

———. *Response to Modernity: A History of the Reform Movement in Judaism*. New York: Oxford University Press, 1988.

———. *"Without Wissenschaft There Is no Judaism": The Life and Thought of the Jewish Historian Ismar Elbogen*. Ramat Gan, Israel: Bar-Ilan University Press, 2004.

Michael, Reuven. *Heinrich Graetz, Historian of the Jewish People* [in Hebrew]. Jerusalem: Mosad Bialik, 2003.

Michael, Sami. "There Are Those Who Wish to Keep Us in the Bathtub Known as 'The Culture of the Orient' [in Hebrew]." *Peamim* 11 (Autumn 1999): 12–18.

Mikkeli, H. *Europe as an Idea and as an Identity*. London: Palgrave Macmillan, 1980.
Mintz, Matityahu. "The Place of the Jewish Workers' Movement in the Politicization of the Jewish People [in Hebrew]." In *Iyunim Bitkumat Israel* 8 (1998): 253–65.
Miron, Gai. *German Jews in Israel: Memories and Past Images* [in Hebrew]. Jerusalem: Magnes, 2004.
Monin, Neli. *The European Union and Israel: A Status Report 2003* [in Hebrew]. Jerusalem: Ministry of Finance, 2004.
Montesquieu, Charles de Secondat, baron de. *The Spirit of the Laws*. Translated by Thomas Nugent. Reprint ed. New York: Hafner, 1949.
Moréri, Louis. *Le Grand dictionnaire historique*. Lyon, France: 1674.
Morgan, Philip. "A Vague and Puzzling Idealism: Plans for European Unity in the Era of the Modern State." In *Culture and Society in Europe: Perceptions of Divergence and Unity*, edited by Michael Wintle, 33–51. Avebury, England: Aldershot, 1996.
Mosse, George L. *German Jews beyond Judaism*. Bloomington: Indiana University Press, 1985.
Musil, Robert. "Das hilflose Europa oder Reise vom Hundertsten ins Tausendste." In Musil, *Gesamelte Werke*, edited by Adolf Frisé, vol. 8: *Essays und Reden*, 1075–94. Hamburg: Rowohlt, 1978.
———. *Der Mann ohne Eigenschaften*. Vols. 1–2. Berlin: Ernst Rowohlt, 1930–33.
Nathans, Benjamin. *Beyond the Pale: The Jewish Encounter with Late Imperial Russia*. Berkeley: University of California Press, 2002.
Nedava, Yosef. "Predicting Historical Events and Sensing the Holocaust [in Hebrew]." *Bitfuzot Hagolah*, nos. 83–84 (Winter 1978): 100–107.
Neusner, Jacob. *Sifra in Perspective: The Documentary Comparison of the Midrashim of Ancient Judaism*. Vol. 3. Atlanta, Ga.: Scholars Press, 1988.
Nietzsche, Friedrich. *Beyond Good and Evil: Prelude to a Philosophy of the Future*. Translated with commentary by Walter Kaufmann. New York: Vintage, 1989.
———. *The Dawn of Day*. Translated by J. M. Kennedy. New York: Russell and Russell, 1964.
———. *Human, All-Too-Human*. Translated by J. M. Kennedy. New York: Russell and Russell, 1964.
Nocke, Alexandra. "Yam Tikhoniut: The Place of the Mediterranean in Modern Israeli Identity." Ph.D. diss., Potsdam University, 2007.
Nolte, Ernst. *Three Faces of Fascism*. Translated by L. Vennerwitz. New York: Holt, Rinehart and Winston, 1966.
Nordau, Max. *Paradoxes*. Translated by J. R. McIlraith. London: William Heinemann, 1906.
———. *Zionist Writings: Lectures and Essays* [in Hebrew]. Edited by B. Netanyahu. Jerusalem: Hasifriyah Haziyonit, 1959.
Novalis [Friedrich von Hardenberg]. "Die Christenheit oder Europa." In *Gesammelte Werke*, edited by C. Seelig, 5:9–34. Zürich: Buhl, 1941.

Noverstern, Avraham. *The Lure of Twilight: Apocalypse and Messianism in Yiddish Literature* [in Hebrew]. Jerusalem: Magnes, 2003.

———, ed. *Yaavdu Shamaim Vaaretz: Jewish Apocalyptic Poetry* [in Hebrew]. Translated from Yiddish to Hebrew by Ido Basok. Tel Aviv: Keshev, 2002.

Ofir, Adi, and Ariela Azulai. "One Hundred Years since the First Zionist Congress: An Account [in Hebrew]." *Resling* 51 (Summer 1998): 5–13.

Opalski, Magdalena, and Israel Bartal. *Poles and Jews: A Failed Brotherhood.* Waltham, Mass.: Brandeis University Press, 1992.

Orluc, Katiana. "Decline or Renaissance: The Transformation of European Consciousness after the First World War." In *Europe and the Other and Europe as the Other*, edited by Bo Stråth, 123–55. Brussels: P.I.E.-P. Lang, 2000.

Ortega y Gasset, José. *The Revolt of the Masses*. Translated by Anthony Kerrrigan. New York: Norton, 1993.

O'Sullivan, Emer. *Friends and Foes: The Image of Germany and the Germans in British Children's Fiction from 1870 to the Present*. Tübingen, Germany: G. Narr, 1990.

Oved, Yaakov. "Nineteenth-Century Utopias and *Altneuland* [in Hebrew]." *Zmanim* (Winter 1981): 70–83.

Oz, Amos. *A Tale of Love and Darkness*. Translated by Nicholas de Lange. Orlando, Fla.: Harcourt, 2004.

Pagden, Anthony, ed. *The Idea of Europe: From Antiquity to the European Union*. Cambridge: Cambridge University Press, 2002.

Parker, W. H. "Europe: How Far?" *Geographical Journal* 126 (1960): 278–97.

Passerni, Luisa. "The Last Identification: Why Some of Us Would Like to Call Ourselves Europeans and What We Mean By This." In *Europe and the Other and Europe as the Other*, edited by Bo Stråth, 52–56. Brussels: P.I.E.-P. Lang, 2000.

Payne, Stanley G. "The Concept of 'Southern Europe' and Political Development." *Mediterranean Historical Review* 1 (1986): 100–115.

Paxman, Jeremy. *The English: A Portrait of a People*. London: Michael Joseph, 1998.

Peabody, Dean. *National Characteristics*. New York: Cambridge University Press, 1985.

Pegg, C. H. *The Evolution of the European Idea, 1913–1933*. Chapel Hill: University of North Carolina Press, 1983.

Peled, Rina. *The "New Man" of Zionist Revolution: Hashomer Hatzair and His European Roots* [in Hebrew]. Tel Aviv: Am Oved, 2002.

Peleg, Yaron. *Orientalism and the Hebrew Imagination*. Ithaca, N.Y.: Cornell University Press, 2005.

Penrose, Boies. *Travel and Discovery in the Renaissance, 1460–1620*. New York: Holiday House, 1962.

Penslar, Derek J. *Zionism and Technocracy: The Engineering of Jewish Settlement in Palestine, 1870–1918*. Bloomington: Indiana University Press, 1991.

Perlmann, M. "The Education of Salama Musa." *Middle Eastern Affairs* 5 (1954): 17–25.

Phillips, Melanie. Londonistan: How Britain Is Creating a Terror State Within. New York: Encounter, 2006.

Pinder, John. *European Community: The Building of a Union*. New York: Oxford University Press, 1995.

Pinsker, Leon. *Autoemancipation! Mahnruf an seine Stammesgnossen von einem russischen Juden*. Berlin: W. Issleib, 1882.

Pinto, Diana. "The Third Pillar? Toward a European Jewish Identity." *Contemplate* 4 (2007): 15–22.

Pulzer, Peter. *Jews and the German State: The Political History of a Minority, 1848–1933*. Cambridge, Mass.: Blackwell, 1992.

———. "Legal Equality and Public Life." In *German-Jewish History in Modern Times*, vol. 3, *Integration in Dispute, 1871–1918*, edited by Steven M. Lowenstein et al, 153–95. New York: Columbia University Press, 1997.

———. "The Response to Antisemitism." In *German-Jewish History in Modern Times*, vol. 3, *Integration in Dispute, 1871–1918*, edited by Steven M. Lowenstein et al., 252–80. New York: Columbia University Press, 1997.

———. "The Return of Old Hatreds." In *German-Jewish History in Modern Times*, vol. 3, *Integration in Dispute, 1871–1918*, edited by Steven M. Lowenstein et al., 196–251. New York: Columbia University Press, 1997.

———. *What about the Jewish Non-intellectuals in Germany? Some Remarks on the Image of Pre-1933 German Jewry*. Bar-Ilan University Braun Lectures in the History of the Jews in Prussia, 7. Ramat Gan, Israel: Bar-Ilan University Press, 2001.

Rabau, Tziona. *I Am a Tel-Avivi* [in Hebrew]. Tel Aviv: Misrad Habitahon, 1984.

Rabinovitz, Yaakov. "Al Maamadenu Hatarbuti [On our cultural situation]." In *Sefer Hashana shel Eretz Israel* [The Jewish Palestine yearbook]. Tel Aviv: 1934–35.

———. "The Crisis of Culture as Seen through the Philosophy of History [in Hebrew]." *Hedim* 4 (May 1926): 89–98.

———. "On the Orient and the West [in Hebrew]." *Hatekufah* 15 (1922): 433–54.

Raz-Krakotzkin, Amnon. "A Few Comments on Orientalism, Jewish Studies and Israeli Society [in Hebrew]." *Jama'a* 3, no. 2 (1998): 34–61.

———. "The Zionist Return to the West and the Mizrahi Jewish Perspective." In *Orientalism and the Jews*, edited by Ivan Davidson Kalmar and Derek J. Penslar, 162–81. Waltham, Mass.: Brandeis University Press, 2005.

Reiner, Elchanan. "On the Roots of the Urban Jewish Community in Poland in the Modern Period [in Hebrew]." *Gal-Ed* 20 (2006): 13–27.

Reinhard, Wolfgang. *Lebensformen Europas: Eine historische Kulturanthropologie*. Munich: Beck, 2004.

Reinharz, Jehuda. *Chaim Weizmann: The Making of a Zionist Leader*. Oxford: Oxford University Press, 1985.

———. *Fatherland or Promised Land: The Dilemma of the German Jew, 1893–1914*. Ann Arbor: University of Michigan Press, 1975.

———. "Ideology and Structure in German Zionism 1882–1933." *Jewish Social Studies* 42 (1980): 119–46.

———. "Jewish National Autonomy: Defining the Ideological Parameters [in Hebrew]." In *Kehal Yisrael: Jewish Self-Rule through the Ages*, edited by Israel Bartal, vol. 3: *The Modern Period*, 251–67. Jerusalem: Merkaz Zalman Shazar, 2004.

———. "The Response of the Centralverein deutscher Staatsbürger jüdischen Glaubens to Antisemitism in the Weimar Republic [in Hebrew]." In *Israel and the Nations: Essays in Honor of Shmuel Ettinger*, edited by S. Almog, 85–110. Jerusalem: Merkaz Zalman Shazar, 1987.

Remba, Isaac. *Jabotinsky to the World and His People* [in Hebrew]. Vol. 2. Jerusalem: 1943.

Renier, Gustaaf Johannes. *The English: Are They Human?* London: 1931.

Reuveni, Jacob. *The Administration of Palestine under the British Mandate 1920–1948: An Institutional Analysis* [in Hebrew]. Ramat Gan, Israel: Bar-Ilan University Press, 1933.

Revel, Jean-François. *Anti-Americanism*. Translated by Diarmid Cammell. San Francisco: Encounter, 2003.

Richarz, Monika. "Jewish Women in the Family and Public Sphere." In *German-Jewish History in Modern Times*, vol. 3, *Integration in Dispute, 1871–1918*, edited by Steven M. Lowenstein et al., 68–102. New York: Columbia University Press, 1997.

Richman, H. *The Image of America in the European Hebrew Periodicals of the Nineteenth Century*. Austin: University of Texas Press, 1971.

Rieger, Bernhard. *Technology and the Culture of Modernity in Britain and Germany, 1890–1954*. Cambridge: Cambridge University Press, 2005.

Riesser, Gabriel. *Börne und die Juden: Ein Wort der Erwiderung auf die Flugschrift des Herrn Dr. Eduard Meyer gegen Börne*. Altenburg, Germany: 1832.

Riger, A. *Hahinuch haivri beeretz Israel* [Hebrew education in Palestine]. Vol. 1. Tel Aviv: 1939–40.

Rischin, Moses. *The Promised City: New York's Jews, 1870–1914*. Cambridge, Mass.: Harvard University Press, 1962.

Rodrigue, Aron. *Images of Sephardi and Eastern Jewries in Transition: The Teachers of the Alliance Israélite Universelle, 1860–1939*. Seattle: University of Washington Press, 1993.

Röhr, R. *Graf Keyserling's magische Geschichtsphilosophie*. Heidelberg: 1939.

Rose, Ernest. "China as a Symbol of Reaction in Germany, 1830–1880." *Comparative Literature* 3 (1951): 57–76.

Rotenstreich, Nathan. "Hermann Cohen: Judaism in the Context of German Philosophy." In *The Jewish Response to German Culture Culture: From the Enlightenment to the Second World War*, edited by Jehuda Reinharz and

W. Schatzberg, 31–63. Hanover, N.H.: University Press of New England, 1985.

Roth, Samuel. *Now and Forever: A Conversation with Israel Zangwill on the Jews and the Future*. New York: R. M. McBride, 1925.

Rousseau, Jean-Jacques. *Considérations sur le gouvernement de Pologne* [Thoughts on the government of Poland]. 1772. Reprint, Paris: Editions Granier, 1960.

Rozen, Mina. "Pedigree Remembered, Reconsidered, Invented: Benjamin Disraeli East and West." In *The Jewish Discovery of Islam: Studies in Honor of Bernard Lewis*, edited by Martin Kramer, 49–75. Tel Aviv: Tel Aviv University, 1999.

Rozin, Orit. "Term of Disgust: Hygiene and Parenthood of Immigrants from Muslim Countries as Viewed by Veteran Israelis in the 1950s [in Hebrew]." *Iyunim Bitkumat Israel* 12 (2002): 195–238.

Rubaschoff, Salman. "Erstlinge der Entjudung: Drei Reden von Eduard Gans im Kulturverein." *Der Jüdische Wille* 1, no. 2 (1918): 108–15.

Rubinstein, Amnon. *The Zionist Dream Revisited: From Herzl to Gush Emunim and Back* [in Hebrew]. Jerusalem: Schocken, 1980.

Rühs, Christian Friedrich. *Historische Entwicklung des Einflusses Frankreichs und der Franzosen auf Deutschland und die Deutschen* [The historical development of the French influence on Germany and the Germans]. 1815.

Rumford, Chris. *The European Union: A Political Sociology*. Oxford: Blackwell, 2002.

Ruppin, Arthur. *The Sociology of the Jews* [in German]. 2 vols. Berlin: Jüdischer Verlag, 1930–31.

Russell-Wood, A. J. R., ed. *An Expanding World: The European Impact on World History, 1450–1800*. 31 vols. Brookfield, Vt.: Ashgate Variorum, 1995.

Rustow, D. A. *Politics and Westernization in the Near East*. Princeton, N.J.: Princeton University Press, 1956.

Sachar, Howard M. *Israel and Europe: An Appraisal in History*. New York: Knopf, 1998.

Said, Edward. *Orientalism*. New York: Pantheon, 1978.

Said, Suzanne. "The Mirage of Greek Continuity: On the Uses and Abuses of Analogy in Some Travel Narratives from the Seventeenth to the Eighteenth Century." In *Rethinking the Mediterranean*, edited by W. V. Harris, 268–93. Oxford: Oxford University Press, 2005.

Salzberger, Eli, and Fania Oz-Zalzberger. "The Hidden German Origins of the Israeli Supreme Court [in Hebrew]." In *Law and History*, edited by Daniel Gutwein and Menachem Mautner, 357–94. Jerusalem: Merkaz Zalman Shazar, 1999.

Saul, John Ralston. *Voltaire's Bastards: The Dictatorship of Reason in the West*. New York: Free Press, 1992.

Schatzker, Chaim. *Jewish Youth in Germany: Between Judaism and Germanism, 1870–1945* [in Hebrew]. Jerusalem: Merkaz Zalman Shazar, 1989.

Schechtman, Joseph B. *Rebel and Statesman: The Vladimir Jabotinsky Story*. Vol. 1. New York: T. Yoseloff, 1956.

Schidorsky, Dov. *Libraries and Books in Late Ottoman Palestine*. Jerusalem: Magnes, 1990.

Schmidt, Francis. "Jewish Representations of the Inhabited Earth during the Hellenistic and Roman Periods." In *Greece and Rome in Eretz-Israel: An Anthology of Studies*, edited by A. Kasher, G. Fuks, and U. Rappaport, 119–34. Jerusalem: Yad Ben Zvi, 1990.

Schmidt, H. D. "The Establishment of 'Europe' as a Political Expression." *Historical Journal* 9 (1966): 172–78.

Scholem, Gershom. *Devarim Bego: Pirke Morashah Utehiya*. Tel Aviv: Am Oved, 1975.

Schor, Ralph. *L'antisémitisme en France dans l'entre-deux-guerres*. Paris: Editions Complexe, 2005.

Schorsch, Ismar. *From Text to Context*. Tauber Institute for the Study of European Jewry Series. Waltham, Mass.: Brandeis University Press, 1994.

———. *Jewish Reactions to German Anti-Semitism, 1870–1914*. New York: Columbia University Press, 1972.

Schorske, Carl E. *Fin-de-Siècle Vienna: Politics and Culture*. New York: Knopf, 1979.

Schroeter, Daniel J. "Orientalism and the Jews of the Mediterranean." *Journal of Mediterranean Studies* 4, no. 2 (1994): 183–96.

Schulte, Christoph. "Max Nordau: The First of Nietzsche's Critics [in Hebrew]." In *Nietzsche, Zionism, and Hebrew Culture*, edited by Jacob Golomb, 67–80. Jerusalem: Magnes, 2002.

Schwab, Raymond. *The Oriental Renaissance: Europe's Rediscovery of India and the East 1680–1880*. Translated by G. Patterson Black and V. Reinking. New York: Columbia University Press, 1984.

Schweid, Eliezer. *Judaism and the Solitary Jew* [in Hebrew]. Tel Aviv: Am Oved, 1974.

Segal, Dimitri. "The Impact of Russian Literature and Culture on the Emergence of the Jewish Liberation Movement [in Hebrew]." In *Hebrew Literature and the Labor Movement*, edited by Pinhas Ginossar, vol. 1: *1919–1920*, 1–16. Beersheba, Israel: Ben-Gurion University of the Negev Press, 1989.

Segal, Howard P. *Technological Utopianism in American Culture*. Chicago: University of Chicago Press, 1985.

Segel, Harold F., ed. *Strangers in Our Midst: Images of the Jew in Polish Literature*. Ithaca, N.Y.: Cornell University Press, 1996.

Sela-Sheffy, Rakefet. "The *Yekkes* in the Legal Field and Bourgeois Culture in Pre-Israel British Palestine [in Hebrew]." *Iyunim Bitkumat Israel* 13 (2003): 295–321.

Servan-Schreiber, Jean-Jacques. *The American Challenge*. Translated by Ronald Steel. New York: Atheneum, 1968.

Shaanan, Avraham. *Studies on the Literature of the Haskalah and the Influence of French Literature* [in Hebrew]. Merhavia, Israel: Sifriyat Poalim, 1952.

Shafer, Shlomo. *Ambiguous Relation: The American Jewish Community and Germany since 1945*. Detroit, Mich.: Wayne State University Press, 1999.

Shapira, Anita. "Israeli Perceptions of Anti-Semitism and Anti-Zionism." *Journal of Israeli History* 25, no. 1 (March 2006): 245–66.

———. *Visions in Conflict* [in Hebrew]. Tel Aviv: Am Oved, 1989.

Sharett, Y., ed. *Moshe Sharett and the German Reparations Controversy* [in Hebrew]. Tel Aviv: Haamutah lemoreshet Moshe Sharett, 2007.

Shavit, Uria. "A Fifth Column in the West?" *Middle East Quarterly* 14 (Fall 2007): 13–21.

Shavit, Yaacov. "Ahad Ha-'Am and Hebrew National Culture: Realist or Utopianist?" *Jewish History* 4, no. 2 (Fall 1990): 71–78.

———. *Athens in Jerusalem: Classical Antiquity and Hellenism in the Making of the Modern Secular Jew*. Paperback ed. London: Littman Library of Jewish Civilization, 1997.

———. "Eschatology and Politics: Between 'Great Prophecy' and 'Minor Prophecy': The Case of Uri Zvi Greenberg [in Hebrew]." In *Hamatkonet vehadmut: Studies on the Poetry of Uri Zvi Greenberg*, edited by Hillel Weiss, Yehudah Friedlander, Avidan Lipsker, and Lilian Dabi-Guri, 327–36. Ramat Gan, Israel: Bar-Ilan University Press, 2000.

———. "First Encounters: East European Jewry Discovers Pre-Balfour England." In *Global Politics: Essays in Honour of David Vital*, edited by Abraham Ben-Zvi and Aharon Klieman, 283–306. London: F. Cass, 2001.

———. "From Admission Ticket to Contribution: Remarks on the History of an Apologetic Argument." In *The Jewish Contribution to Civilization: Reassessing an Idea*, edited by Jeremy Cohen and Richard I. Cohen, 151–64. Oxford: Littman Library of Jewish Civilization, 2008.

———. "The 'Glorious Century' or the 'Cursed Century': Fin de Siècle Europe and the Emergence of Modern Jewish Nationalism." *Journal of Contemporary History* 26 (1991): 553–74.

———. "My Heart Is in the East, and I Am at the Edge of the West [in Hebrew]." *Keshet* 42 (Fall 1972): 149–59.

———. "Regulations of the First Colonies: From Communal Regulations to an Experiment in Practical Utopia [in Hebrew]." *Cathedra* 72 (June 1994): 50–62.

———. "The Scent of the Lemon Tree [in Hebrew]." *Etmol* 29 (July 2004): 4–6.

———. "'Shall a Nation Dwell Alone?' The Myths of Eretz-Israel's Geo-Historical and Geo-Cultural Belonging [in Hebrew]." In *Myth and Memory: The Transfiguration of Israeli Consciousness*, edited by David Ohana and Robert S. Wistrich, 321–34. Tel Aviv: Hakibbutz Hameuhad, 1996.

———. "The 'Spirit of France' and the 'French Culture' in the Jewish Yishuv in Eretz Israel (1882–1914) [in Hebrew]." *Cathedra* 62 (December 1991): 37–53.

———. "The Status of Culture in the Process of Creating a National Society in Eretz-Israel: Basic Attitudes and Concepts [in Hebrew]." In *The History of the Jewish Community in Eretz-Israel since 1882: The Construction of Hebrew Culture in Eretz-Israel*, edited by Zohar Shavit, part 1, 9–29. Jerusalem: Mosad Bialik, 1998.

———. "Vladimir Zeev Jabotinsky [in French]." In *Les Juifs et le XXe siècle: Dictionnaire critique*, edited by Élie Barnavi and Saul Friedländer, 589–601. Paris: Calmann-Levy, 2000.

———. "Window on the World [in Hebrew]." *Kesher*, no. 4 (November 1988): 3–10.

———. "The Works of Henry Thomas Buckle and Their Application by the *Maskilim* of Eastern Europe [in Hebrew]." *Zion* 49, no. 4 (1984): 401–12.

———. "The *Yishuv* between National Regeneration of Culture and Cultural Generation of the Nation [in Hebrew]." In *Jewish Nationalism and Politics: New Perspectives*, edited by Jehuda Reinharz, Gideon Shimoni, and Yosef Salmon, 141–57. Jerusalem: Merkaz Zalman Shazar, 1996.

——— and Gideon Biger. *The History of Tel Aviv*. Vol. 1: *The Birth of a Town (1909–1936)* [in Hebrew]. Tel Aviv: Ramot, 2001.

——— and David Mendelson. "The Discovery of Italy and the 'South' in Western Literature [in Hebrew]." In *A Mediterranean Anthology*, edited by Yaacov Shavit, 15–76. Tel Aviv: University of Tel Aviv, 2004.

——— and Liat Shtayer-Livni. "Who Cried Wolf? How Did Zeev Jabotinsky Understand the Nature and Intentions of Nazi Germany? [in Hebrew]." In *In the Eye of the Storm: Essays on Zeev Jabotinsky*, edited by Avi Bereli and Pinhas Ginossar, 345–69. Sde Boker: Ben Gurion Institute, 2004.

Shavit, Zohar, ed. *The History of the Jewish Community in Eretz-Israel since 1882: The Construction of Hebrew Culture in Eretz-Israel* [in Hebrew]. Jerusalem: Mosad Bialik, 1998.

Shechter, Rivka. *Auschwitz, Faust-Kingdom*. Tel Aviv: Sifre Leyad Hotsaat "Achshav," 1986.

Sheffi, Naama. "Anatomy of Rejection: Israeli Society and its Attitude toward German Culture [in Hebrew]." In *Germany and the Land of Israel: A Cultural Encounter*, edited by Moshe Zimmermann, 217–34. Jerusalem: Magnes, 2004.

———. *The Ring of Myths: The Israelis, Wagner, and the Nazis* [in Hebrew]. Haifa: University of Haifa Press, 1999.

Shenhav, Yehouda, ed. *The Arab-Jews: A Post-colonial Reading of Nationalism, Religion, and Ethnicity*. Stanford, Calif: Stanford University Press, 2006.

Sheva, Shlomo. *O Seer, Go, Flee Away: A Biography of Chaim Nachman Bialik* [in Hebrew]. Tel Aviv: Dvir, 1990.

Shimoni, Michal Tur-Kaspa, Dana Pereg, and Mario Mikulincer. *Psychological Aspects of Identity Formation and Their Implications for Understanding the Concept of Jewish Identity: A Review of the Scientific Literature* [in Hebrew]. Ramat Gan, Israel: Bar-Ilan University Press, 2004.

Shoham, Shlomo Giora. *Valhalla, Calvary and Auschwitz*. Tel Aviv: Tcherikover, 1992.
Shore, Cris. *Building Europe: The Cultural Politics of European Integration*. London: Routledge, 2000.
Shulman, Kalman, ed. *Sefer Divrei Yemei Olam* [A history of the world]. 2nd ed. 9 vols. Vilna, 1868–84.
Silber, Michael K. "The Emergence of Ultra-Orthodoxy: The Invention of Tradition." In *The Uses of Tradition: Jewish Continuity in the Modern Age*, edited by Jack Wertheimer, 23–84. New York: Jewish Theological Seminary of America, 1992.
Simmel, Georg. "Die Idee Europa." In Simmel, *Aufsätze und Abhandlungen, 1909–1918*, edited by Klaus Latzel, 2:112–16. Frankfurt: Suhrkamp, 2000.
Simon, Josef. "Nietzsche on Judaism and Europe." In *Nietzsche and Jewish Culture*, edited by Jacob Golomb, 101–16. New York: Routledge, 1997.
Siu, Paul C. P. "The Sojourner." *American Journal of Sociology* 58 (July 1952): 34–44.
Slezkine, Yuri. *The Jewish Century*. Princeton, N.J.: Princeton University Press, 2004.
Sluchovsky, Moshe. "Eschatological Anxieties: Historical Fact or Historiographical Construct? [in Hebrew]." In *Fins de Siècle: End of Ages*, edited by Yosef Kaplan, 111–27. Jerusalem: Merkaz Zalman Shazar, 2005.
Slutsky, Yehuda, ed. *Poalei-Tzion in Eretz-Israel 1905–1919 (Documents)* [in Hebrew]. Tel Aviv: Tel Aviv University Press, 1978.
———. *The Russian-Jewish Press in the Nineteenth Century* [in Hebrew]. Jerusalem: Mosad Bialik, 1970.
Slutzky, A. Y., ed. *Shivat Zion: Collected Articles of the Great Thinkers of the Generation in Praise of the Settlement of Palestine, 1891* [in Hebrew]. Jerusalem: Magnes, 1998.
Smilansky, Moshe. "Maaseinu [Our deeds]." In Smilansky, *Collected Works*, vol. 12. Tel Aviv: Hitahdut Haikarim Beeretz Israel, 1937.
Smith, M. L., and P. M. R. Stirk, eds. *Making the New Europe: European Unity and the Second World War*. New York: Pinter, 1980.
Smolenskin, Peretz. "Am Olam" (An Eternal People). In Smolenskin, *Essays*, 1:1–163. Jerusalem: 1925.
———. *Hatoeh Bedarkei Hahayim* [Stumbling through the paths of life]. Vilna: 1910.
Smooha, Sammy. "Is Israel Western? [in Hebrew]." In *Israel and Modernity: In Honor of Moshe Lissak*, edited by Uri Cohen, Eliezer Ben-Rafael, Avi Bar'eli, and Efrayim Yair, 49–83. Beer Sheva, Israel: Ben Gurion University of the Negev Press, 2006.
———. "Jewish Ethnicity in Israel: Symbolic or Real?" In *Jews in Israel: Contemporary Social and Cultural Patterns*, edited by Uzi Rebhum and Chaim I. Waxman, 47–80. Waltham, Mass.: Brandeis University Press, 2004.

Sokolow, Nahum. "A Journey to Poland in 1934 [in Hebrew]." In Sokolow, *Hatzofe Lebeit Israel*, 240–335. Jerusalem: Hasifriyah Haziyonit, 1961.
Sombart, Werner. *The Jews and Modern Capitalism*. Translated by M. Epstein. New York: Dutton, 1913.
Sorkin, David. "The Invisible Community." In *The Jewish Response to German Culture: From the Enlightenment to the Second World War*, edited by Jehuda Reinharz and W. Schatzberg, 100–19. Hanover, N.H.: University Press of New England, 1985.
———, ed. *Profiles in Diversity: Jews in a Changing Europe, 1750–1870*. Detroit: Wayne State University Press, 1998.
Spencer, Lewis. *Will Europe Follow Atlantis?* London: Rider, 1942.
Stampfer, Shaul. "Literacy among East European Jewry in the Modern Period: Context, Background and Implications [in Hebrew]." In *Transition and Change in Modern Jewish History: Essays Presented in Honor of Shmuel Ettinger*, edited by Shmuel Almog et al., 459–83. Jerusalem: Merkaz Zalman Shazar, 1987.
Stanislawski, Michael. *For Whom Do I Toil? Judah Leib Gordon and the Crisis of Russian Jewry*. New York: Oxford University Press, 1988.
———. *Zionism and the Fin de Siècle: Cosmopolitanism and Nationalism from Nordau to Jabotinsky*. Berkeley: University of California Press, 2001.
Stern, Fritz. *The Politics of Cultural Despair: A Study in the Rise of the Germanic Ideology*. New York: Anchor Books, 1965.
Sternhell, Zeev. "Reflections on the Turns of Centuries: On Historicism and the Campaign against the Enlightenment [in Hebrew]." In *Fins de Siècle: End of Ages*, edited by Yosef Kaplan, 343–65. Jerusalem: Merkaz Zalman Shazar, 2005.
Stiftel, Shoshana. "Nahum Sokolow: From Judaic-Polish Positivism to the Zionist Movement [in Hebrew]." Ph.D. diss., Tel Aviv University, 1994.
Stråth, Bo, ed. *Europe and the Other and Europe as the Other*. Brussels: P.I.E.-P. Lang, 2000.
Straus, Janine. "France and the French People in Y. L. Gordon's Works." In *Proceedings of the World Congress of Jewish Studies*, 3:93–100. Jerusalem: World Union of Jewish Studies, 1994.
Strauss, Leo. "Progress or Return?" In *The Rebirth of Classical Rationalism: Essays and Lectures by Leo Strauss*, edited by Thomas L. Pangle, 227–70. Chicago: University of Chicago Press, 1989.
Swart, Koenraad W. *The Sense of Decadence in Nineteenth-Century France*. The Hague: Nijhoff, 1964.
Syrkin, Nachman. "Al Miftan Meat Haesrim: Hashkafa Al Hitpatchut Hamadaim Bishnot Hamea Ha-19 Veteudatam Leyamim Yavou [At the threshhold of the twentieth century . . .]." In *1900 Yearbook*, edited by Nahum Sokolow, 212–29. Warsaw, 1900.

———. *The Collected Works of Nachman Syrkin*, compiled by Berl Katznelson and Yehezkel Kaufman. Tel Aviv: Davar, 1938.

———. "In the Press [in Hebrew]." *Kuntres* 5 (1918–19): 8–12.

———. "Letters from Europe [in Hebrew]." *Kuntres* 9 (1923): 3–5.

Tal, Uriel. "Myth and Solidarity in the Zionist Thought and Activity of Martin Buber [in Hebrew]." *Zionism* 7 (1981): 18–35.

Talfir, Gabriel. "Enemy No. 1 [in Hebrew]." *Gazit* 5–6 (1943): 1–2.

Talmon, Jacob L. *The Myth of the Nation and Vision of Revolution: The Origins of Ideological Polarization in the Twentieth Century*. Vol. 1. London: Secker and Warburg, 1980.

Tanaka, Stefan. *Japan's Orient: Rendering Pasts into History*. Berkeley: University of California Press, 1995.

Tauber, Zvi. "Envisioning the 20th Century: Heinrich Heine's Historical Prognoses." In *Deutsche Geschichte des 20: Jahrhunderts im Spiegel der deutschsprachigen Literatur*, edited by Moshe Zuckermann, 13–26. Göttingen, Germany: Wallstein, 2003.

Tedeschi, J. P. "The Myth of the Jews and the Myth of the Germans [in Hebrew]." In *Hagut Ivrit Beeyropa: Studies on Jewish Themes by Contemporary European Scholars*, edited by Menahem Zohori and Arie Tartakover, 189–91. Jerusalem: Berit Ivrit Olamit, 1969.

Teich, Nikulas, and Roy Porter, eds. *Fin de Siècle and Its Legacy*. New York: Cambridge University Press, 1990.

Tennyson, Alfred, Lord. *Tiresias and Other Poems*. London: Macmillan, 1885.

Teveth, Shabtai. "A-Historiographical Non-Historiographical Historiography [in Hebrew]." *Alpayim* 20 (2000): 117–28.

———. *Ben-Gurion and the Holocaust*. New York: Harcourt, Brace, 1996.

———. *Kinat David: The Life of David Ben Gurion* [in Hebrew]. Vol. 1. Jerusalem: Schocken, 1976.

Tibi, Bassam. *Der Islam und Deutschland: Muslime in Deutschland*. Stuttgart: Deutsche Verlags-Anstalt, 2000.

Todd, Emmanuel. *After the Empire: The Breakdown of the American Order*. Translated by C. Jon Delogu. New York: Columbia University Press, 2003.

Todorova, Mavia. *Imagining the Balkans*. New York: Oxford University Press, 1994.

Toller, Ernst. *I Was a German: The Autobiography of Ernst Toller*. Translated by Edward Crankshaw. Reprint ed. New York: AMS Press, 1991.

Toury, Jacob. "Emancipation and Assimilation: Terms and Concepts." *Yalkut Moreshet* 2 (1964): 167–82.

———. "The Jewish Question: A Semantic Approach." *Leo Baeck Institute Year Book* 11 (1966): 85–106.

———. *Prolegomena to the Entrance of Jews into German Citizenry* [in Hebrew]. Tel Aviv: Hamakhon Leheker Hatefutsot, 1972.

Trigano, Shmuel. "Is There a Future for French Jewry?" *Azure*, no. 20 (Spring 2005): 45–61.

Tripp, Charles. "Sayyid Qutb: The Political Vision." In *Pioneers of Islamic Revival*, edited by Ali Rahnema, 154–58. London: Palgrave MacMillan, 1994.

Tristram, Henry Baker. *The Land of Israel: A Journal of Travels in Palestine*. London: Society for Promoting Christian Knowledge, 1865.

Troen, S. Ilan. *Imagining Zion: Dreams, Designs, and Realities in a Century of Jewish Settlement*. New Haven, Conn.: Yale University Press, 2003.

Tsur, Yaron. *A Torn Community: The Jews of Morocco and Nationalism, 1943–1954*. Tel Aviv: Am Oved, 2001.

Tubin, Yehudah. "Berl Katznelson before the Holocaust: An Examination of His Views [in Hebrew]." *Yalkut Moreshet* 42 (December 1986): 81–110.

Tuchman, Barbara. *The Proud Tower: A Portrait of the World before the War, 1890–1914*. New York: Macmillan, 1966.

Tunaya, Tarik Zater. *Westernization Movement in Turkish Political Life* [in Turkish]. Istanbul: Cumhuriyet, 1999.

Tutungi, Gilbert. "Tawfiq al-Hakim and the West." Ph.D. diss., University of Indiana, 1966.

Tzahor, Zeev. "Chaim Arlosoroff and His Attitude towards the Rise of Nazism." *Jewish Social Studies* 46, nos. 3–4 (Summer–Fall 1984): 321–30.

Ullmann, Walter. *The Carolingian Renaissance and the Idea of Kingship*. London: Methuen, 1969.

van Rahden, Till. "Circumstantial Ethnic Belonging in Contrast to Identity Defined by 'Milieu' [in Hebrew]." In *The German-Jewish History We Inherited: Young Germans Write Jewish History*, edited by Henry Wassermann, 214–41. Jerusalem: Magnes and Leo Baeck, 2004.

Vital, David. *A People Apart: The Jews in Europe 1789-1939*. Oxford: Oxford University Press, 1999.

Volkov, Shulamit. *Germans, Jews, and Antisemites: Trials in Emancipation*. New York: Cambridge University Press, 2006.

———. "Jews among the Nations: A National Narrative or a Chapter in National Historiographies [in Hebrew]." *Zion* 61, no. 1 (1996): 91–111.

———. *The Rise of Popular Antimodernism in Germany: The Urban Master Artisans, 1873–1893*. Princeton, N.J.: Princeton University Press, 1978.

Von Laue, Theodore H. *The World Revolution of Westernization: The Twentieth Century in Global Perspective*. New York: Oxford University Press, 1987.

Vyverberg, Henry. *Historical Pessimism in the French Enlightenment*. Cambridge, Mass.: Harvard University Press, 1958.

Wagner, Peter. *A Sociology of Modernity: Liberty and Discipline*. New York: Rouledge, 1994.

Waldo, Frank. *The Discovery of America*. New York: Charles Scribner's Sons, 1929.

Walicki, Andrzej. *A History of Russian Thought from the Enlightenment to Marxism*.

Translated by Hilde Andrews-Rusiecka. Stanford, Calif.: Stanford University Press, 1979.

———. *Philosophy and Romantic Nationalism: The Case of Poland*. Oxford: Clarendon Press of Oxford University Press, 1982.

———. *The Slavophile Controversy: History of a Conservative Utopia in Nineteenth-Century Russian Thought*. Translated by Hilde Andrews-Rusiecka. Notre Dame, Ind.: University of Notre Dame Press, 1975.

Walk, Joseph. *The Education of the Jewish Child in Nazi Germany: The Law and Its Execution* [in Hebrew]. Jerusalem: Yad Vashem, 1975.

Wallace, Alfred Russel. *The Wonderful Century: Its Successes and Its Failures*. New York: Dodd, Mead, 1898.

Wassermann, Jakob. *Josef Kerkhovens dritte Existenz* [Josef Kerkhoven's third existence]. Amsterdam: Querido, 1934.

———. "Der Jude als Orientale." In Wassermann, *Mein Weg als Deutscher und Jude: Reden und Schriften 1904–1933*, edited by D. Rodewald, 29–32. Bonn: Bouvier Verlag Herbert Grundmann, 1984.

Wasserstein, Bernard. *Vanishing Diaspora: The Jews in Europe since 1945*. Cambridge, Mass.: Harvard University Press, 1996.

Webber, Jonathan, ed. *Jewish Identities in the New Europe*. Oxford: Littman Library of Jewish Civilization, 1994.

Weber, Eugen. *France: Fin de Siècle*, Cambridge, Mass.: Harvard University Press, 1986.

———. "Stereotypes of France." *Journal of Contemporary History* 5 (1990): 293–305.

Wechsler, Elchanan Hyle. *Ein Wort der Mahnung an Israel*. Würzburg, Germany: 1881.

Weeks, Theodore R. *From Assimilation to Antisemitism: The Jewish Question in Poland, 1850–1914*. DeKalb: Northern Illinois University Press, 2007.

Weill, Claudie. *Étudiants russes en Allemagne: Quand la Russie frappit aux ports de l'Europe*. Montreal: Harmattan, 1996.

Weitz, Yechiam. "Between the Poet and the Diplomat: Alterman's Attitude to Israeli-German Relations and His Debate with Moshe Sharett, 1952 [in Hebrew]." *Israel* 5 (2004): 99–112.

———. "The Path to the 'Other Germany': David Ben-Gurion and His Relationship with Germany, 1952–1960 [in Hebrew]." In *Independence: The First Fifty Years*, edited by Anita Shapira, 245–66. Jerusalem: Merkaz Zalman Shazar, 1998.

———. "Political and Ideological Conflicts: The Prague Trials and the Debate over the Reparations Agreement [in Hebrew]." In *General Election and Governmental Crisis*, edited by Yechiam Weitz, 116–45. Tel Aviv: Open University Press, 2001.

Weizmann, Chaim. *The Letters and Papers of Chaim Weizmann*. Series A: *Letters*. Vols. 4 and 7, edited by Leonard Stein; vol. 5, edited by Hanna Weiner and

Barnet Litvinoff; vol. 6, edited by Gedalia Yogev, Shifra Kolatt, and Evyatar Friesel. Vols. 1–5: London: Oxford University Press, 1968–80. Vols. 6–7: Jerusalem: Israel Universities Press, 1974–75.

———. *Speeches* [in Hebrew]. Vol. 4. Tel Aviv: 1938.

Werses, Shmuel. "'Awake, My People': Hebrew Literature in the Age of Modernization [in Hebrew]." *Sadan* 4 (2000): 13–26.

———. "The French Revolution through the Viewpoint of Hebrew Literature [in Hebrew]." In Werses, *Awake, My People: Hebrew Literature in the Age of Modernization*, 117–56. Jerusalem: Magnes, 2001.

———. "Nachman's Last Speech: and Its Sources [in Hebrew]." In *Moznayim/Jubilee Book*, 280–91. Ramat Gan, Israel: Ayala, 1979.

———. "On the Threshold of the Twentieth Century [in Hebrew]." *Sadan* 4 (1994): 52–53.

Wheen, Frances. *Karl Marx: A Life*. New York: Norton, 2000.

White, Hayden. "The Discourse of Europe and the Search for European Identity." In *Europe and the Other and Europe as the Other*, edited by Bo Stråth, 67–86. Brussels: P.I.E.-P. Lang, 2000.

Williams, Robert C. *Culture in Exile: Russian Emigres in Germany, 1881–1941*. Ithaca, N.Y.: Cornell University Press, 1972.

Wilson, K., and J. van der Dussen, eds. *The History of the Idea of Europe*. London: Routledge, 1995.

Wintle, Michael, ed. *Culture and Society in Europe: Perceptions of Divergence and Unity*. Avebury, England: Aldershot, 1996.

———. "Europe's Image: Visual Representations of Europe from Earliest Times to the Twentieth Century." In *Europe and the Other and Europe as the Other*, edited by Bo Stråth, 52–96. Brussels: P.I.E.-P. Lang, 2000.

Wistrich, Robert S. *European Anti-Semitism Reinvents Itself*. New York: The American Jewish Committee, 2005.

———. *Laboratory for World Destruction: Germans and Jews in Central Europe* [in Hebrew]. Jerusalem: Magnes, 2006.

———. "Radical Antisemitism in France and Germany [in Hebrew]." In *Between Israel and the Nations*, edited by Shmuel Almog et al., 157–84. Jerusalem: Merkaz Zalman Shazar, 1987.

Witzthum, David. "Germany in Israel: Perceptions, Culture, and Communication [in Hebrew]." In *Germany and the Land of Israel: A Cultural Encounter*, edited by Moshe Zimmermann, 188–216. Jerusalem: Magnes, 2004.

Wolff, Larry. *Inventing Eastern Europe: The Map of Civilization in the Mind of the Enlightenment*. Stanford, Calif.: Stanford University Press, 1994.

Wright, John Kirtland. *The Geographic Lore of the Crusades: A Study in Medieval Science and Tradition in Western Europe*. Reprint ed. New York: Dover, 1965.

Yeivin, Yehoshua Heschel. "The Foreign Legion Comes Home [in Hebrew]." In *Collected Works*, 365–450. Tel Aviv: Havaadah Lehotsaat Kitve, 1969.

Yovel, Yirmiyahu. "Nietzsche and the Jews: The Structure of an Ambivalence."

In *Nietzsche and Jewish Culture*, edited by Jacob Golomb, 117–34. New York: Routledge, 1997.

———. "Nietzsche contra Wagner on the Jews." In *Nietzsche, Godfather of Fascism? On the Uses and Abuses of a Philosophy*, edited by Jacob Golomb and Robert S. Wistrich, 126–43. Princeton, N.J.: Princeton University Press, 2002.

Yunas-Dinovitz, Yael. "Between Integration and Detachment: Polish Immigrants to Palestine between Two World Wars and Their Encounter with the Zionist Melting Pot [in Hebrew]." Master's thesis, Hebrew University, 2004.

Zabarenko, Judith. "The Negative Image of America in the Russian-Language Jewish Press (1881–1910)." *American Jewish History* 15, no. 3 (March 1986): 267–79.

Zangwill, Israel. *The Melting Pot: A Drama in Four Acts*. New York: Macmillan, 1911.

Zeira, Moti. "Trembling, But Not Because of the Cold [in Hebrew]." *Etmol* 59, no. 4 (March 2004): 9–21.

Zilbersheid, Uri. "Herzl's Social and Economic Vision [in Hebrew]." *Iyunim Bitkumat Israel* 10 (2000): 614–40.

Zimmermann, Moshe. *German Past—Israeli Memory* [in Hebrew]. Tel Aviv: Am Oved, 2002.

———, ed. *Germany's Singular History* [in Hebrew]. Jerusalem: Magnes, 1989

Zunz, Leopold (Yom-Tov) Lipmann. *Die Gottesdienstlichen Vorträge der Juden historisch entwickelt* [Jewish sermons and their historical evolution]. 2nd ed. Berlin: 1892.

———. "Zur Geschichte und Literatur." In *Gesammelte Schriften*, vol. 1. Berlin: Louis Gerschel, 1875.

Zur, Eli. "A Difficult Divorce: Mapam and Soviet Orientation, 1942–1958 [in Hebrew]." *Shvut*, n.s., 12, no. 28 (2004–5): 105–34.

Zuta, H. L. *The "Melamed" and the "Teacher"* [in Hebrew]. Jerusalem: 1914.

Zweig, Stefan. *The World of Yesterday: An Autobiography*. Introduction by Harry Zohn. Lincoln: University of Nebraska Press, 1964.

INDEX

Abramovitsh, S. Y. *See* Mendele Mokher Seforim
absolutism, enlightened, 27–29
acculturation, 2, 59, 63–65, 214n24, 220n120; as cause of antisemitism, 98; as coercion, 162; limits of, 66, 69–70, 74, 78; prevention of, 96; results of, 84–85; values/norms and, 81–83. *See also* assimilation; integration
acculturation, reverse, 168
Achimeir, Aba, 122–23, 132, 148
Ahad Haam, 51, 121, 126, 130, 144–45, 164
Aizman, Moshe, 139
Alexander II (czar), 28
Allgemeine Zeitung des Judentums (periodical), 31–32
Altman, Arieh, 182–83
Altneuland (Herzl), 37–38, 91, 144–46, 208n55, 208n63
America. *See* United States
Americanism and Americanization, 170, 175–77, 185. *See also* anti-Americanism; culture, American
"An einen Mann von Stande" (Mendelssohn), 18
Angell, Norman, 102
anti-Americanism, 175–77, 194–95, 250nn5–6
anti-Europeanness, 162–67, 241–42n31. *See also* Europe/Europeanness: rejection of
anti-Jewish literature. *See* literature
anti-Jewishness. *See* antisemitism
antinomy, East-West, 2, 136, 139, 162, 167–69, 196, 243n42, 243–44n48

antisemitism, 4–5, 86–99, 108–9, 136–37, 179, 189; 19th century and modern, 30–32, 89, 90, 212n10; causes/sources of, 87, 92–94, 97–98, 112–13, 222n2, 250n11; French, 186–87, 249n28; German, 72, 87–88, 97, 111, 119, 182, 184; Polish, 80, 94–95, 104, 115–16; rebirth of, 9, 198n17; role in the Orient, 141; Russian, 88, 90, 185; socialist view of, 94; types of, 94–96, 186. *See also* blood libels; Judeophobia; pogroms
anti-Westernness. *See* anti-Americanism; anti-Europeanness
Appelfeld, Aharon, 250–51n12
Arabs, 135–37; Jewish view of/kinship with, 139, 152, 167; Western culture and, 148–49, 165–67, 241–42n31
archetypes, Jewish, 56
Arlosoroff, Chaim, 111, 148–49
Aronson, Aharon, 107
Ascher, Shaul, 105–6
Ashkenaz, 108, 238–39n3
Ashkenazi Ape (German anti-semitism), 97
Asia and Asiatics, 136–37. *See also* Orient, the
assimilation, 59, 62–63, 65, 107, 214n24; antisemitism and, 93, 97–99; fear of, 156, 236–37n40; German Jews and, 90, 138; limitations of, 77–78, 90; Polish Jews and, 80–81; prevention of, 142. *See also* acculturation; integration
Auerbach, Berthold, 44
Autoemancipation (Pinsker), 61, 93

automobiles. *See* science and technology

Baeck, Leo, 74
Balkans, the, 200–201n23
Baron, Salo Wittmayer, 65
Bar-Yosef, Hamutal, 202–3n44
Beilinson, Moshe, 116
Ben-Aharon, Yitzhak, 182
Benedict, Leopold. *See* Winchevsky, Morris
Ben Gurion, David, 51–52, 116, 119–20, 149, 193–94
Ben-Hillel Hacohen, Mordechai, 158
Ben-Yehuda, Eliezer, 206n43
Berdichevsky, Michah Yosef, 4–5, 30
Bergman, Shmuel Hugo, 83–84
Bernfeld, Shimon, 48–49, 126
Beyond Good and Evil (Nietzsche), 121–22
Bialik, Chaim Nachman, 113–14, 173–74
Bible, the, 3, 143, 203n46
Bilu movement, 38, 64, 151
Birnbaum, Nathan, 61–62, 77–78
Bismarck, Otto, 14, 22, 97, 107
"Blind Generation, The" (Brandstaetter), 115
Bloch, Ivan, 102
blood libels, 30–31, 86–88, 90–91. *See also* pogroms
Borochov, Ber (Dov), 52, 91, 142, 209n2
Brainin, Reuven, 49
Brandstaetter, Roman, 115
Brandstetter, Yehoshua, 151
Brenner, Y. C. (Yosef Chaim), 146–47, 158, 164–65, 243n40
Breuer, Isaac, 82–83
Britain/the British. *See* England/the English
Buber, Martin, 39, 78, 137–38, 140–41
Buchanan, Patrick, 179–80
Bund (Jewish Socialist movement), 98, 118, 127

Burckhardt, Jakob, 246–47n71
Burke, Edmund, 13

characteristics, cultural. *See* character traits; *culture entries*
characteristics, national. *See* character traits; stereotypes
Characteristics of Paris (Rapoport), 125
character traits, 14–15, 60–62, 122, 160, 200–201n23, 215n27
Charlemagne, 12
Chekhov, Anton, 42, 44
Christianity and Christians, 11–12, 181, 198nn6–7
Christian-Jewish relations. *See* Jewish-Christian relations
Churchill, Winston, 193–94
Cohen, Bernhard, 89
Cohen, David, 80
Cohen, Gustav, 89
Cohen, Hermann, 73
Cohen, Richard, 60
colonialism, cultural, 169, 244–45n55. *See also* Occidentalism and Occidentalists; Orientalism and Orientalists
communism, 14, 185
conversion, religious, 77
"Correspondence of an English Lady on Judaism and Semitism, The" (Graetz), 1, 46–47
cosmopolitanism, 5, 55, 123, 200n14, 202–3n44, 209n2, 213n15
counterculture, 150–51
Croce, Benedetto, 102–3, 226n13
cross-Europeanism, 13–14, 16, 18–20, 200n14
cultural assets, 157–61. *See also culture entries for various nationalities*
cultural perceptions, 123–26
cultural pessimism, 42–53, 177, 210n11
cultural polarization, 194–95
cultural reality. *See* acculturation

culture, amalgamation/transplantation of, 144–45, 156–57
culture, American, 166–67, 170–77, 194–95, 246n68, 246n71
culture, Ashkenazi, 123, 155, 166–68, 238–39n3
culture, Eastern. *See* Orient, the
culture, English, 124, 129
culture, European, 124–26, 145, 154–78. *See also* culture, Western; *culture entries for various nationalities*; Hellenism/Hellenization
culture, French, 124–29, 232n27
culture, German, 19, 111, 135; influence of, 124; Israeli view of, 184–85; uniqueness, 108
culture, Hebrew, 155. *See also* culture, Israeli; culture, Jewish
culture, Israeli, 169–70. *See also* culture, European; culture, Hebrew; culture, Jewish; culture, Western
culture, Jewish, 132, 145, 156–57, 169
culture, Russian, 124, 231n14
culture, Western, 4–5, 171, 175–77, 196, 197n2, 243–44n48; Arabs/radical Muslims and, 188, 241–42n31; Egypt and, 241–42n31; Israeli/Jewish Palestine view of, 142–45, 162–63; loyalty to, 143; participation of Jews in, 59; rejection of, 163–66; Turkey and, 241–42n31; universalization of, 141. *See also* culture, American; culture, European; Hellenism/Hellenization

Damascus Affair (blood libel), 87–88
"Dank" (Jacobowski), 75
Darwinism, 36, 48, 50–51
Dawn of Day, The (Nietzsche), 84, 187
Death of the West, The (Buchanan), 179–80
"Derech Eretz or Atheism" (Luzzatto), 45, 126

Der Israelit (periodical), 31, 66, 74
Der Mann ohne Eigenschaften (Musil), 100
Der Untergang des Abendlandes (Spengler), 100
"Deutschland, Ein Wintermärchen" (Heine), 106
Deutschtum und Judentum (H. Cohen), 73
Die Judenfrage und die Zukunft (G. Cohen), 89
"Die Zukunft des Judentums" (Freund), 109–10
Doctor Faustus (Mann), 72, 107
Dostoevsky, Fyodor, 41, 122, 209n2
Druyanov, Alter, 79
Dubnow, Simon, 31, 50, 61, 65–66; view of influence of Judaism, 68–69; view of political reactionism, 90; view of the Orient, 136, 234–35n10; view of United States, 171–72
Dubnow, Vladimir Zeev, 142
Duel, The (Chekhov), 42

East, the. *See* East and West; Orient, the
East and West, 136–37, 146–47, 165, 167, 240n24. *See also* antinomy, East-West
Eastern culture. *See* Orient, the
Egypt, 241–42n31
Ehrenpreis, Mordechai, 21, 200–201n23
Ein Wort der Mahnung an Israel (Wechsler), 92
Ein Zukunftsbild (Eisler), 47
Eisler, Edmund Menachem, 47
Elbogen, Ismar, 90
electricity. *See* science and technology
Elon, Amos, 184
Elyashiv, Vera, 184
Emden, Jacob, 125

emigration, Jewish, 156, 171. *See also* immigrants
"End of the Century, The" (Brainin), 49
"End of the Century, The" (Levin), 48
England/the English, 130–31; cultural pessimism, 42, 210n13; as a model/influence of, 129–33, 232n37, 233–34n60; stereotypes, 121–22, 125
Enlightenment, European, 28–29, 84, 139, 186–87
Enlightenment, Jewish. *See Haskalah*
Erasmus Mundus educational program, 247n8
ethnic groups/ethnicity, 121, 168, 222n133
Eurocentrism, 6–7, 193, 241–42n31
Europe, Eastern, 65–66, 103–4, 133, 185. *See also* Balkans, the; Jews, East European; Jews, Polish; Jews, Russian
Europe, Western, 14–15, 65, 177–78; cultural pessimism and, 40; decline of, 179; United States and, 175–76, 194–95, 250nn5–6. *See also* Jews, German; Jews, West European
European heritage. *See* Europe/Europeanness
Europeanization, 1, 56–57, 141, 164, 205n23
Europe-Asia antinomy. *See* antinomy, East-West
Europe/Europeanness, 1–10, 15–16, 179–81, 200–201n23, 221n131, 250–51n12; decline of, 100, 179–81; duality of, 6, 170, 193, 196; Israeli view/identification, 2, 8–10, 21, 152, 178–81, 194; Jewish view/identification, 2–6, 9–10, 18–21, 196; post–World War II, 179–91; regionalism, 14, 200–201n23; rejection of, 150–53, 162–66, 169, 241–42n31; transferring to Orient, 142, 151–53; United States and, 175–76, 194–95, 250nn5–6; unity of, 13–14, 16, 50, 101–3, 181, 202n36, 226n14, 247n8. *See also* culture, European; culture, Western; Europe, Eastern; Europe, Western; Hellenism/Hellenization

Europe on the Brink (radio program), 179
Europhobia, 43. *See also* cultural pessimism; Europe/Europeanness

"Fall of European Jews, The" (Mann), 111
fascism, German. *See* Nazism
fatherland. *See* homeland, concept of
Fathers and Sons (Mendele Mokher Seforim), 64
Feierberg, Mordechai Zeev, 46, 138
Feuchtwanger, Leon, 110–11
Fichte, Johann Gottlieb, 22
fin de siècle, 43–44, 50, 203–4n3, 210n11
France/the French, 127–28; antisemitism, 186–87, 249n28; stereotypes, 122–26, 230–31n12
Frankel, David, 25
French Revolution, 17, 26–28
Freund, Ismar, 109–10
Friedberg, A. S., 108–9
Friedman, Eliezer Eliyahu, 80
Frischman, David, 137, 171, 195
"From the Days of the Flood" (Harcabi), 96
Fuenn, Shmuel Joseph, 28–29
Future of the Jews, The (Lynx), 111
Future of War, The (Bloch), 102

Gans, Eduard, 19, 20, 25, 138
Geiger, Abraham, 67–68, 73
Gellner, Ernest, 201n29
"General Outlook on the Year 1879 and Its Significance for Our Jewish Brothers, A" (Sokolow), 65
German language, 73–74
Germanomania, 105–6

Germany/the Germans, 108–9; antisemitism, 87, 182, 184; Israel and, 182–83, 248n25; nationalism and Nazism, 182–84; stereotypes, 121–22, 123, 125. *See also* culture, German
Geschichte der Juden in Deutschland (Elbogen), 90
Ginsberg, Asher Zvi. *See* Ahad Haam
Ginsburg, A., 115
globalization, 197n10
Gobsch, Hans, 53
Goethe, Johann Wolfgang von, 121
Goldmann, Nahum, 110
Goldstein, Moritz, 20–21
Gordon, Y. L., 19, 29–30, 61, 67, 70–71, 139, 215n34
Gottlober, Abraham Baer, 108
Graetz, Heinrich (Zvi), 1, 46–47, 68, 107, 196
Great Britain/the British. *See* England/the English
Great Illusion, The (Angell), 102
Greenbaum, Yitzhak, 112
Greenberg, Uri Zvi, 8, 101, 138, 181; view of antisemitism, 94, 95, 104–5; view of Europe, the Orient, and Palestine, 105, 149–50; view of Nazi Germany, 116–17; view of Zionism and Messianism, 149–50
Guizot, François, 13
Günsburg, Karl Siegfried, 64
Gurion, Y., 115

habitus, 58, 81–83, 152, 161, 213n18, 241n28
Hakitza Ami (Y. L. Gordon), 29
Hamagid (periodical), 21–22, 32, 124
Hameassef (periodical), 26–27
Hamelitz (periodical), 88–89
Harcabi, Vladimir, 96
Hardenberg, Friedrich von. *See* Novalis (Friedrich von Hardenberg)

Hashomer Hazair, 150–51
Haskalah, 26, 70–71, 74, 206n39. *See also maskilim*
hatred of Jews. *See* antisemitism
Hatzfira (periodical), 33, 95, 206n43
Hazan, Yaacov, 182
Hazit Haam (periodical), 118
Hebrew Bible. *See* Bible, the
Heine, Heinrich, 13, 72, 87, 106, 122, 245n60
Hellenism/Hellenization, 69, 163–64
Herder, Johann Gottfried, 19, 66
Herschberg, Avraham Shmuel, 127, 143–44, 159
Herzl, Theodor, 204n7; Ahad Haam and, 144–45; economic, political, and social views, 36–39, 128, 227n34; view of antisemitism, 89–91, 98; view of England/the English, 131; view of France/the French, 126, 128; view of technology, 34–39, 145, 207nn47–48, 208n63; view of Western culture versus the Orient, 134–35; Zionism and, 68, 145, 155, 157, 237n51
Hess, Moses, 74, 87, 106–7, 128, 135
Hirsch, Shimshon Raphael, 97
Hissin, Haim, 64
Histoire générale de la civilization en Europe (Guizot), 13
history, perceptions of, 221n128
Hitchcock, William, 194–95
Hitler, Adolph/Hitlerism, 110–13, 115–20. *See also* Nazism
Hobsbawm, Eric, 201n29
homeland, concept of, 64–66
Hugo, Victor, 23–24

Ichpoesie (self-centered writing), 44
identity, crisis of, 74–75
identity, cultural, 77, 166, 244n49. *See also* Europe/Europeanness; Orient, the; Palestine

identity, European, 199n12, 200n19; Christian, 12, 181, 198nn6–7; cultural and geographical, 11–13, 18–20, 198n4, 202n33
identity, Jewish, 59, 250–51n12, 250n10
identity, national, 76. *See also* nationalism
identity, religious, 77. *See also* identity, European: Christian; identity, Jewish
immigrants: cultural assets and, 157–61, 169, 231n14; European, 162, 169; German, 161, 240n25, 241n28; Muslim, 186–88; Polish, 160–61, 240n25, 241n28
individualism, 82–83. *See also* cultural pessimism
"In Exchange for Shoes" (Gordon), 71
"In Malchus fun Tzelm" (Greenberg), 95
integration, 62–66, 74; impossibility of, 77; of Jews, 25, 40, 60–69, 84, 96, 222n134. *See also* acculturation; assimilation; Jews
intellectuals, Russian, 42, 209n4, 230–31n12
intellectuals/elite, Jewish: cultural pessimism and, 44–45; England/the English and, 129–30; nineteenth century and, 24, 29, 41; view of Europe, 18–20, 93; Vilna (Russia) and, 79; worldview, 92
intelligentsia, Oriental, 165–68
intelligentsia, Russian, 209n4, 230n12
interwar period, 103–4
Islam, 140, 147, 165–66, 187–91. *See also* Arabs
Islamophobia, 186, 189–90
Isocrates, 13
Israel: contrast with Europe/West, 177–78; identity of, 8–9; United States and, 170, 174–77, 246–47n71;
view of/identification with Europe/Europeanness, 2, 8–10, 21, 170, 178–81, 194. *See also* culture, Israeli; Palestine

Jabotinsky, Zeev, 2–3, 5, 63, 79–80, 94, 210n11; political predictions, 52, 118–20; view of antisemitism, 90; view of English political culture, 131–32; view of European and Oriental cultures, 147–48; view of Germany/the Germans, 112, 116; view of nineteenth and twentieth centuries, 41; view of United States, 246n68
Jacob, Margaret C., 200n14
Jacobowski, Ludwig, 75, 218n87
Jaffa, Israel, 158
Jellinek, Adolf, 61
Jewish-Christian relations, 64
Jewish State, The (Herzl), 36
Jews: Europeanization of, 56–59, 84, 142–44; identification with a specific nation, 59, 61, 63, 215n34; role of, 250n11, 250–51n12; Westernization of, 212–13n12, 213n14. *See also* immigrants; *under various nationalities*
Jews, American, 194–95
Jews, Arabized, 167
Jews, East European, 76, 78, 83; German Jews and, 58, 61; influence of England and France, 124–29
Jews, European, 1–5, 19–22, 61, 74–75, 189–92, 203n46; contributions to culture, 3–5, 66–69, 146–48, 216nn51–52, 217n59, 250–51n12; population figures, 250n10; status of, 7–8, 55, 135. *See also* Jews, East European; Jews, West European; *under various nationalities*
Jews, German, 61, 72–78, 83, 112–16, 213–14n19; contributions to

culture/integration of, 109–10, 216n51; duality of, 76–77, 222n134; liberal, 73–74, 77; neo-Orthodox, 74, 77, 98. *See also* Germany/the Germans: antisemitism; immigrants, German

Jews, Polish, 62, 65, 118–19, 238n3; acculturation/contributions to culture, 80–81, 220nn115–116; antisemitism and, 94–95, 104, 111–13, 115. *See also* immigrants, Polish; Poland/the Polish: antisemitism

Jews, Russian, 60–65, 90, 219n105; contributions to culture/integration of, 78–80; equal rights and, 29–30, 97; persecution, 185. *See also* Russia/the Russians: antisemitism

Jews, Sephardi, 243n42

Jews, West European, 76, 156

Jews and Muslims, 168, 189–91, 243n43

Jews as Race and as Culture, The (Kahn), 164

Jost, I. M., 88

Judaism, 165–66, 250n11; Europe and, 19–22, 68–77, 83, 146–48; liberal, 73–74, 77; Orthodox, 74, 77, 98, 117–18, 163; revival of, 138, 157, 164, 180–81

Judenjahrhundert. *See* nineteenth century

Judeocentrism, 7–8

Judeophobia, 93. *See also* antisemitism

Kahn, Fritz, 164
Katznelson, Berl, 115–16
Kaufmann, Yehezkel, 112–13
Kehiliateinu, 1922 (Tzur), 150
Klatzkin, Jakob, 73
Klausner, Josef, 88–89
Kley, Eduard, 64
Kohler, Kaufmann, 89
Kohn, Hans, 141

Kolisher, A., 114
Kook, Zvi Yehuda, 163
Kultur, 82
Kulturpessimismus. *See* cultural pessimism

Land Haunted by Its Past, A (Elon), 184
Langbehn, Julius, 108
Laqueur, Walter, 203–4n3
Lazarus, Moritz, 32, 73
Le'an? (Feierberg), 46
Lehmann, Emil, 32
Lessing, Michael Benedict, 58
Levanda, Lev, 79, 88
Levin, Yehuda Leib, 44–46, 48–49
Levinsky, Elchanan Leib, 49–50, 126–27
Levinsohn, Isaac Baer (Rival), 17–18, 67
Lévi-Strauss, Claude, 189
Lilienblum, Moshe Leib, 3–5, 22, 71–72, 96–97, 128; cultural pessimism and, 49; view of East-West antinomy, 139; view of French Revolution, 27
Lindau, Baruch, 60
literature, 55, 98, 103–4, 136–38
Livneh, Eliezer, 180–81, 247n5
love of country. *See* homeland, concept of
Lowenthal, Marvin, 111
Luzzatto, Shmuel David (Shadal), 45, 126
Lvov, Poland, 104

machines. *See* science and technology
Mandelstam, Benyamin, 125
Mann, Thomas, 103, 107, 111, 122, 225–26n7
Marr, Wilhelm, 92
Marx, Karl, 23
"Masa Leeretz Israel Bishnat 2040" (Levinsky), 49, 126–27

maskilim, 17–18, 28, 129; faith in progress, 32, 45; radical, 127, 171. See also *Haskalah*; *under individual names*
Mauschel (degenerate Jew), 98
Mediterraneanness, 244n53
Mefisto (Greenberg), 101
Meirovitz, Menashe, 144
"Melamed" and the "Teacher," The (Zuta), 164–65
melting pot, the, 172–73
Mendele Mokher Seforim, 64, 96, 129
Mendelssohn, Josef, 18
Mendelssohn, Moses, 18, 27, 207n48
messianism, 38–39
Mikonis, Shmuel, 182–83
modernism/modernization, 159; East European Jewish culture and, 243n45; Jews and, 68–69, 80, 81–85; Oriental model, 167
Monbron, Louis Charles Fougeret de, 199n13
Montesquieu, Charles-Louis de Secondat (baron), 14, 16, 200n20
multiculturalism, 173, 190–91, 244n53
Musa, Salama, 241–42n31
Musil, Robert, 100, 103

Napoleon and Napoleonic wars: Jews and, 18, 26; vision of Europe and, 17, 202n36
nationalism, 5, 17, 180, 201n29; acculturation and, 63; ethnonationalism, 247n3; French, 127; German, 107, 182–84; Jewish, 70, 164; "solutions," 50; Western, 235n20. *See also* identity, cultural; identity, national; identity, religious
Nazism, 107, 111–16, 119, 182
neo-Orthodoxy. *See* Orthodox, the
newspapers. *See* periodicals
Nietzsche, Friedrich, 13–14, 121–22; Jews and, 16, 54–55, 187, 200n16, 212n2; view of antisemitism, 91

nineteenth century, 23–41; contrast with end of 15th century, 43; Jewish view of, 24–31; *Judenjahrhundert* (the Jewish century), 54–55; negative aspects, 30–31; positive aspects, 25, 30–32, 205n23; social and moral decline, 46–49
Nordau, Max, 31, 39–40, 44, 50, 145–46
Notes from the Underground (Dostoevsky), 42
Novakhovitsh, Benzion. *See* Winchevsky, Morris
Novalis (Friedrich von Hardenberg), 13, 199n13
Nuremberg Laws, 112

Occidentalism and Occidentalists, 100, 134–35, 176, 241–42n31
Odessa, Russia, 78, 219n105
Oppenheimer, Franz, 76
Orient, the, 144, 152, 234–35n10; Europeanization of, 139–42, 147–48; negative aspects, 134–36; positive aspects, 137–39; values of, 166–67
Orientalism and Orientalists, 147, 167
Ortega y Gasset, José, 14, 16–17, 102
Orthodox, the, 98; in Germany, 74, 77; view of Western culture, 163. *See also* ultra-Orthodox, the
Other Germany, The (Elyashiv), 183–84
Ottoman Empire, 12, 51–52, 199n7, 243n43

Palestine, 36–38, 152, 154–78; cultural aspects, 140–49, 160–61, 168–69, 238–39n3; immigrants, 137–39, 142, 231n14; influence, Western, 2, 124, 131–33, 147–49, 151, 196, 235n14; transference, 193, 236n40; view of United States, 174. *See also* Israel; Zionism and Zionists
Panegyricus (Isocrates), 13

Pan-European Union, 103
Paris, France, 124–25
patriotism, 65–66
periodicals: *Allgemeine Zeitung des Judentums*, 31–32; *Der Israelit*, 31, 66, 74; *Hamagid*, 21–22, 32, 65, 124; *Hamashkif*, 115; *Hameassef*, 26–27; *Hamelitz*, 88–89; *Hashachar*, 88; *Hatzfira*, 33, 104, 206n43; *Havatzelet*, 158; *Hazit Haam*, 118; *Judisk Tidskirt*, 114; *Shulamit*, 25; *Voskhod*, 93
pessimism, cultural. *See* cultural pessimism
Piccolomini, Aeneas Silvius. *See* Pius II (pope)
Pinsker, Leon, 61, 93
Pius II (pope), 12
Poale Tzion party, 155–56
pogroms, 70; causes of, 97; Polish, 104; Russian, 30, 49, 64, 88, 90. *See also* blood libels
Poland/the Polish, 80–81, 200–201n23, 216n42; antisemitism, 94–95, 104, 111–13, 115–18; as Ashkenaz, 238–39n3. *See also* Jews, Polish
Polonization. *See* Jews, Polish
progress, 29, 32, 36–41, 88–89, 129, 209n2. *See also* cultural pessimism; science and technology
Prussia, 28

Qutb, Sayyid, 241–42n31

Rabinovitz, Yaakov, 133, 142–43
Rabinowich, Osip, 79
race, concept of, 121
racism, 95–96, 112–13, 186
Ranke, Leopold von, 107
Rapoport, Shlomo Yehuda Leib, 125
Rathenau, Walter, 76, 139–40
Reform Jews. *See* Jews, German: liberal

Rembrandt als Erzieher (Langbehn), 108
revolutionary consciousness, 156
Riesser, Gabriel, 72
riots. *See* pogroms
Rival. *See* Levinsohn, Isaac Baer (Rival)
Rosenzweig, Franz, 73
Roth, Samuel, 100–101, 172–73, 225n6
Rousseau, Jean-Jacques, 13, 27, 204n17
Rühs, Christian Friedrich, 122
Rülf, Isaak, 93, 98
Ruppin, Arthur, 69
Russian language, 79, 219n110
Russia/the Russians, 28–31, 64–65, 122–24, 193; antisemitism, 90–91, 97, 108–10; cultural pessimism, 42–44; Europe and, 205n23; intelligentsia, 209n4; Israel and, 231n14; modernization, 205n23; stereotypes, 123. *See also* Jews, Russian
Russification, 78–79

Sanhedrin, the, 18
Schlegel, August Wilhelm, 19
Schocken, Gershom, 184
Scholem, Gershom, 78
Schorsch, Ismar, 189
science and technology, 32–35, 207n47, 208n63; creation of model societies, 145; distinguishing from spiritual culture, 164; Jewish perception of, 39–40, 206n39
Sefer Divrei Yemei Olam (Shulman), 17
self-hatred, Jewish, 99. *See also* antisemitism
Shadal. *See* Luzzatto, Shmuel David (Shadal)
Shakespeare, William, 130–32
Shapira, Zvi Hermann, 33
Sharett, Moshe (formerly Shertok), 115, 183
"Sheelot Hazman," 45–46

"Shem and Japheth on the Train" (Mendele Mokher Seforim), 96
Shertok, Moshe. *See* Sharett, Moshe (formerly Shertok)
Shulamit (periodical), 25
Shulman, Kalman, 17, 27–28, 66–67, 129–30
Simmel, Georg, 103
Smilansky, Moshe, 236–37n40
Smolenskin, Peretz, 88, 125–26, 130
Smooha, Sammy, 177–78
socialism, 36, 94, 128, 150–51. *See also* Bund (Jewish Socialist movement)
societies, multinational and multi-ethnic, 127
society, Israeli. *See* culture, Israeli
society, Jewish, 173. *See also* culture, Jewish
Society for Culture and Science of the Jews (Verein für Kultur und Wissenschaft der Juden), 18–19
Society of Friends (Gesellschaft der Freunde), 18
Sokolow, Nahum, 65, 94–95, 113
Soviet Union, 185, 248n13. *See also* Russia/the Russians
Spencer, Herbert, 36
Spencer, Lewis, 225n6
Spengler, Oswald, 100
Staël, Madame de, 14
stereotypes, 60–62, 177, 215n27; American, 173, 176; of England/the English, 121–22, 125, 128; of France/the French, 122, 125–27, 128; of Germany/the Germans, 121–22, 128; national, 121–23, 127, 161
Strauss, Leo, 163–64
subcultures, 160–61
"Swastika Crusade, The," 118
Syrkin, Nachman, 34, 94, 104, 157

Tamuz, Benyamin, 246–47n71
Tel Aviv, Israel, 150–52, 158, 239–40n17

Teutons. *See* Germanomania
thinkers, English, 130–31
"Thoughts and Deeds" (Levinsky), 49
Time Machine, The (Wells), 42
"Toward the End of the Nineteenth Century" (Bernfeld), 47–48
traits, cultural. *See* character traits
transference, 156, 193, 236n40
Travels of Benjamin the Third (Mendele Mokher Seforim), 129
Treitschke, Heinrich von, 92
Troeltsch, Ernst, 188
Turkey, 241–42n31. *See also* Ottoman Empire

ultra-Orthodox, the, 117–18
United States: cultural pessimism, 43; decline of, 195, 250n8; Europe and, 175–76, 194–95, 250nn5–6; images of, 171, 245n60; Israel and, 174–77, 246–47n71; Israeli/Jewish view of, 166, 195; Muslim view of, 195
universalism, 19–22, 108, 250n11
Ussishkin, Menachem Mendel, 112

values and norms, 59; American, 170–71; European, 69–71, 160–63, 245n56; Western, 164–65, 195. *See also* culture, Western
Verne, Jules, 208n63
"Vial of Perfume, A" (Gordon), 70
Volk, 19
Volkist movement, 108
Volkskultur, 163–64
Voltaire, 13
Vor dem Sturm (B. Cohen), 89
Voskhod (periodical), 93

Walicki, Andrzej, 200–201n23
Wallace, Alfred Russel, 38
Wassermann, Jakob, 110, 140
Wechsler, Elchanan Hyle, 92

Weizmann, Chaim, 52, 91–92, 124, 156; view of antisemitism, 99, 113; view of East-West antinomy, 140–41; view of English culture/England, 131, 233n54
Wells, H. G., 38, 42
Werther, der Jude (Jacobowski), 218n87
West and East. *See* East and West
When the Sleeper Wakes (Wells), 38, 42
Will Europe Follow Atlantis? (L. Spencer), 225n6
Winchevsky, Morris, 121, 230n1
Wolfskehl, Karl, 75
Wonderful Century, The (Wallace), 38
World of Yesterday, The (Zweig), 57
world war, threat of, 102–4, 111–12, 115–17, 120, 182
World War I, 51–53, 101

Yaari, Meir, 21
Yeats, William Butler, 53
Yeivin, Yehoshua Heschel, 114, 164
yekkes (German immigrants), 161, 240n25, 241n28
Yiddish language, 79

Yishuv, culture of, 156–59, 174, 185
Young Palestine group, 165
Yudlevitz, David, 143–44

Zangwill, Israel, 172
Zimmermann, Moshe, 184
Zionism and Zionists, 105, 111, 155; East-West antinomy and, 137; German, 110; prerequisites, 149–50, 153, 157, 160; prophecies of catastrophe, 118; role in the Orient, 236–37n40; United States and, 170–71, 174, 195; view of assimilation, 98; view of England/English, 130–33; view of Soviet Union, 185. *See also under individual names*
Zionist socialism, 132, 174. *See also* Hashomer Hazair; Poale Tzion party
Zunz, Leopold (Yom-Tov) Lipmann, 20, 25–26, 30
Zuruf an die Jünglinge (Günsburg and Kley), 64
Zuta, H. L., 164–65
Zweig, Stefan, 53, 57, 218n90